THE HUENEFELD GUIDE TO BOOK PUBLISHING

Revised Fifth Edition

John Huenefeld

Mills & Sanderson, Publishers
Bedford, MA • 1993

Published by Mills & Sanderson, Publishers
41 North Road, Suite 201 • Bedford, MA 01730
Copyright © 1993 John Huenefeld

Library of Congress Cataloging-in-Publication Data
Huenefeld, John, 1928-
 The Huenefeld guide to book publishing / John Huenefeld. -- Rev.,
5th ed.
 p.   cm.
 Includes index.
 ISBN 0-938179-33-0 : $35.00
 1. Publishers and publishing--United States--Management. 2. Book industries and trade--United States--Management. 3. Little presses--United States--Management. I. Title.
Z471.H84 1993
070.5'0973--dc20   92-36477
                                                         CIP

Printed and manufactured by Capital City Press.
Cover design by Lyrl Ahern.

Printed and Bound in the United States of America

CONTENTS

FIGURES

List of Figures:

INTRODUCTION
Building Creative Enterprises
for the Information Era

Two fundamental impacts of computerization on our emerging universal culture will have tremendous effects on book publishing from now far into the twenty-first century.

First, our exploding ability to record, organize, manipulate, recover and reproduce information now makes it virtually certain that such readily-accessible and easily-replicated information "packages" as books (and periodicals, video- or audio-cassettes, computer software, on-line databases, cd rom, seminars, etc.) will be among humanity's most treasured and salable commodities for decades to come. Multimedia information (including its variants: instruction, inspiration, advocacy, entertainment) packaging and distribution is truly an industry approaching its moment in the sun. And books have a special edge in that industry, since they're among the least capital-consuming, lowest priced, and most "user friendly" of information packaging formats (media). They require no special hardware to use ... and they always move at the user's preferred pace.

Second, the computer's ability to sort marketing (address) databases into an ever-changing, overlapping variety of special-interest groupings is shifting significant power away from the several-dozen large publishing conglomerates that now control over 75 percent of U.S. book-industry dollar volume, toward smaller enterprises that can better serve the needs of more specialized, discriminating audiences. Just as the late-twentieth century has seen the decline of mass magazines (*Saturday Evening Post, Collier's, Life, Look,* etc.) and a matching proliferation of more specialized periodicals ... and the decline of the major television networks, with a matching proliferation of specialized cable broadcasters ... and growing difficulty in the efforts of mass market paperback houses and mass-culture movie-makers to please people millions-at-a-time rather than on a more limited and specialized basis—so twenty-first century book-readers will certainly demand more discriminating attention to their specialized interests and concerns and levels of sophistication. The computer is rapidly freeing us from the low common denominators of mass-think!

Clearly, in the twenty-first century this enormous shift from mass-think toward more discriminating, demanding individuality will extend far beyond the information packaging industry. CAD-CAM technology (itself a form of information packaging) is making it easier and easier for capital-equipment producers to offer industry the tools to provide consumers with a more varied, creative array of special-purpose products to meet very specific needs of small markets at reasonable prices. Even in the socio-political arena, we're already seeing the break-up of population masses into smaller, more individualistic units (from new nations to new churches) which can usefully cooperate without all having to salute the same flag, speak the same language, or worship the same deity.

Perhaps more significantly, for book publishers, there are already symptoms of a future collapse of mass-mind retailing. Many publishers (especially the smaller, more flexible ones) are discovering that readers are increasingly less willing to pigeon-hole themselves by media packaging formats—by seeking information (or instruction, or entertainment) specifically in *book* stores or *record* shops or even the now-in-vogue *video* stores. More and more, they expect to find *all* of their needs relative to any important interest (including information packages in *all* popular media formats) available in one place—a gardening center, an outdoor recreation store, a teacher-supply store, an office-products center, a therapist's office, a travel agency, etc.

When such outlets are not available to serve a particular interest, entrepreneurs are increasingly using those same address databases to launch phone-response catalogs combining information packages with a wide range of related products; eventually, we can expect more and more of these to take the form of special-interest-oriented "shopping programs" on cable television. In this rapidly-approaching landscape of integrated, interest-oriented "one-stop-shopping," books won't simply compete with other books—or even other media; they'll compete on-the-spot with knapsacks and microscopes and travel tickets and a thousand other ways to enrich one's pursuit of any given personal interest.

This suggests that the book wholesaler of the future may well be a franchiser of subject-sorted, multimedia information displays and constantly replenished inventories to those "one-stop-shopping" outlets that also sell supplies and equipment and services—and to a wide range of catalogers and cable television retailing programs.

These trends have already made their mark on book publishing. The number of ISBN-registered U.S. book publishing entities more than tripled in the single generation following the introduction of personal computers—with some 20,000 new publishers joining the fray. Though the conglomerates kept swallowing each other and getting bigger, the "independents" swarmed like gnats and rapidly took charge of more and more (though still a minority) of the book market.

But even more importantly, those smaller independents are proving far more *creative* than their conglomerate competitors. Because they tend to focus on restricted, specialized subject-interests, their decision-makers usually know a lot more about their audiences' compelling needs than do their counterparts in the conglomerated houses. Because those decision-makers are usually *part* of the special audiences they serve, they're closer to changing trends, and to the cutting-edge of new knowledge in their subject-areas. And because they're smaller, more personal organizations—they can *change direction* to respond to changing needs and trends much, much faster than any conglomerate. As a result, even the conglomerates have learned that the easiest, safest way for one of them to "create" a new product line or invade a new market is to *buy a small publishing house* that has already established a bridgehead.

But the speed with which small publishers are able to change direction can be a two-edged sword; it frequently propels them into uncharted waters. And their limited capital bases give them very little margin for error. A conglomerate's myriad budget-lines contain thousands of opportunities for robbing Peter to cover Paul—when Paul takes a gamble that fails. (Such coverage also masks and makes bearable a lot of incompetence on Paul's part!) But a single six-digit miscalculation can literally wipe out the typical modest-sized independent publisher.

Nevertheless, many of those smaller "independents" (both commercial enterprises and the numerous not-for-profit organizations that have discovered the advantages of packaging information for their constituencies in book format) have learned to use their PCs to manage their affairs every bit as sophisticatedly and (dollar-for-dollar) as profitably as their giant competitors. Thus they approach the Twenty-First Century Information Era with some of the same advantages smart, flexible, fast-moving little mammals enjoyed at the end of the Dinosaur Era. They are generally in a much better position to serve the increasingly sophisticated, differentiated, fast-changing needs of *specialized audiences* than are the safe-but-clumsy conglomerates—at a time when much of humanity has finally found the "breathing space" to refocus on such special interests. And frankly, their people lead more interesting professional lives (because of their more creative environment)—so every year, more and more of the better publishing people desert the conglomerates for the independents. And every year, more and more of the better authors follow them!

When the PC boom (and the collapse of mass-mind strategies) got under way a generation ago, virtually all of the models (in books, trade journals, seminars, etc.) that one could consult on how to publish books were based on the conglomerates—big organizations with vast capital pools, rigidly pyramided into highly specialized (and often monotonous) divisions of labor, seeking huge markets by emphasizing low common denominators (both in editorial selection and promotional language). It was just about then (in 1968) that my little band of colleagues and I started working with non-conglomerated, independent (entrepreneurial and not-for-profit) publishing organizations to identify or invent *new* models and strategies more appropriate to the fast-moving, highly-creative, but very *risky* dynamics of the small work group. The pages that follow update the insights gleaned from the quarter-century exploration of those dynamics that we've since shared with over 300 varied but collectively-representative client publishing organizations.

Perhaps the most important thing we've learned in that quarter-century is that productivity in a fast-moving, creative enterprise like a book publishing house can best be enhanced by focusing each *individual* player on only one of several *synergistic*—and impersonally quantifiable—performance goals. If the publisher (the traditional title for the chief operating officer) can get one group of people to accept responsibility for maximizing sales volume (the marketing function), another to take responsibility for maximizing the contribution of "yeasty" new products to that volume (editorial acquisition), a third to be responsible for getting those new products onto the printing press on time with the lowest feasible absorption of front-money capital (pre-press development), and a fourth (business operations) to manage the fiscal and physical assets *and* the corrective, strategy-enlightening data-feedback of the enterprise in such a way as to maximize operating margin (profit)—that publisher (and that publishing house) can hardly fail. Each of those groups competes not with another group, but with its own past performance—so while there's enormous peer pressure for productivity (group success), it tends to be *synergistic* rather than divisive.

Here, then—in the 40 chapters and several appendices that follow—is what we've learned from several hundred often-brilliant, often-struggling, often-triumphant, sometimes-tearful independent publishing organizations about how it's done. One tip as you begin this exploration. When the text cross-references one of the illustrative samples elsewhere in the book, the "figure" number by which it is identified will always refer to the chapter in which that sample can be found. A numerical listing of all those samples appears at the end of the (foregoing) table of contents.

John Huenefeld
18 August 1992

PART I

Context

CHAPTER 1
A Profile of Contemporary American Book Publishing

Over 200,000 organizations (commercial and not-for-profit) throughout the world are serious enough about book publishing to have registered with the International Standard Book Numbering system (a comprehensive industry program for identifying individual books and their sources). Of these, some 28,000 are located in the United States of America. But of that 28,000, only about 4,000 are seriously engaged in building on-going publishing organizations (by continuing to introduce *more than one* new title to the market each year).

Less than 1 percent (40) of those 4,000 serious American book publishing entities have more than $30 million in annual sales, or more than 150 employees—thus dictating that only those 40 must normally operate by the cumbersome, rigidly hierarchical, off-line decision-making style typical of large organizations. The remainder are able (assuming their managers are smart enough) to function by much-more-flexible "small group dynamics"—whereby key decision makers interact face-to-face on a routine day-to-day basis, and have the authority (and necessary perspective) to make far-reaching decisions on-the-spot ... while their supporting colleagues "network" with a shifting variety of contacts throughout the organization to get the day's work done. This book is primarily about and for those serious "small" American book publishers—though much of it will be relevant to publishing outside the United States, to publishing as practiced in the conglomerates, to entrepreneurs only contemplating potential publishing ventures, and to organizations packaging and/or distributing information in other media formats besides books.

Because official statisticians have traditionally focused almost all of their attention on the conglomerates, and tended to under-estimate the impact of smaller entities, data about the scope of so-called "independent" (non-conglomerated) book publishing is at best spotty—but educated estimates are possible. Of the 4,000-or-so serious small book publishers, about half are the book publishing arms of not-for-profit organizations; we'll take a closer look at their special concerns in the next chapter. The other 2,000 are commercial entrepreneurships. Perhaps 300 new ones enter the field each year—and about 200 recent start-ups fall by the wayside. Because we are in an era of rapid technological changes which constantly present new information packaging and distribution opportunities—and because book publishing requires comparatively little capital to launch a new venture (see Chapter 3)—the industry has attracted many recruits in recent years.

Roughly speaking, Americans buy and use about $18 billion worth of books every year—three-fourths of them from those very few conglomerates. Perhaps three billion of these dollars go to non-publishing distribution middlemen (bookstores and wholesalers) for serving as conduits between the publishers and bookstores, libraries or schools. Most of the rest is split between four generalized markets: bookstore, paperback-rack and library patrons (about 30 percent—much of it through wholesaling middlemen), end-users (individuals or organizations) who buy books directly from publishers (about 30 percent), classrooms (about 30 percent), and organizations distributing books in non-conventional ways (from specialized religious ministries to dispensers of promotional merchandise premiums—accounting for perhaps 10 percent of total industry sales).

Books that reach their audiences through bookstores and libraries (and the wholesalers who supply them) are referred to in the jargon of the industry as "trade" books; the trade market is divided among bookstores (general, college, religious), public and school libraries, and "mass market" book-racks (primarily for inexpensive paperbacks) in such heavily trafficked areas as airports and drugstores.

Books that are purchased directly by their eventual readers are referred to as "direct response" (or, more archaically, "mail order") books. This segment of the industry is divided between consumer-oriented (general interest) books—often doubling as "trade" books—and "professional" (business, scientific, law, medical, scholarly, etc.) books intended for use in one's work.

Books that find their audiences (willing or not) in the classroom are known as "adoption" books (because the *educators* adopt them as sanctified teaching aids and learning resources for their charges). This segment of the industry is divided between "el-high" (elementary and secondary), college, and religious-curriculum (church school) books.

Book distribution through other organizations outside these three major, conventional channels (trade, direct-response, classroom adoption) is referred to as "special marketing." In the early 1990s, for example, 15 percent of independent publishers were achieving at least 35 percent of their annual sales volume from retail outlets *other than bookstores* (garden shops, gift shops, computer stores, etc.).

Licensing of other print or non-print media (or even other book publishers) to adapt and use all or part of a book manuscript in a different media "package" or book "edition" or language translation is referred to as "subsidiary rights" marketing; perhaps 2 percent of all publishing revenues pad the budgets of *more than one* publishing house through such licensing.

It is these marketing channels (and the economics they enforce) that govern the principal differences between book publishing houses. "Trade" publishers must give 40-50 percent of the end-purchase (retail) value of most sales to *distribution middlemen* (bookstores, and wholesalers who service both stores and libraries) in order to keep those conduits functioning. The trials and tribulations of operating on as little as half of the total cash flow from their products make trade publishers different from other types (though "special market" publishing tends to be somewhat similar). While considerable subject specialization is still possible, such publishing puts a premium on *broad consumer appeal*—conducive to long press runs, bulk purchasing by middlemen, and large-lot order processing/shipping. To meet even modest financial expectations, a successful trade book must normally sell at a rate of 3,000-or-more each year as long as it remains on the market.

Trade publishing, as practiced by small independent houses, has been beset in recent years by a subtle form of unfair discrimination practiced by some of America's largest book distribution outlets (a segment of the industry far more centralized and conglomerated than publishing itself). Some—but fortunately, not all!—trade wholesalers, and most bookstore chains have (through incompetence or indifference) declared it impractical to evaluate the books of, and deal *directly* with, most small publishers. Therefore they insist on buying the books of a vast majority of non-conglomerated "independents" (if they buy them at all) through an extra echelon of middlemen—so-called "trade distributors," who demand 55-70 percent discounts because they claim (even while insisting that promoting each book is still primarily the publisher's responsibility) that they play a more active sales role in "moving books along the trade pipeline" than do conventional wholesalers. These additional middlemen absorb 10 percent or more of the total cash flow from the books they handle—and that essentially wipes out the typical small publisher's profit margin. This extra tariff is *not* required of the large conglomerates with whom the independents must compete—since the chains and wholesalers all buy directly from them at their normal discount schedules.

Most of these so-called "trade distributors" have proven relatively ineffective *except* for exercising their privileged franchises as conduits to those few, major, discriminatory chain and wholesale outlets who insist on such extra-layer processing. (They survive primarily by garnering most of the cash flow of a constantly changing population of naive "self-publishers"—writers who print and peddle their own works.) And yet such distributors manage to perpetuate among quite a few legitimate small publishers the preposterous contention that simply moving a finished book through the distribution pipeline—from publisher's warehouse to eventual reader—is worth *more* of the reader's dollar (those 55-70 percent discounts) than the *combined* work of the author, the publisher, the printer and the paper-maker. And every small publisher who falls for this demeaning proposition makes it harder for others to stand their ground and demand more reasonable terms.

So far, unfortunately, the independent publishers (and their not-very-aggressive regional and trade associations) have not united around effective antidotes to this insulting proposition (such as the Netherlands' industry-wide cooperative Central Bookhouse distribution center). But small publishers are certainly not the only victims of this widespread distribution discrimination. The reading public is thus deprived of reasonable access to many important books—and hundreds of gifted writers are deprived of the audiences they deserve. Nevertheless, a number of efforts to interest members of Congress in this public deprivation have met with indifference.

Classroom "adoption" publishers, on the other hand, have arrived at a much happier, tacit accommodation with the educational establishment which dominates their distribution prospects. As budget-conscious public servants, educators have traditionally insisted on the lowest feasible prices for the taxpayers or students or church-school budget-planners who must "go along with" the book selections those educators make for them. And since the educational establishment either buys direct, or controls most of the distribution channels (college bookstores, textbook depositories, etc.) through which those adopted texts flow, it has been willing to swap *low discounts* for *low prices*. Thus the typical textbook bears only about two-thirds of the price it might if channeled toward consumer bookstores—because the traditional "short" discount (if any) that publishers give the middlemen on bulk purchases (except for very large wholesale quantities) is only 20 percent.

Yet by definition, this is a bulk-buying (one-per-student) market. And once a textbook is "adopted" for a course, that bulk purchase tends to be repeated for several seasons with relatively little additional sales expense. Classroom adoption publishing, therefore, is perennially the most profitable, stable major segment of the industry. And because it has so much to lose ... and because its patrons (the educators) live in political fishbowls ... it also tends to be the most conservative.

Direct-response publishers have the special luxury of being able to operate at their own individually-chosen paces. And because people buying books *for themselves* are generally less price-resistant than people buying for others (either as trade middlemen or as classroom "adopters"), it is feasible for direct-response publishers to price books high enough to make a reasonable profit on a modest press run—thus facilitating a high degree of subject-specialization. Whereas sales of 3,000-or-more of a given title are normally required to recover one's "front money" investment in a new trade title (while contributing reasonably to such on-going costs as marketing and order fulfillment)—you can do it with 1,000-or-less of a book with highly *specialized* value to an easily-targeted direct-response audience. While this low-volume capability makes direct-marketing particularly appropriate (and predominant) in professional/vocational-book publishing—where "on-demand printing" now makes it possible to inventory high-priced books just 10-to-20 at a time!—it does not deter the *consumer-oriented* direct marketer, once it confirms mass appeal by preliminary testing, from "rolling out" its promotion to a large audience and matching the units-per-title norms of the trade houses. And exactly *because* of such pre-testing possibilities, direct-response publishing (particularly in its higher-priced professional book segment) tends to be less risky, and thus more profitable, than trade publishing.

Since direct-marketers don't have to split the proceeds with middlemen, they have considerably more latitude to experiment with marginal books and new authors. It is because of both this flexibility, and of the plausibility of operating on a more modest scale (promoting only to the extent of their current resources, and testing-before-plunging), that direct-response publishing has become the favorite arena of small, "independent" publishers—and particularly of limited-capital "start-up" ventures.

Every major type of book (trade, adoption, direct-response, special-market) has some subsidiary rights prospects—for adaptation to different book channels (such as book clubs that convert trade titles to direct-response items), different media (such as audio cassettes, cinematic or stage dramatizations, or accessible-by-modem databases), or different languages (largely for re-publication overseas). But increasingly (especially among secular and religious not-for-profits, who often have comprehensive information-packaging responsibilities to their constituents), successful experience in marketing subsidiary rights has encouraged flexible, independent publishers to launch *multimedia* operations on their own. Once you zero in on your own special audience, you find that they'll buy cassettes and disks from the same catalog pages that sell them books—and those other media packages can easily be stored and shipped from the same facilities, in the very same containers.

Needless to say, most small publishers function in more than one of the basic marketing channels—and thus display hybrid characteristics in their resulting organizational structures, strategies, and emphases. This diversity is one of the few "safety nets" available to them in their high-risk role as the industry's innovators and talent scouts. But most tend to reflect a "primary" style keyed to one of the major marketing channels—the "go-for-broke" riverboat gambler style of the trade world, the methodical probe-then-plunge (at your own pace) style of direct-response publishing, or the thoughtful conservatism of most classroom publishing.

All in all, less than 100,000 people work in those 4,000-or-so publishing houses (including the 40-or-less "big" publishers) that accomplish most of American book publishing. Thus, both in total work force and total sales volume, this entire sub-industry is smaller than several of America's largest single manufacturing and transportation corporations. (Shop-lifters garner twice as much of the gross national product as book publishers; drug-peddlers dwarf them!)

Basically, these 100,000 people do five kinds of work—with some sub-specialties. Roughly 24 percent of the total work force is involved in each of the four major interacting functional work groups of the publishing dynamic—

acquisition (planning/obtaining new products), pre-press development (getting those new products ready for the printing press), marketing (generating and inputting customer orders), and business operations (managing physical and fiscal assets and data feedback so as to assure profitability)—with the remaining 4 percent *coordinating* that interaction (general management and its immediate support). That latter figure would suggest that all 4,000 serious publishing houses have one-person "publisher's offices"; the fact is that while some general managers have assistants, many also wear a second hat (as the editor-in-chief, business manager, etc.). It all evens out around a one-per-enterprise average.

In small, independent publishing houses, *general management* consists of the publisher (chief operating officer) and any immediate clerical ("administrative assistant") and *alter ego* ("executive assistant") support assigned to the publisher's office—seldom more than one of each.

The *acquisition* function consists of the editor-in-chief, individual acquisition "series" editors (most effectively assigned by subject-series specialties), and appropriate clerical/administrative support.

Pre-press development, headed by the managing editor, consists primarily of manuscript-polishers ("copy editors") and page-generators (increasingly, "desktop typesetters").

Marketing consists of (a) a promotion function (one or more creative specialists in *communicating with people-in-categories* by such mass media as mail, package inserts, print or broadcast ads, telemarketing scripts, and book covers) and (b) a sales function (formerly traveling field or commissioned sales reps, but now increasingly in-house telemarketing order-processors) which *communicates personally with prospective customers one-on-one* to interface the publisher's product list with each customer's specific needs or interests. Usually, one of these specialized sub-teams is personally headed by the over-all marketing manager, the other by an assistant manager (coordinating either promotion or sales).

Business operations normally consists of a business manager (usually doubling as the chief financial officer), assisted (as appropriate to the organization's size and needs) by financial administrators (computer-centered bookkeepers), inventory handlers (shippers—and possibly a print buyer), and facilities personnel (an office manager, receptionist, clerical pool, etc.).

The work these people do, and the ways they're organized to do it, are undergoing significant and continuing change in the last decade of the twentieth century—due largely to the impact of small computers. As noted above, telemarketers are rapidly replacing field sales reps (whether staff or commissioned)—and making it possible for trade publishers to dispense with the dubious and expensive services of those extra middlemen, the "distributors." And because of the sophistication of easily available, "off-the-shelf," publishing-specific order processing software, those telemarketers are frequently able to enter transactions directly into the computer while talking to the customer by phone—thus eliminating piles of paperwork, the errors inevitable in redundantly processing it, and the hours necessary to file and recover it.

This transfer of order-entry chores from the business office (the inventory handlers) to the marketing function has made it easier for the former to accept responsibility for print-buying—recognizing this latter function as essentially (and more logically) "financial management" rather than "production."

And the business manager's acceptance of print-buying responsibility (following pre-determined printing specifications) has freed up the managing editors (the pre-press development successors to traditional "production managers") to master and coordinate new technologies for electronic manuscript handling/polishing (via word processing) and page-generation (formatting and typesetting, via "desktop" systems)—so as to virtually eliminate the traditionally externalized interior design, typesetting and "paste-up" processes.

By integrating copy editing with page generation, the managing editors of the pre-press development function have freed the acquisition editors from laborious "paper-grading" chores—thus enabling these often-expert subject-specialists to concentrate their precious knowledge and time on finding and working with competent authors to extend the "state of the art" in their respective subject areas.

Naturally, many publishing organizations have (some for good reasons, many more from simple inertia) resisted these computer-driven changes in the traditional ways of "making books." Some still use their Ph.D. series editors to correct authors' punctuation, pay external designers for unique page formats for every book, give distributors 25 percent commissions over-and-above 45 percent trade discounts to serve as middlemen between them and the bookstores, let the marketing people decide the inventory print quantities, tie themselves to inflexible fiscal-year budgets and seasonally distorted (partial) fiscal-year-to-date feedback, and scribble down written notations of all those phone orders—to be laboriously deciphered and redundantly keypunched somewhere in the back recesses of the business office. But what we'll present in the pages that follow is how the *most effective* publishers handle these chores.

It is in the tight integration of these very different, very complex functions that small group dynamics really comes into its own. By organizing and streamlining the "pipelines" (process steps) by which proposals, manuscripts, orders, actual books and money flow through each function—and by focusing each of those functions on a *different* accountability index (goal) that supports the over-all effort without competing directly with other functions—an imaginative publisher (general manager) is able to generate synergy (an end result greater than the literal sum of its parts) ... and take advantage of the fast-change capability of small group dynamics to compete effectively in a swamp of gigantic, safe, slow-moving, uncreative conglomerate dinosaurs.

Thus the marketing team accepts responsibility for improving sales volume, the acquisition team seeks to give that volume more "effervescence" (and to obsolete competing books) with imaginative new products, the pre-press team underwrites work-efficiency and profitability by getting those new products onto printing presses *on time* with the lowest feasible front-money investment, and business operations handles the assets and feeds back analytic data so as to maximize that profitability. Keeping them all moving in the same (and right) direction is the publisher's job.

It's as simple as that. But it'll take 39 more chapters to prove it!

CHAPTER 2
What's Different About Not-for-Profit Publishing?

About half of the 4,000 serious American book publishing houses are "not-for-profits": tax exempt publishing programs established by religious denominations or missions, trade or professional or academic associations, foundations, universities or other educational institutions, and similar organizations—to assist them in serving their constituencies or promoting their causes. (Roughly a third of those are religious organizations, two-thirds are secularly oriented.) Even though making money is not properly listed among the prime objectives of such publishing ventures, in most years they average a slightly better "bottom line" (before-tax operating margin) than their commercial competitors—not only because of the savings they achieve on the subsidized nonprofit bulk rate postage they use for a major portion of their marketing outreach, but because of the captive membership audiences they can (if they have useful books to offer) so easily tap.

But these special advantages of their not-for-profit status are mixed blessings. Unless their parent-organization leadership is realistic, disciplined and supportive of-and-about publishing, not-for-profit publishers must often make major decisions (from new title selection to pay raises, from promotional strategy to discounts) in a highly politicized environment. And unfortunately, managers of such not-for-profit publishing programs sometimes use (or accept) that politicized environment as an alibi for sloppy decision-making or inept execution of the publishing plan.

One sees clear evidence of such unrealistic, undisciplined institutional leadership in the inventory accounting typical of not-for-profits. Because write-offs of obsolete inventory must (to explain resulting declines in accumulated capital-investment values) be treated as operating losses at the time they are officially recognized, parent organization officials often conspire with their Directors of Publications to convince the institution's auditors that unsalable accumulations of inventory are *not really* obsolete. This makes the organization's annual financial report look better—but further complicates the eventual, inevitable reckoning with yesterday's acquisition and print-buying mistakes. As a result, end-of-1991 inventory accumulations of not-for-profit book publishers averaged about 39 percent of annual sales volume—over half-again more than the 22.5 percent averaged by commercial publishers! That's pulling a lot of institutional wool over a lot of members' eyes!

Perhaps the next most common "intellectual sleight-of-hand" used by some not-for-profit managers to justify poor performances is the contention that they're required, for the public good, to publish controversial or highly specialized "quality" material which "the commercial houses won't touch" because of bottom-line consciousness. Actually, competent commercial publishers have long since learned that *controversy sells*; it's the not-for-profit (worried about member-politics) houses who're most inclined to shy away from it. And as for specialized "quality" books—it's the well-documented willingness of specialized audiences to pay four or five times normal book prices for really *useful* material of this sort that has made short-run professional book publishers (including many not-for-profits) one of the most profitable segments of the industry.

So despite such occasional lapses, the decade of the 1980s largely demolished the old stereotype of the not-for-profit publisher as a bumbling do-gooder who'd never survive in the "real world" of commercial publishing. A number of the best-run, and most profitable, mid-sized publishers in America today are not-for-profits. Several of those the author has worked with in recent years (mostly secular, but also a few religious houses) routinely boast "bottom line" operating margins of 20-40 percent—offsetting losses in (and thus making financially feasible) significant other aspects of their parent organizations' programs. It is to such successful examples that we must look for useful models of not-for-profit publishing.

The most effective of these programs are rooted in a parent organization's identification *of itself* (whether association, denomination or other type of not-for-profit entity) as essentially an *information network*. If it sees itself primarily as a clearing house for information and related resources (from propaganda to teaching aids to interface opportunities) for a constituency of individual members or local chapters (be they churches, clubs or professional societies), it tends to organize itself in a manner highly conducive to effective, profitable information packaging and distribution—not only in book format, but in a variety of other media.

Purposeful organizations which regard themselves primarily as information networks are usually more receptive to multi-media information packaging than are commercial enterprises (whose bottom-line fixations prompt them, once beyond break-even, to cling more fervently to the replication of past success formulas than to the invention of new ones). As a result, the not-for-profits as a category are well ahead of the rest of the information industry in the integration of their book publishing programs with the creation and marketing of video- and audio-cassettes, special-interest journals and newsletters, pragmatic software for their member-practitioners, seminar and conference programs, and other information packaging formats.

Such a religious or secular information-packaging network usually focuses most of its activity on *interaction with a special constituency*—either its members, or a segment of the general public that it hopes to persuade or enlighten or convert. And it quickly discovers that successful interaction is a *two-way* proposition. What it learns from (or about) its constituency (everything from phone numbers to performance-ratio norms) can usually be refined and repackaged for use by that constituency. As a book publisher, it often gets its authors and its readers from the same pool of interest-sharing contacts.

Organizing this two-way interaction as a self-financing conduit (and refiner/reorganizer) of helpful informational resources for its constituents is a highly technical business—best pursued with maximum professionalism and minimum politicizing. Judging from the couple-hundred not-for-profit publishers with whom the author has worked over the past two decades, the most effective of them (whether secular or religious) have been organized something like this:

Figure 2a—The Not-for-Profit Organization as Information Network

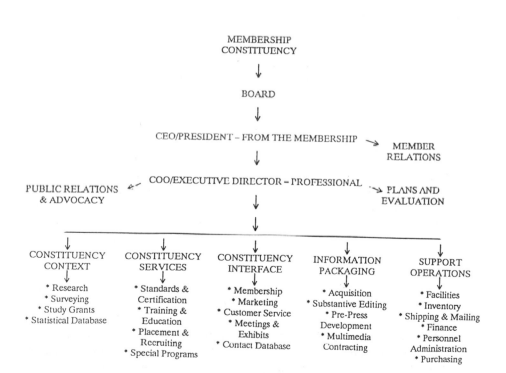

Note that this model leaves the membership constituency ultimately in charge (at the top as voting stockholders, at the bottom as customers)—but injects a layer of political management (the president/CEO) between that constituency and the headquarters organization. Also note that it isolates the most politics-prone aspects of that headquarters operation (public relations, advocacy, analytical feedback on the working of the organization itself) as special concerns of top management (the executive director/COO)—thus insulating the day-to-day interplay between most of the staff from those highly political activities.

This model avoids one of the most common errors of not-for-profit information-packaging organizations. It does *not* set up any distinct medium (books, journals, video, etc.) as a self-contained empire. It locates marketing and physical distribution outside the "packaging" function—so that their primary loyalties can be to the constituency—not to any medium, or any editorial team. Thus, the same catalogs and carton inserts and other member-resource presentations sell everything from memberships to books to placement services to videos to conference registrations to professional certification to journal subscriptions—as long as it's appropriate to the particular audience of each such presentation. Revenue is thus generated at a fraction of the cost of maintaining separate marketing programs for each medium—and separate renewal programs for memberships, subscriptions, etc.

The Information Packaging unit (typically headed by a "Director of Publications") may acquire manuscripts from the internal "Constituency Context" function—as when publication rights are a standard condition of study grants or membership surveys. Or it may look outward—to conference papers, to the general membership, or even to conventional acquisition from non-member specialists—for its raw material. The resulting books and other information packages may be used internally (in training or other "special" programs), offered primarily to the membership, or aggressively marketed to external audiences. But because books are among the *least expensive* and most universally usable (without special hardware) of all information packages—book marketing is very often (and very wisely) the "point activity" by which the association or denomination scouts for new recruits to its membership constituency.

In such a set-up, the Director of Publications is almost inevitably caught up in a managerial ambiguity not usually encountered in commercial publishing houses. While normally responsible for both acquisition and pre-press activities, this Director is typically a *peer* (rather than the "boss") of the institutional managers who control marketing and business operations (including finance). Thus, while said Director of Publications is normally charged with making the publications program pay off (or at least not operate at a significant deficit), this individual does not really command two of the functions (marketing, finance) whose basic strategies are absolutely critical to publishing success.

To resolve any conflicts arising from this ambiguity, it is important that the sponsoring organization's COO/Executive Director delegate to the Director of Publications responsibility/authority to conduct *weekly* coordinating meetings of key publishing people *and* those institutional marketing and finance managers—with the COO herself chairing a monthly "issues resolution" meeting between the Director of Publications, marketing manager and finance officer. Then it becomes largely irrelevant whether the Director of Publications or the Executive Director assumes the formal title of "Publisher."

In such a publishing environment, the membership and its leaders can serve constructively not just as authors and as customers, but in a variety of other supportive roles. Among them:

(1) *A Low-Cost Cooperative Communication Channel:* The not-for-profit publisher is usually able to include promotional materials in institutional information packets to local chapters or congregations, or announce new books in ads in organizational periodicals, at a fraction of commercial costs for comparable promotional outreach.

(2) *A Test or Survey Audience:* Organizational leaders are usually delighted when the publishing program gives members evidence that "your association/denomination listens"—by using a cross-section of the membership list for useful opinion-polling about resource needs, constituency trends, etc.

(3) *Free, Expert Technical Advisors:* Unpaid member-panels or advisors usually delight in the prestige (within their professions or their communities-of-interest) derived from their service on institutional advisory committees that provide the publishing program with diverse and often-expert kibitzing on general management policies, editorial project selection or author-competence evaluation, marketing themes or contacts, financial strategy, applying new technology—from computer software to desktop formatting, or evaluation of timely issues—such as the practicality of new media formats or price ranges.

(4) *Political Allies in Parent-Organization Deliberations:* Though Directors of Publications have to be very diplomatic about how they accomplish it, inviting organizational leaders (from influential committee chairs to such headquarters functionaries as the Treasurer) to advise on the development of budgets, ambitious expansion plans, etc., often converts them into powerful allies (and partisan spokespersons) when such issues or proposals finally come to an institutional vote.

(5) *Actual Retail Sales Outlets:* Major organizational conferences provide a great setting for impromptu retail bookshops that make useful resources from the publishing program available for immediate purchase or near-future delivery. And local churches/chapters can often be persuaded to set up their own informal bookshops as continuous outlets for such resources—especially if you'll offer normal trade discount terms to make this a fund-raising opportunity for them.

(6) *Traveling Exhibit Caretakers:* Organizational specialists who conduct "field programs" among the membership, or attend many regional meetings, are often delighted to take along portable resource-exhibit kits from the publishing program—complete with easy-order forms or toll-free order-phone numbers.

(7) *New Product Launching Pads:* Membership "book clubs" or "standing order plans" that offer either individuals or chapters automatic early delivery of all appropriate new titles at substantial discounts are an easy-to-promote method for (a) generating new product front-money, and (b) instigating early word-of-mouth support for those new products.

But those seven special advantages of not-for-profit publishers are more-or-less offset by seven characteristic disadvantages:

(1) *Departmental Turf Warfare:* Because marketing, finance and administrative support are frequently (and for good reasons) performed in departments not directly answerable to the Director of Publications, the publishing program does not always have the close cooperation from those functions it could expect in a commercial publishing house. Unless the parent organization's CEO and COO are understanding and far-sighted (which, unfortunately, is too-often not the case), priorities are established on the basic of short-term membership or office politics rather than long-term institutional health. Membership solicitation competes with book promotions for postage money; new titles compete with new office equipment for capital funds.

(2) *Budgetary Inflexibility:* When annual membership meetings approve budgets, institutional officers are reluctant (and perhaps legally unable) to change them as changing circumstances during the year warrant. Often, the only effective way to deal with this is to budget (for membership votes) in very general terms—leaving the line-by-line details to the discretion of the COO (who must still muster the occasional courage to make bold adjustments to new problems or opportunities).

(3) *Membership Discount Prices:* Not-for-profits are often encumbered, when they seek to sell their useful resources in broader non-member markets, by having to carry two sets of prices (member/non-member) in the catalog, so the membership will be politically impressed by this added dividend it gets for supporting the publishing program. This appropriate bonus can be handled a lot less awkwardly—both in promotion, and in accounting—by simply giving members an across-the-board percentage discount, which can be emphasized when appropriate (as in membership promotion) and ignored when not (as in general public or trade sales efforts).

(4) *Public Image Timidity:* Most marketing veterans will tell you that controversial copy gets high reader-attention, and helps sell more books (or other media packages). But parent organization officers are frequently so afraid of controversies (which may require them to defend themselves at the

next annual meeting) that the publishing house is reduced to a milque-toast approach to ad slogans, book titles and cover designs, catalog copy, and even acquisition decisions. On this score, you'll inevitably fare no better than the quality of your institutional leadership.

(5) *The "Tyranny of the Mission"*: While not-for-profit Directors of Publications must be careful not to let acquisition editors "cover themselves" on weak selections by claiming that the "special mission" of the institution overrode other aspects of critical judgment—they must also recognize that the mission does have some legitimate claims on their publishing priorities. And those claims can usually be met (in such undertakings as institutional histories, biographies of outstanding leaders, conference proceedings, or advocacy of unpopular causes) by careful, realistic fine-tuning of prices, print quantities, and marketing plans in advance of publication.

(6) *Assessments for Inappropriate Facilities*: Many a not-for-profit publishing program has been unable to plan its budgets or evaluate its results in the light of normal publishing experience because it is *arbitrarily assessed* for a share of elaborate computer programs, warehouse space in a high-rent district, cumbersome personnel administration programs, etc., which it would never (in its right mind) have considered worth-the-money had it been on its own. At the very least, the institutional controller should be willing to lump such excess charges in one convenient category—so they can be subtracted from financial data and ignored whenever the publishing program needs to compare itself with industry norms.

(7) *Inappropriate Accounting Systems*: The thirst for uniformity among institutional accountants often results in budgeting and financial feedback formats that make it very difficult to isolate the *publishing program* from such dissimilar operations as membership maintenance, professional certification, or institutional research. Ideally, controllers should listen to their information packaging specialists to learn how easily they can include sub-sections in each function's chart-of-accounts (from research to membership to the mail room) to isolate true publishing costs from other costs. Those costs can then be reassembled on the publishing program's own PCs to give it much more meaningful feedback than is likely from comprehensive institutional scorekeeping.

Despite these disadvantages, not-for-profit organizations have proven to be very advantageous platforms for information packaging and distribution. Those that become the paramount institutional voice of a given profession, academic discipline, trade, religion or consumer special interest essentially have a "franchise" as the most-trusted source of information in their subject area. Private operators are persistent in attempting to persuade them that they "shouldn't really be in business"—but should license rights to package and distribute their members insights *back to those members* under a joint imprint implying the organization's "seal of approval." Year-by-year, fewer and fewer are willing to give away their institutional birthright in this manner—and are finding that "a little business on the side" is not such a bad idea.

Hopefully, the chapters that follow will help make that assessment valid for quite a few more.

CHAPTER 3
Starting a New Publishing House

Because book publishing enjoys high social prestige, can easily be both moderately profitable and extremely rewarding in psychic benefits, and often requires less capital backing than is inherent in a contemporary home-owner's mortgageable equity (or the typical not-for-profit's endowment collateral)—new publishing houses crop up in America at the rate of almost one-per-day. But more than two-thirds of them will fall by the wayside before they become self-sustaining enterprises. The odds that any given entrepreneur, or not-for-profit sponsor, will succeed at this complicated business are substantially related to the degree of care given to pre-start-up planning.

There are six basic phases in the launching of a new publishing venture: First you must choose an editorial "niche." Second comes the preliminary planning phase (writing a business plan)—all on paper, not costing you anything but sleep. Third, you have to raise (or otherwise assure yourself you can afford) the "front money" (capital investment) necessary to get the enterprise to a self-sustaining "break-even point." Fourth comes the "acquisition" phase—when establishing an adequate flow of publishable manuscripts (or comparable "raw material") is the life-or-death top priority of the venture. Fifth, you enter the "marketing" phase—when you race to build a large-enough sales volume (and thus, cash flow) to have a reasonable chance of "breaking even" (replacing revenue as fast as you must spend it); if you've planned well, that should happen in two or three years, at about $250,000-a-year in sales volume. And finally, sixth, comes the "institutionalizing" phase—when you adjust all those earlier compromises you made, and refocus staff assignments, to insure long-term viability (which, in one form or another, essentially means "profitability").

The first sensible start-up task, then, is to identify the "editorial niche" one expects one's new publishing house to occupy in the vast terrain of the industry. A "niche" is a cohesive combination of subject matter and intended audience that enables the publisher to accumulate and exploit editorial insights and marketing contacts efficiently. Unless you're very well financed, it is difficult to succeed in a niche already precisely occupied by very many other, established publishers—unless those others are all doing bad jobs of it.

So at the very beginning of your new-venture planning process, get yourself a blank piece of paper, and list as succinctly as possible the subject area(s)—intellectual disciplines, professions or vocations, consumer activities, etc.—within which you are contemplating publishing books. Now spend some time in the section(s) of the library card-file you think would represent your best source of information if you were pursuing the same subject(s) as a persistent reader. See how many books you can find on the topic(s) you've listed, and write down the names of their publishers. Visit the best-stocked bookstore in your area, and do the same with the books on its shelves. Study the book ads and reviews in appropriate periodicals, and list any publishers who are bringing out new material in your preferred subject area(s). Check all closely-related subject categories in the current *Subject Guide to Books in Print* (from your library or R. R. Bowker Co.—see Appendix 2). Keep adding to your accumulative list of publishers' names.

The publishers you've listed, then, are your potential competitors. Now write to all of them and request a copy of their current book catalog. You'll find their addresses in *Subject Guide to Books in Print* or *Publishers, Distributors & Wholesalers of the U.S.* (another Bowker directory). While some may ignore you, most will respond.

From those catalogs (and the prior research), you should be able to develop a fairly clear idea of who's doing what in your chosen field(s) of interest. Do *not* skimp on this preliminary competition-research; originators of new book ideas are constantly surprised to discover that someone else in this creative world of publishing has already had their favorite brainstorm. And the odds against success increase geometrically when there is direct competition already in the field!

But an even more important product of this research will be your discovery of what *isn't* being done. Look carefully for aspects of the subject(s) which interest you that haven't been developed by other publishers ... or for segments of the potential audience whose needs have not been addressed. Have competing publishers ignored the professionals or the amateurs, the old or the young, the teachers or the practitioners, the nostalgics or the avant-garde? What significant schools of thought or points of view are not being represented? In short, what is there left for you to do that *nobody else* in the field is doing adequately?

This unfulfilled service to some defined audience, then, is a feasible new editorial niche. The more untouched that niche is, the better. It is sometimes feasible to start a new publishing venture in the face of existing competition—but only if you have specific advantages (author contacts, marketing insights, production short-cuts, etc.) that will help you outdistance that competition, and only if you have enough money to stay in the race until those advantages begin to pay off.

Once you've identified your niche, you're ready to begin developing a "business plan." Whether or not you need a written plan to convince other investors, its creation is an *absolute prerequisite* to the safeguarding of your own sanity, and perhaps your life-savings. One's natural enthusiasm for new dreams tends to distort critical judgment. Until you can get others you trust to agree (by reviewing your plan) that you've really got your act together—you're an automatic candidate for that majority of start-ups that fail.

A sound business plan should essentially consist of the seven basic "strategic planning documents" described in greater detail in later chapters—except that a conventional "budget" might better be replaced by a "cash flow forecast" (as described later in this chapter). But you'll be well-advised to develop the basic strategy documents in a slightly different order than they're presented in Chapter 9.

The first of those basic documents you'll need is a "mission statement"—to provide a context for other strategic planning. The niche-identifying work you've hopefully already done will provide most of the raw material. Chapter 6 will provide a format. But since *all* of your early sales will come from new titles, set acquisition targets in terms of an escalating number of titles-per-season, rather than new-title contribution to sales volume. Instead of specifying a target "growth rate" and "operating margin," spell out in this pre-launch version both the money-investment and time limits within which you aspire to reach break-even.

Remember that in entrepreneuring, "time is money." The faster you can afford to go in terms of early new-product generation and promotional outreach, the sooner you should reach break-even (and stop paying fixed-cost penalties for under-occupied office space, under-utilized people and equipment, etc.)—*if* you know enough, and are careful enough, to spend your front-money effectively. But if you *don't* know enough about publishing—going fast will simply exhaust your capital faster. So pace your expectations realistically—giving yourself time to learn what you don't know.

After that mission statement, the second basic strategy document in your business plan should be an organization chart or other personnel-plotting format that (a) describes the organization as you expect it to exist *when you reach break-even*—and then (b) spells out the approximate timing at which each slot will have to be filled. The easiest way to do this is to chart the break-even organization in one-role/one-person blocks—and then create a matrix estimating *what fraction* of a full-time person each function will require at the end of each three-month (quarterly) period from start-up to break-even. Using that matrix, think through and summarize a "staffing plan" whereby you appropriately combine tasks into very few one-person loads at the beginning, and gradually spin off more specialized assignments to new recruits as your workload grows quarter-by-quarter.

For the third segment of your business plan, skip ahead of the Chapter 9 sequence for a bit—and envision the pre-press development process (sequence of steps) by which you expect to convert each raw manuscript (or body of publishable data) into a ready-to-print repro master or computer disk.

(You'll do well to read Chapters 20-23 at this stage.) The strategy you adopt in this sequence will have a lot to do with the specific scheduling and cost-estimating that must come later.

The fourth section of the business plan should be a financial planning model—a set of assumed ratios and unit cost estimates from which you can not only calculate the incremental investment necessary for each new book, each marketing effort, each staff member, each work station, etc. (on a weekly, monthly, or project-by-project basis), but also project the time-lag and dollar volume of income resulting from each such investment.

The fifth and sixth sections of your plan, then, will be the basic "acquisition" and "marketing" planning/strategy models described in Chapter 9. This is the "fun" part of the planning process for most would-be publishers. But the previous exercises should have prepared you to keep your feet prudently close to the ground.

The final segment of an *already-established* publisher's on-going strategic plan would have been the annualized budget described in Chapter 10. But you'll be starting without the existing sales volume, comparative history and existing function-to-function relationships on which such a budget is properly based. Furthermore, the distinction between capital inventory investments and operating expenses is somewhat academic at this stage—since the printer has to be paid in "new cash" until you've achieved enough sales volume to recycle recovered inventory money ("cost-of-goods") to finance new titles. So you'll find a cash flow projection—spelling out just what you'll need to invest month-by-month until you reach break-even, much more useful ... and much more reassuring to potential investors.

Here's a sample of (and workable format for) such a projection:

Figure 3a—Sample Cash Flow Projection

Yr/mo/day - line item		+/–	accum
10101	Rent Post Office Box	$ -25	$ -25
10101	File Incorporation Papers	-500	-525
10101	Print Stationery	-200	-725
10115	Fall-1 Author Advances (1st instlmt)	-1,200	-1,925
10201	Begin Monthly Key Contact Newsletter	-50	-1,975
10215	Inventory Purchase Queries	-25	-2,000
10301	Monthly Key Contact Newsletter	-50	-2,050
10315	Spring-1 Author Advances (1st instlmt)	-1,800	-3,850
10401	Monthly Key Contact Newsletter	-50	-3,900
10501	Monthly Key Contact Newsletter	-50	-3,950
10501	Start Phone, Office, Equipment Leases	-750	-4,700
10501	Edr/Publr & Adm Asst on Payroll	-1,500	-6,200
10501	Fall-1 Author Advances (2nd instlmt)	-1,200	-7,400
10515	Semi-Monthly Payroll (Hire Desktop Opr)	-2,000	-9,400

Yr/mo/day - line item	+/–	accum
10520 Fall Key Contact Presentations	-500	-9,500
10601 Leases, Newsletter, Payroll	-3,000	-12,900
10615 Payroll	-2,000	-14,900
10615 Freelance Copyediting (Fall Books)	-2,000	-16,900
10615 Fall-1 Author Advances (3rd instlmt)	-1,600	-18,500
10701 Leases, Newsletter, Payroll	-3,000	-21,500
10701 Payroll (Start Marketing Manager)	-3,000	-24,500
10715 Inventory Purchases (From Other Publrs)	-2,500	-27,000
10801 Leases, Newsletter, Payroll	-4,000	-31,000
10801 Sales Visits to Select Key Contacts	-1,000	-32,000
10810 Promotional Mailing (Fall Prepub)	-2,200	-34,200
10815 Payroll	-3,000	-37,200
10815 Spring-1 Author Advances (2nd instlmt)	-1,800	-39,000
10831 Shipping Costs (Fall Advance Orders)	-100	-39,100
10831 AUGUST RECEIPTS	+2,000	-37,100
10901 Leases, Newsletter, Payroll	-4,000	-41,100
10901 Printing, 4 Fall Books	-12,000	-53,100
10915 Payroll	-3,000	-56,100
10915 Minimum State Income Tax	-232	-56,332
10900 Promotional Mailing	-2,200	-58,532
10930 Shipping Costs	-150	-58,682
10930 SEPTEMBER RECEIPTS	+3,000	55,682
11001 Leases, Newsletter, Payroll	-4,000	-59,082
11010 Fall-2 Author Advances (1st instlmt)	-1,800	-61,482
11015 Payroll (Hire Copy Editor)	-3,500	-64,982
11015 Spring-1 Author Advances (3rd instlmt)	-2,400	-67,382
11031 Shipping Costs	-200	-67,582
11031 OCTOBER RECEIPTS	+4,000	-63,582
11101 Leases, Newsletter, Payroll	-4,500	-68,082
11110 Promotional Mailing	-2,200	-70,282
11115 Payroll	-3,500	-73,782
11115 Spring-2 Author Advances (1st instlmt)	-1,800	-75,582
11115 Spring Key Contact Presentations	-500	-76,082
11130 Shipping Costs	-250	-76,332
11130 NOVEMBER RECEIPTS	+5,000	-71,332
11201 Leases, Newsletter, Payroll	-4,500	-75,832
11215 Payroll	-3,500	-79,322
11215 Inventory Purchases (Other Publrs)	-2,500	-81,832
11231 Shipping Costs	-300	-82,132
11231 DECEMBER RECEIPTS	+6,000	-76,132
20101 Leases, Newsletter, Payroll	-4,500	-80,632

Yr/mo/day - line item	+/-	accum
20110 Promotional Mailing	-2,200	-82,832
20115 Payroll (Hire Telemarketer)	-4,000	-86,832
20115 Printing 6 Spring Books	-18,000	-104,832
20131 Shipping Cost	-350	-105,182
20131 JANUARY RECEIPTS	+7,000	-98,182
20201 Leases, Newsletter, Payroll	-5,000	-103,182
20215 Payroll	-4,000	-107,182
20225 Promotional Mailing	-2,200	-109,382
20228 Shipping Costs	-400	-109,782
20228 FEBRUARY RECEIPTS	+8,000	-101,782
20301 Leases, Newsletter, Payroll	-5,000	-106,782
20315 Payroll	-4,000	-110,782
20315 Inventory Purchases (Other Publrs)	-2,500	-113,282
20331 Shipping Costs	-450	-113,732
20331 MARCH RECEIPTS	+9,000	-104,732
20401 Leases, Newsletter, Payroll	-5,000	-109,732
20415 Payroll	-4,000	-113,732
20420 Reprinting 1 title	-3,000	-116,732
20431 Shipping Costs	-500	-117,232
20431 APRIL RECEIPTS	+10,000	-107,232
20501 Leases, Newsletter, Payroll	-5,000	-112,232
20515 Payroll	-4,000	-116,232
20515 Fall-2 Author Advances (2nd instlmt)	-1,800	-118,032
20515 Inventory Purchases (Other Publrs)	-2,500	-120,532
20531 Shipping Costs	-550	-121,082
20531 MAY RECEIPTS	+11,000	-110,082
20501 Leases, Newsletter, Payroll	-5,000	-115,082
20615 Payroll	-4,000	-119,082
20615 Inventory Purchases (Other Publrs)	-2,500	-121,582
20630 Shipping Costs	-600	-122,182
20630 JUNE RECEIPTS	+12,000	-110,182
20701 Leases, Newsletter, Payroll	-5,000	-115,182
20715 Payroll	-4,000	-119,182
20715 Fall-2 Author Advances (3rd instlmt)	-2,400	-121,582
20715 Inventory Purchases (Other Publrs)	-2,500	-124,082
20731 Shipping Costs	-650	-124,732
20731 JULY RECEIPTS	+13,000	-111,732
20801 Leases, Newsletter, Payroll	-5,000	-116,732
20801 Sales Visits to Select Key Contacts	-1,000	-117,732
20810 Promotional Mailing (Fall Prepub)	-2,200	-119,932
20815 Fall-3 Author Advances (1st instlmt)	-1,800	-121,732

Yr/mo/day - line item	+/ –	accum
20815 Payroll	-4,000	-125,732
20820 Reprinting 2 titles	-6,000	-131,732
20831 Shipping Costs	-700	-132,432
20831 AUGUST RECEIPTS	+14,000	-118,432
20901 Leases, Newsletter, Payroll	-5,000	-123,432
20901 Printing, 6 Fall Books	-18,000	-141,432
20915 Payroll	-4,000	-145,432
20915 Minimum State Income Tax	-232	-145,664
20930 Promotional Mailing	-2,200	-147,864
20930 Shipping Costs	-750	-148,614
20930 SEPTEMBER RECEIPTS	+15,500	-133,114
21001 Leases, Newsletter, Payroll	-5,000	-138,114
21010 Spring-2 Author Advances (2nd instlmt)	-1,800	-139,914
21010 Reprinting 3 titles	-9,000	-148,914
21015 Payroll	-4,000	-152,914
21015 Spring-2 Author Advances (3rd instlmt)	-2,400	-155,314
21031 Shipping Costs	-800	-156,114
21031 OCTOBER RECEIPTS	+17,000	-139,114
21101 Leases, Newsletter, Payroll	-5,000	-144,114
21110 Promotional Mailing	-2,200	-146,314
21115 Payroll	-4,000	-150,314
21115 Spring-3 Author Advances (1st instlmt)	-1,800	-152,114
21115 Spring Key Contact Presentations	-500	-152,614
21130 Shipping Costs	-850	-153,464
21130 NOVEMBER RECEIPTS	+18,500	-134,964
21201 Leases, Newsletter, Payroll	-5,000	-139,964
21215 Payroll	-4,000	-143,964
21220 Reprinting 4 titles	-12,000	-155,964
21231 Shipping Costs	-900	-156,864
21231 DECEMBER RECEIPTS	+20,000	-136,864
30101 Leases, Newsletter, Payroll	-5,000	-141,864
30110 Promotional Mailing	-2,200	-144,064
30115 Payroll	-4,000	-148,064
30115 Printing 6 Spring Books	-18,000	-166,064
30115 Sales Tour of Select Key Contacts	-1,000	-167,064
30131 Shipping Cost	-950	-168,014
30131 JANUARY RECEIPTS	+22,000	-146,014
30201 Leases, Newsletter, Payroll	-5,000	-151,014
30215 Payroll	-4,000	-155,014
30225 Promotional Mailing	-2,200	-157,214
30228 Shipping Costs	-1,000	-158,214

Yr/mo/day - line item	+/–	accum
30228 FEBRUARY RECEIPTS	+24,000	-134,214
30301 Leases, Newsletter, Payroll	-5,000	-139,214
30315 Payroll	-4,000	-143,214
30315 Fall-3 Author Advances (2nd instlmt)	-1,800	-145,014
30331 Shipping Costs	-1,050	-146,064
30331 MARCH RECEIPTS	+26,000	-120,064

The dating sequence (year/month/day) used in the first column makes it easy to accumulate a line-by-line database during the planning process—and then reorganize all the entries into chronological order and calculate the running deficit (capital requirement) when you're ready. Obviously, this sample projection was based on a fundamental strategic commitment—to publish four books in the first fall season, and six each 6-month season thereafter until break-even. It also made no provision for pay increases until after break-even.

Before we go any farther, *please* recognize that this is only a format sample—not a recommended strategy or timetable for the launching of *your* new publishing venture. Note, then, that the maximum accumulative deficit in this sample ($168,014) occurs at the end of the twenty-fifth month. This peak indicates the projected break-even point. (But the projection must be extended far enough beyond this point to confirm that it truly is the peak.)

Thereafter the accumulative deficit declines, because more money is expected to come in than go out—and thus the total amount of capital supposedly needed to establish this venture is estimated at that $168,014. But our entrepreneur will be well advised to make certain there's *at least half-again* that much capital available to cover unforeseen contingencies and disappointments. This suggests that she should be reasonably certain of the availability of some $250,000 in start-up capital before she takes the plunge.

Also note that on 15 January of the first year, this plan calls for contracting with initial authors three and a half months before any payroll is established. There's no sense in paying people to sit around waiting for work to arrive. And note those 15 July and subsequent purchases, in the first year, of inventories of related books from other publishers, to improve the selection offered in (and thus the response expected from) the early promotions.

The point of these observations is that a great deal of strategy must be applied to the manipulation of this cash flow projection. Keep in mind the shifting progression of post-financing priorities (phases) described above—from acquisition to sales volume to profitability.

Once you've extended your cash flow projection far enough to identify and confirm the break-even point, study it for obvious possibilities for speeding up self-sufficiency or lowering the total required investment. Now is the time to evaluate the impact of various print quantities, more selective (or more expansive) marketing, faster or slower new-title introduction, etc. Having all of the line entries in a PC-database will make it easier to evaluate such options.

Such adjustments become especially important if your original projection (unlike this sample) does not indicate a steady progression toward break-even in a reasonable time; once momentum is lost, you're likely to reverse direction. Two or three years should provide plenty of time for learning how to operate self-sufficiently, and investors have reason to be uneasy if your plan doesn't anticipate that. But when making adjustments, be sure they are realistic—not wishful thinking you've indulged in just to change the numbers. If you have to violate the assumptions of your earlier "financial planning model" to make things work out, chances are good that yours is not yet a viable plan.

Before you accept your collection of documents as a finished business plan, be particularly sure that you have represented your own salary requirements adequately. As an entrepreneur, you'll have your hands full between launch and break-even, without the distraction of personal financial hassles.

And then, before you can put the plan into effect, there's the little matter of "phase three"—raising the necessary cash.

As we suggested earlier, the largest single accumulative deficit that appears in your final start-up cash flow projection should be marked up about 50 percent to cover contingencies and estimating errors. The resulting number, then, is the amount you should have *firmly committed* to the enterprise before you burn any bridges, make any announcements, or sign any contracts. If you don't have the money lined up in advance, it will be much more difficult to get after you've started—when most financing sources will assume that your need reflects failure of some initial plan/projection (and thus, a crippled venture).

The processes by which not-for-profit organizations make sure there will be enough money available to finance their new publishing programs until they break even are as varied as those organizations themselves. We will not try to detail them here. But let us stress that it is every bit as important for such organizations to go through all of the detailed steps of creating a business plan (including the cash flow projection) as it is for a private entrepreneur to do so. And it is vital that they make sure future money is committed to cover the *entire* pre-break-even period. If you expect to take two years to break-even, but your organization only budgets one year at a time, you'll make yourself an automatic hostage to all sorts of institutional second thoughts and political juggling halfway through, unless you get some kind of clear commitment for that second year's investment support *before* you launch the project.

Most new private ventures in book publishing are financed by one, or some combination, of six basic sources of start-up capital. They are:

(1) *Self-Financing:* Whether you feel like a capitalist or not, *you* are the single most likely source of investment money to cover those anticipated start-up deficits. By putting up personal collateral, you may be able to convince a bank to lend *you* money it would never dream of lending directly to your new publishing house. Second-mortgage equity in family homes has probably

launched more publishing enterprises than any other single source of funds. Accumulated savings, life insurance policies, coin collections, titles to boats and vacation retreats, and other negotiable property have provided the assurance bankers needed to underwrite many more.

But remember, when you mortgage personal assets for working capital, the basic principal of sound entrepreneurial risk-taking: never risk anything you couldn't afford ultimately to lose. Ask yourself how you and your family would be affected if the venture went down the drain. Is the risk small enough, and are the potential rewards large enough, to justify the gamble?

(2) *Friends and Relatives:* The indulgent daddy and the rich aunt have served as founding angels for so many book publishing ventures that they deserve a larger place in our industry's folklore. This is not an excessively expensive business to get into. A well prepared business plan that documents good prospects for success may well bring forth some unexpected offers of support from personal intimates. So if start-up money is your major problem, by all means show the plan around such circles and invite suggestions (but don't circulate multiple copies, in violation of SEC regulations). If you get voluntary family offers to help with the bankrolling, negotiate them through objective third parties (for example, your respective attorneys) to insure fairness and financial discipline.

Unfortunately, friends and relatives most often get into the act late—after you've started with too little money, and run into enough difficulty to make you ask for help—rather than in the beginning, when their support could lend most to the health of the venture. So decide early whether you want such support, and let them know what you're up to if you do.

(3) *Working Partners:* If you can raise part of the money yourself, but need additional help to guarantee solid financing all the way to break-even, you might look about for trusted associates in the publishing world who share your ambition to be self-employed; two house-equity second mortgages are better than one! If your interests and job-skills are compatible rather than competing, and if you're convinced you'll work well together over the long run, inviting one or more such partners to join you in the venture might yield all the additional capital you need. In fact, it might even reduce total capital requirements, since some of these partners might lend part-time assistance while retaining other jobs, or come on the payroll for less than they would demand without an equity stake.

If you make this kind of arrangement, be sure that proportional equity (the percent to be owned by each partner) and salary relationships have been carefully spelled out in advance. Here, again, neutral intermediaries can be useful. Later resentments over inequities or misunderstandings between such partners can be devastating to a new organization.

(4) *Venture Capital:* People with dreams of entrepreneurial triumph often assume that there are legions of wealthy potential backers lurking somewhere, ready to put money into speculative ventures for modest shares of the eventual

(if any) pay-offs. That's hardly accurate even in the best of circumstances—and trying to peddle equity in an untested publishing venture is hardly the best of circumstances.

Nevertheless, if you'll talk forthrightly to enough bankers, probate lawyers, development officers of acquisitive conglomerates, stock brokers, Small Business Administration advisors, and others who stand close to overstuffed portfolios and dormant estates, you will learn the names of some people who *might* be interested in investing in your publishing venture.

If you decide to go this route, before you contact any of those potential angels, call the regional field office of the U.S. Securities and Exchange Commission in your nearest metropolitan center (or the SEC in Washington) and ask for a current publication describing the regulations and restrictions you're required to observe. And before you get in any deeper, you should also discuss what you're doing with an attorney, whose help you'll eventually need in formalizing any such investment deal.

Obviously, the price for whatever amount of equity (percentage of ownership) you're willing to give up must be enough to cover your anticipated needs (including contingencies) until break-even. If you hope to retain eventual control of the venture (as most entrepreneurs do), that means your business plan must convince the investor that even a minority interest is going to earn enough money within a fairly short time to reward him/her adequately not only for the alternate income he/she will have sacrificed, but for the considerable risk in backing a new venture. For the typical venture capitalist, this means potentially getting back three times the original investment in five years or so.

However, you may be able to make a marginal proposition more attractive to the investor (or a temporarily-minority position more tolerable to yourself) by negotiating an agreement whereby one party has an option to buy the other out at a set-but-rewarding price after several years. This could enable you to sell the investor more than 50 percent while still guaranteeing yourself potential control.

(5) *Co-Publishing Advances:* Here's where those conglomerates can be useful! Part of the capital required to launch a small publishing house might very well be put up by a large publishing house—as a way for the latter to share in particularly attractive book projects originated by the former. This will only come about if you have exclusive data and/or very unique ideas for one or more books with sufficiently obvious potential to merit a substantial cash advance from a co-publishing agreement. Under such an agreement, the originating publisher (you) usually provides the manuscript, editing, page design, and typesetting; the secondary publisher takes care of printing, marketing, order fulfillment, and collections. Appropriately, the secondary publisher then keeps about 65 percent of the money collected, and forwards the rest to the originating publisher (who must then pay the author). The advance paid to seal such a deal might be as much as the originating publisher's

share of estimated first-year sales. For a big book—or an extended series—this could add up to a significant part of your capital requirement.

(6) *Barter Deals:* If you talk up (by asking advice about) your proposed new venture enough among the people who hope to sell you manufacturing or fulfillment services, rent you office space, or perform professional services (such as freelance copy-editing or desktop page generation) for you, some may be interested in bartering those services in exchange for stock. But before you invite any such proposals, consider carefully what impact this may later have on your independence to do business with other vendors or professional specialists who might serve you better.

Whatever combination of these (or other) money sources you employ, it is vital to the health of your future enterprise (and perhaps to your own mental health as well) that you make *no* commitments until you're firmly assured of sufficient financial backing to reach break even (with a margin for contingencies). People will be very reluctant to come to your aid later, when the venture looks like a leaking lifeboat. Lack of adequate financial backing has killed off more budding publishing ventures than any other single problem, with the possible exception of managerial immaturity or incompetence.

When you're actually ready to launch the venture (by beginning the fourth, or "acquisition" phase), your initial firm commitments should revolve around *establishing a name, an address, an ISBN, and a legal structure.*

The most common source of publishing company names is the personal name(s) of the founder(s). This not only identifies and distinguishes your publishing house, it associates it with whatever reputation you (for better or worse) have already gained in publishing circles. And for many people, it is a psychological stimulus and reward that can help offset some missed paydays.

Some people use geographic names for their publishing houses; be careful that this doesn't (as in the case of most state names) make you appear to be more regionally focused than you intend. Others adopt names from mythology, legend, or history that have connotations they like (or that they think help define the nature of the venture). Some make up acronyms from initials or word-combinations.

There are advantages to a name that suggests to the world what you do; this makes it easier for customers, authors, and potentially valuable employees to find their way to you. For this reason, such words as "Press," "Publisher," "Publications," and "Books" are popular in the organizational names of new publishing houses. Some publishers also incorporate the major subject area they intend to pursue into their name, though this might tend to be disadvantageously inhibiting in the future.

But none of these common practices is mandatory. The ultimate purpose of the name is to identify your publishing house, distinguishing it from all others so that it can get its mail, make unambiguous contracts, accumulate a reputation, etc. Whatever name you choose for this purpose, ascertain that it is not already being used by, or will not be easily confused with, the name of any previously-existing publisher. Perhaps the simplest way to do this is to check it out against the latest edition of Bowker's *Publishers, Distributors and Wholesalers of the United States* (see Appendix 2 for Bowker's address)—the most comprehensive readily-available listing of American publishing houses, which is particularly useful as a reference because it lists thousands of existing names in strict alphabetical order.

Before you can make any use of this name, of course, you'll need an address where other people can contact your new publishing entity. The only point we wish to make here is that it is not necessary to rent an office or hire a receptionist in order to begin communicating with the publishing community. Until you really need such a location *for work space,* a post office box number or your residential address will enable you to print some initial stationary and start dealing.

Now you're ready to make your formal entry into the publishing industry by obtaining your own, distinctive "ISBN prefix." This is a number that separately identifies each registered publisher in all participating parts of the world, and to which other numbers can be attached to identify each of those publishers' individual books. This identification number program is administered for the American book industry by the International Standard Book Numbering Agency, c/o R.R. Bowker Company, 121 Chanlon Road, New Providence, NJ 07974. Write to them, outlining briefly the scope of publishing you intend to do (number of titles per year), and they'll not only assign you a number, but provide you with instructions for using it. (This will also get your publishing house "on the record" and thus discourage other new publishers from duplicating its name.)

At some point in this initial establishment of an organizational entity, you need to come to terms with its legal structure. The principal question is whether the venture should be separately incorporated, to shield you and your family (or sponsoring institution) from unforeseen liabilities that might arise out of bankruptcy, suits for libel or slander or plagiarism, or damage claims due to some natural disaster. Since it usually costs less than a thousand dollars (depending on your state and your law firm) to incorporate and limit such liabilities, most publishing entrepreneurs decide this is good, inexpensive insurance. But if any of the principals in your venture are in complicated tax situations, you probably should check out all of the implications with your lawyer before you decide. (Particularly make sure you understand the legal implications and potential personal hazards of an unincorporated partnership, before entering into any such arrangement.)

If you incorporate with less than 15 stockholders, you have the option of declaring yourself a "Subchapter S" corporation and avoiding double taxation by IRS on both corporate profits and stockholder dividends; some states also recognize the Subchapter S option. Subchapter S status may inhibit efforts to raise capital, but it can be voluntarily discontinued at the beginning of any tax year by unanimous agreement of the stockholders. For more information, ask your regional IRS forms center for its free booklet entitled "Tax Information on Subchapter S Corporations."

Now you're ready to announce your existence to the world. Use one of those brand new letterheads to create your first of (we hope!) many news releases. Type boldly across the top of the sheet, and underline, the words "NEWS: For Immediate Release." Add, just beneath the letterhead, the name and phone number of some individual (probably yourself) who can answer any questions the release may inspire. Start with a straightforward, newspaper-style headline announcing the birth of your new publishing house. Then devote several paragraphs (but not more than one page) to a newsy account of "who, what, when, why, where, how."

Send the first photocopy of this news release to the primary trade journal of the book publishing industry: *Publishers Weekly,* 249 West 17th Street, New York, NY 10011. Send the second to your local newspaper. Put the third in your corporate history file. Then make plenty of additional copies for the edification of all of the new contacts who, in the weeks just ahead, will need to be made to understand what you're trying to do.

Now you're in business—but there are still seven other important start-up chores that should be dispensed with *before* you open an office—and thus have to pay rent, utility bills, and wages. They are things you can do primarily in off-hours; with an occasional lunch-break phoning session, you can get them started before you give up your prior job. Use your box number return address, and hire a phone answering service if it's inappropriate for people to call you at work. Meanwhile, use that news release you've already prepared to explain who you are as you give your project a head start on gathering momentum in each of these seven areas:

(1) *Establishing a Learning Procedure:* Make an early habit of writing down every significant question about your new publishing task that you can't answer on-the-spot. Periodically consult available informational resources (reference books, experienced publishing acquaintances, trade and professional associations, consultants, etc.) for answers to everything that has accumulated on that question list. Establish this as a formal process as soon as you begin working on your niche definition and business plan; those alone should suggest several pages of questions. The idea is to find out what your real knowledge/experience gaps are *before* you've begun spending (and potentially wasting) serious money.

(2) *Creating an Author Pool:* If you're talking to sharp venture capitalists, you may have already been questioned about who you think you can get to convert hypothetical book ideas into usable manuscripts. As fast as feasible, you should accumulate an address-list of writers and experts who are potential authors of the kind of material you want to publish. As soon as you begin thinking about book ideas, start recording names of, and notes about, every potential author who comes to mind or is suggested by others. Make sure the

recording mechanism is functioning routinely as you start screening prospective writers for that first serious batch of manuscripts you'll need.

(3) *Developing a Promotional List:* Once you start talking to authors and subject-area experts, querying trade associations, and making other contacts, you'll begin hearing about people who might become good customers, good publicity contacts, potential subsidiary rights buyers, etc. So while you're accumulating that address-list of potential authors, start another database of people who should receive any further news releases, catalogs, or other promotional material as it becomes available. While there will be mailing lists of such people available for rental, none of them will ever be as responsive as an accumulated list of personal contacts who have already shown some interest in what you're doing.

(4) *Actual Contracting With Authors:* There's no point in assembling a staff or renting office space for it until it has something to work on. Usually, you don't have that until the first finished manuscript arrives from a previously-contracted author. So certainly one of the first things you want to get started at, before you open an office, is contracting with some of the potential authors you've identified, to write the books you've envisioned in your business plan. Most new publishing entrepreneurs should try to contract with authors for everything they hope to publish *for at least the next year* before they formally open for business, sign a lease, or meet a payroll. And this means you'll also need to develop a basic author contract, along the lines described in Chapter 14.

(5) *Developing Vendor Contacts:* If you will spell out what you want in fairly specific terms (as far as length and deadlines are concerned) in those author contracts, you can then begin making detailed arrangements for the desktop typesetting equipment, paper-printing-binding (manufacturing), freelance copy-editing assistance, promotional graphics and printing and mailing services, warehousing, and whatever else you expect to need in short order once the manuscripts arrive. But you're going to have to match your plans and budget to the capabilities and competitive pricing of your suppliers; you're going to have to synchronize your own procedures with those suppliers' requirements; you're going to have to establish credit once you've chosen the best suppliers. This is all work that can be done before that first rush of distractions that follows the arrival of the initial manuscript and the opening of the office.

The most critical of these vendors will be the printers who'll produce your book inventory. To identify those, start with a form-memo to a generous selection of the specialized manufacturers listed in Bowker's *Literary Market Place* (see Appendix 2), or in the *Directory of Book Printers* published by Ad-Lib Publications (see Appendix 1); just invite their sales reps to call, and you'll be surprised how much free education you can obtain! Meanwhile, be *very wary* of local printers who *don't* have extensive book industry experience;

their learning errors have spelled disaster for many a fledgling publishing house.

Your other vendor requirements can probably be met from the telephone yellow-pages. A copy of your initial news release (announcing the venture) and brief notes inviting them to phone if they think they can help you should be more-than-sufficient to build an adequate database of competitive possibilities in each specialty.

(6) *Scouting for Future Employees:* You may be disappointed if you have to settle for whatever people are currently on the job market at the time you schedule each payroll addition. By being honest about the delayed starting date, you might be able to pre-recruit exceptional people who are already employed, and would be able and willing to stick with their present jobs until you're ready for them.

(7) *Refining Those Initial Manuscripts:* Even the arrival of the first finished manuscript from a contracted author need not necessarily call for the opening of the office and the hiring of regular personnel. If only one or two manuscripts are ready for polishing, you might be able to do that yourself in off-hours, or arrange for a freelance copy editor to do it at home, to put off the beginning of regular overhead costs a little longer. As with all of the other tasks outlined immediately above, your goal should be to get as close to your first publication date as feasible before starting that unstoppable drip of the overhead faucet. Every day you delay opening the office will probably mean another day of "staying power" if you end up in a race between break-even and bankruptcy.

So eventually there comes a day when you have manuscripts in hand, publication dates approaching, a formally-opened office, a payroll to meet—in short, a functioning book publishing house. But even though things are now in high gear, there are still a number of important decisions that can *and should* be postponed.

You're going to learn a lot in those first few months. What you learn will help you make better choices as a publisher and a manager. So there is a lot to be said for delaying any commitments you *don't really have to make* at the beginning, until you've seen enough of your particular niche in the publishing world to refine your first ideas. Make a habit of asking when each significant decision needs to be made (so as not to delay work by colleagues, authors, or suppliers), and then keeping your options open until that deadline. There are six particular areas of decision-making in which you should be careful not to "jump the gun" with premature commitments:

(1) *Designating Key Suppliers:* If you're insecure about handling book production, and some printer's sales rep throws a security blanket around you by promising to explain all future mysteries, there's a natural temptation to promise: "You'll be my printer." But publishing is a far less expensive business if you can keep printers, promotional lettershops, office supply dealers, etc., *competing* for each major job or purchase as it comes along. So be careful not only about premature commitments on specific jobs, but about unnecessary

general commitments that later inhibit your playing one supplier against the next for better prices.

(2) *Basic Equipment Choices:* Many an entrepreneur has reveled in equipment demonstrations and signed leases for everything his/her clerical, accounting and order-entry people will ever need before any of those people are on hand to express opinions and preferences. Generally speaking, if the people who're going to use it aren't there, it's too early to be selecting the equipment. Don't make a long-term commitment to something expensive just because you want to use it yourself an hour a week, before the momentum picks up enough to hire someone to keep it busy. In many cases, the employees you will be adding will have experience with various brands, and can choose between them more wisely than you.

(3) *Hiring Expensive Specialists:* It's fairly easy to get a modestly paid assistant to occasionally make a decision or function in a role that's "over his head." But it is much harder to get a once-pampered veteran of the executive suite to pack books or empty wastebaskets or stuff envelopes in a pinch. Unless you have a backlog of top-level work, much of the time of such experienced specialists is wasted, or vastly overpaid, during the start-up phase. So it's better to depend on freelancers, plus a few hours of occasional coaching from specialized consultants, than it is to prematurely add experienced specialists to your full-time staff. And if you'll wait until you really need such people on a regular basis, you're likely to find that someone on your home-grown original staff has learned how to do the job less expensively, and with more concern for your special circumstances, than any veteran you're able to lure away from some other publisher.

(4) *Designating a Chain of Command:* Somebody in the background (a Board of Directors or a spouse or the executor of your will) should always be empowered and instructed to recruit a replacement should you suddenly become the bull's eye for a falling skid of lethal books, but that may be about as far as you should go in establishing a hierarchy during your first few months of operations. If you don't know the people well, or aren't experienced at staff-building, you're probably in for some big surprises as to who can do what, who can't, and who can be trusted. So resist the temptation to define a pecking order until you've watched your new team work together under a representative range of pressures.

(5) *Settling Final Marketing Details:* Books change as they undergo development; marketing channels are fluid; your expanding contacts offer constant new opportunities. So just because you couldn't sleep one night last year and designed a "dream" mailing piece (complete with headlines) for your first book promotion ... or just because you once used a certain mailing list in your old job that's "just right" for the books you're planning ... don't give in to the temptation to decide marketing details far in advance of promotional typesetting deadlines. Be specific about general approaches and budget

assumptions, but leave the nuances to absorb maximum last-minute information and inspiration.

(6) *Contracting Second-Year Authors:* Eventually, you should be signing contracts with most authors about 18 months before you plan to publish books. But when you're just getting started, you will find it easier to adjust your strategy to the hard lessons of new experience if you keep your options open as long as possible. So for the first year or so, it is probably wise to contract only about one year in advance, except in the special case of a book that will obviously take longer to write or compile.

Once your publishing venture is underway, it's important that you keep score so you'll always know whether you're ahead of, or behind, your expectations. Simply matching the checkbook to your initial cash flow projection will tell you a lot. But in order to know *where* necessary adjustments should be made, you should compare actual results with the assumptions of your initial "financial planning model" at least monthly. Establish a routine of looking at those comparisons in a weekly staff meeting, and discussing possible ways of catching up with whatever schedules or budget projections are in trouble, without spending more money to do it.

Such meetings will sharpen awareness of individual responsibilities, exert peer pressure on habitual laggards, improve coordination, suggest potential modifications in your plans and priorities, and help you sleep at night by providing assurance that nothing is going seriously awry without your knowledge. (As the organization grows, you'll have to convert this weekly full-staff session into a meeting of just the core management group—as described in Chapter 8—and encourage those core managers to hold separate staff meetings for their respective departments.)

But you should resist making modifications to your basic plan for reaching break-even during those casual weekly reviews; such complex plans deserve more deliberate, better-researched critiques and proposals before you alter the direction of the enterprise (financially, chronologically, structurally, or otherwise). Nevertheless, you do need a mechanism for making such basic changes as it becomes obvious that segments of your original plan are failing. Very rarely does a new publishing enterprise succeed without some modifications of its original plans, in response to changing circumstances and the management's expanding knowledge and experience.

A good context for making such changes is the monthly financial report (basically a summary of operating data), tied to a quarterly (every third month) financial planning review. To provide a framework for your review, ask every person responsible for one or more of the basic operating functions to copy from the cash flow projection in your business plan all dates and spending items (or portions of items) that relate to their function(s). Then ask them to prepare a month-by-month budget-and-schedule for fulfilling their responsibilities, on the basis of that original cash flow projection and break-even schedule. Make sure their responses are broken up into monthly segments.

Compare their projections with actual results at the end of each month. Except for emergency situations, simply ask for monthly ideas for possible corrections or improvements. But schedule a serious *quarterly* planning review at which those suggestions will be thrashed out, and possibly adopted. Each time this process alters your cash flow projection, ask them to update their respective budgets-and-schedules accordingly. If they'll do this until you reach break-even, they'll be adequately prepared to move on into more formal budgeting procedures for the long haul.

By devoting one day every quarter (plus whatever preparatory time your managers need) to such basic rethinking of your plans and projections, you should be able to adjust to discrepancies between your original projections and your actual experience fast enough to avoid substantial waste or missed opportunities. This is, in effect, a deliberate mechanism for allowing the learning process to have a direct and prompt impact on the evolution of your enterprise. Making your business strategy dynamic, instead of static, should significantly improve the odds—and reduce the cost—of reaching break-even before you run out of money.

In addition to this financially-focused monitoring and adjustment of your original plans, it makes sense to adjust your definitions of "who does what" as the needs of the organization, and the capabilities of its personnel, evolve. You can do this effectively if you'll establish three simple procedures:

(1) Make sure every person hired is given a *written* memorandum describing the job he/she is expected to do, and the rules under which he/she is expected to do it; these should be written by the member of the core management team for whom each works; originally, that probably means they'll all be written by you.

(2) Until break-even, core managers should spend a few minutes in a one-to-one review of these memoranda *with each employee* every three or four months; put these reviews on your work schedule, and require confirmation that each review has actually been accomplished. Focus these sessions on minor adjustments, and on collecting suggested major revisions for more deliberate consideration. However, anytime the fast pace of evolution characteristic of new ventures causes a certain job or certain procedure to slip seriously out-of-focus, you should add such serious restructuring to the immediate agenda of your next core management meeting.

(3) Once each year (perhaps on the anniversary of each individual's employment), ask the appropriate core manager to sit down with each employee and essentially "renegotiate" the job. Discuss not only changes in procedures and responsibilities, but pay adjustments and such career enhancement benefits as training programs and reference/resource materials. Look back over the job description and any related notes left in the file from

the previous year's review; record appropriate notes to be reviewed (for progress measurement) next year. If major dissatisfactions are expressed by either employee or supervisor, record those as well, in the expectation that they will have evaporated when you re-examine the notes at that next annual job review.

This combination of quick staff discussion of weekly operating indices, monthly comparison of expenses and income with budgeted expectations, quarterly adjustments of operating plans and budgets (and updating of the cash flow projection), and annual job reviews (backed by more frequent supervisory interviews), should keep your publishing house responsive to changing circumstances and opportunities until it is safely beyond break-even. It should also speed up your arrival at that break-even point, by stimulating steady utilization of new things you and your staff learn as you go.

This can be an exhilarating process if things are going as well as you had expected, or better. But it can become very dreary if results are consistently disappointing. If you've followed the planning and adjustment procedures outlined here, and still consistently missed your targets, that in itself is a condition for which you should have a planned response.

At the beginning of your venture, go over the cash flow projections and locate the major points at which you are escalating your financial commitment. These are likely to be those dates on which you turn significant new batches of finished manuscripts over to the typesetter for composition, and before you've given them to the printer. Mark an appropriate sequence of such dates (approximately every six months) on your calendar for a hard-headed reassessment of *whether you still want to found a publishing house*. Sit down with the people you trust to be frank (your spouse, your accountant, your banker, a tough-minded friend or two) on each of those dates, go over the actual performance figures that relate to your cash flow projections, and entertain the question: "What if we quit right now?"

Without pursuing this gloomy side of the planning process any further than necessary, let us simply say that since a majority of new publishing ventures do fail to reach break-even, you'll be wise to recognize this possibility and establish a mechanism for "cutting your losses" early, rather than dragging the struggle out to the point of exhaustion, bankruptcy, and maximum demoralization of all concerned. Having those "Go—No Go" review dates on your planning calendar from the beginning will make it easier.

But with adequate advance planning, a lot of careful attention, and a little bit of luck—the answer should always be "Go!"

Chapter 4
Buying or Selling a Publishing House

Of course, if you've got the money, the simplest (and often safest) way to get into the book publishing business is to buy an already-established publishing house from someone else. Conversely, when you're ready to retire from the business, your needs might best be met by finding some other aspiring entrepreneur (or adventurous conglomerate) who wants to do the same.

Whether you're buying a publishing house, or selling one, the first thing you'll need is a realistic appraisal of how much it's worth. Conventional business appraisals most often try to establish a market value by projecting the recent record of earnings (profit). But since a third of all modest-sized book publishers register operating losses every year, and very promising but incomplete start-ups may have *never* documented any profit—this often suggests that a given enterprise with significant sales volume and even greater potential is worth *nothing*. To estimate market value more realistically, you'll find it useful to project *future potential* rather than *past performance*.

The major question an investor must ask in deciding whether the enterprise is worth a specific price is: "How soon will I get my money back?" But those years in which the publishing program is expected to repay that purchase price will not be governed by the circumstances or the publishing strategies of the past. How much a buyer can afford to pay will depend on what *that buyer* (not the previous owner) can do with the momentum that exists at the time of transfer.

By studying the range of agreed prices in a variety of successful and mutually-satisfactory sales negotiations, we find that a book publishing enterprise is generally salable for somewhere between 4 and 7 years' accumulative after-tax earnings. Those aggressive venture capitalists who insist on *both* recovering their money *and* earning a major equity stake in 3–5 years seldom achieve their aspirations in book publishing. At the same time, the number who lose their total investment when things go sour is considerably lower in book publishing than in many more volatile industries—because of the equity-value others will see in the inventory and the potential salvage of promising start-ups.

Since state and local income taxes on corporations are generally nominal, those are best absorbed into "operating expense" projections when estimating future earnings. Estimated future federal taxes should, however, be subtracted from profits before adding the accumulative earnings—since it's with *after-tax* dollars that a buyer must pay the former owners, and thus it is after-tax dollars the buyer needs to recoup.

Recognizing that earnings potential differs with varying management strategies, you should begin your evaluation by estimating after-tax earnings for each of the next 7 years according to the *present* pattern of operations—as described below. Then make two additional projections (also described later), each based on a different set of assumptions (or "scenarios"). The fourth-, fifth-, sixth-, and seventh-year accumulated earnings according to each of these three sets of assumptions produces a matrix of 12 numbers, representing an appropriate "bargaining range" between buyer and seller. Averaging the 12 numbers in this range will indicate a reasonable "fair market value" for the enterprise in question (whether you're buying it, or selling it ... and subject to some latitude for inventory-value adjustments as described below).

This process frequently produces a suggested price close to the current annual sales volume of the publishing house. That's a very rough, short-cut rule-of-thumb for guessing how much normally profitable, established publishing houses *tend* to be worth—but it is not a safe basis for actually negotiating a transaction. Some publishing houses, because of obvious but untapped potential, are worth much more; others have sales volumes that were ballooned by abnormal circumstances that won't continue, and are worth less. So for a reliable valuation, you need to work through the process step-by-step.

Step 1 is the determination of a base level and ratios from which to project the next 7 years. To do this, study the last three years' financial statements to determine the annual increase in net sales revenue (growth rate), the average percent-of-sales devoted to cost of goods sold (inventory capital absorption), variable marketing costs (including salaries and commissions), other (fixed operating) costs, and resulting before-tax operating margin (profit). Those three categories of costs (cost of goods, variable marketing, fixed operations) behave differently for different types of books and marketing channels, and different strategy scenarios—and thus should be projected separately.

If the publishing program you're evaluating consists of several distinct "profit centers" (sources of earnings—such as distinct media or marketing channels) that reflect different patterns of growth, cost, or profitability—make a separate analysis of each profit center. Then, throughout the process, simply combine the projected before-tax earnings subtotals for all profit centers year by year, before deducting taxes and calculating accumulative over-all earnings.

To establish a projectable growth rate, divide the *most recent* year's net sales (after returns) by the previous year's sales. (Since it's *current* momentum that counts, averaging 3 years' growth rates can mislead you.) To project expenses, separately divide the total *3-year* cost of goods, marketing costs, and fixed operating costs by the combined 3-year net (after returns) sales—to determine what percentage of revenue is normally being eaten up by each of these three categories of expenses.

Then, starting with the current annual sales volume and growth rate, use those ratios to project "normal" (first scenario) revenue, costs, and resulting before-tax profit over the next 7 years. Assume normal corporate income taxes in converting that to after-tax earnings (since any loss carry-overs or tax shelters which might mitigate are separate property of the current owner, and really have no bearing on the future earnings potential of the enterprise).

Do it on a computer spreadsheet, and it will be easy to copy the layout twice more, for transformation into your two alternative scenarios. For the second scenario, project what you believe would happen to sales volume and cost ratios if obviously-advantageous strategic changes were adopted. Strategy changes that might make substantial differences include increases or decreases in the numbers of new titles published in each major editorial series, the development or expansion of new marketing channels, the elimination of unprofitable channels, the elimination of unproductive staff—which often includes the former owner, or the adoption of less-expensive production techniques (such as desktop page generation). Project the impact of the revised ratios over the next 7 years, and create a second set of fourth-, fifth-, sixth-, and seventh-year accumulative after-tax earnings forecasts.

The third scenario you project should assume that the publishing program being appraised will be "dovetailed" into another (already existing) publishing house. This may mean that field selling costs can be eliminated because the buyer already has a field force that can handle the new line of books at little or no extra expense. It may mean that mail order programs can be combined, at considerable postage savings. Office rent may be drastically reduced, and managerial salaries may be virtually eliminated (assuming the buyer's existing management team can direct the additional publishing program with relatively little assistance). Again, you must estimate the impact of these possibilities on the percentage ratios established earlier, and project the changed results.

This third scenario is of particular interest to the publishing conglomerates which frequently buy up smaller enterprises to fill gaps in their product lines; it's how they make money from conglomerating. Even though they will resist paying the previous owner all the fruits of those dovetailing possibilities (since that owner didn't create them), such a scenario clearly reduces price resistance by showing how much margin for error a buyer who's already in the publishing business has in acquiring, essentially, a new imprint.

All three scenarios should start with the same current figures for net sales, cost of goods sold, variable marketing costs, other fixed costs, and tax liability. To be able to use an evaluation in planning sessions—and certainly to be able to communicate it to a potential buyer, in support of your asking price—you must document the financial report basis of those numbers, and save your worksheets and spreadsheet formulas to show how you converted them into 7-year projections.

As we've noted above, the accumulated after-tax earnings from each of the three scenarios described above, at the end of the fourth, fifth, sixth, and seventh years following the sale, produces a matrix of 12 numbers that should represent a fair price range for a book publishing house supported by a "normal" inventory of currently-active titles (which means a capitalized value of about 27 percent of current annual sales volume). Any agreed adjustment for above-or-below-normal inventory value should be made "off the top," after a base price has been agreed. Meanwhile, deciding just where within that 12-number range to strike a deal is what sales negotiation is all about.

Whether or not the situation you're evaluating has an actual prospective buyer who has another publishing operation into which this one can be dovetailed makes little difference. Because of the insatiable conglomerates, the existence of such *potential* buyers can generally be assumed when you're buying or selling a publishing house in America today.

Exactly where any specific negotiation concludes, within the 12-figure pricing range described above, depends on a combination of many factors (including the nerve, and selling skill, of the participants). Before entering into such negotiations, one is well advised to prepare a thoughtful list of characteristics of the publishing house in question that significantly reduce, or increase, the owner's risk. Among factors that decrease risk, and thus would encourage both buyer and seller to consider a price above the average of the range, are (a) a steady pool of key dealer accounts large enough to be unaffected by one or two defections; (b) a significant number of backlist titles that continue to sell well several years after publication; (c) editorial subject areas and distribution contacts that relate to open-ended markets—to potential millions of readers instead of thousands and/or that coincide with growing reader-interests; (d) stability in the recent financial performance of the enterprise (as opposed to erratic performance, or projections built on very short term shifts); (e) firm contracts for enough promising new manuscripts for the next 2 years; or (f) a "captive audience"—through a unique mailing list, special arrangements with associations or similar groups, well-established school adoption accounts, etc.

On the other hand, certain factors increase the buyer's risk, and thus suggest that some of that risk might be ameliorated by settling for a price somewhat below the average of the projection matrix. Such price-depressing factors include: (a) over-dependence on a few very large accounts; (b) over-dependence on a few key authors; (c) over-dependence on a key employee who might defect; (d) strong personal involvement by the seller with key accounts or authors—which might lead that person back into the arena as a future competitor; (e) the existence of aggressive, effective competitors in the same niche; (f) binding long-term commission contracts with ineffective sales agents; (g) undesirable leases on buildings or equipment; or (h) a bad past credit record that might complicate vendor relations.

These, then, are the kinds of things a seller tries to "fix" before entering the market place, and a buyer tries to identify and discount before making a deal.

The sale of a publishing house may include, or exclude, whatever related assets the parties concerned choose to specify. Defining what is included, and what is not, is a significant aspect of both the sales negotiation, and the writing up of the eventual sales agreement.

Generally speaking, it is a good idea to include only such assets as are required to operate the publishing business, and are not normally available from vendors. The pricing approach described above (based on 4–7 years' projected earnings from three alternative strategy scenarios) assumes that the buyer will get a viable publishing operation, with all of the essential ingredients for continuing. These normally include: (a) a *normal* inventory of salable books (with a capital value approximating a normal 27 percent of current annual sales volume, or later adjustment for any abnormal excess or deficiency); (b) all useful files and records of the enterprise since its inception; (c) unrestricted ownership of the company name, and all imprint names, with whatever good will has accrued to them; (d) all mailing lists of actual or potential customers, publicity contacts, authors, and vendors; (e) all author contracts; (f) all publishing-related computer software; (g) all publishing-related reference materials; (h) the individual office furnishings and equipment currently utilized by publishing personnel; and (i) assurances that the seller will not enter into direct competition with the enterprise for a reasonable (specified) period.

There are other assets, however, which are not essential to the continuance of the publishing house, that might better be excluded from the basic transaction *if the prospective buyer desires;* most of them can be sold to other parties in separate transactions. If the buyer, however, should wish to include them in the purchase, their value should be separately negotiated, and added to the sales price arrived at by projecting accumulative earnings. These include: (a) accounts receivable (assuming the seller also assumes responsibility for accounts payable); (b) obsolete inventory—with remainder value only; (c) extraordinary equipment (most frequently automobiles, but potentially anything from sound systems to specialized computer gimmickry not essential to routine operations); and (d) real estate.

As a seller, you're usually well advised to separate all such surplus assets from the basic transaction, so as not to complicate negotiations with buyers who don't need them. As a buyer, you may be able to find some real bargains by expressing a willingness to include such supplementary items if you're going to have to spend money on them (supplementing inventory, renting equipment, etc.) in the near future anyhow.

If you're an aspiring buyer, it is a good idea to wait until you have several potentially-buyable publishing houses identified before you start comparing and evaluating them. To keep things orderly, and make sure nothing gets overlooked, prepare a logbook in which you can enter the name and address, date, source of contact, and other pertinent information on every candidate you eventually identify. Also obtain a supply of large manila envelopes in which you can safely store material received from each of them, until you are ready to digest or discard it.

Now you're ready to start seeking out book publishing houses that might fulfill your ambitions. Generally speaking, there are five good ways to make contact with such prospects. Since the largest possible number of candidates tends to improve your selection, you should probably pursue all five of these approaches simultaneously. They are:

(1) *Reading the "For Sale" ads:* Only a modest number of publishing houses will be formally on the market at any given time. These will be so widely scattered that no single metropolitan newspaper's classified ads or general business magazine will normally include enough to give you a reasonable choice. But *Publishers' Weekly* (249 West 17th Street, New York, NY 10011) is so predominant as the unofficial trade journal of U.S. book publishing that many publishers who are trying to sell out announce their availability in its classified columns. Start there to find your most obvious candidates.

(2) *Consulting business brokers:* You'll find a number of firms that specialize in buying and selling businesses for others listed under "Business Brokers" in your metropolitan "Yellow Pages" phone book. Routine letters to all of those who look appropriate (i.e., who don't indicate some specialty that would exclude publishing properties) may well identify good local prospects; researching brokers' addresses in other major metropolitan areas (from your public library's phone book collection) will multiply the effectiveness of this approach. In a form letter asking such brokers whether they have anything to offer, make it clear that *you are not retaining the broker* to act for you (so the fee won't come out of your pocket). Any broker who's been commissioned to sell a publishing house will be eager to respond, if you indicate that you're interested in buying one.

(3) *Advertising your intentions: Publishers' Weekly,* and such general business periodicals as *The Wall Street Journal,* are regularly and eagerly consulted by people trying to sell publishing companies, as they seek guidance from other advertisements as to the state of the acquisition market. These are good places to identify yourself as a potential buyer—by running a brief ad (with a blind-box return address, c/o the medium, if you prefer not to be identified) describing the kind of publishing property you'd like to acquire. Such an ad is likely to bring responses from some publishing houses that haven't been put formally on the market, and that you probably wouldn't have discovered through other methods.

(4) *Networking through personal contacts:* Particularly if you're willing to wait a bit for your acquisition program to get into full gear, you may discover some interesting possibilities which haven't been openly advertised by spreading the word of your intentions, and your selection criteria, through

strategically-located people you know personally. Acquaintances active in publishing associations, book manufacturers, publishing consultants, bankers, probate lawyers, and other book publishers themselves, are all in positions that make them ideal word-of-mouth intermediaries in your search.

(5) *Asking appealing prospects directly:* Even if a publishing house's owners have not made a decision to sell, they may be amenable to doing so if the right offer is forthcoming at the right time. Examine the catalogs of various publishers in the field you'd like to enter (*Literary Market Place* breaks them down by editorial subject-areas.) When you find one that seems to meet most of your criteria, simply write to its chief executive officer and ask if he/she would entertain a buy-out offer. In fact, you might address such tentative feelers to a number of publishers whose catalogs resemble your target profile, giving statistical probability a chance to produce several candidates for your list. Whether or not this generates immediate prospects willing to sell, it will broaden the word-of-mouth network that is spreading news of your intentions among appropriate segments of the industry.

By pursuing all of these approaches simultaneously, you should be able (within a few weeks) to identify a number of publishing houses that are at least potentially available-for-purchase. Some may be so patently inappropriate that they should just be entered on your prospect-log (so you'll know not to waste your time if they crop up again) and eliminated without further scrutiny. For that purpose, it's a good idea to compose a brief letter that can be re-used throughout your search—to politely reject those that don't meet your requirements, so they won't continue to distract you with their sales efforts.

All the others should be sent a screening questionnaire such as illustrated below, with a cover letter indicating you'll need their answers to proceed (and including a request for their catalog), as soon as they're entered on your prospect-log. The questionnaire is likely to produce a phone call probing whether you're serious or just curious—but it's a good idea (after giving reassurances) to insist that you can't go farther without the questionnaire information. When each questionnaire is returned, establish a file-folder for all material you accumulate on that specific publisher. Any that ignore the questionnaire might be sent one follow-up request—in case your original inquiry went astray—and then disregarded.

Figure 4a—Sample Buy-Out Screening Questionnaire

---

(1) In what year was your book publishing program begun? _____

(2) How many separate titles do you now have in print? _____

(3) What items do you have in inventory other than books? _____

(4) Are you a corporation, unincorporated proprietorship, or partnership?

---

(5) What percentage of your total ownership is included in your offer to sell? _____ If less than 100 percent, explain nature and intentions of the remaining owners. _____

(6) Recent Financial Performance:

FISCAL YEAR BEGAN _____	This fiscal Year to Date	Last Year	Prior Year
Net Sales (after returns)	$_____	_____	_____
Pre-tax Profit (+) or Loss (–)	$_____	_____	_____
End of Period Inventory Value	$_____	_____	_____
* Cash plus Receivables	$_____	_____	_____
* Payables	$_____	_____	_____
" Indebtedness	$_____	_____	_____
Number of New Titles Published	#_____	_____	_____
Number of Titles Reprinted	#_____	_____	_____

(7) Approximately what do you expect the next year's sales to be? $_____ Explain any anticipated increase or decrease.
_____
_____
_____

(8) List major items of property and equipment to be included in sale, and give approximate market value.

Item _____ Value $_____

Item _____ Value $_____

Item _____ Value $_____

Item _____ Value $_____

Item _____ Value $_____

(9) Name the individual who now performs each of the following functions in the publishing house, and indicate ("yes" or "no") whether you think that individual will want to remain in that job after the sale.

Position	Name	Will Stay?
GENERAL MANAGER	_____	
FINANCIAL MANAGER	_____	
EDITORIAL MANAGER	_____	
MARKETING MANAGER	_____	

(10) How many people do you now employ?

Full-time _____; Part-time _____.

(11) Which of the following documents are available for inspection?

[] Written Budget [] Inventory count by value and title

[] Year-to-date results compared to budget

[] Profit/loss statements for past 3 years

[] Financial balance sheets for past 3 years

[] Sales by title for current and recent years; [] Sales by region; [] Sales by customer/account

[] Tax returns for current and recent years

(12) How many unpublished books do you now have under contract with

authors? _____ How many of these are already written? _____

(13) What is the most successful book you've published in the last 5 years?

_____

Year published? _____ Total number sold to date? _____

(14) List the major types of books you publish (by subject, purposes, etc.), and indicate the approximate percentage of your recent new titles represented by each type:

Type _____ Percent _____

Type _____ Percent _____

Type _____ Percent _____

Type _____ Percent _____

Type _____ Percent _____

(15) What approximate percentage of your current sales volume comes from each of the following sources? Make sure it adds up to 100 percent.

Sales to bookstores	_____	percent
Sales to wholesalers	_____	percent
Direct sales to libraries	_____	percent
El-high classroom adoptions	_____	percent
College classroom adoptions	_____	percent
Direct sales to professionals	_____	percent
Direct sales to consumers	_____	percent
Overseas sales	_____	percent
Subsidiary rights sales	_____	percent
Other: _____	_____	percent
Other: _____	_____	percent
Miscellaneous	_____	percent

(16) Rank the following in order of their importance in achieving your marketing results ("1" = most important, "2" = next-most important, etc.):

____ Commissioned sales representatives

____ Representation by another publisher

____ Direct mail-order selling

____ Exhibits

____ Field sales trips by staff

____ Representation by distributor

____ Telephone selling

____ Other (_____)

(17) Do you maintain an up-to-date mailing list of previous customers? _____

If so, how many names does it contain? _____

Only request the further documentation identified in Question 11 of the sample questionnaire above from the *three most attractive possibilities* from whom you receive completed questionnaires (hopefully, after you've seen at least ten). But keep the material you've accumulated from other plausible candidates on file, until you've made a deal and are sure you won't be reconsidering them. As new candidates become known, take them beyond the questionnaire request only if they look more promising than your third-ranked contender.

Now it's time to phone the chief executive officer, or other authorized spokesperson, of each of your top three candidates. Tell them that you have studied the preliminary information they've submitted (through the questionnaire, etc.), and are seriously considering making them an offer. Explain that before you can proceed, you'll need two things: (a) all of the additional documentation identified in Question 11 of Figure 4a, or reasonable substitutes, and (b) the answers to any additional questions that might have arisen as a result of your reading of the screening questionnaires.

If a seller is reluctant to show you such confidential material as recent tax returns at this stage, or answer certain sensitive or nebulous questions, you needn't push. But you certainly should *list* all such touchy issues and subjects, and make certain they've been satisfactorily dealt with before you make any binding commitments.

Use the questionnaires and documents presented by your top three choices to project what you and your associates think you could do with each publishing house if you bought it—and to estimate the fair market value of each. Then arrange a discreet on-site inspection of *the one most-appealing candidate.* Invest a little time in preparing for your visit—especially by dusting off your lists of unanswered (possibly sensitive) questions and advising the candidate (by phone or letter) what you'll need to be shown before you can consider making an offer.

If, at the end of such a visit, you still have *any* unanswered questions—advise the seller that it's now or never. Then, assuming you get satisfactory answers, present your first offer in an informal phone conversation. This will make it easier to adjust minor differences, or to withdraw the offer without leaving behind a lot of dangling commitments if too many difficulties arise.

In such a phone conversation with the seller (or a letter, if you insist), define specifically what you expect to be included in the sale, and what surplus assets you expect to be excluded. Suggest an effective date for the transfer of title, and outline briefly how you propose to handle the receivables, payables, and inventory value-changes. Then—unless the other party has beaten you to the punch—state the price you're prepared to offer, and outline any terms (delayed payments, stock swaps, etc.) upon which your offer is conditional. Tell the seller you'll put it in writing if the offer is acceptable.

If the seller balks, ask for a specific counter-offer; i.e., what would the seller want you to change about your offer, to make it more acceptable? If you are willing to accommodate any suggested changes, offer to incorporate them into your written agreement. If you aren't, either propose a compromise or tell the seller you must withdraw your offer and look elsewhere.

If it comes to the latter option, proceed with your second-choice candidate in the same manner: make an offer, entertain counter-offers, propose compromises, and either settle or withdraw. If it doesn't work the second time, try it with your third candidate. If that doesn't get you the property you want, start over with those other questionnaires waiting in the file folders.

It is very important, during this negotiating process, that you discipline yourself to stand by your previous determination of appropriate price ranges, required settlements terms, and special problems that must be covered by the agreement. Letting yourself be stampeded by impatience to reach a quick agreement can undo all of your careful preparation, and lead you into a deal you'll regret.

If you start near the low end of the estimated price range matrix, you'll have considerable room for compromise. If the property seems like a relatively safe investment, you can easily go up as far as the 12-number average. If it offers untapped opportunities which really excite you, you might even move toward the top of the matrix.

Once you and a seller have informally agreed to a price and terms, offer a modest deposit (so their check-endorsement will document the understanding) in return for a temporary written agreement to consummate the deal within a reasonable period for legal paperwork (usually about a month). You may want to have your own attorney draw up such a temporary agreement in advance, to facilitate prompt settlement once negotiations succeed.

You may find, of course, that the seller has been willing to take the lead by indicating an "asking price"—and if you're very, very lucky, that price may be so well within your acceptable range that you're prepared to accept it without bargaining. But "asking prices" are far more likely to be higher than any outsider's calculation of the appropriate level, since the seller is obviously biased in a different direction. In that case, you simply have to settle the rest of the details and then make what would have been your initial price offer as a counter-proposal. (You'll be surprised how often such proposals are accepted; sellers frequently realize that their asking prices are pipe dreams!)

Be prepared for the possibility that, rather than either accepting or rejecting your first (or subsequent) offer outright, the seller may ask for time to consider it. This is frequently a tactic to keep the bidding open long enough to compare your offer with those expected from other suitors. But it is certainly a legitimate move on the part of the seller, and you should be prepared to accept brief, reasonable delays at this stage. Meanwhile, it is legitimate for you to insist that your offer is not binding on you until there is some sort of temporary agreement—so that as long as the seller leaves the matter open, you are free to consider alternative acquisitions while you wait. Meanwhile, try to get some commitment as to when the seller will give you an answer—to help nudge that other party past any last-minute attacks of indecisiveness.

If the seller wants a delay of more than a week, you might be wise to begin tentative negotiations with your second choice (just to discourage that second choice from selling to someone else before you have a chance to bid). You can probably do this without making any binding commitments, by outlining every aspect of your potential offer except the price, insisting that this second party quote you a price (even if it's ridiculous—and will invoke your later counter-offer), and then asking for some time to think about it.

Once you've make an informal agreement with a seller, and exchanged your deposit for a temporary option, it's time to prepare that final purchase agreement. It would be foolhardy of us to try to tell you how to do it, just as *it would be foolhardy for you to try to write it yourself.* This is a legal exercise, not a publishing exercise. So turn the job over to your corporate general counsel or personal attorney. Explain to the lawyer the nature of book publishing receivables and payables and inventory values, and your understandings with the seller regarding their impact on the final sale price. Explain your need for protection against future returns by customers (for credit or refund), or lawsuits over prior instances of alleged slander or libel or plagiarism or breach of implied-author-contract, which might undermine the value of the enterprise after the sale. Go over any other issues that may have bothered you or the seller during the negotiations. Then ask the attorney to draft a final sales agreement that resolves all such issues fairly and reasonably, and to instruct you as to its execution.

Obviously, then, there's more to buying a publishing house than merely reading the "For Sale" signs and starting to haggle. But you'll find the work not only worthwhile, but potentially fascinating. Perhaps the single most important key to making it *profitable* as well is your willingness to keep looking for candidates until you've identified ten (to give you a good basis for comparison). You can then minimize the demand on your time by limiting your price projections to the top three, and on-site inspections to your first choice (unless/until that negotiation falls through).

Now let's turn to the other side of the coin, and examine this process from the seller's point of view.

A sale is a natural and potentially rewarding way to recruit a new owner/operator when it comes time for the present proprietor to retire. Or it may be an essential step in the settlement of an estate, or a divorce. Sometimes not-for-profit organizations find themselves unintentionally over-involved in their book publishing programs, and conclude that divestment is the best way to refocus their energies on their main purposes. Whatever your reasons for selling, honest analysis of them will probably indicate special requirements for a successful transaction.

The most obvious such requirements have to do with the amount of money you need to realize from the deal, and how soon you need that money. It is important to determine whether the *amount* or the *timing* is most critical to you, since there are often bargaining trade-offs between the two. If, for example, you can offer a buyer delayed payment terms that reduce the amount of immediate cash needed to close the deal, you can often get a significantly better price than if you insist on complete, immediate payment.

However, a seller's requirements and desires are not always limited to money. It may be important (for you, or for the enterprise) that you (the seller) continue your association with the publishing program, at least on a part-time basis, for months or even years after the transfer of ownership. You may have personal or moral obligations to others (such as long term employees) that you want to be confident the new owner will respect. You may even have an ideological concern with the directions in which the new owner will lead the enterprise (particularly in the case of special-purpose not-for-profit organizations divesting themselves of publishing businesses).

Whatever requirements your motives suggest a sale must meet to successfully achieve your objectives should be *written down* before you make any overt moves to sell. And you should review that written statement from time to time, to remind yourself that *if you settle for less than this, you will not have concluded a successful sale.*

Before you formally put your publishing house on the market, you should review steps you might take to reduce pressures for a quick sale. If finances are the problem, for example, can you cut back some marginal activities to give yourself more staying power during the negotiations with prospective buyers? If you're in a hurry to get on to something else, can you shift some responsibilities to co-workers, so that you're only needed on a part-time basis as sales negotiations proceed? Can major new commitments and decisions be rescheduled to eliminate their pressure from the super-charged emotional atmosphere in which you'll operate until the sale is completed? Calm thinking, careful planning, and appropriate consultation with co-workers can take away much of the need for selling quickly, and thus greatly improve your negotiating stance (and your blood pressure!).

Another major preliminary consideration you should face is how you can best present the news of the impending sale to your staff, to creditors, and perhaps even to those authors with whom you have a strong personal connection. There is no foolproof, across-the-boards formula for covering all those situations, but you should be aware that your corporate life is going to get complicated enough during the weeks and months of sales negotiation, without your having to deal with any side-conspiracies growing out of staff or creditor anxiety. So systematically identify the people who might seriously care who owns your publishing house—and ponder in advance when and what you should tell each of them about your plans for selling, and how you think those plans will affect them.

Finally, you should give some thought to whether or not you need specialized, professional help in selling the business. A business broker will cost you perhaps 10 percent of the eventual sales price (some ask for more, some for less, depending on circumstances). Some will ask for an up-front fee for price appraisals, etc. They're worth this to you only if you're convinced they'll increase your net proceeds by more than they'll cost, or if they'll relieve you of a lot of unpleasant work in arranging and executing the sale, at a cost you'd rather pay than do the work.

Good brokers are disciplined and persistent about holding out for the minimum conditions (including the price) you've established; they are better at saying "no" than most of us. Just think carefully through the issue before you make the expensive decision to hire one. But remember that you can always try it by yourself for a while, and bring in a broker later if you decide that you're in over your head.

Only when you've dealt with all of these issues should you begin to make known your desire to sell. Premature disclosure of such intentions can demoralize (or disruptively distract) your staff, make vendors nervous, and even threaten relationships with important authors.

Once you've sorted out those questions, your next concern should be identifying prospective buyers. The more such prospects you are able to contact, the better your chances of concluding a satisfactory sale at the price you want. And the more time you're prepared to allow for such prospecting, the more contacts you're likely to make.

Perhaps the biggest mistake you could make at this stage would be to try to do too much too fast. Focus your attention primarily on writing a classified ad that will attract serious and appropriate prospective buyers. There'll be time to assemble your actual sales presentation while you're waiting for those ads to appear, and for prospects to respond.

A good ad will include six pieces of information: (a) In the opening words which announce that you've got a publishing house for sale, include some positive characterization ("established," "well-known," "growing," "innovative," etc.) that serves notice to the bargain hunters that this isn't a fire sale; (b) Indicate the general editorial niche on which you've focused; buyers are often looking for compatibility with other lines, or their personal interests; (c) Mention briefly the major marketing channels in which you've established contact ("large customer mailing list," "extensive trade and specialty accounts," "solid pattern of classroom adoptions," etc.); (d) Indicate (only by general region) your location, unless the business is easily relocatable (in which case, say so); (e) Drop in a general indication of sales volume (to the nearest half-million), since this will suggest whether you're too big, or too little, for a buyer's game plan; (f) Give a response address that does not (at this time) identify your publishing house—by renting a post office box, using your home address, or making arrangements to route responses through the ad media (many of which offer "blind box" addresses and forwarding services).

When the ad's written, set it aside to "cure" (or pass it around to trusted confidantes), and start determining where it should appear. The most widely used "bulletin board" of the book publishing industry is the classified ad section of *Publishers Weekly*. Perhaps the most widely used (though quite expensive) general business medium for such announcements is *The Wall Street Journal*. You should also consider running the advertisement in smaller publishing periodicals, in other general business magazines, and in the "Business Opportunity" section of the classified ads in appropriate metropolitan newspapers (see *Literary Market Place* for addresses). If your publishing program serves a specialized field of interest, classified ads in trade or professional journals covering that field may get results.

Prepare your list of media, and schedule your ad to run once (or possibly twice) in each selected periodical to give you a comparison of the responsiveness of their audiences. (Use codes, such as a changing set of fictitious initials—"Attn: WSJ"—in your reply addresses to identify each ad medium.) Then instruct the several media whose ads produced the *best* responses to keep repeating the message until you tell them otherwise. Prepare to spend some serious money on these ads; remember that only by generating a substantial number of inquiries can you be reasonably sure of finding a good match who'll meet your price requirements.

Even before you place the ad, however, you should prepare a suitable "log" (a written form, or a computer file) on which names, addresses, phone numbers, and other notations regarding *every* contact you make during the selling campaign can be recorded for safekeeping. At the same time, arrange separate file folders to preserve all communications from each of these contacts until you're sure they're no longer relevant.

Now prepare a "fact sheet" to use in responding to the advertisement. Use the same uncompromising address you used in the ad; it's still not the time to go public. Write out (in narrative paragraphs, or as a categorized outline) a more detailed description of what kind of books you publish, how many you have in inventory, how and (generally) where you sell them (with sales volume numbers for each major channel), how many employees you have (and whether they expect to continue with the publishing house after the sale), what kind of facilities you occupy (and whether they're part of the deal), and other such generalized data as will enable a prospect to decide whether the matter is worth pursuing. Offer very clearly to identify your publishing house and send a copy of your catalog *if* the buyer is still interested after seeing the fact sheet.

Perhaps the biggest decision you have to make about the fact sheet is whether to include an "asking price." Unless you do so either at this point, or in the cover letter by which you introduce yourself soon after, you're likely to find prospective buyers significantly understating the fair market value in their opening offers—and you'll be at a "haggling disadvantage" as you work to force the price up. There is a considerable case for stating your asking price (the high side of your expectations) from the beginning, as openly and casually as possible, and letting the other party assume the burden of arguing to change the numbers—while you concentrate on positive sales talk.

You might also use this fact sheet for a selective, unsolicited mailing to business brokers listed in appropriate metropolitan phone "yellow pages"— not with the intention of hiring their services, but in case any are acting as acquisition agents for appropriate buyers. Estate and probate lawyers, and trust officers of major banks, might also be included (again from the yellow pages), in hopes some of them have clients seeking such an investment opportunity. And sending the fact sheet to the presidents (again, see *Literary Market Place*) of large publishing houses might get you tied into several corporate acquisition programs.

There is considerable disagreement as to the value of "word of mouth" promotion of a "For Sale" situation. If your reasons for selling have no negative impact (for example, if you're clearly at retirement age), consider telling your major vendors (printers, typesetters, etc.), sales reps or distributors, and similar contacts that you'd appreciate hearing about any potential buyers they might incidentally encounter; then use the fact sheet to invite those contacts to express direct interest.

Once you've identified a prospective buyer by getting a positive response to your initial fact sheet, you face the challenge of making a sales presentation that will support your asking price (or the minimum price you intend to accept) without unnecessarily exposing the confidential details of your business to the merely curious. The presentation should be made in several stages, to offer varying depths of information according to the prospective buyer's degree of interest. (You might start with *your own version* of the questionnaire displayed in Figure 4a.) At some stage, nevertheless, a good presentation should include:

1) a current copy of your catalog;
2) your last 3 years' financial summaries;

3) a current balance sheet;
4) a current inventory report (by title);
5) a memo outlining intangibles to be included in the sale;
6) a memo describing optional items (real estate, etc.) not automatically included, but for which a separate offer will be entertained;
7) an outline of works in progress (under contract but not yet published);
8) an analysis of the major sources of your sales volume.

A case can even be made for showing a serious prospect your own projection of the next 4-to-7 years' earnings potential, to help demonstrate how soon the buyer can recover the purchase price.

Generally speaking, you can divide what the buyer will eventually need to know into three levels of confidentiality. First, there is "screening information," which only enables that buyer to determine whether or not you meet the general requirements of the property he/she is hoping to acquire; the fact sheet should settle that. Next, there is "sensitive information" from which no competitor could substantially benefit, but that you would not normally be inclined to announce publicly; that's where your answers to the background questionnaire might be appropriate. Finally, there is "strategic information," that would be of value to your competitors, or to anyone starting a new publishing house serving your audiences; now we're talking about per-title sales data, identification of accounts, works in progress, etc.

Generally speaking, any plausible prospects who answer your ad should be eligible for the first level. Only those who've made personal contact and convinced you they're serious should get the second level of information. The third level should be restricted to those who've made at least a tentative offer—and now need to verify the basic facts.

If the offers that result from this process are all very far below your asking price, re-examine your sales presentation; there may be something about it that is not lending appropriate credibility to the value of the enterprise. Try to decipher the buyers' anxieties, and strengthen your presentation to overcome them. If that doesn't yield results, it may be time to recalculate your own "game plan" and evaluation; perhaps you've rationalized your way into unrealistic expectations, or overestimated the condition of the market.

The processes outlined above for selling a publishing house can also be used to sell a single editorial series, or some other segment of your enterprise, without divesting yourself of the core of the company. The preliminary task of analyzing your motives and establishing basic requirements is the same. The process of generating inquiries to identify potential buyers is the same. To a considerable degree, the later stages of sharing strategic information on-site inspections and interviews, and final closing arrangements are the same. But that sensitive stage in which you provide basic but non-strategic financial information (profit-or-loss statements, balance sheets, inventory records, etc.) must be handled differently.

Start by working systematically through your financial statement to see if you can isolate all expenses relative to the series or segment of the business that you hope to sell separately. Certainly your title-by-title sales figures from the past, your inventory records, and book-by-book production expenses can easily be segregated. But for some items (payroll, facilities, etc.), you will have to make percentage estimates as to what portion of a larger total should be charged to the series in question to reflect the true and total cost of developing and maintaining that series.

Using whatever such estimates are necessary (and keeping your worksheets to document their validity), create a retroactive profit-or-loss statement covering the operation of the series or sub-division for the past 3 years. Reproduce only those portions of your larger records as might lend credibility to this after-the-fact financial accounting for the smaller segment. Then deliver this material, along with specific inventory and royalty records for the books involved in the transaction, at the sensitive information stage of your sales presentation.

If the segment of your business thatyyou're selling is substantial, almost self-sustaining, and at least partially staffed, you might even find it advantageous to reorganize it as an autonomous operating entity before you begin promoting its sale, so that you can more easily document its viability. This may also help settle issues as to which employees will go with which part of the company after the split, and thus prevent distractions in your on-going business.

When you sell only a segment of your publishing house, in this manner, it is particularly important that you do a very precise job of spelling out just what is included in the sale, and what isn't. Which mailing lists, which author contracts, which past sales records, etc., is the new owner to have or share—and which remain your exclusive property?

A well-run campaign to sell your publishing house most advantageously will continue classified ad promotion for prospective buyers until at least one viable contender has stayed with you through enough of the follow-up steps to make a serious offer. This means you keep replying to inquiries from the ad with your fact sheet, and then sending any who're still interested after that your catalog and basic sales terms, and then walking the survivors through the semi-confidential financial information, and sharing with those you feel are strong and acceptable prospects a certain amount of strategic information (sales analyses, editorial schedules, earnings projections, etc.).

You can put any number of potential buyers through all of this at the same time, without conflict—since none of it need seriously cost nor compromise any of them. The more prospects working their way through the sequence the better. Just make sure you're maintaining a file folder on each party who's communicated with you about the sale, and a log (with addresses) indicating who's at which stage of the process.

When any prospect finally makes a firm offer that you want to consider, it's time to spend a little money asking a professional credit service for a report on the buyer. Unless you're being paid in full at the close of the deal, the amount of money you're entrusting to the buyer for future payment will be substantial; knowing how well that buyer has performed on similar commitments in the past will be inexpensive insurance.

When a prospective buyer has seen all of your presentation documents, discussed your terms, and accepted your price and conditions or made you a serious counter-offer, you now have to start deciding whether to settle for that particular prospect, or wait for a better one. It is a good idea at this stage to phone every serious contender and make it known that you have to make a decision on at least one firm offer in the near future (in case any are anxious to get their competing bid in beforehand). When you have at least one firm, acceptable offer in hand, and have given others that chance to make their competing commitments, it's time to single out the best firm offer and start trying to close a deal.

Whatever is included (all or part of your business, your own services or consultation, surplus assets, etc.), you should sit down immediately after negotiations and outline on paper (informally, and unsigned) every condition and understanding you believe to be part of the deal, as a result of the preceding exchanges. Invite any close associates who've also been involved in the selling campaign to examine your list for oversights. Review this list with the buyer and, after any necessary adjustments, give it to your lawyer. Inform the attorney that you now expect him/her to see that the negotiation is concluded in such a way as to guarantee you exactly what has been agreed upon.

It is appropriate to suggest that *your* attorney draw up a temporary sales agreement, involving a reasonable deposit, which will be sufficient to cause you to cease negotiations with all other prospective buyers; it is similarly appropriate to suggest that the *buyer's* attorney draft the final sales agreement incorporating all terms and conditions—subject to your own attorney's perusal and approval. In this manner, the party whose need for protection is most complex (at each stage) is put in command of the actual drafting.

PART II
General Management

CHAPTER 5
Staffing and Managing the Publisher's Office

The publisher is the "chief operating officer" of the enterprise—ultimately responsible for recruiting and organizing and developing and supervising the staff ... and for making the financial arrangements that get them (and the vendors) paid. The publisher *may* also be the "chief executive officer"—the *legal* head of the corporate entity—though many organizations make this a separate function (of the chairman of the board, or of a non-operating president representing ownership). This usually depends on whether the publisher also owns a major portion of the stock, or is a principal officer of a parent organization (such as a not-for-profit association). If the publisher actually has little "ownership" clout, the chief operating and executive roles are usually split to put the latter in the hands of someone who does.

In very small publishing houses, the publisher may also retain the role of "chief financial officer." However, to avoid blurring responsibilities, it is best that this role be delegated to the business manager, as soon as feasible.

At any rate, the publisher is properly Janus-faced—representing the duplicitous concerns of the board of directors (owners) to the staff, and of the staff to the board of directors (owners).

The real heart of the publisher's job, however, is the recruitment, coordination, and nurturing of a small "core management group" of specialists to head the basic manuscript acquisition, pre-press development, marketing, and business/finance functions whose interaction is so essential to the success of the publishing process. Though each of these four middle managers should pursue *different* objectives, it is the publisher's job to keep them all moving in the same general direction—so that they achieve *synergy* (a total result larger than the sum of their separate efforts) with respect to the corporate mission statement (as described in Chapter 6).

To achieve synergy, it is vital that the publisher *delegate* clear responsibility to each of the core managers (with their diverse frames-of-reference), rather than attempting to call all the shots in each area of operations. Never-the-less, a wise publisher will *always* keep a watchful eye on the health of the basic operational pipelines along which the work of each function flows. That means he'll always insist that acquisitions show evidence that the author pool is being solicited for a steady flow of new proposals from which new contracts will be filtered, that marketing is always making an adequate number of live promotional contacts from which sales can eventually be developed, that pre-press is always anticipating future roadblocks by allowing time for the adjustments that will avoid publication delays, that business operations is always monitoring the cash flow far enough in advance to massage it through extra collection efforts and prudent timing of disbursements to prevent any impending payday crises.

We might compare this tricky, many-faceted managerial task with "putting socks on an octopus." You'll see that reflected in a typical Publisher's Job Description like the one shown on the next page.

As that job description suggests, the publisher is co-accountable for achievement of the goals of *each* of the supporting "core managers"—for seeing that the editor-in-chief guides the acquisition function so as to generate new titles that make an appropriate contribution to sales volume, and the managing editor controls the pre-press cost of getting those new titles into the warehouse on time, and the marketing manager maintains an acceptable growth rate of sales revenue, and the business manager both guides the enterprise toward an acceptable profit margin *and* keeps inventory investment within the capital-commitment limits set by the owners in the mission statement.

Formalized accountability indices are essential for an effective and disciplined relationship between the publisher and the other core managers. Since such small groups tend, over a period of time, to develop a considerable degree of personal intimacy, it will not always be easy for the publisher to override bad decisions or take strong remedial action when results falter in one function or another. Yet if performance indices for one of the functions (as discussed in Chapter 7) decline for *two straight quarters*—it is unlikely that the responsible manager (despite the best of intentions) will be able to reverse the trend. The obvious remedy—replacement of that core manager—will be a much more humane process for all concerned if the publisher has made known to all of this group from the very beginning that *their jobs (as well as his) depend on satisfactory performance* with respect to those impersonal indices.

Accountability indices at all levels are therefore best framed as *quantitative* goals that can be measured by routine computer feedback of operating data; see Chapter 7 on how to do it. When you start getting *subjective* and *qualitative* about performance expectations, you usually create ambiguous loop-holes that can be used as alibi's. But in addition to his obligation to help the other managers meet their quantitative goals, the mission statement may properly saddle the publisher with additional responsibility for seeking their fulfillment within the context of the owners' *qualitative* aspirations.

Figure 5a—Sample Job Description: Publisher

TITLE: Publisher (General Manager)
Salary Grade: F (Negotiated)
Reports to: Board of Directors
Directly Supervises:
> Editor-in-Chief
> Managing Editor (Pre-Press)
> Marketing Manager
> Business Manager (CFO)
> Assistant to the Publisher
> Secretary to the Publisher

Budget Line Responsibility:
> Lines 210-219 (Management Expenses)
> Line 103 (Borrowing on Credit Line)

Accountability Indices:
> New Title Percentage of Sales
> Pre-Press On-Time Cost-per-Page
> Sales Volume Growth Rate
> Operating Margin
> Accumulative Inventory Investment
> Dollars in Retained Earnings

GENERAL RESPONSIBILITIES:

To function as the chief executive and operating officer of the enterprise, and to represent it as its public and legal spokesperson.

SPECIFIC OPERATING RESPONSIBILITIES:

a) To represent the concerns of the Directors to the employees, and those of the employees to the Board of Directors;

b) To obtain periodic re-confirmation of the Directors' Mission Statement, as a basis for strategic planning;

c) To recruit, instruct, and supervise the core management team (editorial acquisition, pre-press development, marketing, and business managers), as the principal function leaders and strategic planners of the enterprise;

d) To keep available to those core managers current descriptions of all staff positions they are authorized to fill in their respective functions, and such acceptable financial ratios as they will need for effective planning;

e) To coordinate and adjust the strategic plans of each major function of the enterprise so as to achieve maximum fulfillment of the Mission Statement;

f) To recruit and supervise the staff of the Publisher's office;

g) To report the performance, problems, and opportunities of the enterprise accurately and responsibly to the Board of Directors;

h) To take such other actions as said Publisher or the Directors may deem appropriate for maximum fulfillment of the Mission Statement.

And in addition to guiding those subordinate managers toward achievement of each of their specialized goals, the publisher in most publishing houses has another blunt, comprehensive goal—continually adding an acceptable number of *actual dollars* (rather than a comparative percentage) to the "retained earnings" pool from which dividends are paid to stockholders— or transferred back to a parent organization.

The publisher's job is the top prize in this business. But it's obviously not intended for the faint of heart!

The publisher's development and coordination of the core managers should center around their individual "strategic plans" for acquisition, pre-press development, marketing, and financial control (as further described in Chapter 9). But those individual managers can't plan effectively unless they know what resources they'll have to work with. Most of those resources can be expressed in terms of money—budget percentages or dollars. However, it is dangerous to let middle managers convert budget dollars into payroll (by adding people to the staff) unless such commitments are consistent with the publisher's long-term concept of the "shape of the organization."

So in specific responsibility "d," the sample job description suggests that the publisher has an obligation to keep the function managers advised not only as to how many budget dollars they can expect in the foreseeable future— by endorsing or amending the planning ratios proposed by the marketing manager for annual sales growth, and by the business manager for the assumed percentage of those sales or other financing that each function will be expected to use—but by providing an up-to-date organization chart that identifies every staff position they're authorized to fill. In Chapter 7, we'll take a detailed look at how that task is best approached.

The "span of control" required of the publisher by Figure 5a (direct supervision of six people) is the widest span normally advisable in any information packaging organization functioning by "small group" (face-to-face) planning and coordination dynamics (and that should include virtually *every* book publisher with less than 150 employees and/or $20 million in annual sales). Since the publisher in our sample has a two-assistant staff in addition to the four core-function managers, this is probably a well-established enterprise with an annual budget exceeding $1 million. Throughout the rest of the publishing house, no one should be asked to supervise directly more than four or five people.

Why? Because publishing is such a complex business that relatively few people have identical job descriptions. When individual managers try to supervise more than four or five (or in this one case, six) people *who do different things,* they almost always reduce their expectations and instructions to generalized "common denominators" that dilute effectiveness and creativity. And suppression of creativity in publishing is deadly!

Effective publishers delegate most planning and control responsibilities to the specialized middle managers who run each function (acquisition, pre-press development, marketing, business/finance). Note that in our sample job description, only the (usually fairly nominal) expenses of the publisher's office itself (mostly payroll), plus the interest-cost of meeting ownership's obligation to provide necessary working capital, are designated as specific budgetary responsibilities of the publisher. (The decision to meet capital needs by borrowing is an ownership rather than staff decision, and thus the interest-cost of that borrowing is more properly watched over and answered for by the owners' proxy—the top manager—than by a staff finance function ... even when the business manager rather than the publisher functions as chief financial officer.)

We'll deal with the publisher's relationship to the owners, the core managers, and the staff in general in the chapters immediately following. But before we do, let's look further into the staffing and operation of the publisher's office itself.

The publisher's office is the nerve center and command post of the publishing operation. Therefore, it must not only know *what is happening* within that operation at all times ... it must give the core managers, the owners, and other appropriate people *quick answers* to their questions about (and proposals for changing) the existing game plan of the organization.

To stay constantly cognizant of conditions, and provide prompt decisions, the publisher must be reasonably free from distraction. When the organization is very small (as with the typical four-or-five person start up), about all this usually means is a back-room office location and a phone that is screened by the switchboard. But as soon as feasible, the publisher's office should be staffed with an administrative assistant (secretary) who'll shield that Worthy from unwanted interruptions, monitor the appointment calendar, and do clerical chores that might otherwise eat into the publisher's work-day. If feasible, this secretarial assistant should *not* be the company receptionist (who properly works for the business manager)—since that receptionist is usually tied down to a single location, while the publisher's assignments are likely to send one farther afield.

At a later stage in the development of the enterprise (typically at around $2-million in annual sales volume), it becomes feasible (and wise!) to add a second—and very different—assistant to the publisher's personal staff. This is usually an "executive assistant" (most-often titled "assistant to the publisher") who functions as an intellectual *alter ego*. The job should be filled by someone with whom the publisher is very comfortable, and in whom the publisher has absolute trust. All other personnel (including the core managers) should be officially informed that while this assistant gives nobody "orders" (except when delivering those signed by the boss) he/she *does have the authority* to request *any* information (no matter how confidential) about the publishing operation from *anybody*—on the same basis as if the request came from the publisher herself.

In the next six chapters, you're going to read about a number of basic planning and reporting spreadsheets and databases that core managers use to control daily work and coordinate their diverse strategies. A major part of the work of an effective executive assistant is to provide the publisher with reliable, on-line access to all of this other information—and to reorganize it or analyze it to help the publisher assess trends or answer significant questions.

Such computer files include the directors' mission statement, the publisher's own organization chart (which the assistant should regularly update), the functional strategy models (acquisition, pre-press development, marketing, financial—as per Chapter 9), and the line-by-line budget with (historical and current) result-feedback from the finance function. From this feedback and other sources, the executive assistant should then be able to create and maintain the weekly spreadsheet of "key operating indices" and the monthly scorecard of "accountability indices" described in Chapter 8— from which the publisher and other core managers learn who/what is performing well at any given time, and who/what isn't.

The executive assistant may, because of the confidential nature of the role, also function as the basic personnel administrator of the organization. (Very few book publishing houses are large enough to cost-justify a specialized personnel department or manager.) This responsibility will *not* include payroll accounting (properly and routinely handled in the finance office) or leave-time scheduling (best handled by each individual supervisor), but the assistant may maintain confidential employee records (such as recruitment references and past performance reviews) and monitor the scheduling and the results of the supervisors' periodic reviews of their subordinates' performances that normally determine pay adjustments—to see that the publisher is informed of any significant problems or promotions.

Another aspect of the publishing process that executive assistants are well-situated to handle for the publisher (and all concerned) is integrated work scheduling. Chapter 8 will describe the "management events calendar" integrated scheduling approach developed over the years (as PCs replaced card files) by the Huenefeld Publishing Consultants and a number of their clients. The system results in a constant database from which current chronological checklists of those things each function owes the others (indicating who's responsible for doing what by when) can easily be generated prior to each weekly coordinating meeting of the core managers—for their review and adjustment. Maintaining this calendar (largely by entering the adjustments those meetings make) is an appropriate assignment for the publisher's executive assistant—who is frequently the *ex officio* "recording secretary" for (though not an active participant in) those core management meetings. This should assure that the publisher quickly learns (from that alter ego) about serious deadline defaults that effect the progress of the enterprise.

The executive "assistant to the publisher" thus plays a comprehensive "shadow role" touching on all aspects of the enterprise. For this reason, publishers find this a particularly appropriate position in which to "try out" (and train) a good candidate for any anticipated, future core management opening.

Before we move on from the special concerns of the publisher's office, some attention should be given to physical facilities. If you have a computer network from which any eligible party can call up all of those planning and control forms, and feedback indices—the publisher's need for conventional office apparatuses like filing cabinets and typewriters is very limited. But by the nature of the job, publishers typically spend *as much as half* of their total work-time time in *meetings* with other people. The subjects these meetings are often sensitive. So a prime requirement of a properly-conceived publisher's office is that it provide appropriate space for *confidential* conversations.

The cast of the typical "core management meeting"—the publisher, four function managers, and the executive assistant as recording secretary—adequately defines the maximum requirement of that confidential meeting space. Any larger group (such as a board meeting, with supporting specialists—or a general staff meeting) should be moved to a general conference room; with that many participants, it is very unlikely to remain confidential anyhow.

But we do not mean to suggest that most of the publisher's work goes on behind closed doors. The most effective publishers delegate, delegate, delegate—so that somebody else is responsible not only for doing virtually all of the detailed work of the publishing house, but for *seeing that it gets done.* The publisher, then, can and should be a free-floating catalyst and instigator who makes sure that neither significant problems nor legitimate opportunities are overlooked.

CHAPTER 6
Relating to Owners/Directors

In this chapter title, note that we used a slash to suggest that owners and directors are, for all practical purposes, the same entity when it comes to managing your publishing house. The directors of a corporation are the legal proxies for—and speak for—the owners. They (usually organized as a "Board of Directors") constitute the ownership reality with which every top manager (even in a not-for-profit publishing house) must ultimately come to terms.

The laws of the various states that allow people who own group enterprises (business or otherwise) to limit their personal risks to the size of their individual investments by forming a corporation, also set forth rules for continued exercise of the power of ownership through a Board of Directors. Voting for election of directors is normally proportional to each stockholder's relative equity in the enterprise in commercial corporations; not-for-profit organizations follow a great variety of (usually democratic) procedures for such elections. Generally speaking, then, the Board of Directors becomes the "boss's boss," with the authority to overrule or to fire the chief operating officer.

Having to "get your act together" well enough to explain plans and progress (or the lack of same) to a non-operating Board such as this usually has such a beneficial effect on top-echelon perspective and discipline in a publishing house, that even those that are wholly-owned by the management often go through the motions of Board elections and meetings at regular intervals. In fact, it's generally such a valuable exercise that many not-for-profit publishers that are not separately incorporated by their sponsoring organizations set up external "publication advisory committees" to perform the same function.

The existence of a Board, which must be informed and consulted, can make it much easier for management to demand accountability from key staff people who might otherwise attempt to isolate and defend personal fiefdoms within the organization. And the Board provides a forum in which strategy (basic directions and long-term plans) rather than the day-to-day tactics of routine operation become the center of attention. Using this somewhat remote platform to achieve distance from daily details can help management control the general direction of the enterprise despite the vested interests of staff veterans who are threatened by change.

Some Boards of small publishing houses (particularly where ownership is divided among several participants) consist entirely of senior staff personnel. However, such a completely internal Board loses the advantage of external perspective that comes from a wider base of membership. Sometimes members are selected to assure various personal interests, or points of view within a divided ownership or sponsoring membership, that each will be heard (even though the balance of power is—and should be—stacked in favor of a bloc of directors who reflect the attitudes of a majority of the stockholders). Most managers will agree that if minority owner-discontent arises, they'd rather have it out in the open, and fully voiced, than waiting in ambush for the next annual stockholders' meeting.

If the Board is expected to make an active impact on corporate strategy, members may also be chosen because of their professional insights into non-publishing fields that have a bearing on those strategies: education, bookselling, banking, printing, etc. (Be careful, however, about including potential vendors who'll use the position to make you a "captive account"; you can avoid that by having *two* from any vendor industry represented.) Not-for-profit publishing programs frequently seek directors from commercial publishing houses to re-enforce such insights.

State laws establish certain rules regarding not only the election, but the conduct, of a Board of Directors. If your incorporation is competently handled by a qualified lawyer, these requirements will be spelled out clearly in your corporate by-laws. (Such professionalized incorporation usually costs less than a thousand dollars, and is worth every cent of it.) A copy of those by-laws should be made available to every Board member. Needless to say, the publisher/COO (and the Board chairperson, if that's a different individual), should become especially familiar with them.

More is at stake in the manner in which your Board is organized, and operates, than legal niceties. Corporate law and proper Board procedure exist primarily to make sure that all equity holders (partial owners) are treated fairly. In small, personal enterprises such as most book publishing houses, this is more important than among bigger enterprises. If hard feelings about unfairness develop here, it will usually be among close working associates, friends, and even family members—far more disruptive than impersonal disputes among absentee investors that can be fought out in court without sentiment.

Along with ground rules for the composition and election of the Board, your by-laws should establish a clear and acceptable parliamentary procedure for its functioning. Again, the best approach generally is to retain competent legal counsel, who will have available basic, time-tested guidelines for fair and effective organization of the group, conduct of its meetings, and making of decisions. But in any case, as long as the by-laws enable a majority of present directors to override a parliamentary ruling of the chair, an essential minimum of fairness is virtually guaranteed.

Once the by-laws are established and directors are duly elected, the first significant question that must be decided is: "Who will lead the group?" In small publishing houses whose top manager owns a controlling interest, it is common for that individual to chair the Board in addition to heading the staff; however, some COOs prefer that someone else chair the Board, so they'll be freer to campaign vigorously for partisan points of view within that forum.

In not-for-profit publishing programs, the chairperson is frequently a non-publishing watchdog from the parent organization. But whether the publisher/general manager heads the Board, sits as one of its members, or merely attends meetings on a non-voting ex officio basis, that individual has a major stake in the selection of issues with which the Board chooses to deal, and in how it deals with them. In fact, most Boards look to general management to tell them what issues need to be addressed, and use management's proposals as points of departure for forging their decisions.

Keep in mind that chairing the Board can be a very important part of the effective management of a publishing enterprise. Because it is the forum of last resort, usually speaking with all of the clout of outright ownership, a Board can (unless wisely restrained by leadership) interfere disastrously in a process as complex and specialized as book publishing. But that is not usually the main challenge to Board leadership; publishing loses much more from Boards that fail to live up to their contributive potentials than from those that over-involve themselves. Making the Board a positive force for achievement of the owners' objectives is one of the ways a good chief executive officer earns her/his pay.

The services of the publisher's office and staff are normally made available to the Board (and to its chairperson, if that's not the publisher), for purposes of reproducing and distributing meeting notices, minutes, background reports, etc., for making physical arrangements for meetings (from conference table to lunch), for reimbursing members' travel expenses, seeing that they get any prescribed honorariums, and for meeting other legitimate logistical expenses of the Board. Such expenses are usually charged to the publisher's management section of the budget, since both the Board and the publisher are involved in the general management of the enterprise.

Whether you're chairperson, or a non-chairing publisher, you'll find that one major key to an effectively functioning Board is the manner in which its meeting agenda are established. Normally, the best procedure is to establish an accumulative file of agenda items (on a database or in a folder) in which carry-over topics may be recorded at the previous Board meeting (as questions arise or items are pushed forward for further study), and to which the chairperson may make additions at any time. You'll be wise to establish a procedure by which other Board members may also place questions on the agenda, but the authority of the chairperson to eliminate the trivial or inappropriate, combine items, and otherwise shape the agenda to the time constraints of a plausible meeting should be clearly established.

In practice, however, most of the agenda items will come from the publisher. If the chairperson is a different individual, these two should confer well in advance of each meeting to identify agenda items that meet the organization's need for decision making (and owner support), without overtaxing the Board.

A great deal will depend, of course, on whether your Board convenes just to make sure the enterprise remains on the "up and up," without getting seriously involved—or whether it attempts to help run the company by making policy and plotting strategy. Deciding which of these two basic types of Board you want is one of the major early issues of organizational strategy.

A good case can be made for either a standoffish Board that merely fulfills legal meeting requirements, hears the chief operating officer out, and then says yea or nay—or a deeply involved Board that lends a variety of perspectives and insights to actual planning and decision making. The former might appropriately be referred to as a trustee-type Board, and the latter as an activist Board.

The relatively unobtrusive trustee Board is most appropriate when the expectations of the owners are clear-cut and not very likely to change. Under those circumstances, what the owners primarily need to know is whether management is pursuing those objectives honestly and competently, with diligence and common sense. If the Board should decide at any time that the answer is "No," its most effective course of action will be to dismiss and replace the publisher. (If that individual happens to own the publishing house, and cannot be replaced, members of an honorable trustee Board will usually conclude that their duty lies in making their doubts about the course of events clear—by themselves resigning.)

Unless things are going badly, trustee Boards tend to be unanimous and uncontentious. For the long-term health of the enterprise, it is a good idea to shuffle membership in such groups regularly, and to seek strong personalities of unquestioned integrity, so you can depend on someone to stand up and sound off when and if it becomes obvious that "the emperor has no clothes."

If you expect to be involved in a publishing program of considerable complexity, or one that is expected to change with the times, or grow by its own momentum, an activist Board is probably more in order. Even if the publisher is a sole owner, such a Board can serve as a powerful brainstorming resource, helping the publishing program compensate for the blind spots of that owner. And in any type of enterprise, a good activist Board helps overcome that awesome isolation that frequently surrounds a top manager who must steer an enterprise through threatening shoals without demoralizing the staff by confronting them with too many stark vistas.

But an activist Board is a much more complicated creature for management to deal with than is a group of relatively unobtrusive trustees.

Considerable attention must be given to the selection of directors, to achieve a group that interacts positively, but not syncophantically. If there is no controlling stockholder bloc, skilled political maneuvering may be required to accomplish this. Be particularly careful to avoid a hostile Board majority that could actually wrest control of overall strategy from the publisher's office for political reasons, rather than managerial incompetence.

To avoid that possibility, it is usually wise to make an activist Board fairly large and diverse. While three conscientious people may be enough "watchdogs" to insure the integrity of the enterprise as trustees, it becomes much too easy for two of them to gang up on the third (or the publisher) if they are actively helping plot the direction of the publishing program.

When you opt for an activist Board, the professional qualifications of the members also become much more important. If they are going to be empowered to make significant decisions about publishing strategy, it behooves you to choose people who know something about publishing—or about such vital components of the publishing process as finance, production, or distribution. However, as we noted above, care should be taken not to include potential vendors who will compromise your freedom-of-choice—or at least, to include them in competing pairs to "keep each other honest." A particularly good alternative is to seek directors from among your principal authors and customers—who bring not only their own useful perspectives, but often some insight into how your competitors operate.

This is not to say that *all* directors must offer publishing insights; it may be necessary to include some innocents in order to see that particular stockholder or membership interests are adequately represented. A diverse group that includes both a number of professionally experienced people, and enough open-minded non-professionals to mediate the disagreements between the pros, will be hard for anyone to manipulate.

Not-for-profit publishers often pay their directors nothing except expenses, viewing their time as a contribution to a good cause. Commercial enterprises who do pay honorariums over and above travel expenses must remember to report these to the Internal Revenue Service, and so advise each director on the prescribed form (1099-Misc) at year's end. Obviously, with so much more expected of them than is expected of a trustee-type Board, activist Boards normally receive more substantial honorariums (fees in compensation for their services). In small publishing houses, Board honorariums typically range from $50 to $200 per meeting.

The law generally requires not only that advance notice be given all directors of all Board meetings, but that a written record of the results of those meetings be maintained. By the simple parliamentary device of reviewing and approving each set of minutes at the next meeting, the Board can effectively guard against the possibility that such records might be slanted, or inaccurate.

Since the act of incorporation is enshrined in law, the subsequent decisions of corporate directors are legally binding with respect to the assets and obligations of the enterprise. Therefore it is important that the record of those approved minutes, from the organization of the enterprise throughout its existence, be maintained in chronological sequence as a basis for researching or documenting such instructions and restraints as the directors may have established for management's operation of the publishing house.

However, wading through years of Board minutes every time a relevant policy question arises can be very time-consuming. Furthermore, since decisions recorded at one point may well have been rescinded at some later time, it's risky to take short cuts by simply trusting someone's recollection that "we decided that three years ago last summer." So it behooves the chair and the publisher to maintain a summary of past Board actions that limit the staff's (or the Board's) options—regularly updated whenever subsequent action revises such policy guidelines.

Another way of making the Board minutes easier to consult is to index them. Brainstorm a list of appropriate policy-area topic headings, establish a database code for each topic on your computer, add consecutive page numbers to your permanent file of meeting minutes. Then simply indicate on each topic-file in the database every page in the record where that subject is significantly mentioned.

The kinds of Board decisions that should be included in such an easy-reference file include ground rules for budgeting, borrowing money in the company's name, making significant investments in capital equipment or real estate (i.e., buying instead of renting), increasing the accumulated inventory investment, and perhaps even adding people to the payroll. All of these constitute obligations against corporate assets about which directors may well insist on being consulted.

A record of dividend decisions should also be easily accessible. Presumably, the corporate finance officer will report regularly (in person or through the publisher) the amount of after-tax money accumulated in the "retained earnings" account. It is up to the Board, then, to decide how much (if any) of this accumulation will be paid out to stockholders in the form of dividends. This is a more complex decision than is immediately apparent. Sometimes this money is sorely needed for other purposes (such as increasing the inventory investment). Sometimes there are big tax advantages in using it to fund a deliberate deficit in the following year—through operating practices that will increase the value of the company later (such as extensive mail order list screening to enlarge a customer base). Whatever guidelines the Board has established in the past for reaching such decisions (percentage allocations, customary quarterly or annual pay-outs per share, etc.), along with up-to-date data on the status of the retained earnings account, should always be immediately available.

Board records can also be used as the basis of an accumulative written statement of personnel policy, covering everything from working hours and benefits to termination policy, and incorporating a chart of the various pay levels sanctioned for different degrees of skill or responsibility (as per Chapter 11). Making the personnel policy statement and salary structure creatures of the Board, rather than the management, may help the publisher explore ideas and proposals with the staff without compromising corporate options—since the publisher is not free to make commitments on-the-spot, but must take the issue "off line" for more detached consideration by the Board.

Just as the corporate by-laws become the "constitution" governing the function of the Board, then, an orderly and accessible record of Board actions on specific issues becomes a "constitution" for the operating managers of the publishing program. But the Board may wish to give management more than "ground rules" for operating the enterprise. And management itself should insist on knowing explicitly what results are expected of it. This can be dealt with by including in that accumulative, updated summary of Board decisions a "mission statement."

A mission statement is a formal expression of what the Board expects the paid staff of the enterprise to accomplish. Obviously, this can be stated in broad generalities, or in specific and numerical detail. A significant percentage of the mission statements of publishing houses (especially not-for-profits dedicated to good causes) unfortunately have relatively little impact on operations or strategy, because they are litanies of platitudes rather than decision-making guidelines.

The best mission statements (those that do make an impact) are no more than a page long. They are fairly explicit about *what* the directors expect the organization's books to do for/to *whom*, thus giving both editors (seeking new manuscripts) and marketers (seeking new audiences) some real guidelines for the direction and dimensions of their searches. They also establish realistic, but not unchallenging, numerical performance goals for each major function of the enterprise—along the lines suggested in Chapter 7. Doing a little math on those performance goals (often expressed as percentage ratios) also produces an explicit earnings target (in actual dollars) that can be used to estimate future dividends or reserves. In a commercial operation, this may well be the ultimate index by which the top manager's performance is measured.

It is particularly appropriate that the mission statement be explicit about the amount of the owners' capital (either as a percentage of annual sales volume, or as an exact dollar figure) the staff will be allowed to "lock up" in the warehouse in the form of unrecovered inventory investment.

Such an explicit statement of corporate goals makes some managers and their key associates uneasy, because it provides benchmarks for documenting unsatisfactory performances by those managers, and the departments for which they are responsible. But effective management teams tend to *like* explicit mission statements from their Boards, because they also provide standards for documenting *success*. This assumes, of course, that the directors will set realistic goals—based on gradual improvement of actual past indices. Failure of a Board to be realistic destroys its credibility with key personnel— with potentially destructive morale and turnover impact.

If your publishing program does not currently have an explicit statement of what its owners/sponsors expect the publishing team to accomplish, it behooves the management team to prod the Board into adopting one. The best way to do this is for the core management group to prepare its own version of a realistic statement, and present it (through the publisher) to the Board as "our current understanding of what we're supposed to be doing." Then ask the Board either to adopt the statement as its own, or to amend it so the staff will have specific, realistic goals. This mission statement (sample shown on next page) then becomes the starting point for all strategic planning—and a comparison of results to goals should be a routine item on every Board meeting's agenda.

Periodically reviewing and updating the corporate by-laws (rules for its own functioning), the accumulative index of policy guidelines it has adopted (from meeting minutes), a statement of personnel and pay policy clarifying its contract with the staff, and a mission statement establishing goals for overall results, may give your Board as much as it wants to do—to look after the interests of whoever owns your publishing house. But once these basic documents are created, changes should normally be relatively modest and gradual; with staff recommendations as a starting point, this is within the grasp of even an unobtrusive trustee Board.

If you wish the Board to be more significantly involved in setting policy and plotting strategy, it is important that you identify some specific focal points to which the members of the Board can most effectively apply their insights. Otherwise, Board meetings will become generalized bull sessions that produce a lot of entertaining rhetoric, but no specific guidance for the operating staff.

Perhaps the easiest way to provide such focus, and give the Board some real leverage for influencing strategy, is to share with it the basic planning documents by which general management controls the direction and scope of the publishing program—as described in Chapter 9. In addition to the Board's own mission statement, these should include the publisher's organization chart, the strategic planning models of the four functions (acquisition, pre-press development, marketing, finance), and the budget (with historical background and current comparative results.

Given an opportunity to consult updated copies of each of the seven basic planning documents prior to each meeting (and perhaps review them more thoroughly at the meetings on a rotating basis), to question any changes, and to comment on the options suggested by management, intelligent Board member members can make an enormous contribution to both management's perspective, and its identification of options. An activist Board with a diverse membership drawing on professional experience in related areas (finance, distribution, etc.) that is willing to kibitz these planning documents periodically and make constructive suggestions, without making detailed demands, can contribute positively to the evolving strategy of the enterprise.

The Board should be reminded, however, of the myriad background details that go into any one of those strategy models. While its overview will be helpful, and occasional specific suggestions may be adopted verbatim by the staff planners, it is generally unwise of a Board to try to dictate details of these basic planning documents unless it has decided that the management team is clearly incompetent—and is ready to take strong remedial action.

Figure 6a—Sample Mission Statement

Twenty-Fifth Century Publishers, Inc., exists to publish and distribute information packages (primarily books—but with an openness to other media) relevant to natural history and outdoor recreation. It is the expectation of the Board of Directors (as confirmed at its meeting on 10 October 1992) that the managers and employees of Twenty-Fifth Century Publishers will, until instructed otherwise:

Acquire, refine, and publish approximately 3,000 book-page equivalents of new product in the first half of 1992, and increase that volume by 5% (accumulatively) in each subsequent 6-month publishing season,

Maintain an annual growth rate in sales dollar-volume of not less than 12.5%,

Achieve at least 30% of that volume from the sale of products less than a year old;

Realize a before-tax operating margin of not less than 10.0% of that dollar volume, and

Limit accumulative inventory investment, at any given time, to not more than 27.5% of the current annual sales volume.

It is also the expectation of the Board of Directors that the managers and staff will periodically review prospects for enhancing the financial position of the company, the job-satisfaction of the employees (without jeopardy to the position of the company), and the interests of the stockholders in furthering both public education in natural history, and public access to informational resources for the enjoyment of outdoor recreation.

As you consider possibilities for making your Board of Directors a more constructive player in your publishing program, pause a moment over the realization that Board actions are *real*. If you're incorporated, the law has vested the power to speak with the force of ownership in this body. Future lawsuits (about everything from employee rights to stock values, from the validity of author contracts to the tax status of a sponsoring institution) may be settled on the basis of the wording of Board motions and the recording of Board votes.

And when the person who chairs that Board (whether the publisher or an outsider) speaks or signs on behalf of the corporation, the world is entitled to believe that your publishing house has expressed its definitive position. Obviously this suggests reasonable caution about public statements, or even private commitments; oral contracts with both authors and key employees have proved expensive and awkward for many a publishing house with an irrepressible chairperson.

But perhaps of greater significance is the *internal* credibility of the Board. Because it speaks with near-final authority, it can be a major force for change and progress if it is so inclined, and adequately led. But this force is primarily exerted in terms of the weight the Board carries with the publishing staff. A vacillating, poorly informed, unimaginative Board will inevitably be ignored by the people who run the publishing house. An informed, decisive Board will help mobilize staff energies and discipline staff coordination behind the strategies adopted by the publisher and other core managers.

And an effective Board helps prevent professional isolation of these core managers. It brings in external perspectives, and its individual members can make major contributions by sharing their knowledge of new technologies with appropriate staff members.

Above all, the Board has authority to sanction change—and this is especially important when that change is risky. Operating personnel are normally cautious about sticking their necks out beyond the boundaries of their own specialties; they may be excessively inhibited by the realization that it's not their money. Simply by being willing to *sanction risk,* a Board of Directors can motivate a publishing staff to move much more imaginatively and boldly than it would move on its own.

The Board, too, must be reminded in this context that its actions are *real.* It speaks for the legal entity that is the publishing house; it must not speak capriciously. Its diversity and experience and general competence (Boards do not tend to be made up of ineffective people) must be counted on to identify *excessive* risks that the enterprise can't afford to chance. At the same time, its perspective and experience should enhance the self-confidence that enables an organization to move boldly forward in changing circumstances.

The chief executive officer and/or publisher who works intelligently at harnessing the potential clout of such a body has a much better chance of instigating effective publishing than does one who sees the Board as only an awkward legal necessity.

CHAPTER 7
Organizing to Generate Synergy

In work as complex (and often ethereal) as publishing, it is not always easy for individuals to see just how their efforts fit into the total process—or how they effect group results. This can lead to misdirected energy-waste, divided loyalties, and confused priorities. But if one is clearly identified as a member of a specific segment of the organization—and if the goals of that segment are clearly and appropriately stated, impersonally measured, and openly reported—it becomes much easier to focus one's thoughts and labors. And if those measurements are routinely posted side-by-side with the results being achieved by other groups within the organization, subtle but powerful peer pressure is exerted on each staff member "not to let their team down" in hopefully-friendly competition with those other groups.

Therein lies the key to effective organization of your publishing house. If the publisher can get one group of people to dedicate themselves to maximizing the sales volume (that's *marketing*), a second to assume responsibility for finding new books that will give that marketing effort maximum support (we call that *acquisition*), a third group who'll put those new products into the inventory on time with a minimum utilization of capital (the *pre-press development* function), and a fourth who will look after the fiscal/physical assets in such a manner that the publishing house gets to retain a maximum percentage of its sales revenue as "profit" (the *business operations* function)—then that publisher can hardly fail! And with the coordinating publisher's office separately identified as general *management,* we've defined the five basic staff components of an intelligently organized publishing house.

Early in the development of a publishing program, it will be necessary for some people to serve more than one master—to "wear multiple hats" by dividing their focus between two or more of those quantitative goals. When they do so, it is essential that they stop from time to time and remind themselves *which* focus (and thus, which end result) they're supposed to be serving at the moment. It may, in fact, be helpful for such divided souls to set aside specific times of day to work on each different function.

But it is important to begin identifying each person with a single, constant function as soon as feasible—so that all except the publisher's office will have no doubt as to which specific end result takes top priority in their planning and decision-making.

If there are only two people in the entire enterprise, you should make certain—regardless of which is the publisher—that one of them has the primary *acquisition* responsibility and the other the primary *marketing* responsibility. These are the two most strategic functions—with acquisition controlling the direction in which your publishing program is evolving, and marketing controlling the speed of its development. One looks at the world through the eyes of the author, the other those of the reader/customer; it is almost impossible to keep both of those perspectives crystal-clear in a single mind. From free-wheeling interplay between the two, you get synergy. But if one of them can "lord it over" the other, and make its priorities paramount— that synergy dissipates. Maintaining a truly balanced peer relationship that ignites the refining fires of honest contention between these differing acquisition and marketing frames-of-reference will always be one of the most important challenges facing the publisher.

As a "bootstrap" venture grows beyond those two people, it usually makes sense to identify *the next two people* with the remaining major functions—pre-press development and business operations. Get specific individuals to work organizing the strategies, the procedures and the files of each of the four basic functions *as early as possible* in the evolution of the enterprise. As long as the civility of mutually respectful professionals is maintained, one of the four can also safely continue "chairing" the group as publisher for several years—but that individual will have to be very careful not to "pull rank" in support of their particular operating function, thus throwing the synergy of honest contention among all four functions into imbalance. (By the time the organization is big enough to require a *full-time* publisher, the core function managers should be mature enough not to be blinded by rank-pulling ... and the publisher should be tough enough to exercise any necessary clout or discipline when things get sticky.)

But it is the people who perform basic tasks within each of these functions, but don't get to call the shots as managers, who are most effected by organizational ambiguity and divided loyalty—because they're not in position to see the "big picture" as clearly as the function managers. Until you get the four basic functions defined, it's really best to make *everybody a core manager;* nobody gets a secretary or other assistant until the *fifth* employee is justifiable. And beyond those first four, you should try hard to avoid multiple hats and divided loyalties. Though all four functions may need clerical support by the time you hire that fifth person—make him a subordinate to the business manager, performing diverse (but simple) individual tasks *as negotiated with that business manager* by the other core managers. *I.e.,* give him only one "boss"—and make that boss's primary accountability index (in this case, profit margin) this employee's own ultimate goal.

So beginning with that fifth person, it should be possible to avoid further functional ambiguities—except for the publisher herself—by assigning each new staff member to one-or-another of the basic teams. (And if you recall Chapter 5, the publisher is in clear control of this evolutionary process through her authorship of the organization chart which authorizes hiring by identifying all approved positions.) How fast you add additional personnel should be determined by the cash flow available to pay them.

When the typical start-up enterprise reaches the quarter-million-dollar annual sales volume normally necessary to "break even," it has 3.5 full-time-equivalent employees (thus, one or more part-timers)—and has already sorted out the four basic functions so that all new recruits will belong clearly to one-or-another (even if more part-time hiring is necessary). Now the publisher must keep a careful eye on the total number of full-time-equivalent employees on the payroll for each $100,000 in annual sales volume—only authorizing new positions (whether full- or part-time) that can be justified within the ratio assumed in the current financial planning strategy model (see Chapter 9). The average at the typical $250,000 break-even level is 1.4 full-timers per $100,000; the average for all under-$20-million publishers is 1.0 per $100,000; 0.8 per $100,000 is typical of truly *profitable* small publishing organizations.

The "organization chart" by which the publisher identifies authorized staff positions may simply be the table-of-contents of a file of job descriptions. But you'll find it more useful to display each position in relation to the others, on a single sheet of paper—so that reporting channels and networking relationships are made clear. Publishing personnel tend to be much too creative and individualistic for such rigid hierarchies as the military-style pyramids typical of manufacturing organizations. And because very few people in a typical independent publishing house have identical assignments, physically and administratively grouping them so as to facilitate easy networking in support of each function's specialized performance goals (marketing's growth rate, acquisition's new title contribution, pre-press's per-page cost, business's operating margin) enhances coordination without over-loading the function managers who must facilitate such teamwork. With that in mind, then, the typical contemporary publishing house operating by highly-creative small group dynamics is organized something like the one depicted in Figure 7a, on the next page.

Note that each of the functional "core managers" has *two places* on the organization chart—one as head "facilitator" of the specialized work of his/her group (in pursuit of their defined accountability index), the other at the publisher's conference table as a member of the coordinating "core management group." The publisher also has this double identity—as the chair of that core management group, and as one of the participants (whether as chair, member, or reporting COO) in the deliberations of the Board of Directors.

Figure 7a—Sample Organization Chart

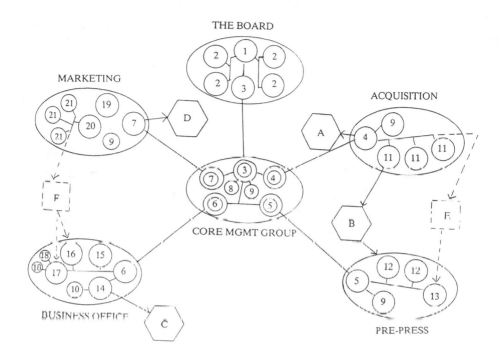

A = "Launch Meeting"
B = "Transmittal Conference"
C = "Facilities Committee"
D = "Exploitation Conference"
E = Desktop Page-Gen Computer
F = Order Processing Computer

1 = Chairman of the Board (CEO)
2 = Directors
3 = Publisher (COO)
9 = Administrative Assistants
8 = Exec. Asst. to Publisher

4 = Editor-in-Chief
11 = Series Acquisition Editors

5 = Pre-Press Managing Editor
12 = Copy Editors/Project Mgrs
13 = Desktop Operator

6 = Business Manager
14 = Facilities
10 = Receptionist/Adm Asst
15 = Print Buyer/Purchasing Adm
16 = Finance Administrator
17 = Shipping Administrator
18 = Shippers

7 = Marketing Manager
19 = Promotion Coordinator
20 = Customer Service Coordinator
21 = Customer Service TeleReps

As we said in Chapter 5, the publisher's office may eventually consist not only of the general manager (COO), but of an administrative assistant for clerical chores, and an executive assistant as spreadsheet monitor and *alter ego*. Seldom does the publisher's office (general management function) in an under-$20-million publishing house really need to be any bigger than this.

This suggests that as many as six people (the four core managers, plus the two assistants) might report to—and expect supervisory support from—the publisher. This relationship with a set of directly-reporting subordinates is known as a "span of control." When people are doing work as diverse as that of a publishing house, this six-person span is *the largest* that should be required of any manager in the organization. None of the others (the functional "middle managers" or their section leaders) should be asked to directly supervise more than five people; beyond that scope, assistant managers should be added to the structure.

The *acquisition* function (often recognized as "first among equals" in synergistic interaction—though the marketing people will contest that) is traditionally headed by an editor-in-chief (who may also double as a series acquisition editor), and consists of acquisition editors assigned to specific product categories ("series"), plus necessary (and usually "pooled") administrative assistants.

The *pre-press development* function is traditionally headed by a managing editor (who may also double as the star copy editor and project manager). Its basic specialists are the copy editors (or "project managers") who take over raw manuscripts from the acquisition editors, make sure they are correct in spelling, punctuation, and syntax, query the author (through the acquisition editor) on unclear or unconvincing passages, and arrange for their conversion into camera-ready pages or "desktop" disks from which the printer can eventually prepare plates.

Reflecting the most revolutionary trend in publishing houses in recent years, the remaining members of today's optimal pre-press team for most situations are page compositors (or "desktop operators," or "typesetters")— who format pages and compose finished type by manipulating the copy editors' word-processed manuscript files with "desktop publishing" software, using laser printers to show the copy editors (and through the acquisition editors, if necessary, the authors) exactly how each eventual book will appear. In some very small publishing houses, the copy editors also function as desktop operators.

The *marketing* function should be organized to perform a one-two punch. Its "promotion" sub-function communicates with people *by audience categories* (through such mass media as bulk mail, package inserts, print or broadcast ads, telemarketing scripts, portable exhibit displays, and book covers) to generate the initial responses that will "qualify" prospective customers for more expensive, intensive, or extensive future attention. Its "sales" sub-function "drops the other shoe" by communicating *personally* with thus-qualified prospective customers *one-on-one* (by visit, phone, or mail)—to interface the publisher's product list with each customer's specific needs or interests. One of these specialized sub-teams is usually personally headed by the over-all marketing manager, the other by an assistant manager (coordinating either promotion or sales). In trade houses, the marketing manager is usually also the sales coordinator; in direct response and adoption houses, he's more likely (because of the paramount role of that sub-function) to double as the promotion coordinator.

The promotion coordinator sometimes functions without additional staff—using a lettershop or ad agency to execute scheduled promotions—but that will depend on the size and circumstances of the publishing house; as you get bigger, you may need to add copy writers, mailing or list-maintenance clerks, a production administrator, or project managers for each separate *on-going* audience dialogue (campaign) on the marketing strategy model. The sales coordinator may oversee a network of (usually external, commissioned) field sales representatives or distributors—but is increasingly more likely to orchestrate all such customer interface *internally,* through customer service "telereps" who enter orders into the computer, process returns credits, answer customer queries, and follow up specific qualifying leads (such as requests for sample books) while monitoring a telephone headset, a computer keyboard, and a well-sorted stack of incoming mail.

The *business operations* function is traditionally headed by the business manager (who also usually doubles as the chief financial officer). As noted earlier, he is assisted (as appropriate to the organization's size and needs) by financial administrators (bookkeepers), inventory handlers (shippers—and possibly a print buyer), and sometimes by centralized facilities personnel (an office manager, receptionist, clerical pool, etc.).

Those hexagons in the sample organizational chart in Figure 7a above play an important role in the organizational strategy of effective publishing house managers. Those are inter-departmental "ad hoc" groups called together from time to time, as needed, to offer either information or ideas relative to some specific problem/concern. They are properly chaired by the person most responsible for dealing with the issue. They may be "standing committees" with representatives from each concerned function, which reassemble whenever needed ... or they may be reconstituted by the core management group for each appropriate situation.

As we'll suggest in the next chapter, scheduling meetings of such ad hoc groups to pool information, or brainstorm, in support of any staff member facing a problem or opportunity that merits such attention, should be a regular agenda item for each weekly core management coordinating meeting. But the people designated as the chairs (and principle beneficiaries) of such meetings should be repeatedly reminded of two critical principles of effective ad hoc "committee" utilization:

(1) They're only supposed to keep their colleagues tied up in such a meeting for whatever time it takes to extract such relevant ideas and information as those participants have readily available; these should not be intended as ponderous "study" or planning sessions; 10-minute meetings are usually a much better use of staff time than 30-minute meetings.

And (2) the convening of such a brain-swap meeting *does not relieve* the party most concerned with the problem from responsibility for its solution. *Don't* let such superficial meetings "make decisions" (by voting or otherwise); in most cases, that only diffuses responsibility—so that nobody's really accountable when things go wrong. That does *not* tend to inspire the development of a dependable staff or management team.

The Japanese-inspired (post-Deming) vogue of "team management" and "collegiality" has produced some very creative approaches to organizational endeavor. But it has also produced some disasters. Because it tends to give the intuitive right-brainers center stage (since hard-headed left-brained evaluation is properly employed only *after* the brainstorming is over), letting such groups actually make decisions is dangerous stuff!

After making clear which critical operating ratio each functional team is expected to improve—year-to-year growth rate of sales volume for marketing, new-title contribution as a percentage of that sales volume for acquisition, per-page capital costs for *on-time* new title development for pre-press, operating margin (profitability) for business operations—the publisher should arrange for either the executive assistant-to-the-publisher (if one exists), or the business manager (who'll have easy access to the same necessary data) to post or otherwise distribute a *routine* monthly update of each function's actual performance with respect to those indices. (Because of the more diverse responsibilities of the business office, it [or the publisher] may also want business operations performances measured by such additional indices as the print-buying cost per page-impression, accumulated inventory value as a percent of annual sales, and/or return [annualized profit] as a percentage of that inventory investment.)

You'll make this feedback much more useful—and flimsy alibis for declining indices much more obvious—if you'll *annualize* the data (by generating a most-recent-12-months summary at the end of *every* month, to even out all seasonal distortions and short-term flukes). Do this by simply entering the *raw* monthly base for each index (the number of press-ready pages finished, page impressions printed, before-tax margin dollars, etc.) on a spreadsheet *at the end of every month* and then programming that spreadsheet to *re-total the most recent 12 months* at that month-end closing (and, for year-to-year growth rate trends, the net sales figures for the *previous* 12 months as well). Then just divide appropriate sub-totals to generate percentage ratios for each critical index. Figure 7b shows the result (though it would normally be lengthened to show the entire past year's trends).

Once these indices start appearing on the bulletin board—or the open computer network—at the end of every month, you're going to see one department strutting and another cringing as their respective "scores" move up and down. It will be very easy for all concerned to see which functions (and as a corollary, which core managers) are bringing home the bacon—and which are holding back the progress of the publishing house.

Figure 7b—Sample Performance Index

PERFORMANCE INDICES	Jan 93	Dec 92	Nov 92	Oct 92	Sep 92
Month's Net Sales	$71,099	$91,633	$91,964	$99,722	$104,778
Annualized Growth Rate	3.1%	8.4%	12.5%	21.8%	27.2%
Month's New Title Sales	$24,014	$34,461	$43,259	$39,143	$32,339
Annualized Contribution	38.5%	38.3%	38.9%	38.1%	37.9%
Month's Pre-Press Expense	$20,831	$35,606	$33,124	$24,729	$25,488
Month's Pages Completed	961	1234	1178	1071	1102
Annualized Cost-per-Page	$24.79	$25.30	$24.34	$24.02	$24.99
Month's P/P/B Expense	$17,760	$0	$2,913	$3,504	$3,150
Month's P/P/B Impressions	2280000	0	319680	405312	355344
Annualized Imprsn Cost	$0.0087	$0.0092	$0.0092	$0.0092	$0.0093
Month's Operating Margin	$9,125	$9,433	$8,482	$7,478	$8,154
Annualized Margin	7.9%	7.7%	6.6%	5.4%	4.4%

The inevitable result is strong peer pressure within every department for every member (including the supervisor!) to "carry his weight" and help save the team from public embarrassment. *It works!* It's based on the same fundamental principle of human relations that drives those tough drill sergeants in basic training centers: "No soldier ever willingly died for his country—but lots have given their all for the guy in the next foxhole."

Generally speaking, if the performance index of a major function *continues to disappoint you* for six straight months, you can safely assume that the function manager responsible is not capable of (or sufficiently dedicated to) turning it around. It's at that point (and sometimes sooner) that the publisher has to earn her pay by being tough enough to replace that core manager.

As the enterprise grows, and the core managers compete over who gets the next live body (when sales volume justifies more hiring), you need a systematic procedure for determining just how many people you really need in each function at any given time. One that has proven effective is the "task analysis" process created over a number of years by the Huenefeld Publishing Consultants for-and-with several of their client publishers.

The idea of "task analysis," essentially, is to estimate the weekly workload (in tenths-of-a-person/hour, for easy computer subtotals) that various external or time-triggered stimuli put on each of the basic functions (general management, acquisition, marketing, pre-press development, business operations)—and on each level-of-responsibility within each function.

Start by brainstorming (function-by-function) a list of stimuli to which the organization must respond. Be especially certain that you've included all basic steps in the major "pipeline" by which each function does its principal work: how acquisition progresses from identifying potential authors to signing contracts, how marketing moves from each scheduled exposure to copywriting, etc. You should come up with an expanded version something like Figure 7c.

Figure 7c—Sample Checklist of Task Stimuli

Management
-- Annual Stockholder Meeting
-- Annual Management Retreat
-- Quarterly Board Meeting
-- Quarterly Budget Update
-- Quarterly Schedule Extension
-- Monthly Out-of-Stock Report
-- Weekly CMG Meeting
-- Payroll Vacancy Report
-- Job Review Report

Acquisition
-- Quarterly Strategy Review
-- Manuscript Proposal Received
-- Publishing Decision Requested
-- Raw Manuscript Received
-- Rough Pages/Proofs Received
-- Author Newsletter Mailing

Pre-Press
-- Transmittal Conference
-- Rough Pages Completed
-- Equipment Malfunctions
-- Proof Corrections Returned

Marketing
-- Quarterly Strategy Review
-- Quarterly Promotion Schedule
-- On-Line Station Occupied (Daily!)
-- New Title Contract Notice

Business
-- Annual Vendor Review
-- Annual Financial Close/Open
-- Annual Payroll Close/Open
-- Annual Requisition Close/Open
-- Monthly Financial Closing
-- Monthly Inventory Report Ready
-- Daily Mail Arrives
-- Payable Bill Received
-- Payment Received
-- Print Bids-and-Materials Received
-- New Inventory Received
-- Merchandise Return Received

Next, stimulus by stimulus, you should brainstorm *each task* that has to be performed to *completely* and adequately resolve or exploit that situation. A "task" should be defined as the more-or-less uninterrupted sequence of steps one individual takes to either complete the organization's optimal response to a stimulus, or effectively move responsibility along to the next person.

Circulate the list until you're satisfied it's complete. Then ask *every* staff member to estimate (to the nearest tenth) how many hours she/he must spend at each of these tasks in an average week (dividing once-a-year chores by 52, quarterly chores by 13, monthly chores by 4.3 to convert them to weekly workloads). Ask supervisors to adjust or endorse their subordinates' estimates before this data is processed further. Typical sequences of tasks for responding to stimuli look like Figure 7d.

Figure 7d—Task Responses to Common Stimuli

Stimulus	*Tasks*	*Dept*
Proof Corrections Returned	Editorial Proof Review	Acq
	Revision Conference	Acq/PrPr
	Corrections Input	PrPr
	Print-Buy Preparations	PrPr
	Print Order Executed	Bus
Quarterly Board Meeting	Minutes, Honoraria Mailed	Mgmt
	CMG Follow-Up Review	Mgmt
	Next Notices etc. on MEC	Mgmt
	Meeting Pre-Planning	Mgmt
	Background Info Mailed	Mgmt
	Next Meeting Attended	Mgmt
On-Line TeleRep Hired	Phone Answer Procedure	Mark
	Phone Entry Procedure	Mark
	Entering Mail Orders	Mark
	Tracing Claims/Queries	Mark
	Reference Data Updates	Mark

Meanwhile, ask each core (function) manager to indicate the lowest level-of-responsibility (according to pay grades, as illustrated in Figure 11a—Chapter 11) to which each task can safely be delegated. Then enter everybody's workload estimates into a database file set up something like Figure 7e.

Figure 7e—Sample Task Analysis Data-Form

```
┌─────────────────────────────────────────────────────────────┐
│  12-07-1992          Sample Task Analysis DataForm      10:39 │
│ Task[_____]            │
│ Dept[_____]  Section[_____]                      │
│ Person[_____]  Level[_____]  Wkly Hrs(___.__)          │
│ Notes[_____]            │
└─────────────────────────────────────────────────────────────┘
F1=EXIT   F2=DUPE FIELD NO.   F4=DICTIONARY    F5=RESTORE PAGE   F9=UPDATE
```

Now print out a database report, reorganizing the weekly time estimates per task by *organizational function,* subtotaled by *level of responsibility* (lowest feasible pay grade). You should get a five-column function-by-function print-out, with tasks in each column (for each department) grouped by descending levels of responsibility.

In each function, block off approximately the top 30 hours of most-responsible work for the function manager—the remaining time being left for situational supervision. (In general management, only block off 20 hours for the publisher; the rest of each week should be available for contingency fire-fighting.) Then block off descending 35-hour blocks as feasible workloads for additional staff members in that function. The result (for each department) should look something like Figure 7f, on the next page.

So what did we learn? This publisher now knows that two people are needed in the Marketing Department. After the Marketing Manager (who should also, obviously, be the promotion coordinator in this particular situation) assumes responsibility for everything at levels 5 and 4, he still has time to take on about six additional hours of weekly responsibility (still leaving ample time for "fire-fighting"). He might decide to sort the mail, get journal summary print-outs from the computer as needed, and handle the phone follow-ups of complimentary books ("comps") that were sent on request to bookstores.

That's going to leave 37 hours of weekly work on levels 3 and 2 for his assistant (who obviously covers the order-phone). But since they'll need to arrange for a small amount of weekly clerical help (from a pool or a part-timer) to handle level 1 anyhow, some of that 7 hours of copying and mailing of news releases can be delegated to reduce the assistant's job to a manageable total.

Optimally, you should avoid assigning any individual (position) responsibility for tasks more than one pay level below their actual salary grade. It doesn't make sense to increase the need for higher-level personnel by letting some of them "loaf" at work that can easily be done by lower-paid juniors.

When you have *more* than 35 hours of work within a two-level span in any function, the core manager has an opportunity to build in some useful specialization—by splitting the load between two peers who focus on different types of activity, and utilize different skills.

Figure 7f—Sample Task Analysis Print-Out: Marketing

Level	Task	Wkly Hrs
5	Attending CMG Meetings	2.0
	Updating Strategy Model	0.3
	Arranging Cover Art	1.0
	Sales Estimates	0.2
	Reviewing Daily/Weekly Journals	1.5
	Departmental Meeting	1.0
		6.0
4	Conference Exhibits	1.6
	Creating Promo Copy Packages	5.0
	Special Marketing Queries	2.0
	Updating Key Contact List	0.2
	Planning/Executing Mailing Pieces	7.0
	Planning/Eceouting Print Ads	2.0
		17.8
3	TeleMarketing Follow-Ups of Comps	2.5
	Sorting Marketing Mail	2.0
	Tracing Claims/Queries	1.0
	Sales Journal Print-Outs	1.5
	On-line Reference Updates	0.5
	Answering Order Phone	15.0
	Departmental Meeting	1.0
	Entering Mail Orders	10.0
		33.5
2	Updating Addresses (General)	1.5
	Preparing Comp Labels	1.0
	Copying/Mailing News Releases	7.0
		9.5
1	Distributing Author Brochures	1.0
	Advance Book Photocopying/Mailing	3.0
		4.0
		========
		70.8

Once you've done this exercise for the entire organization, and gotten a print-out for each function (department), you're likely to find a number of places in which workloads can be evened-out as full-time equivalents by "farming out" bottom-level work to a clerical pool in the business office (as a centralized service of its "facilities administration" responsibility).

The task entries on these summary print-outs provide the raw material, then, for detailed job descriptions. And each task will eventually require a "procedure guide"—a checklist of the steps required for its completion. We'll look at that in greater detail in Chapter 11.

CHAPTER 8
Developing and Using the Core Management Group

When the top manager of a publishing houses insists on making all the critical decisions and calling the major creative shots in every aspect of the business, certain undesirable things almost always happen. Among them:

(1) The overall performance of the enterprise is limited to that manager's *weakest* suit (be it marketing, finances, or whatnot)—where poor decisions cancel out the effects of strong performances elsewhere;

(2) The boss overlooks danger signals and opportunities because too many people (an excessive span of control) are reporting to him to keep everything straight;

(3) Critical insights from other people are less likely to forecast and prevent problems, because most people are not good at talking back critically to the boss;

(4) Subordinate managers lose most of their credibility with the people they're supposed to supervise, because they're so frequently over-ruled;

(5) Decisions are made too late for maximum effectiveness, because the publisher's office has become an overworked bottleneck through which all projects must flow.

To avoid such problems, effective top managers delegate major responsibility for planning, decision making, and supervision of the principal specialized functions to their most responsible and capable subordinates (who in turn delegate specific tasks to those they supervise). As we've suggested before, the most effective pattern of such delegation in most book publishing houses is to make one subordinate manager responsible for acquisition of new products, another for pre-press development of those products, a third for all marketing activities to generate customer orders, and a fourth for managing the physical and fiscal assets of the enterprise. We'll suggest detailed job descriptions for each of these specialized managers in the chapters discussing basic organization of each of their functions.

Whether it's formally recognized or not, the managers who head these functions constitute, along with the publisher, a "core management team"—because what they do essentially determines the success or failure of everyone else's contribution. By focusing primarily on the development and continuing interplay of this team, the publisher can direct and enhance the complex, subtle, volatile flow of interactions (between people, situations, and statistical possibilities) of the entire publishing house with considerable precision.

The personal character of the core management team in any serious publishing organization is a matter of great importance not only to that organization, but to the members of the team. Over a period of time, they will almost inevitably spend more time together than any of them spend with most members of their families. Their professional careers and emotional well-being will depend very heavily on each other. To reach sound decisions and achieve synergy, they must respect and trust each other. All must be unafraid to speak out openly; only telling the boss just what she wants to hear is one of the most serious viruses that infect weak management teams. Effective inter-action can only be achieved in such a group by maintaining a high level of personal honesty in dealing with each other—a pattern for which the need must be stated, and the good example set, by the publisher.

Without being too insistent, we might suggest that good editors-in-chief and marketing managers tend to be intuitive "right-brained" types ... while good pre-press and business managers tend to have analytical (left-lobe-dominant) brains. The synergistic interplay between the two brain-types can be extremely creative *if* the publishers keeps a low enough profile to let right-brain ideas get a full airing before they're squelched by left-brain skepticism.

Recruiting, training/developing, and continually coordinating such a team is by far the most important single job the publisher must perform. If that job is done well, it is virtually impossible for the organization to fall far short of realistic mission statement goals. If it is done poorly, the potential for disaster is too obvious to require comment.

It is useful, then, for every publisher to think of himself from time to time as one who doesn't *do* much actual and direct publishing work, but who primarily *facilitates* publishing accomplishments by the other members of the core team (who should in turn see their primary work as facilitating achievements by their own subordinates).

But no matter how confidently a publisher delegates responsibility for day-to-day operations to the other core managers, facilitates the implementation of their plans, and enlists their combined insights in decision making—ultimate responsibility for the end results of the publishing enterprise still rests *with that publisher.* So eventually, that individual's wishes should prevail when important choices have to be made. How do you best make that happen?

The most admired managers of earlier times, when the martial hierarchy dominated the publishing industry's organizational thinking, were the strong and fearless types who called all the tough shots and took full responsibility for results (while occasionally tossing a modest compliment to the troops in the trenches). But the style most compatible with the entrepreneurial networks and self-directed workforces of contemporary publishing houses is that of the patient consensus-builder.

President Jules Nyerere of Tanzania is reputed to have pointed, when an American visitor lamented the lack of a strong opposition party in his government, to a gathering of village elders talking in the shade of an enormous tree. "Sooner or later," paraphrasing Nyerere, "their chief will announce his decision about whatever problem they're discussing without taking a vote, and you'll complain that he wasn't democratic about it. What you're ignoring is that he'll keep them there, and keep them talking, until they're all saying the same thing. Then, when they start getting bored by the repetition, he'll announce what they're saying as his decision."

Any important issue confronting a core management group should be discussed until there is no doubt how each member of the team feels. An effective top manager will *insist* that everyone in the core group answer the question: "What do you think we should do?"; this is no place for shrinking violets. Then he will keep the topic moving around the table (making sure each participant gets to finish his/her statement before the next one takes the floor) until everybody is essentially saying the same thing.

If a consensus *doesn't* develop in a reasonable time with this approach, the publisher must hazard an opinion (and invite others to do likewise) as to whether the decision can wait until the next (weekly or otherwise) meeting; you'll be surprised how many knotty problems can be simplified by "creative procrastination." One or more members might even be delegated to look into background facts more extensively in the meantime.

But if the decision can't wait, or consensus doesn't develop despite the delay, or even if the publisher is convinced the consensus of the others is wrong—it is essential that said publisher intervene with his/her own solution. It should be stated as diplomatically as possible ("I may be wrong but ..."), with a summary of principal reasons supporting the decision, and with full assumption of responsibility by the publisher.

Maintaining the freedom to ask advice, without being obligated to take it, is a subtle art that every good manager eventually masters. You earn that freedom by demonstrating thoughtful respect for the other members of the group—by making sure each gets ample opportunities to express contrary views, by listening and listening and listening, by being willing to give reasons when you over-rule the consensus, by avoiding petty finger-pointing and accepting personal responsibility.

In the long run, if you can't master the arts of both *building* and occasionally *over-ruling* consensus in the core management group, it will be difficult for you to get peak results from any good, creative publishing organization.

The core management group, then, should make the key decisions by which the publishing house operates. To make those decisions in a supportive, self-checking group process without delaying operations and thus discouraging initiative, the group must meet regularly. The most common frequency for routine meetings is weekly—with additional special meetings whenever urgent situations arise. However, to keep larger issues in perspective, the core group should also schedule other meetings at different levels of concern. Usually, their coordinating responsibilities can be fulfilled through recurring meetings on four levels—as follows:

Figure 8a—Basic Core Management Meeting Cycles

Weekly Coordinating Meetings - @ 2 Hours

1. Review Key Operating Indices to determine if there are any fires the publisher needs to help fight;
2. Review Management Events Calendar (integrated deadline schedule) to negotiate adjustments;
3. Arrange Inter-departmental "brain-swap" meetings;
4. Discuss other issues on which the publisher seeks to determine a managerial consensus.

Monthly Feedback Reviews - @ 1 Hour

1. Explanations (to publisher and to each other) of any significant variances from budget or anticipated results;
2. Joint preparation of agenda for 1 hour "full staff meeting" to be chaired by publisher (for presentation of "performance indices," other information, and general staff's opportunity to ask questions.)

Quarterly Planning Updates - @ 3 Hours

1. Agree (after review of financial feedback) how much should now be added to, or cut from, total annual-level budget;
2. Determine (by talking through reverse-zero-base proposals) on which budget lines these changes should be made;
3. Critique each manager's proposal for three-month extension of his function's strategy model on that basis;
4. Adjust intervening quarters accordingly.

Annual Strategy Review

Core Managers participate in over-night (or week-end) retreat asking: "If we were starting over, what might we change about ...?"

1. The Mission Statement
2. The Organization Chart
3. The Financial Planning Model
4. The Acquisition Strategy Model
5. The New Title Development Checklist
6. The Marketing Strategy Model
7. The Budgeting and Feedback Format

While each participating manager will naturally be most concerned with the needs of the particular function she/he heads, the publisher should insist that core meetings on all levels focus on *general* concerns—not on things one manager could handle alone. (They have plenty of time outside these meetings to deal with limited problems within their respective functions; they shouldn't use the group as an emotional security blanket regarding parochial issues.) All participants should be heard on all critical or interdepartmental questions on the agenda. And the agenda should be *open* to topics proposed by any of them (perhaps with a requirement that they submit those topics to the publisher in advance, so they can be included on a written agenda outline to help keep each meeting moving).

If the core management group normally meets only once a week (typically for a couple of hours) to coordinate on-going, routine operations, how can it expect to address *all* of the concerns of the diverse people and functions of a publishing house? The trick lies in identifying what really *needs* to be addressed, and by-passing those things that require no managerial intervention (an approach popularly referred to as "management by exception"). By restricting most of their weekly meeting time to the first three agenda items suggested in Figure 8a above (though still making provision for occasional important agenda items that don't fit that format), effective core management teams find that 2 hours a week is quite adequate.

The "Key Operating Indices" (see Figure 8b) and "Management Events Calendar" (see Figure 8d) are continuously-updated documents most properly maintained by the publisher's office. Publishers who don't have executive assistants to do such work are well advised to consider *doing it themselves*. Once these two reporting/coordinating formats are established (as detailed below), the simple mechanics of making inter-office calls (or circulating a short response-form) once a week to collect the results-data needed to update "key operating indices" ... and noting schedule changes on the current "management events calendar" as the group adjusts commitments during its weekly meeting, so you can make quick changes in the database file after the meeting and provide each manager with an updated version ... can help the publisher stay abreast of the day-to-day pulse of the publishing house without awkward "snooping"—and with very little time commitment.

The first suggested agenda item, then, was a review of the "key operating indices." Each of these indices is a "vital statistic" of the publishing program that *somebody* should be routinely able to give you, in a few seconds, at any given time. The core management group should brainstorm a representative selection that will tell it (at any weekly meeting) which aspects of the publishing program are "on target" and which are lagging. Along with indicating negative performances, the report should also enable the managers to spot fortuitous circumstances that might be profitably exploited. A typical weekly report of key operating indices (with recent weeks still displayed on the spreadsheet to make trends more obvious) looks like this:

Figure 8b—Sample Key Operating Indices

KEY OPERATING INDICES	Oct 9	Oct 16	Oct 23	Oct 30	Nov 6	Nov 13	Nov 22	Dec 1	Dec 8	Dec 15	Dec 29	Jan 5
MEC Deadlines Missed	11	9	13	14	15	15	15	14	9	9	8	14
Acqui Dept	3	3	4	4	4	6	4	5	4	4	3	5
PrePress Dept	5	3	6	7	9	9	10	8	4	5	5	8
Marktg Dept	1	1	2	0	1	0	0	1	0	0	0	0
BusOps Dept	2	2	1	3	1	0	1	0	1	0	0	1
Oldest Order (days)	6	4	4	3	4	4	3	5	4	4	6	4
Total MTDC Days Behind	7	9	7	6	7	10	8	10	9	7	10	8
Receivables	$79,752	$81,114	$80,788	$82,495	$83,671	$85,884	$84,993	$85,383	$87,472	$87,869	$86,793	$87,201
Payables	$28,484	$28,795	$28,116	$27,447	$27,539	$27,334	$26,792	$27,569	$27,737	$27,991	$19,684	$21,677
Checkbook Balance	$4,788	$3,444	$7,162	$8,931	$6,835	$9,669	$7,467	$7,311	$10,897	$7,118	$1,934	$3,712
Month-to-Date Sales	$3,351	$15,111	$20,777	$32,872	$14,040	$39,007	$49,285	$66,829	$18,196	$31,572	$111,533	15,378
Promotional Exposures	53,212	17,936	0	2,134	0	1,309	2,777	17,681	0	0	47,823	39,752
Bookstore/Whsl %	55.2%	24.5%	21.5%	22.3%	0.0%	3.0%	7.9%	6.0%	8.4%	6.3%	3.8%	10.3%
Distributor %	15.4%	56.7%	60.2%	55.3%	99.0%	80.0%	73.3%	75.1%	60.0%	68.3%	84.4%	74.1%
Special Acct %	29.3%	15.2%	12.9%	16.7%	1.0%	16.0%	17.0%	16.7%	13.8%	13.2%	5.7%	3.3%
Direct-Response %	0.0%	3.6%	5.4%	5.7%	0.0%	1.0%	1.8%	2.1%	4.7%	3.4%	3.9%	2.5%
Sub-Rights %									13.2%	7.6%	2.2%	9.8%
Mo. Proposals This Wk	13	9	4	12	11	12	13	15	12	9	2	11
Proposals Under Study	29	28	25	28	27	26	30	31	29	26	23	27
Mss. Under Contract	37	37	38	36	38	39	40	39	38	38	38	38
Mss. In-House	11	11	12	10	10	11	12	11	10	10	10	9
Pre-Press Pgs m/t/d	81	150	219	279	63	144	199	212	67	139	117	0

The sample above reflects only one set of possibilities. But note how clearly the spreadsheet alerted the group during November to some kind of slowdown or logjam in the pre-press department ... and how quickly it became apparent at their meeting following December 29 that there might be a cash flow squeeze developing in the checkbook balance. Both situations are automatic candidates for managerial intervention. Meanwhile, it's obvious that the other functions are operating on an even keel, requiring no special attention from the publisher. "If it ain't broke, don't fix it!"

The design of the key operating index (as with any other on-going monitoring, planning, or control format) should be open-ended. When any element ceases to be useful, it should be eliminated; when the core managers identify other indices that would be useful, they should be added (as with that index of subsidiary rights sales in the sample above).

This regular feedback of key operating indices is one of the best methods available to keep the publisher informed of the health of those basic operational pipelines mentioned at the beginning of Chapter 5—that sequential series of events that leads acquisition to a steady flow of feasible book proposals, and marketing to an adequate feast of good sales opportunities ... and that steers pre-press development away from serious schedule delays, and business operations away from short-term cash flow crises. The weekly trend of "Manuscript Proposals This Week" and "Promotional Exposures" tells him whether the strategic prima donnas (acquisition and marketing) are keeping up the pressure in the pipelines. By scanning the line reporting "MEC Deadlines Missed" in the pre-press department, he can anticipate the development of serious scheduling logjams. By monitoring the week-by-week difference between receivables and payables, he can spot threatened cash flow crises.

Adjusting their scheduling commitments to each other—Item #2 of the agenda suggested by Figure 8a, under *weekly coordinating meetings*—will always be a principal concern of the core managers. To facilitate this process, the publisher should organize an *integrated* scheduling system that records all of those commitments—and makes feasible their quick review and revision within the context of the weekly core management meeting. One of the simplest effective systems for accomplishing this is a "Management Events Calendar." By "management event," we mean an individual task that, if not finished on schedule by the responsible party, is likely to delay the timely performance of other work—and upset the intricate timing or strategies of other groups or functions.

To create such a calendar, set up on your computer a brief database form whereby each deadline entry can be made in a manner of seconds. The format illustrated below has proven adequate in a wide variety of publishing organizations:

Figure 8c—Sample Management Events Scheduling Data-Form

```
 12-07-1992          MANAGEMENT EVENTS CALENDAR          11:48

  Completion Date[_____]  Dept[_____]  Person[____]
  Task[_____]
  Project[_____]
  Notes[_____]
```

Enter all desired completion dates as six-digit numbers, with the first two digits representing the year, the next two the month, and the last two the day of said month. Then, once an accumulation of forthcoming individual deadlines has been amassed (as single entries in the database), it is a simple matter to have the computer rearrange them chronologically and print out a variety of calendars. The one that concerns us at the moment—for weekly review by the core managers—will integrate *all* deadlines (regardless of function or department) into a single chronology something like Figure 8d.

Figure 8d—Sample Management Events Calendar

When?	Who?	What?
920620	All	General Staff Meeting 9:15
920620	RMS	Complete Edison Copy Editing
920620	JJK	Martin Rough-Pages Available
920620	GDS	Check/Service Postage Meter
920621	MTM	Order Library Mailing Labels
920621	DDD	Mail July Board Meeting Notice
920921	RMS	Mail "Tidbits" to Author Pool
920622	MTM	Hanson Promo Copy Package Done

Etc., etc., etc., for whatever time-span you wish

Immediately *after* each weekly core management meeting, the person maintaining the calendar should call up from the database all entries for which the managers negotiated changes (revised completion dates)—under Item #2 of the *weekly coordinating meeting* agenda suggested in Figure 8a. Make those changes in the database, and then print out a new calendar re-integrating all deadlines, for all functions, for *the next 2 weeks*. Distribute copies to all core managers—who should in turn make copies for all members of their respective departments. It will then be the responsibility of each core manager to determine, on the eve of the *next* core meeting, which of the current week's deadlines *have not been met*—and which of the forthcoming week's deadlines (also shown on that two week print-out) *are not likely to be met*. As each manager confesses those failures of their function to their colleagues during that next weekly meeting, the publisher or executive assistant records the agreed adjustments on his copy of the calendar, to begin the revision cycle all over again.

By using the "project" space on the dataform to indicate forthcoming new titles, major meetings, on-going marketing campaigns, etc.—the keeper of the calendar is able to print out specialized schedules for such individual books or projects, as needed by the core managers or other parties. By entering the responsible party's department, they're able to produce separate calendars for each core manager if desired. Printing a personal calendar for a single individual, for vacation planning or other purposes, is very easy. The "notes" blank is used to amplify far-in-advance entries—for reference if people forget what's involved by the time they show up on a print-out.

Although new items will inevitably be added to the database by the core managers at (or between) each of their weekly meetings (especially as they learn from experience what a useful "tickler file" it can become), most of the entries can be made three-months-at-a-time, as a *quarterly-update* responsibility of the person maintaining the calendar. It will take perhaps half-a-day each quarter—but that half day (itself listed on the calendar) will make such an enormous contribution to the coordination of the entire, complex publishing operation that it will be an appropriate expenditure of time (even the publisher's, if no assistant is available for the task).

The basic quarterly calendar entries will come from three places—from the managing editor's continuous new title development checklist (see Figure 9d), the marketing manager's strategy planning spreadsheet (Figure 9b), and an accumulative checklist of recurring items maintained *on the scheduling database itself* by that "keeper of the calendar."

To create that checklist, just enter all *recurring* deadline items as they're identified with an *alphabetical first-digit date entry* (so they'll never show up when the computer prints out chronological calendars for numerically-specific time periods). Core management brainstorming should begin the accumulation of the checklist, but new additions can be made at any time. Use the next two digits of each checklist date entry (after that alphabetical code) to indicate how many times a year it re-occurs (52 = weekly, 12 = monthly, etc.); use the next two digits to indicate the time-period within that cycle (which month of the year or quarter, which week of the month or fortnight, which day of the week) in which the event should normally take place. Then, whenever you want the checklist as a guide to updating the calendar, just have the computer print out (by department) everything beginning with your code-letter. Assuming "X" is the checklist code, it will look something like this:

Figure 8e—Sample MEC Extension Chart

Dept	Date	Person	Task
All	X5201	All	Core Managers Meet 1:15
	X5205	All	KOI Reports to NN
	X1202	All	Security Disks to PC
	X1201	All	Turn in Leave Slips
	X0401	All	Budget Change Proposals to NN
	X0403	All	Strategy Model Updates
Aqui	X5205	LE	Proposal Screening Meeting 10:00
	X0103	LE	Review/Update Author Brochure
Bus	X1201	PC	Review Inventory for Reprints
	X0401	PC	File Sales Tax Return
Mgmt	X0108	NN	Annual Stockholder Meeting Notices

Etc., etc., etc., etc., etc.

That first line tells you that the core managers meet 52 times a year (weekly), on the first day of the week. In the quarterly update, then, the schedule-keeper should indicate such a meeting for 1:15 on each of the next 13 Monday afternoons.

Once they've reviewed the Key Operating Indices to determine whether top management intervention is needed anywhere in the routine operations of the publishing house, and gone over both the past week's and the next week's Management Events Calendar to make necessary schedule adjustments, the core managers might well devote most of the remainder of each weekly meeting to scheduling *subsequent* meetings (which will immediately appear on the calendar) at which their subordinates can thrash out problems, share ideas in "brain swap" sessions, or coordinate interactions too specialized for core management direction.

Such near-future "brain swaps" between appropriate individuals from various functions can help the acquisition editors improve book titles, help promotion copywriters strengthen brochure titles or offers, coordinate all concerned as to which promotional inserts should be added to which out-going book cartons, help telcreps devise scripts for answering customer queries, or give the office (facilities) manager guidance on stocking the supply room or painting the hallways. Each such meeting should be chaired by the person whose problem or opportunity it addresses—and that won't necessarily be the top-ranking attendee.

The capacity of individuals playing modest roles to contribute useful ideas and information to each others' endeavors is too-often overshadowed by unreasonable disdain for meetings. The assertion that "most meetings are a waste of time" is usually a confession that the person speaking doesn't know how to plan or conduct a meeting effectively. All-in-all, face-to-face meetings are the fastest way to exchange large amounts of information accurately—and advance ideas through several generations of give-and-take evolution; all six senses are transmitting and receiving for each participant, with a minimum of intermediate mechanics (like writing).

Effective meetings (whatever the setting or scale) should be planned around a recurring sequence of *five processes* relative to any issue at-hand. Most staff "brain swap" sessions scheduled by the core managers for their subordinates will (and should) only deal with a single, specific issue. But a monthly full-staff meeting, or a quarterly budget review by the core management group, might subject an extensive agenda of topics (one by one) to this five-step treatment.

In the first step, the person chairing the meeting simply *defines the issue*—states as clearly and succinctly as possible what the group is trying to accomplish (suggest alternative solutions to a problem, become informed about recent developments, etc.). In the second step, the chair then provides whatever background information is deemed necessary to enable the others to contribute effectively. (If the main purpose of the meeting is to inform the group—as with a routine general staff meeting—this step, repeated for each major topic, may consume most of the meeting time.) Third, the chair then invites questions intended to *clarify* (not to solve) the issue at hand; an effective chair doesn't let things go beyond this point until *everybody understands the question* being addressed. Fourth, the chair invites feedback—ideas, opinions, objections, etc. And finally, the chair states what he/she now intends to do relative to the question and the feedback.

Management cannot too often stress to all staff members that such brain-swap meetings do not relieve the individuals asking for help (and thus chairing such sessions) of their personal responsibility for the problem-solution or follow-up-strategy they eventually select from the group input. Too often, insecure people pretend that citing "group consensus" diffuses ultimate responsibility through that group; it's amazing how often middle-managers *boast* about letting such groups make decisions, rather than taking responsibility themselves, as they're paid to do. Almost always, when this happens, strategies get fuzzier and accountability evaporates.

Furthermore, the minute the group is made to feel that (even if the guilt is collectively shared) it will be blamed if things go wrong—all those wonderfully intuitive right-brained idea-people clam up, or start hedging their bets until they lose their sparkle. Remember, these brain-swap sessions belong in the horizon-defining part of the creative process; the hard work of bringing things back to earth should still reside with the question-asker.

When core managers schedule a few people from two or more departments to meet sometime in the next week-or-so to deal with a specific issue, the person chairing that subsequent session (the one who needs the ideas, information, etc., that will result) should be reminded of the respectability of short meetings. Asking others to meet you in the conference room doesn't require you to *waste their time proving it was important*—by keeping them 30 minutes when five will suffice! Get their ideas and information as fast as possible—and let them get back to their self-directed tasks.

It's a good idea for the publisher's office to make available (and to circulate via the core managers, whenever such brain swaps are added to the management events calendar) a written reminder for the people asked to chair such meetings that:

(1) They should only keep the group for as long as that group is making significant contributions to the solution of their problem;

(2) They should have that problem (or sequence of problems—for a more complex meeting) spelled out as a *written* agendum; preferably distributed to the participants beforehand, to elicit their preparation or forethought;

(3) Once they've stated the issue/question/problem, provided necessary (but not verbose) background information, and answered any clarifying questions, they should now call on the participants *one at a time* for such feedback as might be offered; they should continue going around-and-around the group asking for individual comments—making sure that everybody gets to speak (or chooses to "pass") without interruption—for as long as new information or ideas are forthcoming;

(4) In small "brain swap" meetings, the chair should assume responsibility for "taking notes"—for recording all of the useful suggestions made—unless it is felt that tape-recording the meeting will be more practical; for more

complex meetings, the chair might appoint someone else to keep notes (as when the publisher's executive assistant is invited into the core management meeting itself);

(5) If a consensus is needed and hasn't developed, or an adequate fund of ideas hasn't emerged, the chair may restate the question/issue as it has evolved during the meeting, and (repeating the process) invite further feedback;

(6) The chair should seldom attempt to shift responsibility for *making a decision* to the meeting participants; this is not usually a sound environment for actual decision-making;

(7) But the chair should never forget that final step—telling the meeting what will subsequently happen—so as to uphold the credibility of the process. This could take any form from "I'll put a memo on the bulletin board" or "I'll send you all a copy of my minutes" to "Let's get together again in a couple of weeks to go over my final draft." If nothing more is expected of the group—let 'em off the hook!

Reviewing the Key Operating Indices, adjusting the Management Events Calendar, and scheduling brain swap meetings between appropriate members of their departments on a weekly basis should enable the core management group (and especially the publisher) to "stay on top of" what's happening in the publishing house—and focus most of their remaining attention on the specialized work of their respective functions. Of course, the publisher should invite "other appropriate business" at the end of each of these meetings—but should resist attempts to absorb this high-powered group in petty issues that can best be handled within a single department, or by fiat from the publisher's office. And these weekly meetings provide a forum in which the publisher can probe for "managerial consensus" on policy issues as they arise.

But such weekly coordinating meetings will inevitably (and properly) focus on the "trees" rather than the "forest"—on operational details rather than grand strategy. Yet no matter how smoothly the work of the publishing house is coordinated, it won't lead to maximum fulfillment of the owners'/ directors' mission statement unless the controlling game plan is effectively and continuously adjusted to the inevitably-changing circumstances within which it operates.

To facilitate such adjustment, we've suggested (Figure 8a) additional core management meetings on *three other levels.* For the first, as soon as each month's financial results are available, the group should assemble around the business manager's updated feedback (hopefully in the budget-and-trend-relating format suggested by Figure 10a) and discuss all budget lines for which results are more than nominally above-or-below expectations. This can probably be done by simply adding another half-hour to that week's coordinating meeting.

It shouldn't actually be necessary to plan remedial action (or exploitation of new opportunities) at these monthly feedback reviews. Leave responsibility for modest, gradual refinement of their plans to the individual managers. But as we've noted before, if a manager has to go on offering alibis for the same seriously missed targets for *6 straight months* (despite the corrective opportunities of intervening quarterly budget adjustments), it is unlikely that said manager is ever going to be able to correct the situation; it's time to start thinking of a replacement.

At the end of each fiscal-year quarter (three months), however, the core management group should assemble for a special session (in addition to their weekly meeting) to make formal changes in the budget. If you're a not-for-profit or a remote subsidiary locked into a budget endorsed by an annual meeting—hopefully you'll have kept budget categories so general that a great deal of adjustment is still possible in specific line items.

We'll examine the budgeting-and-review process in considerable detail in Chapter 10. For the moment, let it suffice to say that this special quarterly gathering of the core management group should first agree—in the light of recent financial results—how much money can be added to, or must be cut from, the annual-level (12 month) spending pattern reflected in the current operating budget. Then *each manager* should be asked to explain the two-or-three places additional money devoted to their function would produce the best results—or, in the case of a budget reduction, the places they'd prefer to cut if they had to reduce their overall spending by a given percentage. Each suggestion should be explained in the light of the changes it makes in that function's basic planning strategy (see Chapter 9). The publisher should be concurrently listing these adjustment possibilities—preferably on a black-board or chartboard, so all can review them at a glance.

Then the publisher should lead the group in deciding item-by-item which increases they think would most benefit the house—or which cuts would effect it least. The best way to do this is to take turns inviting each manager to "nominate" one of the proposed increases or cuts on the list for adoption; talk that one out until consensus emerges or the publisher is ready to make a decision—and then go on to the next manager and the next nomination. Keep the process rolling until the budget has been increased or decreased to the desired level.

Each manager should be noting changes on her respective departmental strategy model as this process takes place. Those models should then be updated after each quarterly budget adjustment. But for more thoughtful re-integration of strategic themes, you should set aside 1 to 3 days every year for a "strategy review" retreat. Take the core managers away to some remote location. Let them go back to "ground zero" and reconsider the publishing house's most basic planning assumptions and strategic commitments as though they were starting anew. You can do this very simply by asking them how they'd rephrase any of the basic strategic planning documents indicated in Figure 8a (earlier). Make sure you keep going around the group—document by document—listing suggestions on the blackboard, and then talking them out one-by-one, until you've incorporated everything your core managers have learned since the last retreat into your basic publishing game plan.

Through patient repetition, then, of the overlapping cycles of weekly coordinating meetings, monthly financial-feedback reviews, quarterly budget adjustments, and annual strategy retreats—the publisher should be able to nurture and polish the core management group into a high-powered, delicately balanced team more than up to the on-going challenges of the publishing process.

CHAPTER 9
Strategic Planning

Some independent publishers shy away from "strategic planning"—attempting to map the major directions and assumptions of each function as "ground rule" guidance for specific operating tactics—because they fear the exercise is too grandiose and too complex for a small organization. But in fact, because of the relatively small margin-for-error inherent in the limited financial reserves of the typical independent publisher, strategic planning is more essential in this segment of the industry than among the conglomerates. By getting the "big picture" assumptions of the various functions more-or-less in step with each other, and steering all concerned clear of discernible fallacies and conflicts, you can substantially improve the statistical probability that "it'll all lead you where you want to go" in the end.

Because (no matter which major market you pursue) book publishing is a highly cyclical business, your strategic planning should focus (and continually refocus) on the generalized question: "Given a specific amount of money to spend over the next year (about as far ahead as you should prudently pretend you can control events with any precision)—how can we best spend it to maximize desired results?" But for practical purposes, always think of that year as extending *five quarters* (15 months) into the future. You'll usually generate more chaos than improvement by trying to change things scheduled for (and already under way in) the *current* quarter—so it's the strategy (and budget) for those 12 months *following* the current quarter on which your planning and refining should concentrate.

A budget is simply the summation of all of your plans and predicted results for any future period of time. In the next chapter, we'll explore the mechanics by which you thrash out the details and officially sanction the spending of money by each of the basic (acquisition, pre-press, marketing, business) functions. But first, let's see how the publisher can most easily lead the core managers to "get their acts together" as a basis for budgeting.

The key is to require *each* core manager to maintain, at all times, a spreadsheet model that quickly and clearly communicates to the others the game plan by which his respective function is operating. Because it controls the frame-of-reference in which the others must work (and for other reasons we'll spell out in Chapter 12), you should insist that the *acquisition* strategy always be mapped *3 years* into the future. Because of the cyclical nature of the publishing year, marketing and finance models should always reflect—at any planning point—*the next 12 months*. Pre-press development models should extend far enough into the future to encompass all books currently in the developmental pipeline (usually a matter of 7 or 8 months).

Each functional plan starts with the owners'/directors' mission statement (see Figure 6a). In pursuit of that general summation of goals, the publisher should then tell the core managers (through the organization chart—see Figure 7a) how many people (in what roles) each can commit the publishing house to pay regularly, and otherwise nourish, until further notice. Given said mission statement and organizatio.1 chart, then, each core manager should be asked to chart—on a *single,* easily-displayed spreadsheet—the "grand design" which they believe will best focus their department's personnel and budget on *maximum* achievement of thcir particular accountability index (growth rate of sales volume for marketing, new title contribution to that sales volume for acquisition, per-page on-time new title development cost for pre-press, operating margin [profit] for the business office). It is important that each of these models be confined to a single spreadsheet or chart (even if most of them do exceed normal page-sizes)—scanable at a single glance—so they can be easily communicated, understood, and interactively manipulated in core management sessions. (Those 20-40 page "plans" middle-managers sometimes attempt to foist on their colleagues reflect not only a lack of respect for those co-workers' time, but probably a great deal of fuzziness about what/why/how the originator really hopes to meet assigned goals.)

Because the first question each manager will ask is: "How much money am I allowed to spend to do the job?"—the wise publisher asks the *business manager* (as finance officer) to go first in unveiling a basic strategic plan. This *financial strategy model* should be a simple table proposing how anticipated cash flow should be divided between funding of each of the functions (and their major sub-functions), and the business manager's own goal—left-over contribution to operating margin. (In earlier editions, we referred to this as an "economic model"; over thc ycars, readers have convinced us that "financial strategy model" is a more accurate name for it.)

In addition to recapitulating the basic performance goals (from the mission statement) for each function, this financial model might also propose planning-and-monitoring assumptions for such commitments as personnel additions (subject, of course, to the publisher's willingness to revise the organization chart), new title introductions, inventory investment or write-offs, discount range, and price-setting.

It is important to remember that this model (as with all the other strategy models) should only be viewed as a *recommendation* (from the finance officer) until it has been formally endorsed (or amended) *by the publisher.* Such endorsement of any function's strategy model (not only this one, but those from acquisition, pre-press and marketing) should only come after the publisher has heard adequate discussion by the entire core management group.

Figure 9a, on the next page, shows a good format for a financial strategy model (with numbers generally appropriate for a million-dollar annual publishing program ... though they are intended only as an illustration, *not as a recommendation,* since optimum patterns differ by type as well as size of publisher).

Remember, the ratios in Figure 9a are merely typical. Your own business manager should develop actual figures from the most recent 12 months of *your own* publishing activity, and in a side-by-side column recommend how (if at all) each of those numbers should be changed for near-future planning and performance-evaluation purposes. A realistic business manager (and they're all supposed to be that way!) will only seek reasonable improvements over actual recent ratios—adjusting each line-target by mere tenths of percentage points. There'll be plenty of those future quarterly reviews to introduce further, gradual re-targeting.

There are circumstances in which a publishing house is well advised to have two or more parallel financial strategy models—or two or more alternatives for certain specific planning guidelines. This is most common when the publisher functions simultaneously in two-or-more markets (such as trade and adoption) or two-or-more media (such as books and videos) in which operating ratios are significantly different—or when a major portion of the publisher's business is distribution of *other publishers'* products. In those cases, the business manager must simply be asked to create parallel guidelines—and plans and budgets must be sub-divided accordingly.

But only do this reluctantly. Note that the *budgeting* differences between various types of publishers are nominal; you'll be surprised how often that's true for most aspects of different media, too. To keep your strategy intellectually manageable, try to operate with a *single* financial strategy model—asking function managers to make market-focus or media decisions on the basis of *which pays off best* within the context of your mission.

Only when *the publisher* has approved or revised the entire column of proposed ratios (hopefully, after full discussion in the core management group) does the business manager's financial strategy model become (until further notice) the *official* basis on which all managers are asked to plan. And if you follow our advice, it'll all be up for grabs again 3 months later.

Perhaps the most critical number in the financial strategy model is the assumed *growth rate* of sales volume. This tells you what percentage increase (or occasional decrease) the core managers should assume from the *most recent 12 months'* sales volume, in anticipating how much revenue will flow into the publishing house (and thus, what their respective budget-percentages of that money will add up to in cold, hard dollars) over the *coming* 12 months.

Figure 9a—Sample Financial Strategy Model

Function Goals

Sales Volume Growth Rate	11.0% over previous year
New Title Contribution	35.0% of sales volume
Pre-Press Page Cost	$20.00 (including copy-edit)
Operating Margin	11.0% of sales volume
Inventory Investment	25.0% of annual sales level

Budget Ratios (percent of anticipated revenue)

Publisher's Office (Mgmt)	7.0% *
Acquisition Staff/Expenses	5.5%
Royalty Liability	9.0% **
Pre-Press Editing/Page Prdn	10.0% ***
Marketing (Sales, Promo)	17.5%
Business Mgr's Office	2.0%
Financial Administration	2.5% ****
Paper/Printing/Binding	22.5% ***
Warehousing and Shipping	4.0%
Rebillable Transport Charges	3.5%
Facilities & Equipment	5.5%
Operating Margin	11.0%

(* includes interest costs)
(** includes royalty advance cost-of-goods)
(*** as expensed via cost-of-goods recovery)
(**** including bad debt and inventory write-offs)

Planning Assumptions

Payroll/Benefits	24.0% of revenue
F/t/e Employees*****	1.0 per $100,000 sales
Returns	7.0% of sales volume
Bad Debts	0.7% of sales volume
Inventory Write-Offs	1.0% of sales volume
Average Discount	35.0% off list price
Maximum Regular Discount	50.0% off list price
Per-Page Pre-Press Cost	$20.00 including copy-edit
Per-Impression P/P/B Cost	$0.01 per copy per page
Pricing Multiplier	5.8 x unit inventory cost

(***** F/t/e = full-time equivalent)

A smart business manager will always review this number with the *marketing manager* before recommending a growth rate target for any initial budget, or in any quarterly review. That does not mean the business manager is obligated to accept the marketing manager's proposed target; the proposed financial model (and subsequent changes) represent the *business manager's* best professional estimate. But if they disagree, the difference should be talked out in a core management group review *before* the publisher sanctions use of the strategy model for future (or revised) planning by all functions.

This endorsement of an officially-sanctioned growth rate is the single most critical (and perhaps most audacious) commitment and gamble a publisher is asked to make—because it will eventually authorize all concerned to start committing the house to spending money that *hasn't actually arrived on the scene.* If the projected sales volume (growth rate) is not achieved—and appropriate adjustments are not made *in time* at those quarterly reviews—a serious financial crisis is likely ... and the publisher's job is probably in jeopardy!

So let's look next at the planning format by which a competent marketing manager can best show the rest of the team how and why she hopes to maximize that growth rate (or minimize any temporary decline) to meet the planning target (and thus keep the corporate checkbook balanced). Broad marketing strategy is most clearly expressed in terms of the frequency of exposure to, relative expenditure on, and tactics for communicating with a prioritized list of specific *audiences* that the marketing manager believes are the most important influencers of your ultimate customers' purchasing decisions. In a direct response program, these audiences will consist primarily of the customers themselves; in a classroom adoption program, they'll consist almost entirely of educational decision-makers—who're seldom either the actual buyers or the actual readers; in trade houses, the primary audiences will be a mix of customers, background influencers, and distribution middlemen.

The first element in a strategic marketing plan, then, is identification and prioritization of audiences. The second is selection of specific on-going tactics (which over a period of time constitute individual "campaigns") the marketing manager and his colleagues believe will most effectively expose each of those audiences of the house's product line (of both new and backlist titles). The third is determination of a frequency-of-exposure to top-priority audiences that the marketing manager believes will maximize sales results.

A basic principle of sound marketing strategy is to *maximize exposure* to one's top-rated audience (up to a point of diminishing returns) before diverting any money or effort to lower-rated audiences; then maximize exposure to the *second-best* audience before moving on to the third, etc., etc. You maximize exposure by increasing the frequency of communication—recognizing that most people pay so little attention to most promotional and sales messages that most of the *repeated* exposures are essentially falling on virgin ground.

Except for seasonal "dead spots" (such as December), many direct marketers (including publishers) find that every-2-week repetitive exposure goes on pulling the same results time after time, for year after year. Even among the most attentive audiences, very few experience diminishing returns at every-4-week intervals. But we'll save the nuances of marketing strategy for Chapter 24.

At any rate, then, a typical marketing strategy model will be a spreadsheet projecting the chosen strategy (a combination of on-going campaigns to prioritized audiences) 15 months into the future—so you can review-and-manipulate over a full cyclical year *without* disrupting the quarter already-in-progress. It should look something like Figure 9b, on the next page.

When asked to sanction any initial or revised marketing strategy model, the publisher should especially insist on being convinced that the marketing manager has paid attention to those "operational pipelines" referred to at the beginning of Chapter 5. If a marketing manager can identify a single, sizable (open-ended) audience that predictably yields an especially-profitable response to a single, pre-tested, updatable presentation—either *directly* or *indirectly* (by generating good promotion leads for sales follow-up), *the entire scale of the publishing house's operations can be expanded simply by concentrating financial resources on exploiting that one "multiplier" link in the basic marketing pipeline.* Looking for and cashing in on such statistically predictable "multipliers" (which may be as simple as more frequent mailings to your own direct customer list) is usually the single most decisive strategic move a publishing house can take to improve its "place in the world."

Given this conduit to its audiences (the marketing plan), the acquisition function should now be asked to display a *3-year* plan of the pattern of new title development in each of the defined product categories ("series") that it envisions. Three years not only gives the other functions adequate forewarning (with their annual cycles) of significant changes of direction; it creates rational "slots" for future projects, in keeping with the editor-in-chief's game plan, before the vested interests of specific, individual (and often politically-weighted) projects cloud acquisition decision-making.

Essentially, sound acquisition strategy planning begins with identification of product categories ("series"—as reflected by the vertical columns of Figure 9c) that will enable the house to (1) accumulate editorial expertise in particular subject areas and reader-usages, and (2) concentrate its limited marketing resources (especially money) on highly-targeted audiences who share their devotion to those subjects and usages. Next it identifies (horizontally in Figure 9c) a seasonal planning and work-ganging pattern to coincide with marketing's need to "wake the audience up" with something new.

Figure 9b—Sample Marketing Strategy Model

MARKETING STRATEGY MODEL — Week ending >>>>>>>>>>>>
(Assuming 10 titles next xt 12 mos)
PUBLICATION DATES >>>>>>>>

COUNT	TACTIC	@ UNIT	$ YR	Jan 8 Harr (Mill2)	Jan 15 (Jone3)	Jan 22 (Adam1)	Jan 29 (Clar1)	Feb 5 Jone (Mill3)	Feb 12 (Mill1)	Feb 19 (Adam2)	Feb 26 (Clar2)	Mar 5 Mill (Mark1)	Mar 12 (Mill2)	Mar 19 (Adam3)	Mar 26 (Clar3)	Apr 2 Adam (Mark2)	Apr 9 Clar (Parml)
AUDIENCES:																	
KEY CONTACTS:																	
356	Catalog (3 @ year) [Reviewers]	$0.88	$940	$313													$313
149	NRs with Comp Offers x2 [Talk Shows]	$0.35	$1043	$52	$52	$52	$52	$52	$52	$52	$52	$52	$52	$52	$52	$52	$52
113	NRs with Comp Offers x2 [Sub-Rights]	$0.35	$791	$40	$40	$40	$40	$40	$40	$40	$40	$40	$40	$40	$40	$40	$40
14	NRs with Comp Offers x2 [Special Marketing]	$0.35	$98	$5	$5	$5	$5	$5	$5	$5	$5	$5	$5	$5	$5	$5	$5
10	NRs with Comp Offers x2 [Comp Requests]	$0.35	$70	$4	$4	$4	$4	$4	$4	$4	$4	$4	$4	$4	$4	$4	$4
open	Comp books (inc auto)	$2.00	$4000	$400				$400				$400				$400	$400
BOOKSTORES:																	
69	NRs with Comp offers x3 [Key Acts]	$0.35	$725	$24	$24	$24	$24	$24	$24	$24	$24	$24	$24	$24	$24	$24	$24
412	NRs with Comp offers x3 [Open Acts]	$0.35	$4426	$216	$216	$216	$216	$216	$216	$216	$216	$216	$216	$216	$216	$216	$216
937	Catalog (3 @ year) [Prospects]	$0.88	$2474	$825													$825
open	ABA Exhibit (ditto)	$2000	$2000														
LIBRARIES:																	
72	NRs with Comp offers x2 [Big Systems]	$0.35	$504	$25	$25	$25	$25	$25	$25	$25	$25	$25	$25	$25	$25	$25	$25
11	NRs with Comp offers x3 [Wholesalers]	$0.35	$116	$4	$4	$4	$4	$4	$4	$4	$4	$4	$4	$4	$4	$4	$4
1288	Catalog (3 @ year) [Prospects]	$0.88	$3400	$1133													$1133
CLASS ADOPTION:																	
147	NRs with Exam Forms (4x3) [Exam List]	$0.40	$706		$59	$59	$59	$59	$59	$59							
2413	Flyer w/Exam Offer (3) [Discipline]	$0.33	$2389		$796							$75		$796			
open	Conference Exhibit (ditto)	$1500	$1500								$1500						
DIRECT BUYERS:																	
9885	Basic Mailer [Customers]	$0.30	$60000	$3000	$3000			$3000		$3000		$3000		$3000		$3000	
1500	Test Mailers (3) [Cust. Split]	$0.40	$1800			$600						$600					
open	Basic Mailer - 1000 x5x20 [Screening Lists]	$0.35	$7000	$350	$350	$350	$350	$350	$350	$350	$350	$350	$350	$350	$350	$350	$350
open	Highlight Mailer - 2000 x4 [Test Lists]	$0.35	$2800			$700						$700					
Print Ad Circ:																	
open	Page Display [Proven Media]	$500	$5500	$1000				$1000	$500			$1000					$500
open	Quik-Spot Ad [Test Media]	$50	$2000	$200				$200				$200				$200	$200
OVERHEAD																	
	Promotion	$465	$24050	$465	$465	$465	$465	$465	$465	$465	$465	$465	$465	$465	$465	$465	$465
	Sales/Telerep	$750	$39900	$1500	$1500	$1500	$1500	$1500	$1500	$1500	$1500	$1500	$1500	$1500	$1500	$1500	$1500
	Management	$350	$18200	$700	$700	$700	$700	$700	$700	$700	$700	$700	$700	$700	$700	$700	$700
TOTAL MARKETING COST	[Approx. Budget]		$185430	$10256	$3918	$7240	$4144	$7859	$3444	$6385	$4944	$8660	$4585	$7055	$3818	$5985	$6756

Third, the editor-in-chief confers with the business manager to project recovery and recycling of inventory capital (via "cost of goods"—as further explained in Chapter 12) and estimate how many new products the enterprise can afford to introduce in each season for the next 3 years *without additional investment.* With a retrospective look at average per-project "front money" costs in recent months, the editor-in-chief should then be able to convert that recovered capital (after a prudent deduction for backlist reprinting) into a specific number of anticipated new products (books or other media packages) for each forthcoming season. (Once the model is established, of course, the editor-in-chief simply adds a season 3-years-out every time the one closest-at-hand is completed—and makes necessary adjustments in the intervening seasons).

An acquisition strategy *may,* of course, propose a greater number of new titles for any future season than can be financed (as initial inventory) by sales recovery of cost-of-goods. But this will require delicate, long-term negotiations (through the publisher) with the Board of Directors—to obtain permission for the house to borrow, earmark a portion of anticipated earnings, or raise new capital to finance such additional inventory.

The tantalizing strategic issue for the editor-in-chief is to decide which distribution of those affordable future new titles (projects) between the various series will most enhance new title contribution to sales volume—the essential acquisition performance index. That product mix is reflected by distributing *blank lines* for forthcoming books on the model 3 years out—and then gradually filling in the blanks as specific proposals are nominated and approved for each slot. Figure 9c, on the next page, shows just such an acquisitions strategy model.

Now that the business, marketing, and acquisition managers have "weighed in" with their basic strategy models, it's time for the pre-press managing editor to pick up the pieces by plotting how the messiest part of the execution of those plans—the conversion of each of those hypothetical new products from raw manuscript to actual inventory—will be accomplished. As noted before, it is not a good idea to saddle the pre-press function with the *financial* decisions of inventory buying, but if pre-press comes up with printable masters, specifications, and vendor bids, the business office will have no trouble (by adjusting print quantities) "taking it from there" within the guidelines of their own financial strategy model and inventory-investment limits.

To set the table for such print-buying decisions, the managing editor must anticipate all of the steps through which a project must pass *between raw manuscript and finished book.* It is important that publishers ask their managing editors to include non-production steps (for promotion, data processing, etc.) as well as those in which pre-press is directly involved—since delays in one function may upset (or make irrelevant) intricate timetables in others.

Figure 9c—Sample Acquisition Strategy Model

SAMPLE ACQUISITION PLAN	Travel Agency Mgmt	Consumer Travel Tips	Travel Destination Guides	Experimental
Prototypes	Starting an Agency (1433) Selling Cruises (1379)	Don't Drink the Water! (3772) If You Take the Kids (4441)	Marx: Moscow (2758) Carsn: Back to Montreal (3857)	Don't Drink the Water! (3732)
1993: Spring	MALCOLM: ADVERTISING	JONES: ALL ABOUT CRUISING	EDWARDS: HAITI Marshall: New Zealand	
Fall	George: Recruiting/Training	Finney: Vacation Packing	Jacobs: Canadian Maritimes Henry: The Amazon VIDECKI: JAPAN	HARRIS: JAMAICAN COOKBOOK
1994: Spring	(Malcolm: Accounting)	_____	Marshall: Australia Miller: Poland (_____: Vietnam Revisited) (_____: Antarctica)	
Fall	_____	_____	Edwards: Windwards/Leewards Jacobs: Siberia _____ _____ _____	(Audio: Washington, DC) Seminar: Planning a Cruise
1995: SPRING	_____	_____	_____ _____ _____ _____ _____	
Fall	_____	_____	_____ _____ _____ _____ _____	(Video _____)

___ = No Proposal   ( ) = No Contract   CAPS = Ms. in House

The managing editor, then, should take the first shot at identifying steps (column 1 of Figure 9d), estimating time-lapses (the numbers in column 2—each representing the approximate number of days prior to formal publication when that step should be completed), and confirming departmental responsibilities for getting each task finished on time (the initials in column 2). Then the other departments should be invited to comment, object, suggest alternate time lapses, or add steps in their own areas of which they'd like to be routinely reminded.

Once this proposed checklist has been thrashed out in the core management group and approved ("until further notice") by the publisher, individual books (each claiming a column—as indicated by the author-name codes at the top in Figure 9d) can then be entered onto the spreadsheet (and into the pre-press pipeline) whenever acquisition is willing to commit to a manuscript-delivery date (line 3). The managing editor uses the time-lapse numbers to estimate an *approximate* schedule for each book; subsequent refinements and adjustments are made project-by-project and week-by-week (often in conjunction with—and sometimes instead of—the core management group's weekly review of the "management events calendar").

Figure 9d—Sample New Title Development Scheduling Model

	1	2	3	4	5	6	7	8
	1 AUTHOR CODE >>>>> 2	Who/When	Melb	Sinc	Will	Dunb	2nd Sprg	3rd Sprg
3	Raw Ms. Delivered	Acqu-250	1217	0107	0214	0610	0710	0810
4	Dev Schedule Entered	PrPr-245	1222	0112	0219	0615		
5	Input to Word Processor	PrPr-240	1227	0117	0224	0620		
6	Subst Edg Transmitted	Acqu-180	0227	0317	0424	0820		
7	Launch Meeting	Acqu-180	0227	0317	0424	0820		
8	Special Publicity Inputs	Acqu-175	0304	0322	0429	0825		
9	Info/Photo File to Promo	Acqu-175	0304	0322	0504	0830		
10	Interior Art Transmitted	Acqu-170	0309	0327	0509	0904		
11	Title Finalized	Acqu-170	0309	0327	0509	0904		
12	CIP Data Sent	PrPr-165	0314	0401	0514	0909		
13	ABI Data Sent	PrPr-165	0314	0401	0514	0909		
14	Promo Copy Pkg Done	Mark-165	0314	0401	0514	0909		
15	Pre-Page Offer to SubRts	Mark-160	0319	0406	0519	0914		
16	Special Marketing Queries	Mark-160	0319	0406	0519	0914		
17	Author Brochures Offered	Acqu-160	0319	0406	0519	0914		
18	Cover Concept Approved	Mark-160	0319	0406	0519	0914		
19	First Copy-Edit Done	PrPr-160	0319	0406	0519	0914		
20	Page Format Set	PrPr-155	0324	0411	0524	0919		
21	Cover Art Arranged	Mark-155	0324	0411	0524	0919		
22	Rough Pages Ready	PrPr-140	0408	0426	0509	1004		
23	End Papers Inserted	Mark-130	0418	0506	0519	1014		
24	Print Specs Ready	PrPr-125	0423	0511	0524	1019		
25	Printing Bids Invited	PrPr-120	0428	0516	0529	1024		
26	Cover Art Ready	Mark-120	0428	0516	0529	1024		
27	Ads (if any) Placed	Mark-115	0503	0521	0603	1029		
28	Second Edit Completed	PrPr-115	0503	0521	0603	1029		
29	Author/Ed Changes Input	PrPr-110	0508	0526	0608	1104		
30	Price/Quantity Check	Bus-105	0523	0611	0623	1119		
31	Final Pages Approved	PrPr-100	0518	0606	0618	1114		
32	Printer Confirmed	Bus-100	0518	0606	0618	1114		
33	Pages to SubRts, Pre-Revs	Mark-95	0523	0611	0623	1119		
34	Repro Disk Ready	PrPr-95	0523	0611	0623	1119		
35	Print Order Sent	Bus-90	0528	0617	0628	1124		
36	Announcement NR#1	Mark-90	0528	0617	0628	1124		
37	ABI Data Updated	Mark-90	0528	0617	0628	1124		
38	Local Store/TV Letters	Mark-85	0603	0622	0703	1129		
39	Blues, Cover Proofs OK	PrPr-75	0613	0702	0713	1209		
40	Announcement NR#2	Mark-75	0613	0702	0713	1209		
41	Inventory File Initiated	Bus-75	0613	0702	0713	1209		
42	Product File Input	Bus-70	0618	0707	0718	1214		
43	Printer Shipments Set	Bus-65	0623	0712	0723	1219		
44	Warehouse Alerted	Bus-60	0628	0717	0728	1224		
45	Comp Labels Ready	Mark-55	0703	0722	0803	1229		
46	Bound Bks Checked In	Bus-50	0708	0727	0808	0103	0201	0301
47	Comps Shipped	Bus-48	0710	0729	0810	0105		
48	Advance Orders Shipped	Bus-45	0713	0801	0813	0108		
49	Editorial Comps Shipped	Bus-40	0718	0806	0818	0113		
50	Copyright Registered	PrPr-25	0803	0821	0902	0128		
51	Printer Art Recovered	PrPr-25	0803	0821	0902	0128		
52	Permanent File Opened	PrPr-20	0808	0826	0907	0203		
53	Store Phoning Finished	Mark-20	0808	0826	0907	0203		
54	Formal Publication Date	Mark-0	0828	0915	0922	0223	0320	0420

The result, then, is what's called a "new title development checklist"—the basic pre-press strategy model and on-going scheduling device. Carefully monitored and regularly adjusted, it often becomes (with good reason!) the day-to-day nerve center of the publishing operation. It looks something like Figure 9d, on the next page.

Note that we've occasionally referred to each strategy model as a valid planning/coordinating guide "until further notice." As each is developed, it should be subjected to the commentary of the entire core management group, and amended and/or officially sanctioned by the publisher, *before* any money is spent or any contractual commitments are made to carry it out. And after each quarterly budget review, each core manager should update his model to reflect changes endorsed by the publisher during that review. Each updated model should be submitted for the publisher's approval (with particular attention to marketing's sensitivity to pipeline multipliers), and subjected to core group discussion if the publisher so desires, before it is considered official—again, "until further notice."

Such tentativeness about strategic plans bothers some middle-managers; they feel they can't "count on" their basic assumptions for the long run, because top management keeps inviting quarterly changes. But effective publishing is a fast-changing response to a fast-changing market—and that tentativeness is the price we have to pay for flexibility ... for the independent publisher's capacity to out-create and out-maneuver the conglomerate dinosaurs! Middle managers who prefer the complacent comfort of static guidelines and assumptions are really too inflexible for key roles in the highly creative, high-risk world of small group publishing dynamics.

As long as you keep those models projected well into the future—and remember that *the current quarter* is best changed only in dire emergencies (always focusing instead on the 12 months *following* that quarter)—a competent core management team should be able to adjust as frequently as its collective grasp of possibilities (reflected by those models) expands, changes, and matures.

CHAPTER 10
Budgeting as the Culmination of Planning

When all four basic functions (acquisition, pre-press development, marketing, business operations) have mapped out their game plans on the strategy models described in the previous chapter, you're ready to get on with more detailed planning for achieving the goals inherent in each function's accountability index. But the costs resulting from those plans must be synchronized with the income they're expected to produce (unless you've got a lot of very rich, very supportive, very old aunts and uncles). This means budgeting.

One of the most glaring differences between poorly-managed and well-managed publishing houses is that the former tend to make budgets (if at all) simply by projecting past results—and then subjecting the answers to some hopeful manipulation by the publisher or business manager. Well-managed publishing houses, on the other hand, require the people who'll be spending the money to demonstrate that they've done some real (and realistic) planning, before they're authorized to make any financial commitments in the name of the enterprise.

A budget is, essentially, a precise summary of all plans—reduced to the clear common denominator of money. Budgets have traditionally been prepared for *fixed* periods of time (fiscal years). Unfortunately, this means they have to be re-created each time such a fixed period ends; that results in a lot of redundant effort, and costs you a lot of top-scale payroll time.

But in the era of the spreadsheet, publishing managers have learned that it's practical, less time-consuming, and usually much more useful to budget on an *on-going* basis. This means you create a beginning model of what *the next full year* (four quarters) is expected to look like—in terms of spending limits and income expectations—and then simply adjust-and-extend that model quarter-by-quarter to keep it always looking 12 months ahead. (Since too-rapid changes can be very disruptive—those four quarters should never include the *current* one—so to extend the plan another quarter, you actually need to look 15 months ahead.)

Such constantly-extended, frequently-adjusted budgeting is sometimes uncomfortable for people in whom accounting classes, IRS, and annual stockholder or membership meetings have deeply ingrained the concept of (and guilt trips associated with) the fiscal year—an explicit 12-month planning-and-accounting period. But there is nothing sacred (and there is a great deal confusing) about these artificial fiscal years. If you're always (via quarterly extension) projecting income-and-expenses a year ahead, and summarizing results by constantly retotaling *the most recent 12 months* at the end of *every* month, it's a simple matter to "stop the projector" at any point (by printing out a selected slice of your spreadsheet) to give an annual meeting a budget for any *specific* future 12 months—or a tax collector a return for any specific past 12 months (or quarter, or what-not).

If you're "starting from scratch" on a full year's budget, there are essentially ten basic steps to doing it right. You'll need about 7 weeks to complete them—so you should begin *about 2 months before* you expect to authorize people to make commitments on the basis of that budget, or before you have to submit a proposed budget to anyone else (a Board of Directors, etc.) for approval. For a quarterly extension of a continuous budget, you can probably compress the process into four steps, all done in a couple of weeks.

As raw material, you'll need actual most-recent-12-months (or estimated current fiscal year) line-by-line totals from your basic "chart of accounts"—that display of the financial categories to which the accountants assign all income and expense transactions; it will provide both a point-of-departure and a format for the new budget. Since it will help clarify the process, we'll risk boring you by exhibiting a sample chart-of-accounts and budgeting spreadsheet here (on the next two-page spread), even though it will be repeated (and more thoroughly explained) in Chapter 35.

For annual budgeting, the first budget-planning step (in the first week) is a preliminary general strategy review by your core management group (the publisher and major function/department heads). They should re-examine your basic mission statement (Figure 6a), and update the organization chart (Figure 7a) to identify *every* payroll position your new budget is expected to cover. Then they should review together the basic strategy models (Chapter 9) of your acquisition, pre-press, and marketing functions.

Next (Step 2), the business manager should restudy her existing financial strategy model, and prepare *currently updated* recommendations for financial performance goals, budget allocation ratios for each significant function or category, and basic financial planning assumptions—similar to the sample illustrated in Figure 9a. She best accomplishes this by first calculating the house's *current, actual* annualized (most-recent-12-months) numbers for each line item in her model, and then changing specific items if/as she deems appropriate, to improve/adjust them as recommended goals for the new year.

The resulting, updated Financial Strategy Model should then be "talked through" by your core management group, and either amended or endorsed by the publisher (hopefully as consensus emerges)—as a basis for planning the year ahead. Acquisition, pre-press and marketing managers should be expected to speak up aggressively for their respective functions in this process—or forever hold their peace about the size of their budgets.

In Step 3 (still in that first annual-planning week), the business manager should use the growth rate in the updated (publisher-approved) financial strategy model to project (from current sales volume) the expected sales revenue for the year ahead—and add to it any additional investment capital, borrowing capacity, etc., that the publisher says can be spent in that year—to set the *total* budget target (covering both expenses and margin/earnings). Then she should multiply that total by the approved strategy model budget percentages to project *each function's proper share* of that anticipated budget.

In the second week (as Step 4), the business manager should multiply *every line's total* on the last-12-months chart by the targeted growth rate (from Financial Strategy Model) ... and then multiply all of those results *by 1.1* ... to come up with a dollar figure for each line that is a 10 percent *larger* share of next year's anticipated revenue than was spent on that item in the current year. The chart showing those inflated totals for each line should be distributed to all departments to indicate *maximum spending limits* for each item.

In that same week (as Step 5), the business manager should propose (and the publisher should approve or amend) which lines throughout the chart of accounts are to be *automatically projected* by the business office because they are matters of fixed contracts (rent, equipment leases, royalties, etc.), or because they have a relatively fixed relationship to sales volume rather than specific plans (cost-of-goods, returns, bad debts, etc.). As soon as these fixed line projections are made, they should be entered into the budget column of the chart format in place of the inflated "planning limit" numbers from Step 4.

The remaining lines, then, are the "variable" items that should be creatively *planned* rather than mathematically projected. In this second week, *all* function managers should (as Step 6) assign some specific individual the task of planning how the maximum amount available on *each* line in their respective sections of the chart could best be spent in the year ahead. This means the person most concerned with exhibits will be asked to plan how marketing will spend its maximum exhibit-line budget, etc., etc.

Whether you should treat payroll and benefits as "fixed"—to be adjusted on an across-the-boards basis by the publisher's office, and allocated to the various departments—or as "variable"—subject to individual planning by each function manager—should depend on how much real control those managers have over personnel costs. Unless you're bound by rules of a larger (sponsoring) organization, it's usually best to leave each department's payroll (plus a percentage mark-up for benefits, etc.) as a "variable"—and let all managers choose between staffing and alternate ways of getting their work done (free-lancers, etc.).

Now, for Step 7, give those individual line-planners in each department the next 2 weeks (3 and 4) to develop worksheets showing (by schedules, checklists, charts, etc.) just how they believe the *maximum spending limit* (Step

Figure 10a—Sample Chart of Accounts and Budgeting Format

1	2	3	4	5	6	7	8	9
1 SAMPLE CHART OF ACCOUNTS	Jul 93	Aug 92		Jun 93	Last 12 Mos.	Actual %	Budg %	Budget
2 **************								
3 Trade Book Sales	$56,882.84	$51,194.55		$58,521.44	$731,517.96	70.2%	68.3%	$750,000.00
4 Special Market Book Sales	$13,776.95	$12,399.25		$14,173.81	$177,172.65	17.0%	18.2%	$200,000.00
5 Direct Response Book Sales	$14,448.24	$13,003.42		$14,864.45	$185,805.59	17.8%	18.2%	$200,000.00
6 GROSS BOOK SALES	$85,108.02	$76,597.22		$87,559.70	$1,094,496.20	105.0%	104.8%	$1,150,000.00
7 Return Credits	$6,442.31	$5,798.08		$6,627.89	$82,848.67	7.9%	7.7%	$85,000.00
8 NET BOOK SALES	$78,665.71	$70,799.14		$80,931.80	$1,011,647.53	97.0%	97.0%	$1,065,000.00
9 Sub Rights Revenue	$214.22	$192.80		$220.39	$2,754.87	0.3%	0.3%	$3,500.00
10 Shipping Reimbursements	$2,101.01	$1,890.91		$2,161.54	$27,019.20	2.6%	2.6%	$28,000.00
11 Other Revenue	$75.96	$68.36		$78.14	$976.80	0.1%	0.1%	$1,221.61
12 TOTAL NET REVENUE	$81,056.90	$72,951.21		$83,391.87	$1,042,398.40	100.0%	100.0%	$1,097,721.61
13								
14 MANAGEMENT COMPENSATION	$5,697.12	$5,127.41		$5,861.24	$73,265.47	7.0%	6.7%	$73,619.46
15 Mgmt Professional Fees	$0.00	$0.00		$0.00	$0.00	0.0%	0.0%	$0.00
16 Mgmt Travel/Entertainment	$165.19	$148.67		$169.94	$2,124.30	0.2%	0.2%	$2,356.69
17 Board Honoraria	$155.52	$139.97		$160.00	$2,000.00	0.2%	0.2%	$2,000.00
18 Board Expenses	$34.04	$30.64		$35.02	$437.81	0.0%	0.0%	$500.00
19 Interest	$18.01	$16.21		$18.53	$231.62	0.0%	0.0%	$300.00
20 Misc Mgmt Expenses	$53.04	$47.73		$54.57	$682.08	0.1%	0.1%	$1,000.00
21 TOTAL MGMT EXPENSE	$6,122.92	$5,510.63		$6,299.30	$78,741.28	7.6%	7.3%	$79,776.15
22								
23 ACQUISITION COMPENSATION	$4,057.39	$3,651.65		$4,174.27	$52,178.36	5.0%	4.8%	$52,520.78
24 ROYALTY ADVANCE C/G/S	$1,822.49	$1,640.24		$1,874.99	$23,437.40	2.2%	2.2%	$24,450.00
25 Roy Liability Accrued	$6,166.43	$5,549.79		$6,344.06	$79,300.80	7.6%	8.0%	$87,486.63
26 Honoraria/Prof Fees	$27.22	$24.49		$28.00	$350.00	0.0%	0.0%	$500.00
27 Acqui Travel & Entrmt	$54.18	$48.76		$55.74	$696.80	0.1%	0.1%	$750.00
28 Misc Acqui Expenses	$151.87	$136.69		$156.25	$1,953.10	0.2%	0.2%	$2,200.00
29 TOTAL ACQUI EXPENSES ·	$12,279.58	$11,051.63		$12,633.32	$157,916.46	15.1%	15.3%	$167,907.41
30								
31 PRE-PRESS COMPENSATION	$4,006.88	$3,606.20		$4,122.31	$51,528.87	4.9%	4.7%	$52,077.20
32 COPYEDITING C/G/S	$3,084.27	$2,775.84		$3,173.12	$39,663.95	3.8%	3.7%	$40,750.00
33 PAGE-PREP C/G/S	$1,033.64	$930.28		$1,063.42	$13,292.74	1.3%	1.5%	$16,300.00
34 Pre-Press T&E	$0.00	$0.00		$0.00	$0.00	0.0%	0.0%	$200.00
35 Misc Pre-Press Expenses	$60.57	$54.51		$62.31	$778.90	0.1%	0.1%	$800.00
36 TOTAL PRE-PRESS EXPENSE	$8,185.36	$7,366.83		$8,421.16	$105,264.46	10.1%	10.0%	$110,127.20
37								
38 MARKETING COMPENSATION	$4,919.63	$4,427.67		$5,061.35	$63,266.85	6.1%	5.8%	$63,727.27
39 Publicity	$806.49	$725.84		$829.72	$10,371.50	1.0%	1.0%	$10,717.71
40 Trade Selling	$4,142.37	$3,728.13		$4,261.70	$53,271.20	5.1%	5.1%	$55,609.66
41 Co-op Ad Credits	$317.26	$285.53		$326.40	$4,080.00	0.4%	0.4%	$4,102.53
42 PROMO C/G/S	$1,321.51	$1,189.35		$1,359.57	$16,994.67	1.6%	1.5%	$16,300.00
43 Special Market Selling	$1,088.89	$980.00		$1,120.26	$14,003.23	1.3%	1.3%	$14,402.48
44 Direct Response Selling	$297.28	$267.55		$305.84	$3,823.00	0.4%	0.4%	$4,381.12
45 Marketing T&E	$3,478.58	$3,130.72		$3,578.78	$44,734.81	4.3%	4.1%	$45,000.00
46 Misc Marketing Expense	$265.22	$238.69		$272.86	$3,410.70	0.3%	0.3%	$3,500.00
47 TOTAL MARKETING EXPENSE	$16,637.22	$14,973.49		$17,116.48	$213,955.96	20.5%	19.8%	$217,740.77
48								
49 BUS/OPS COMPENSATION	$4,446.46	$4,001.81		$4,574.55	$57,181.82	5.5%	5.3%	$57,790.31
50 Fulfillment Supplies	$374.45	$337.01		$385.24	$4,815.50	0.5%	0.5%	$5,200.00
51 Mfg. Freight In	$628.90	$566.01		$647.02	$8,087.70	0.8%	0.8%	$8,314.65
52 Prepaid Pstg/Trans Out	$1,643.92	$1,479.53		$1,691.28	$21,141.00	2.0%	2.1%	$23,438.38
53 External Storage/Handling	$782.82	$704.54		$805.37	$10,067.14	1.0%	1.0%	$10,590.18
54 Misc Fulf Expenses	$19.44	$17.50		$20.00	$250.00	0.0%	0.0%	$300.00
55 Fin Adm Prof Fees	$0.00	$0.00		$0.00	$0.00	0.0%	0.0%	$0.00
56 MFG (PPB) C/G/S	$14,510.82	$13,059.74		$14,928.82	$186,610.30	17.9%	16.7%	$183,000.00

Figure 10a—Sample Chart of Accounts and Budgeting Format (cont.)

	1	2	3	4	5	6	7	8	9
1	SAMPLE CHART OF ACCOUNTS	Jul 93	Aug 92		Jun 93	Last 12 Mos.	Actual %	Budg %	Budget
2	###############								
57	INVENTORY WRITEOFF C/G/S	$1,227.40	$1,104.66		$1,262.76	$15,784.44	1.5%	1.5%	$16,300.00
58	Bad Debt Write-Offs	$91.36	$82.22		$93.99	$1,174.90	0.1%	0.1%	$1,200.00
59	Misc Fin Adm Expenses	$124.05	$111.65		$127.62	$1,595.30	0.2%	0.1%	$1,500.00
60	Rent and Utilities	$2,177.51	$1,959.76		$2,240.24	$28,002.98	2.7%	2.7%	$30,021.11
61	Equipment Lease/Maint	$2,213.92	$1,992.53		$2,277.70	$28,471.19	2.7%	2.9%	$31,643.62
62	DEPRECIATION	$98.71	$88.84		$101.55	$1,269.43	0.1%	0.1%	$1,300.00
63	Office Supplies	$1,122.67	$1,010.40		$1,155.01	$14,437.62	1.4%	1.3%	$14,000.00
64	Routine Postage	$286.79	$258.11		$295.05	$3,688.10	0.4%	0.4%	$4,112.41
65	Phone/Wire/Courier	$1,167.47	$1,050.72		$1,201.10	$15,013.77	1.4%	1.4%	$15,000.00
66	Ref/Libr Materials	$57.40	$51.66		$59.05	$738.17	0.1%	0.1%	$823.17
67	Misc Facility Exp	$165.84	$149.25		$170.62	$2,132.69	0.2%	0.2%	$2,400.00
68	TOTAL BUS/OPS EXPENSE	$31,139.93	$28,025.94		$32,036.96	$400,462.05	38.4%	37.1%	$406,933.83
69									
70	TOTAL GROSS REVENUE	$87,499.21	$78,749.29		$90,019.77	$1,125,247.07	107.9%	107.7%	$1,182,721.61
71	RETURNS/REFUNDS	$6,442.31	$5,798.08		$6,627.89	$82,848.67	7.9%	7.7%	$85,000.00
72	TOTAL NET REVENUE	$81,056.90	$72,951.21		$83,391.87	$1,042,398.40	100.0%	100.0%	$1,097,721.61
73	TOTAL COST OF GOODS	$23,000.12	$20,700.11		$23,662.68	$295,783.50	28.4%	27.1%	$297,100.00
74	TOTAL OPERATING REVENUE	$58,056.77	$52,251.10		$59,729.19	$746,614.90	71.6%	72.9%	$800,621.61
75	TOTAL OPERATING EXPENSES	$51,364.89	$46,228.40		$52,844.54	$660,556.71	63.4%	62.4%	$685,385.36
76	TOTAL OPERATING MARGIN	$6,691.88	$6,022.70		$6,884.66	$86,058.19	8.3%	10.5%	$115,236.25
77									
78	REFERENCE ACCOUNTS#####								
79									
80	Mfg C/G/S to Bus/Ops	$14,510.82	$13,059.74		$14,928.82	$186,610.30	17.9%	16.7%	$183,000.00
81	Inv Writeoffs Exp'd to Fin	$1,227.40	$1,104.66		$1,262.76	$15,784.44	1.5%	1.5%	$16,300.00
82	Roy Adv C/G/S to Acqui	$1,822.49	$1,640.24		$1,874.99	$23,437.40	2.2%	2.2%	$24,450.00
83	Copy-Ed C/G/S to Pr-Pr	$3,084.27	$2,775.84		$3,173.12	$39,663.95	3.0%	3.7%	$40,750.00
84	Page-Prep C/G/S to Pr-Pr	$1,033.64	$930.28		$1,063.42	$13,292.74	1.3%	1.5%	$16,300.00
85	Promo PPB C/G/S to Marktg	$1,321.51	$1,189.35		$1,359.57	$16,994.67	1.6%	1.5%	$16,300.00
86	COST OF GOODS SOLD	$23,000.12	$20,700.11		$23,662.68	$295,783.50	28.4%	27.1%	$297,100.00
87									
88	Royalty Advances	$1,788.48	$1,609.63		$1,840.00	$23,000.00	2.2%	2.3%	$25,000.00
89	Copy-Editing Investment	$3,031.33	$2,728.20		$3,118.66	$38,983.20	3.7%	4.0%	$43,753.21
90	Pre-Page Investment	$2,715.18	$2,443.66		$2,793.39	$34,917.40	3.3%	3.4%	$37,668.43
91	New Title P/P/B Investment	$8,394.67	$7,555.20		$8,636.49	$107,956.12	10.4%	10.8%	$118,113.92
92	Reprinting P/P/B Investment	$4,194.50	$3,775.05		$4,315.33	$53,941.60	5.2%	5.0%	$54,886.08
93	TOTAL INVENTORY INVESTMENT	$20,124.16	$18,111.74		$20,703.87	$258,798.32	24.8%	25.5%	$279,421.64
94	RECOVERED C/G/S	$23,000.12	$20,700.11		$23,662.68	$295,783.50	28.4%	27.1%	$297,100.00
95	NET INVENTORY INVESTMENT	($2,875.97)	($2,588.37)		($2,958.81)	($36,985.18)	-3.5%	-1.6%	($17,678.36)
96									
97	Capital Equipment Investment	$0.00	$1,000.00		$0.00	$1,432.00	0.1%	0.1%	$1,097.72
98	Depreciation Expensed to #62	$0.00	$0.00		$0.00	$1,269.43	0.1%	0.1%	$1,300.00
99	NET EQUIPMENT INVESTMENT	$0.00	$1,000.00		$0.00	$162.57	0.0%	0.1%	($202.28)
100									
101	Non-Capitalized Salaries	$16,853.21	$15,167.89		$17,338.69	$216,733.62	20.8%	19.9%	$217,922.82
102	Contract Labor	$141.52	$127.37		$145.60	$1,820.00	0.2%	0.2%	$2,000.00
103	Company FICA Contrib	$1,119.91	$1,007.92		$1,152.17	$14,402.08	1.4%	1.3%	$14,535.00
104	Other Payroll Taxes	$538.75	$484.88		$554.27	$6,928.40	0.7%	0.6%	$7,000.00
105	Employee Benefits	$48.99	$44.09		$50.40	$630.00	0.1%	0.1%	$700.00
106	Payroll Insurance	$319.16	$287.24		$328.35	$4,104.40	0.4%	0.4%	$4,200.00
107	Personnel Miscellaneous	$99.07	$89.16		$101.92	$1,274.00	0.1%	0.1%	$1,300.00
108	TOTAL NON-CAPL COMPENSATION	$19,120.60	$17,208.54		$19,671.40	$245,892.50	23.6%	22.6%	$247,657.82

4) for each variable line could best be spent. Emphasize the importance of sufficiently *detailed* and *documented* worksheets—which they (or their function managers) will need later, to defend and modify their spending proposals as the budget planning process continues.

At the end of 4 weeks, by this process, you should have proposals for all of the variable lines ... which exceed by about 10 percent their projected shares (proportional to the previous year's spending). The before-tax *operating margin* projected by the business manager (who as finance officer is most properly responsible for that line) will have been equally inflated.

In the fifth planning week (Step 8), each function manager should be asked to assemble his line-planners, total their routinely-projected "fixed" lines and the purposefully inflated "variable" lines, and *cut back* that function (departmental) total (without changing any of the fixed lines) to 1.05 times (5 percent over) the function total established in Step 3. To accomplish this, the function manager should ask each participant to outline and defend their proposals to the group. Now ask each participant to nominate the one item they'd be most willing to cut from their own proposal. Talk through this list of possible cuts one-by-one, until the manager is ready to decide which cuts to make. Then ask for another round of suggestions, and repeat the process until the function total is down to 1.05 times (*i.e.,* 105 percent of) its Step 3 dollar-share. Each function manager should be able to complete this cut-back process during that fifth planning week.

This approach gives good over-budget ideas in one part of a department's program the opportunity to take money away from weak (budget-padding) ideas on another line. The end result is an effective reshuffling of available resources.

For Step 9, put all of the variable-line results of these function-by-function sessions— plus all of the automatic fixed line projections from Step 5—in the budget-column on the spreadsheet, and print out copies for each core (function) manager. In the next (sixth) planning week, assemble the core management group, and go through the same process described in Step 8—until the publisher is prepared to decide (hopefully by consensus) which proposed cuts he'll accept to reduce the *total* budget to the exact (100 percent) spending level indicated by Step 3. As these final-round cuts are made, remember that it is the proper role of the business manager to campaign vigorously for cuts elsewhere that could divert money to the *operating margin* line. Maximizing that "bottom line" is his fundamental performance goal (accountability index).

Be very conscious of the vital importance of asking those line-planners (in Step 7) to *over-budget* by that extra 10 percent which was built into their maximum planning limit (in Step 4) ... and of having each core manager come into the Step 9 showdown still 5 percent over. It is the free-wheeling cutback of these overages—as weak ideas in one area compete against strong ideas in another—which gives intellectual muscle and financial discipline to the process!

Now that you have a budget, instruct each function manager (Step 10—in the seventh planning week) to go back to her respective strategic plan and modify the model to reflect any *de facto* changes made during this budgeting process. Then you're all set to repeat the same steps the next year—or better still, to update every 3 months by adding that fifth-quarter out.

A good quarterly budget review/extension can be accomplished by your core management group in just four specific steps, in about 2 weeks:

(1) Determine how much can safely be added to, or must be cut from, the total annual-level spending limit previously authorized by the existing budget. This should be decided by the publisher, after reviewing the last 3 months' performance results and listening carefully to the views of the core management group (especially the marketing manager's latest sales projections).

(2) Then allow at least a week for each function manager to submit a priority-ranked (written memo) list of changes in *his function's own existing budget*, showing item-by-item how he'd propose (over the 12 months beginning with the *next* upcoming quarter) to use any-or-all of that potential increase—or where he'd cut his own budget to absorb any necessary annual-level reduction—assuming the *entire* adjustment had to be made within that one function. Circulate copies of all of the function memos to each core manager. And as in the original budgeting process, warn them that they'll need documentation (from their subordinates) to support these proposals.

(3) Now convene the formal quarterly budget review of the core management group. Ask them to take turns proposing (from the memo-lists) one specific addition or cut (in their own department or another) to the existing annual-level budget total, over those 12 months beginning with the next quarter. Let them call in subordinates to argue the implications of proposed changes in specific budget lines as they are needed. Continue discussing each option until the publisher either accepts a consensus, or makes a decision on the item-at-hand. Continue the process until the budget for the 12 months beginning with the next quarter has been revised and extended to equal your revised annual target/total.

(4) Record all resulting, publisher-authorized changes in annual level limits (and any projected monthly distributions you may have previously shown) on the financial spreadsheet—and instruct all concerned to adjust their plans accordingly "until further notice."

It is critical, in such a process, that the publisher give considerable weight to the recent performance indices (Chapter 7) recorded by various functions. When proposals conflict, precedence should normally be given to the function that has best demonstrated that it knows how to get the desired results from the money it's allowed to spend. (That not only tends to maximize effectiveness; it adds to the healthy peer pressures for better departmental and individual productivity!)

Budget changes cannot, however, always be made solely on the tactical basis of who makes the best case for the money. There are also some strategic considerations, reflecting the organization's circumstances and the publisher's grand design for the months ahead, that should be taken into account. Generally speaking, if you need a fast increase in revenue, you try to shift extra money to marketing (because that's the only function that can turn it around very quickly). If you're trying to change your long-range stance in the industry, you favor acquisitions (usually by adding to the staff). Since they're both keyed to cost-effectiveness, pre-press development and business operations will have difficulty contending for larger *proportional* shares of the budget—except on the "bottom line."

In a million dollar publishing house, a tenth-of-a-percent change in a budgeting ratio is worth a thousand dollars to the function whose budget is thus increased. A few such potential percentage-shifts may mean marketing can put in its bid for a three-shot special-offer mailing to the trade account list, the acquisition program can propose a new product category, or the pre-press function might speed up new product delivery by supplementing its staff with temporary freelance aid—while the business manager insists that simply banking the improvement as pre-tax margin is the prudent course. Out of just such healthy contention does synergy magically emerge!

CHAPTER 11

Personnel Development, Supervision, and Administration

As we noted earlier, the publisher must provide the core management group with two basic resources for achieving their respective accountability goals—money and people. Having looked at the basic ways he can guide them toward the most effective use of that money—let's now examine what he can do to help them use the available, supporting people better.

Managing the "people side" of a publishing house is different from bossing an assembly line or construction job. The publishing workforce normally consists of individuals with more-than-average intelligence, education and world-awareness—and as a corollary, larger-than-average egos. Many of them are chosen for their special talents, creativity, and vivid imaginations. All of this tends to make them *potentially* very productive—but at the same time, more difficult to manipulate interchangeably ("manage"), or to discipline.

This supervisory challenge is further complicated by the wide variety of staff specialties required to perform the intricate publishing process. A typical well-managed million-dollar publishing program has 10 or 11 employees—with *no two of them* assigned to the same basic tasks. At twice that size, they *may* have two or three customer service telereps, acquisition editors, copy editors, and/or shippers—but that'll be about as far as job-overlaps go.

Because of this variety, it's virtually impossible for the "bosses" in a publishing house to understand everything about everybody's job. After a few months of give-and-take with the keyboard and the headphones, customer service telereps know a lot more about the trials and tribulations of using their organization's particular order-entry software than do their supervisors. Experienced promotion copywriters usually create better brochure teasers than publishers themselves. Copy editors learn nuances of the stylebook that the editor-in-chief may never discover. Desktop typesetters seem, to most of their seniors, to be playing mysterious space-age computer games as they magically push manuscripts into shape for the printing press. Bosses who "micro-manage" by trying to call all of the detailed shots for these specialists almost always drag down the quality of end results.

Because most of this (from cover designs to marketing analyses) is creative work—reaching out vicariously to thousands of distant minds through esoteric combinations of linguistics, visual art, psychology, cybernetics and statistical probability—it is often the *quality* of work performed, rather than the quantity, that determines eventual productivity (*i.e.,* impact on those functional performance indices that define most of the enterprise's goals). And there is normally a much wider range in quality than in quantity, between what two similar people accomplish in any given hour—or even what any single individual accomplishes on different days.

For all of these complicated reasons, then, top managers of small publishing houses find that their best approach to maximizing over-all productivity from any given number of person-hours (and their best chance of achieving synergy from the interplay of different functions) is to *design a system* that appropriately (but flexibly) links the people doing all of these specialized tasks, establishes the necessary ground rules for their association with each other and with the corporate entity, provides a level of facilitational support to "keep the machinery greased"—and then largely "gets out of the way" and lets each member of this highly individualized workforce "do her own thing" most of the time.

The basic linkage-planning takes place in the publisher's development and evolution of the organization chart (Chapter 7). The ground rules get spelled out in personnel policies, job descriptions, accountability indices, procedure guides, and policy files (discussed below). But because those are so entwined in employee/supervisor relationships—which provide most of that necessary "facilitational support"—let's look at this aspect of staff development first.

At this point, we should make an arbitrary distinction between management and supervision. Generally speaking, *management* involves manipulating the interplay of *all* available resources (people, money, databases and other accumulated information, goodwill, etc.) to achieve stated goals at a continually satisfactory level of productivity. In most well-run publishing houses, this depth of resource-manipulation is only expected of the publisher and the four supporting "middle managers"—that core group heading acquisition, prepress development, marketing, and business operations.

Supervision is the more limited art of day-to-day, personalized direction of just the *people* involved; it is concerned not only with synchronizing their movement(s) in the right direction(s), but with fine-tuning that subtle mixture of work environment, individual development and occasional discipline that enhances qualitative as well as quantitative productivity. The publisher supervises the middle managers, who supervise section coordinators (series editors, promotion coordinators, shipping supervisors, etc.) within their respective functions. The section (sub-function) leaders supervise the foot soldiers of the publishing process.

Sadly, supervision is too-often viewed by its practitioners in terms of carrots and sticks: reward those who do what you tell 'em, punish those who don't. Because of this simple-minded, archaic concept, the small work group (whether an entire publishing house, a functional department, or a sub-section within a department) can too-easily become an emotionally miserable setting in which to spend half or more of one's waking hours.

To guard against such petty, destructive tyrannies, publishers are usually well-advised to "depersonalize" both discipline and conventional (financial) reward—by linking them to appropriate, quantitative (and thus impersonal) performance indices. In other words: "Score appropriately on the computer, and you can normally expect routine pay raises and minimal supervisory intervention (except when you ask for help) ... but if your quantitative indices (selected to measure qualitative impacts as well) lag—your supervisor is duty-bound to either find ways to help you correct the deficiency, or (after a reasonable corrective effort) replace you."

To some people, that seems heartlessly cybernetic. But if performance indices are well-chosen (to reflect qualitative impact on quantitative measurements), it is generally more fair to all concerned than the subjective judgments of personally-involved—and often inexperienced—supervisors. So just as the publisher exerts impersonalized performance discipline on the core managers by holding each of them accountable for the mission statement goals of their respective functions (growth rate for the marketing manager, new title contribution for the editor-in-chief, per-page on-time pre-press costs for the the managing editor, operating margin for the business manager)—that publisher should identify further indices throughout the operation that will help middle managers and supervisors gauge how well their subordinates are performing. This has the two-edged result of also giving each employee a basis for *documenting his own productivity* (proving success) without the subjective agreement of a supervisor.

It's important, then, to go right down the organization chart and ask: "What quantitative indices will reveal strong performances, as well as problems?" in each job position. Don't get yourself caught up in water-cooler legalisms on this one. The indices are not likely to be perfect and inarguable. But they can provide sufficient *approximate* productivity feedback to indicate whether an employee deserves a raise, reassurance, a scolding, or dismissal. (The extreme responses—raises and dismissals—should always be subject to appeal, by either supervisor or employee, to the publisher. But that publisher is well advised to think long and hard—and require strong evidence—before over-ruling a supervisor. Otherwise, the delicate supervisory role of "disciplined facilitation" may lose all its clout.)

The group performance indices of their basic function (growth rate for marketing, etc.) should be stressed as *part of every employee's responsibility.* But in addition to seeing those numerical peer-pressure generators posted on the (wall or computer) bulletin board at the end of every month, you'll lend powerful aid to your supervisors' efforts by broadening the scorecard to include such indices as:

... growth rate break-downs for each marketing audience segment, promotion medium or campaign, or territorial area on which marketing job assignments are based;

... invoice-lines entered per month by each on-line telerep;

... cost-per-useful-response indices for your promotion program;

... new-title contribution (percent-of-total-sales) break-downs for each product category on which acquisition assignments are based—or each series acquisition editor;

... finished pages-per-month for each acquisition editor (putting substantively-edited manuscripts into the pre-press pipeline), each copy editor, and each desktop typesetter;

... total shipping cost-per-unit and cost-per-order;

... book units shipped per shipping person/hour;

... trend of financial administration and facilities costs as percentages of total cash flow;

... Management Events Calendar (integrated schedule—see Chapter 8) deadlines missed in each function/section.

But while negative performance pressures (competitive peer pressure to improve past indices) will keep your publishing staff awake, they won't guarantee the positive commitments that create "learning curves"—those accumulative self-improvements that make individuals more useful to the enterprise month by month and year by year. For that, a more positive force is required.

A lot has been said about the considerable "psychic rewards" of working in book publishing. It is indeed a more interesting way to spend one's life—at least in the eyes of the literate types who gravitate to this industry—than many of the rote tasks (whether physical or mental) by which the vast majority of the human race earns its daily bread. And publishers are well advised to do whatever they can to celebrate and enhance such psychic rewards—as one of the best ways to keep their best people from seeking new jobs as their learning curves improve.

Reviewing the experiences of the several hundred organizations with which the Huenefeld Publishing Consultants have worked intimately, we conclude that (in addition to the sound training and skill-development procedures discussed later in this chapter), two specific strategies (one very simple, the other rather complex) have proven especially practical ways of enhancing psychic rewards for employees. The first has been merely a matter of *personalizing basic work stations*—by making certain that each employee not only has a little space to call his own (with assurance that designated files or drawers won't be disturbed in his absence), but considerable leeway in differentiating that space—with everything from distinctive wall paint to photos to hanging plants.

The second widely-used strategy is managerial encouragement of "intrepreneuring"—empire-building. This means carefully encouraging each person who has been assigned responsibility for performing or managing an on-going function or process to "own" that function or process by redefining (with step-by-step supervisory endorsement) its strategies and procedures and styles ... by taking the lead in proposing practical changes in planning models and report formats and job descriptions and form letters for *that specific function or process,* as long as it is not incompatible with larger strategies and policies and work-sequences of the organization. You eventually want each manager to think of her/his sub-group as *"my* department," each acquisition editor to think of the appropriate subject-area segment of the acquisition author-pool as *"my* authors," each telerep to think of appropriate customers as *"my* accounts."

Some managers fear that encouraging people to personalize their work in this manner will enable them to achieve "hostage" proprietorship—making themselves indispensable (and thus, impervious to discipline) by building work-enclaves no one else knows how to operate. A basic system of accumulative job descriptions, procedure guides, and policy files—as described later in this chapter—will go a long way to prevent that. But perhaps the surest antidote (and a good practice for other reasons as well) is a comprehensive understudy program.

Such a program designates at least one (sometimes two) specific other staff members *besides the incumbent* who are to be generally familiarized with, and kept up-to-date about the circumstances of, *every* position in the organization—as a basis for emergency (and usually temporary) pinch-hitting. This means that one or two *extra* people are generally briefed on how to function as publisher, and one or two on how to function as a telerep (and input orders), and one or two on how to acquire new titles. There is, of course, no point in assigning "understudies" to purely clerical positions that primarily respond to direction from others.

It's appropriate for *all* core managers to understudy the publisher. Meanwhile, if their particular assistants aren't of sufficient caliber to understudy them, that publisher may actually serve as the emergency understudy for one or more of these specialized function leaders.

When you have two or more people functioning in similar jobs (as series editors, copy editors, or telereps), they can obviously and easily understudy *each other.* But in small organizations, the opportunity to understudy other jobs very diverse from one's own adds an extra measure of interest and adventure to the workplace.

The first requirement of a sound understudy program is that each appropriate individual be provided a copy of the job description for any alternate position they've been assigned to understudy—and be added to the routine routing list for any future changes in that job description. Second, every person being understudied should be required to give their potential emergency replacement *at least 1 hour* of initial, no-question-barred explanation of what they do—and how, and why. This should include identification and location of all appropriate strategy models, performance indices, schedules, databases, etc. Third, a half-hour update (current projects and concerns, etc.) between each understudy and each incumbent should be scheduled *every month*. Once the program is established, this means each staff member will spend no more than an hour or two a month both briefing someone else about their job, and being briefed about one or two alternate jobs.

Such a program, then, will make it very difficult for any rogue, intrepreneurial "empire builder" to hold a segment of the organization or the publishing process hostage. It will also provide upwardly-mobile members of your staff with a good means of assessing their assistants (and others) for promotion as their replacements, when they themselves move on to positions of greater responsibility. And it will, obviously, accomplish its public function—by providing emergency pinch-hitters when key people are suddenly unavailable.

But eventually, you have to come face-to-face with the fact that a major element of job satisfaction and productivity-motivation is *pay*—not only because it provides employees with physical rewards, but because it's generally seen as the most specific, unarguable acknowledgment of each individual's worth to the organization.

Whether or not pay scales for all jobs should be public information is a matter of some controversy among managers of small organizations. Some people contend that having others know (or be able to guess fairly accurately) one's pay is an invasion of privacy. Others believe that openly announced pay schedules tend to minimize unfairness and favoritism, as the available payroll is parceled out amidst the complicated personal relationships of a small organization.

The experience of the Huenefeld Publishing Consultants generally supports this latter view. Even when management tries to keep pay levels confidential in a small organization, the grapevine usually spreads fairly accurate estimates. But the absence of some rational pattern for relating financial compensation to an individual's responsibilities and contribution often leads to unfairness and exploitation of the weaker personalities in the group (no matter how much work they do).

A sensible salary schedule will reflect significant increases in base pay for each progressive level of responsibility or professional insight, since these are factors that contribute substantially to the development of the enterprise. It should also provide smaller "merit raise" differentials on each responsibility level to reward seniority; while continuity has some benefits for the organization (as people acquire experience and contacts), it contributes less than the exercise of greater professional responsibility.

Figure 11a (below) utilizes a 20 percent "responsibility increase" in base pay from level-to-level through Level D, a 30 percent increase for Level E, and an open-ended top level (for Board negotiation with the publisher)—to create real incentive for people to seek and exercise greater responsibility. The 5 percent step-raises on each level are intended as seniority rewards *if merited* at the time of annual job reviews. With this particular schedule, the only way to get a raise after 5 years is to win promotion to a more responsible job; thus this publisher bluntly discourages any long-term accumulation of potential, unambitious "deadwood."

This sample schedule is primarily intended to illustrate a format for addressing the issue—not to suggest appropriate salaries for any given publishing house. Never-the-less, these pay levels were typical of $1-million-a-year publishing programs in 1990. The first line in each block indicates hourly base pay, the second weekly gross pay (based on 37 hours), and the third annual pay (based on 52 weeks).

Figure 11a—Sample Salary Schedule

Grade	Start	Step 1	Step 2	Step 3	Step 4	Step 5
A (Cooperative Live Body)	$6.50 $240.50 $12506.00	$6.83 $252.53 $13131.30	$7.17 $265.15 $13787.87	$7.52 $278.41 $14477.26	$7.90 $292.33 $15201.12	$8.30 $306.95 $15961.18
B (Process Responsibility)	$7.80 $288.60 $15007.20	$8.19 $303.03 $15757.56	$8.60 $318.18 $16545.44	$9.03 $334.09 $17372.71	$9.48 $350.80 $18241.35	$9.95 $368.33 $19153.41
C (Skill Talent)	$9.36 $346.32 $18008.64	$9.83 $363.64 $18909.07	$10.32 $381.82 $19854.53	$10.84 $400.91 $20847.25	$11.38 $420.95 $21889.61	$11.95 $442.00 $22984.10
D (Experience + Supervision)	$11.23 $415.58 $21610.37	$11.79 $436.36 $22690.89	$12.38 $458.18 $23825.43	$13.00 $481.09 $25016.70	$13.65 $505.14 $26267.54	$14.34 $530.40 $27580.91
E (Function Manager)	$14.60 $540.26 $28093.48	$15.33 $567.27 $29498.15	$16.10 $595.64 $30973.06	$16.90 $625.42 $32521.71	$17.75 $656.69 $34147.80	$18.64 $689.52 $35855.19
F PUBLISHER	Negotiated Annually by Board					

In Figure 11a, jobs pegged to Pay Grade A would require little except daily presence and willingness; typical examples are mailing and shipping clerks. Grade B assumes the job-holder has accepted responsibility for on-going, "self-starting" performance of certain basic procedures and processes; departmental administrative assistants usually belong in this category. Grade C involves not only such on-going process responsibility, but specialized knowledge, skill or talent—as with a copy editor, typesetter, promotional copywriter, or telerep. Grade D assumes significant professional experience, usually in combination with supervisory responsibility for directing other employees—as with a financial administrator, shipping supervisor, sales or promotion coordinator, or acquisition series editor. Grade E is intended for those middle-managers of the publisher's core group who assume over-all responsibility for one of the major functions (acquisition, marketing, pre-press development, business operations).

In periods of significant inflation, a Board of Directors may occasionally decide to apply an *across-the-boards* percentage increase to the entire schedule (assuming the profitability to finance it). In addition (or instead), a Board may choose to provide such other financial benefits as company-paid insurance, retirement-fund credits, or contributions of a stated portion of any larger-than-expected margins to a company-wide profit-sharing pool (to be distributed proportionally to each employee's percentage of the total payroll).

Financial generosity is clearly the most effective of all productivity and longevity incentives in small publishing organizations. However, it has its limits. In recessionary 1991 (according to the extensive annual survey of the Huenefeld Publishing Consultants), the *major* difference between the operating ratios of independent publishers who *made money* and those who *lost money* was that the former were able to hold total payroll-and-benefit compensation down to only 29 percent of sales volume, while the latter (the losers) let it escalate up to 57 percent! And the data clearly indicates that the major difference was not in how much they paid for each job (the money-makers paid better than the losers), but in how effectively they organized and motivated personnel—to maximize productivity and minimize the head count.

Only when routine pay increases (those step raises in Figure 11a) are pegged to some assessment of job performance does the pay structure truly and directly encourage productivity via the learning curve. The easiest way to relate performance and pay is to require the appropriate supervisors to evaluate *every* employee's work periodically. Such evaluations can become condescending and patronizing (even counter-productive), unless they are conducted as *two-way* reviews in which employees also evaluate how well the company (via the facilitating supervisor) is fulfilling its obligations to them.

It is hard to maintain objectivity (and encourage candor) in such personalized exchanges between people who work closely together every day (especially when/if the situation is compounded by relative inexperience of a lower-level supervisor). Therefore, many publishers stimulate dialogue by requiring (for a first-review after a probationary 3 months, and then on each subsequent anniversary of an employee's hiring) both the supervisor and the employee, *separately and independently,* to complete both Section A (rating the employee's performance) and Section B (rating the company's support) of a checklist similar to this:

Figure 11b—Sample Performance Review Checklist

Subject_____ Date_____

Appraisal by_____

Rate each statement below in the following blank, according to how well you believe it applies in this case:

0 = "not applicable to this employee"   3 = "maybe" or "more-or-less true"
1 = "strongly and exceptionally untrue" 4 = "definitely but moderately true"
2 = "definitely but moderately untrue" 5 = "strongly and exceptionally true"

A. Over the past 12 months _____ (name) has:
    a) been reasonably available during normal working hours ____
    b) worked consistently and productively during those hours ____
    c) been cooperative with, and supportive of, co-workers ____
    d) become more productive by learning from experience ____
    e) sought other resources for becoming more productive ____
    f) kept up with technical and socio-economic changes relative to his/her work ____
    g) demonstrated acceptable productivity through measured performance indices ____
    h) sought and accepted increased responsibility ____
    i) been inventive in developing better work procedures ____
    j) demonstrated creativity at work ____
    k) kept personal distractions to a minimum during working hours ___

B. This organization owes _____ (name):
    a) modestly more pay (in same salary grade) ____
    b) substantially more pay (in a higher grade) ____
    c) reassignment to a more responsible job ____
    d) commendation among co-workers for exceptional performance ___
    e) more public recognition ____
    f) more cooperation by co-workers ____
    g) more management support among co-workers ____
    h) more supervisory guidance in performing work ____
    i) more appreciation of temporary personal distractions ____
    j) more resources to help improve immediate productivity ____
    k) more resources to help increase personal capabilities ____

Complete Together after Discussion:

Indicate (by letters) the three items from Part A which the employee agrees to concentrate on improving during the next year:

____   ____   ____

Indicate (by letters) the three items from Part B on which the supervisor agrees to seek improvement by the organization, with respect to subject employee, in the forthcoming year:

____   ____   ____

Once they've made their independent assessments, supervisor and employee should then exchange forms—and make a prompt date to sit down and discuss any differences they reflect. Then, together, they should thrash out *which three* points the employee will concentrate on improving, and which three the supervisor will commit to by seeking more company support for said employee.

Point B/a is the in-grade "merit increase" that employees in many companies are encouraged to believe is almost automatic if their work is satisfactory. A supervisor's refusal to commit to B/a would essentially constitute a stern warning to the employee to "shape up—or start polishing your resume." It's often very hard for gentle or inexperienced supervisors to say that "in so many words"—but much easier for them to apply this often-necessary pressure in the context of such a routine performance review. Thus the forewarned deadwood often thins itself by seeking other employment.

Both copies of each performance review checklist should be retained in the employee's confidential personnel folder for a year—to settle any "who said what" arguments. And if you'd like to carry this process to further refinement, the publisher's executive assistant might create an anonymous spreadsheet with a row for each rating topic (in both halves of the checklist) and a column for each employee. By putting those anonymous columns in some order known only to the (very discreet!) executive assistant, and programming the spreadsheet to automatically *re-average* the entire set of last-time-around evaluation ratings (using supervisors' ratings of the employees, and employees' ratings of the company's support) after each individual annual review updates the numbers in a specific column, this process will give management a constant index of the changing competence of its staff (as seen by the supervisors), and an excellent index of company morale (through the employees' support-ratings).

The publishers' office is really the most appropriate place for such confidential personnel data—as well as any personal files relative to each employee. This basic personnel administration—because of its sensitive nature—is an appropriate assignment for the alter-ego "executive assistant," if the publisher has one. Leave data, vacation schedules, etc., might best be accumulated here, as well—to make sure the publisher is always informed about staff availabilities. All payroll or other financial records and accounting, however, belong in the finance section of the business office (see Chapter 36).

It goes without saying that, before operating personnel can be effectively utilized, they need to be properly instructed as to exactly what they're expected to do. If you'll refer back to the "task analysis" discussion in Chapter 7, you'll see (Figure 7f) how this technique produces blocks of single-line task descriptions that can be combined (in 35-hour-a-week blocks) to define individual job responsibilities. These individual task-lines, then, become the basic raw material for written job descriptions (the "specific responsibility" sections illustrated in various job-description samples throughout this book).

It is absolutely essential that such a written job description for *each staff position* be created *before* anyone is hired to fill that position (while the issues are still relatively impersonal)—and that review and potential amendment of these descriptions be a part of each individual performance review. It is through this constant, disciplined refinement of job descriptions that a publishing organization adapts to changing circumstances—rather than becoming mired in inflexible responses to yesterday's problems.

Furthermore, organizational and supervisory documentation of what is expected from employees should be carried one step farther down than the written job description. A well-organized publishing house will ask the people actually performing each task identified in the "task analysis" process of Chapter 7 to prepare a *quick* checklist of the steps necessary for each successful performance of that task. The appropriate supervisors should then review, embellish, and "flesh out" these checklists to produce single-sheet reference instructions for accomplishing each normally-recurring task in the entire process. These reference sheets are most commonly known as "procedure guides," and they look something like Figure 11c, on the next page.

Once your staff has brain-stormed, and your supervisors have polished, procedure guides for all normally recurring tasks, these should be accumulated in a master notebook or (probably better) on the basic computer network—so they can be consulted as needed, and updated as appropriate. You'll find them not only essential to the training of new personnel, but a valuable focus for periodic searches for *better ways* of performing the daily routines.

In addition to this accumulative file of procedure guides for accomplishing routine, recurring tasks, establish a similar (notebook or computer) file of management-approved policy solutions to *rare* situations. Encourage all core managers (and even section supervisors) to identify memos, letters, and other documents that explain approved handling of such important and/or sensitive situations—and assign the publisher's executive assistant (or any other appropriate party) to maintain an accumulative file, with a regularly-updated "table of contents" or index. You'll find such a policy file not only prevents embarrassing inconsistencies, but saves many hours of managerial re-invention of already-perfected wheels.

Perhaps the first entry in such an accumulative policy file should be a general statement of employment terms (personnel policy). Yet small publishing houses are often diffident (or overly self-conscious) about formalizing the relationship between the individual staff members (from top to bottom) and the organization. Too many publishers convince themselves that just *because their organizations are small,* they don't need formal personnel manuals or other written statements of policy concerning terms of employment.

Figure 11c—Sample Procedure Guide

Who: First Open TeleRep Work Station

What: Answering Order-Phone

1) Answer ear-phone signal with "Miracle Publishing House ... one moment, please."

2) Finish paper order you were in process of entering. Select "To Enter New Order" on terminal menu.

3) Then say into mouthpiece: "Hello, my name is ___. May I help you?" [If not occupied with paper order, just say: "Miracle Publishing House, (your name) speaking. ... May I help you?"]

4) If caller wants another department, say: "I'm sorry, this is a dedicated line only connected to the customer service department. To get the party you want, it will be necessary for you to call #_____."

5) When caller indicates desire to order, ask for zip code and company name or individual surname (for personal orders). Enter same into finder screen on terminal and press #6 (for "Search").

6) If computer has file for party you're talking with, proceed to Item #7 below. If not, press #7 ("Open New Account File") on terminal and ask for name and address. Determine and enter customer type (see reference sheet) for discount coding.

7) Query method of payment—credit card for individuals, billing plus shipping for organizations.

8) If credit flag appears on screen, say "One moment, please," and buzz supervisor. Otherwise, proceed as follows ...

9) If credit card order, press #4 ("Activate Card Check") and ask/enter Card Number with Expiration Date.

10) Press #3 ("Enter Order") on terminal sub-menu. Ask caller to identify titles wanted, and quantity of each. Enter stock numbers (from alpha/reference) and quantities.

11) Confirm or change default shipping method. Explain shipping charges.

12) Say: "Could you please tell me how you learned about this book (our books)?" Code answer in "Source" blank on screen (as per source-reference chart).

13) Then say: "Before we hang up, would you like to hear briefly about ...?"—and add the query-line from your current "upsell" script. Add stock numbers and quantities of any additional items ordered to screen.

14) Press 11 ("Preview Invoice/Receipt"). Quickly repeat/confirm address, titles and quantities, discount percentage, shipping charge, and total dollar-amount.

15) Say "Thank you very much. You should receive your book(s) in about a week (UPS) ... three weeks (book post) ... etc." (See reference chart.)

But the intense personalization of individual relationships tends to extend throughout a small organization. Either friendships or strong dislikes may develop between any two members of the staff. These relationships can work against both parties (and the enterprise itself) when hard decisions about promotions, terminations, or mutual obligations have to be made.

In a large organization, such decisions can always be bucked "up the ladder" far enough that they're made by someone not involved in such personal complications. In a small organization, it is far more important (though less likely) that the ground rules be clearly spelled out *in advance*—so that personally complicated interpretations after-the-fact are not required. One of the most likely ways to undermine motivation (and thus sap productivity) in a creative organization is to leave people wondering "where they stand" whenever their interests clash with those of the organization.

Such written statements of personnel policy in small and middle-sized publishing houses vary from two-or-three-page memos to thick booklets reproducing group insurance policies and expense account forms. It is important that these personnel policy statements spell out such fundamentals as office hours, adherence to public holidays, when paychecks are written, who gets keys and parking spaces, etc.—to avoid not only future misunderstandings, but oversights in orienting newcomers. Absolute clarity should be sought in defining what other "fringe" benefits employees will receive besides their agreed pay, and how leave time eligibility will be calculated and recorded. Rules regarding individual expenditure of company money when traveling, or entertaining on behalf of the organization, should conform to legal guidelines (which your regional Internal Revenue Service field office will be happy to provide).

A good personnel policy statement formalizes the commitment to periodic performance and pay reviews, and establishes fair rules of advance severance notice and terms (such as pay for unused leave) if the employment relationship is terminated by either party. You may or may not decide to include a statement of the pay scale you've established for different levels of responsibility and seniority, as discussed earlier.

The easiest way to initiate a formal personnel policy statement is to conduct a full-staff brainstorming session as to what the section headings should be; then assign specific and responsible staff members to draft their interpretations of the existing, informal policy on specific topics. Once you've assembled all of those drafts, ask for comments from the core management group and incorporate appropriate revisions in a proposed comprehensive policy statement. Submit this comprehensive statement to your Board of Directors (or any absentee owner or institutional sponsor) for amendments and/or endorsement; there should be absolutely no question of its legitimacy. Then append it to your basic policy file, where it will always be accessible to anyone who wishes to consult it.

From this accumulation of job descriptions, salary schedules, procedure guides, personnel policy statements, etc., you should then find it fairly easy (and worthwhile) to assemble a basic "employee handbook" with *personalized* sub-sections—as a reference for each staff member, and an important tool for recruiting and orienting new people.

Obviously, the level of productivity of a publishing house (what it gets for each thousand payroll dollars) is greatly affected by the quality of personnel it recruits to work for it. And this quality is somewhat proportional to the number of candidates the managers are willing to screen before selecting each new employee. One of the greatest mistakes publishing managers make is to advertise a position until they've received a dozen or so applications, interview those, and assume their top choice must be good because "he was in the upper quartile."

When recruiting any member of the core management group—a publisher, editor-in-chief, managing editor, marketing manager, or business manager—you should be very insistent about *continuing to advertise* the opening until you've received at least 100 resume responses. It's probably safe to cut this to 30 when recruiting lower-echelon supervisors or specialists, and 15 when looking for administrative or clerical help.

Unless you're able to use a post office blind-box address, state clearly in your ad for any position that further information is available only to those who submit *written* resumes; otherwise, your phones may become generally unavailable to customers, authors, etc., for days at a time. If you'll identify in advance two or three basic qualifications that you believe are absolutely essential, you'll normally be able to eliminate two-thirds of the applications as inappropriate or unacceptable after only a couple of minutes of resume-scanning.

To those who survive this first screening, send a (personalized) word-processed letter summarizing the job, the nature of your publishing house, and the approximate pay/benefits level; amplify this with a copy of the job description and your current book catalog. Also enclose a blank application form which will enlarge on the candidate's resume by providing specific answers that can be compared with those of other applicants. That form might look something like Figure 11d (though you'd eliminate the questions about budget responsibility and number of people supervised, for low-level jobs that didn't involve such qualifications).

Recruiting experience suggests that about half of the applicants who survived your first screening will eliminate themselves from the competition at this point, by declining to return this form. (The main reason you want to indicate the pay range in that cover letter is so that those who insist on more will *eliminate themselves* and avoid a mutual waste of interview time.)

Figure 11d—Sample Second-Round Employment Application Form

Name_____ Home Phone_____

Address_____

Social Security No._____ Date_____

1. YOUR PRESENT OR MOST RECENT JOB:

Dates of Employment: from _____ (mo/yr) to _____

Employer:_____ City _____
Your Initial Title:_____
Your Major Responsibilities:_____
_____

Your Present or Final Title:_____
How have (did) your responsibilities changed?_____
_____

What is the largest annual budget for which you had personal responsibility?
$_____

What is the largest number of people you regularly and directly supervised?
_____

What were your major specific accomplishments on this job? _____
_____

What were your main disappointments in this job?_____
_____

Why are you now seeking other employment?_____
_____

[Repeat the questions under the heading:"YOUR NEXT-MOST-RECENT JOB," and ask for addresses/phones for three references on back]

The ideal approach is to go on recruiting until you have at least ten nominally-qualified candidates (interested enough to return this second-round form) for any core management position, five for any lesser supervisory or specialist position, or three for any administrative position. In every circumstance, it's essential that you develop a *choice* between candidates who can be directly compared. Without this, you have to depend on very subjective hunches (which are very often wrong) for decisions that have major impact on the quality of your publishing team.

When you receive second-round applications, then, take the time to check the references they give you. The people they list will be reluctant to talk in great detail—because of nervousness about personal or business relationships, or even fear of legal liability. But if you'll make it easy for them, by simply sending each a brief questionnaire such as that illustrated in Figure 11e below (along with a stamped, self-addressed response envelope), at least one of them can usually be depended on to warn you of anything very *negative* (major addictions, honesty issues, etc.) about which you should know.

Figure 11e—Sample Employment Reference Questionnaire

(Name of candidate)

1) How long have you known this person?_____

2) What is your present or past relationship with the candidate?

_____

3) What was the job/position this person held at the time you were most closely associated?_____

4) What do you believe were this person's most important *specific* accomplishments in that job?_____

5) Please indicate below, on a scale of 0 to 5, how true you think each of the following statements is regarding this candidate.

(0 = absolutely untrue, 1 = almost entirely untrue, 2 = only slightly true, 3 = moderately true, 4 = generally true, 5 = very true.)

    a) Relates well to seniors/superiors ____
    b) Relates well to juniors/subordinates ____
    c) Accepts responsibility for getting results ____
    d) Is reliable about meeting deadlines ____
    e) Is an effective planner ____
    f) Makes good use of time ____
    g) Is seldom distracted by personal problems ____
    h) Is not over-dependent on vendors ____
    i) Is honest in relating to others ____
    j) Is good at analyzing results and making adjustments ____
    k) Organizes complex assignments well ____
    m) Works well under pressure ____

6) At what specific job skills does this person excel?_____

_____

7) Why, in your opinion, did this person leave (or plan to leave) the job situation in which you knew him/her?_____

_____

8) Please comment briefly on anything else about this person you feel a prospective employer should know:_____

_____

9) Should further questions arise in our final selection process, may we phone you? ____ (Number, please_____)

YOUR NAME_____

[Thank you! This questionnaire will be kept in strictest confidence.]

Then it's simply a matter of ranking the candidates who've made it through the process (by receiving and returning the second-round application form), determining how many you want to interview, and sending them word-processed letters telling them who to phone if they'd like an interview. Only after those interviews do you have to make those scary, somewhat-subjective decisions that so greatly effect their careers and the quality of your publishing team.

One dilemma common to the managers of most small publishing houses, when they set out to fill important staff vacancies or newly created positions, is whether to promote somebody from another position or "go outside" to hire someone with greater relevant experience. Going outside does have the potential advantage of bringing in comparative insights from other publishing houses to enlarge your perspective. On the other hand, any experienced specialist another publisher is willing to let you lure away may not be as good a bargain as surface appearances suggest. Publishing houses tend to export their personnel failures a lot more often than their successes.

On balance, it is probably best (for both staff quality and staff morale) to concentrate your recruiting on entry-level positions, and promote from within to fill more senior vacancies. Good copy editors usually have the articulate skills, and may quickly acquire the subject-area familiarity, needed to make them effective acquisition editors or promoters; good telereps often become good sales coordinators or marketing managers. Having the perseverance to wade through those herds of eager graduates and re-entry empty-nesters who answer entry-level ads—and the patience to "grow your own" managers and specialists, tailored to your specific situation—frequently pays enormous people-power dividends.

PART III

Acquisition

CHAPTER 12
Developing Your Acquisition Strategy

Independent book publishers normally receive about a third of their month-by-month sales from books published within the previous 12 months—the so-called "front list." While these frontlist sales are somewhat volatile (due to the varying market appeal of individual titles), the general stability of the publisher's sales volume (which makes it possible to plan effectively) is sustained by that other two-thirds from more-predictable older books: the "backlist."

Strategizing maintenance of the backlist is a fairly simple matter: try never to print more than a 1-year supply of any book as long as it's in the "front list"—or *at most,* a 3-year supply (though preferably still only a 1-year supply) once it is performing dependably in the "backlist." This gives the publisher's print-buyer reasonable flexibility for achieving economies of scale, while preventing the deadly accumulation of obsolete inventory.

But the most intense, continuous focus of the publishing house must almost always be fixed on development of that volatile frontlist—the selection and introduction of *new titles* that will make the publisher's product line more useful, more compellingly unique, to its intended audience(s) than it was the month or year before. While you can do relatively little to improve backlist sales patterns once they are established, the nature and quality of the new titles can make a very big difference in frontlist sales—and thus, in the future budget funds available from cash flow.

Before we look at the people and processes by which new title introduction is achieved, let's examine carefully how specific targets for this process are established ... how a competent publishing house decides what kind of, and how many, new books to look for at any given time. This process—strategic acquisition planning—should begin with periodic review and refinement of the organization's chosen publishing "niche."

Your chosen niche (as described in Chapter 3) is that general combination of subject-area and anticipated end-uses that reflects "what you're trying to do for whom" in your selection, development, and marketing of books. Being clear about this niche helps you do two essential things: (1) confine your operations to an arena not already saturated with competition, and (2) accumulate both author and market contacts that—because of the concentrated subject area—will be useful time-after-time in the future. Any modest-sized publishing house that cannot accomplish these two things is very likely to be swamped by the wake of the conglomerate dinosaurs.

It is, of course, conceivable to serve more than one niche; some small publishers feel that there's less risk in dividing their efforts (and fortunes) between two or three. However, since it is difficult enough to achieve break-even momentum with modest capital when concentrating on a single niche, the distraction of keeping your eyes (and mind) trained simultaneously on several disparate targets merely compounds that difficulty. So most independent publishers conclude that it's wiser to seek the safety-of-diversification by developing several related product "series" within a single niche.

A "series" is a product sub-category that utilizes your general subject-area contacts and expertise to create resources for a *specialized* segment of the niche-audience—or a *specialized* end-usage by that audience. For example, a publisher whose niche is geography might create one line of books (a series) for general public usage, another for classroom teaching, and a third for field reference by travelers. The subject-area expertise acquired in developing any one of these series will be useful in working on the others; the pool of author contacts accumulated for any one may well serve the others; while some specialized marketing contacts will be required for each series, there will obviously be much useful overlap. Meanwhile, the differences in anticipated end-usage will create additional contacts and insights appropriate only to the individual series—and open additional markets.

Do not confuse end-use "series" definitions with "media categories" (hardcover, paperback, audio- and video-cassettes, cd rom, etc.). These media categories may be seen as sub-sections within any series—but for both planning and contact-building purposes, they should be seen as inter-changeable contributors to your "product line" in any end-use series area. People seeking resources to help them learn a specific subject, accomplish a specific task, or serve a specific cause *don't care* whether they meet their needs by buying books or cassettes or seminar registrations. The series definition, planning, and acquisition staff-work should be focused on those *people*—not on the intermediate vendors (printers, recording studios, etc.) who'll convert an author's work (or a database) into such a resource.

By disciplining their project selections to conform to these specific series definitions, the acquiring "series editors" make it possible for the marketing program to accumulate (in addition to its general niche contacts) a reusable pool of customers and publicity contacts for *each series,* which underwrites its on-going viability.

These acquisition series essentially structure the "division of labor" within the acquisition function. As the publishing organization grows, individual series editors are able to specialize further—thus intensifying their accumulation of useful insight and contacts.

Some publishers (wisely, we think) recognize an additional "experimental" series beyond those basic product categories on which their acquisition strategy is focused. This series should be used *only* for books the acquisition team believes might be forerunner prototypes for future new series; *don't* plan any books (or other media products) under this category that (1) won't fit within your declared general niche(s), and that (2) you can't envision as reasonable test-cases and contact-accumulators for a continuous stream of similar, future products. Using an experimental series simply to justify pet acquisition proposals which don't otherwise conform to the discipline of your acquisition strategy planning model is sloppy—and usually unprofitable—publishing.

Such an experimental series is almost always directed (as series acquisition editor) by the editor-in-chief—the core manager responsible for over-all acquisition activities. And it should be limited to a *very small portion* of the total number of new products planned at any given time—since it is sad-but-true that most such experiments fail; too many of them will drag down most of the basic performance indices of the entire publishing team.

Sometimes, because learning to package information products in different media is relevant to the roles of virtually *all* series editors, a publishing house's first venture in a new medium (such as video or cd rom) might best be handled through the editor-in-chief's "experimental" series even though it relates to the subject-area of one of the established series. On-going responsibility for the finished product can then be transferred into the appropriate series—and the procedural lessons of the exercise can more readily be shared with all series editors—and incorporated into future training programs, job descriptions, etc.

Once you've identified the several series through which you intend to discipline new title selections (no more than two or three series at the beginning, with only cautious expansion after break-even), the next step in sound acquisition strategy planning is to determine a seasonal pattern for timing the introduction of new books into your list. This enables the pre-press function to plan its work (and anticipate its staff needs) more effectively; it helps the print-buyer achieve economies of scale by "ganging" appropriate bids; it is absolutely essential to marketing's need for timing of new title introductions to the buying practices of its major audiences—perhaps the predominant factor in determining the optimal seasonal pattern.

Because that's the way their major customers buy, trade (bookstore-oriented) publishers usually organize their acquisition—and subsequent marketing—programs around a two-season year: a "spring" season for January-June new titles, and a "fall" season for July-December titles. El-high textbook houses sometimes recognize only one season—assuming that "if it's not ready in July for pre-September shipments, it'll just sit in the warehouse until the next school year." College publishers are a bit more flexible—with varying semester patterns making either two-season, three-season, or four-season years feasible. Religious curriculum planners normally gear their seasons to the quarterly cycles typical of church school calendars. Direct response publishers have maximum flexibility—and often spread their anticipated books over *monthly* planning blocks (seasons), simply to give their promotional copywriters more opportunities to change headlines.

It is possible (and sometimes smart) to adopt different seasonal patterns for different series. Note in the sample acquisition strategy planning model below that the "geography niche" publisher we conceptualized a few paragraphs ago might well synchronize three different seasonal patterns—by gearing those general books to spring/fall trade buying, the classroom books to the beginning of each el-high school year, and the field guides to peak-period monthly direct-response promotion schedules.

Figure 12a—Sample Acquisition Planning Framework

SEASON	General Books	Classroom Texts	Field Guides	Experimental Books
Spring 94	_____		Feb_____ Mar_____ Apr_____	_____
Fall 94	_____	_____	Sep_____ Oct_____ Nov_____	
Spring 95	_____		Feb_____ Mar_____ Apr_____	_____
Fall 95	_____	_____	Sep_____ Oct_____ Nov_____	
Spring 96	_____		Feb_____ Mar_____ Apr_____	_____
Fall 96	_____	_____	Sep_____ Oct_____ Nov_____	

Note that the seasonal pattern has been projected *3 years* into the future. It is essential to sound strategic planning that the acquisition model always look about this far ahead for two vital reasons: (1) This means that an intelligent pattern for apportioning any feasible number of new titles between series and seasons will normally be established *before* any specific book project is under consideration; acquisition decisions are then more likely to be made in the context of the publishing house's true goals, rather than the personal agenda and political clout of individual authors or editors.

(2) It also gives strategic planners in the other functions (marketing, pre-press, business/finance) a necessary indication of "where we're headed" in time to adjust their own normally-annual strategies, budgets, and staffing plans.

Once the planning framework (Figure 12a) is completed, the next big question the acquisition strategy planner must answer is: "How many new books should we plan to acquire for each indicated season of the next three years?" At this point, a wise editor-in-chief (the primary acquisition strategist) will consult the finance officer (usually the business manager). The latter should be able to project (from recent levels and trends) an anticipated sales *growth rate,* and apply it to the current sales volume to estimate the house's sales revenue for any future season. By multiplying the house's (usually fairly stable) current "cost-of-goods" percentage by that sales volume, the finance officer can estimate with reasonable reliability how much money will be *recovered from inventory investment* in each future season.

The finance officer should then *deduct* the normal percentage of recovered cost-of-goods that must be reinvested in backlist reprinting (to keep good titles in stock) from that anticipated future seasonal recovery of inventory investment. The remaining money will then be available (in that future season) for "revolving" re-investment in *new title inventory development* (to cover only those royalty advance, pre-press, and paper-printing-binding costs normally "capitalized" rather than financed from the operating budget).

By applying current average per-page pre-press development costs to average book lengths, and average per-impression printing costs to normal first-run new title quantities—and then adding normal per-project royalty advances—the business manager (and/or editor-in-chief) should be able to estimate the normal front-money capital cost of adding a new title to the inventory. Dividing this approximate per-project cost into that estimated recyclable cost-of-goods recovery (after backlist reprinting adjustment), that business manager should now be able to tell the editor-in-chief approximately how many new titles the house can afford to add to the inventory in any near-future season *without requiring additional capital.*

(Roughly speaking, after a publishing house has achieved break-even, this tends to add up to about one new title per $100,000 in annual sales volume. But that's only a very approximate indicator; you should go through the whole exercise of projecting and re-investing inventory cost-recovery before the publisher endorses any future season's planned level of new title introduction.)

The editor-in-chief may prefer that the new product "quota" for each season be stated (and allocated among the series) in terms of finished book pages, rather than books. This gives series editors some planning leeway between "mega-projects" and a larger number of smaller books. And as the program gains in multi-media capability, you'll want to establish cost-equivalents for the book page in the other media—so many dollars per minute of packaged audio or video, per megabyte of cd rom, etc. This, then, provides the series editor with budget yardsticks in yet another planning dimension.

For an established publishing house, operating under normal circumstances, this process indicates the optimum number of new titles that the acquisition strategy plan should project. The editor-in-chief or individual series editors may, however, sometimes adjust this by assuming certain major projects will consume the capital normally available for several books—or that two or more inexpensive products can be introduced with the capital normally required for one average book.

If the editor-in-chief creates a future strategy that requires *more* capital in any given season than is likely to be recovered through cost-of-goods, she must then get permission from the publisher (who must subsequently get assurances of additional capital investment or borrowing privileges ... or agreement to earmark a portion of anticipated profits for inventory re-investment ... from the Board, before endorsing the proposed acquisition strategy). It is *not* a prerogative of the editor-in-chief to compromise the financial future of the corporate entity by making unilateral commitments that will require additional capital investment.

Once such an estimate of the number of new titles affordable from available inventory capital has been made (with the understanding that the resulting impact on sales volume should then take care of changes in routine operating costs), the next step in strategic acquisition planning is to allocate those new titles, for that specific season, among the series on the strategy model. Initially (as in Figure 12a above), each anticipated future title should be represented by a blank line in the appropriate series column and seasonal block. How to distribute each season's blank lines between the series in order to maximize the frontlist contribution to sales volume is one of the editor-in-chief's most critical challenges.

Once a 3-year model is created, it should be constantly extended as each season ends—by recalculating how many new titles you'll be able to afford, and then adding (and apportioning) another season's quota of blank lines, 3 years in the future. And as each of these season-by-season extensions is plotted, the editor-in-chief should make any necessary adjustments in intervening seasons (due to changes in financial circumstances—or the timely switching of behind-schedule projects with ahead-of-schedule projects).

Go back to Figure 9c (Chapter 9) to review how a finished model looks. Note that in that sample, the editor-in-chief has listed appropriate backlist titles (with their first-year unit sales in appendices) at the top of each column to communicate more precisely what kind of books each series envisions. Also note at the bottom of the sample how spreadsheet graphics are used to summarize the status of each anticipated project, as the blank lines are gradually filled in with actual books.

The blanks, then, give the acquisition function its walking orders. They tell all concerned how many of each kind of book the editor-in-chief believes (with the publisher's eventual concurrence or amendment) will best achieve the acquisition goal of maximum contribution to sales volume without compromising the owners' control of capital investment, or violating the publishing-niche definition that has grown out of the enterprise's mission statement.

Now all the series editors have to do is to fill in those blanks with good, properly-contracted manuscript titles.

CHAPTER 13
Organizing and Managing the Acquisition Function

Developing and periodically extending that acquisition strategy model we hypothesized in the previous chapter, and then regularly translating it into a smooth flow of good new manuscripts to the pre-press function, is the complex process by which the acquisition function seeks to maximize new title (front list) contribution to sales volume—its essential role in the publishing house. This means that the acquisition work of a number of different seasons is always being pursued and monitored *simultaneously.*

As suggested earlier, the acquisition function should be adding each new season to its planning model about *3 years* ahead of real time. After allowing a reasonable period for managerial amendment or endorsement of each season's strategy, it should then be prepared to discuss long-range projects which support that strategy with prospective authors (or actually invite pre-selected writers to make commitments to house-generated project ideas) as much as *2½ years* before publication. In the period *between 2 years and 1 year* ahead, it should be subjecting those proposals to detailed analyses and actually negotiating contracts with authors. From *1 year to 6 months* out, it should be leaning hard (via nagging inquiries) on previously-contracted authors to deliver complete, raw manuscripts—so the pre-press process can get underway.

The primary responsibility for planning all of this work—and making sure it is being accomplished by continuous, overlapping attention to every anticipated season of the next 3 years—is properly delegated to the editor-in-chief: the traditional title for the head of the acquisition function. The scope of this acquisition manager's responsibilities looks something like Figure 13a, on the next page.

The size of the staff that the editor-in-chief will need, in order to fulfill these responsibilities, will vary with the number of new books the house can afford to add to its product line in any given year. The old rule-of-thumb, that a competent acquisition (series) editor should be able to add *one finished manuscript a month* to the pre-press work flow, is a generally-reasonable indicator of staff needs. If the strategy planning model (previous chapter) only calls for 10-15 books a year, the editor-in-chief should be expected to do virtually all of the acquisition work alone; part-time clerical help, a bright

Figure 13a—Sample Job Description: Editor-in-Chief

TITLE: Editor-in-Chief (Acquisitions Manager)
Salary Grade: E
Reports to: Publisher
Directly Supervises:
> Series Editors
> Administrative Assistant

Budget Line Responsibility:
> 139-145 (Acquisitions Dept.)
> 319 (Royalties)
> 323 (Royalty Advances)

Accountability Indices:
> New Title Sales Contribution
> Manuscript Delivery Dates

GENERAL RESPONSIBILITIES:

To plan and arrange the acquisition and substantive (content) editing of such manuscripts and publishing projects as will best fulfill the objectives of the Mission Statement.

SPECIFIC OPERATING RESPONSIBILITIES:

a) To maintain a strategy planning model indicating the most effective distribution of available new product development capital among the various product categories for 3 years into the future;

b) To recruit, instruct, and supervise series editors assigned to acquire desired publication rights to selected manuscripts or projects;

c) To oversee any administrative personnel assigned to the acquisition function;

d) To oversee the maintenance of an accumulative address database of potential authors;

e) To obtain formal permission from the Publisher before contracting with (or allowing any series editor to contract with) any author for future publication of a designated work;

f) To maintain a secure file of all contracts between the publishing house and its authors – past and present;

g) To keep the (pre-press) Managing Editor informed regarding the status of near-future manuscripts;

h) To oversee the protection of the publishing house's copyrights;

i) To represent the concerns of the acquisition function and staff in the deliberations of the Core Management Group.

Figure 13b—Sample Job Description: Series Editor

TITLE: Series Editor (_____indicate series_____)
Salary Grade: D
Reports to: Editor-in-Chief
Coordinates with:
    Other Series Editors
    Managing Editor (Pre-Press)
    Assigned Copy Editors
Budget line responsibilities:
    Royalties for Series
    Travel & Entertainment for Series
    Editorial Miscellaneous for Series
Accountability Index:
    Trend of percent of Series Sales from New Titles
    Annualized Number of Manuscript Pages Generated

GENERAL RESPONSIBILITIES:
To promote submission of relevant author proposals, and select, acquire and refine manuscripts from those proposals, to meet the manuscript delivery goals of the series as established by the acquisition planning model, while maximizing new title contribution to the annual sales volume of the series.

SPECIFIC OPERATING RESPONSIBILITIES:
- Assist Editor-in-Chief in Periodic Update of Editorial Strategy Model
- Accumulate Idea File of Potential Future Projects in Series
- Accumulate Address/Background Pool of Appropriate Authors
- Promote Author Brochure (for Pool-Building) as Appropriate
- Screen Incoming Proposals/Manuscripts in Subject Area
- Propose Rejection or Development of Each Proposal
- Address First-Round Queries to Selected Authors
- Obtain Background Questionnaires, Photos from Selected Authors
- Verify Literary Competence of Selected Authors
- Complete Competition-Assessment of Each Proposed Project
- Obtain Appropriate Peer Review Assessments of Project Credibility
- Negotiate Proposal Revisions with Selected Authors
- Screen for and Warn of Potential Legal Vulnerability of Projects
- Re-Verify Author Commitment Before Further Analysis
- Submit Acceptable Project Proposals to Editor-in-Chief for Decision
- Support Series Proposals Before Publications Committee
- Negotiate and File Authorized Contracts
- Provide Info/Photo Files to Promotion with Contract Notification
- Monitor Author Delivery Schedules
- Arrange Supplementaries with Authors
- Accomplish Substantive Editing (Content Changes)
- Negotiate Substantive Revisions with Authors
- Verify Authors' Permissions
- Monitor Royalty Statements/Payments to Series Authors
- Make Reprint/Revision Recommendations as Requested

college intern who can screen obviously-inappropriate proposals out of the mail, or an externally-contracted series editor who'll organize a sequence of books and recruit authors for a two-or-three-percent royalty override, can help this one-person department deal with work overloads until the enterprise can afford more staff.

But as soon as the acquisition pipeline is asked to generate more than those 10-15 annual manuscripts, the editor-in-chief should be authorized (required!) to recruit additional acquisition editors—and assign them responsibility for specific product categories (series), so as to focus the accumulation of useful insights, experience, and contacts for maximum future re-utilization. Their job descriptions will include some or all of the responsibilities suggested by Figure 13b, on the previous page.

Basically, you'll need another series editor for each additional 10-15 books. But to avoid the distorting effect of very large or very small books, some editors-in-chief wisely express acquisition workloads (and even planning model distributions between series) in terms of *finished book pages* (estimated typeset cast-off) rather than "books" (new titles). For this purpose, they may define 300 manuscript words as a page—and expect 2,500-3,000 pages a year from each full-time acquisition editor.

At this rate, if the publishing program is (or grows) large enough, the editor-in-chief may be taxed by an excessive span of control. No editor-in-chief should be expected to guide and facilitate the work of more than four subordinate series editors—in addition to the administrative assistant (for correspondence, filing, etc.) who'll inevitably be needed before you reach that point. As you grow larger, then, the editor-in-chief may have to divide supervision of the function with one or more top-level assistants (the most popular title for them is "senior editor")—each (while acquiring titles themselves) overseeing the work of several series editors.

The work of the acquisition function is best organized around a clearly defined "pipeline" of stages/processes by which a manuscript reaches the pre-press function. In all, there are 15 stages of that pipeline in the most effective acquisition departments with which this author is familiar.

(1) *Building an Author Pool:* Accumulating a mailing list of credible writers who *might* submit future manuscript proposals;

(2) *Promoting Author Proposals:* Communicating with that author pool in such a way as to encourage those proposals;

(3) *Initial Screening of Proposals:* Eliminating that 80 percent that will be clearly inappropriate or inept;

(4) *Querying the Authors* of those proposals that survive this first screening—to amplify or clarify the author's intentions, and ascertain receptiveness to further suggestions;

(5) *Verifying Writing Competence:* Examining other work by the prospective author;

(6) *Verifying Author Credibility:* Submitting outline proposals to sub ject-area experts unless the writer's credentials are unquestioningly adequate;

(7) *Verifying Significant Uniqueness* in the author's information or treatment which will compel readers who already have libraries on the topic to buy this additional book;

(8) *Verifying the Strategic Appropriateness* of the project, by identifying the precise slot on the acquisition planning model which it may be proposed to fill;

(9) *Warning of Legal Vulnerabilities* on which the publisher may want advice-of-counsel before contracting;

(10) *Establishing the Financial Feasibility* of the project, by subjecting it to interdepartmental analysis by marketing, pre-press, finance, etc.;

(11) *Massaging the Proposal* to negotiate with the author changes that your evaluation suggests would improve the end result;

(12) *Obtaining Permission to Contract*, by submitting the proposal to whatever "Publishing Decisions" mechanism the publisher has prescribed;

(13) *Negotiating a Contract* with the author that assures the publishing house not only of the right to reproduce and market its intended edition(s), but to appropriately control—and share revenues from—subsidiary rights licensing of other editions, or adaptations to other media or languages;

(14) *Obtaining Manuscript Delivery* in a timely manner—by monitoring and disciplining author progress;

(15) *Negotiating Content Changes* in the first-draft manuscript which the acquiring editor believes will improve the book—before it is transmitted to the pre-press function for production.

We'll look at details of major segments of this pipeline in the chapters that immediately follow. Meanwhile—once the acquisition strategy model exists, and the pipeline stages have been defined—it's important that the editor-in-chief establish a regular *weekly* procedure (a brief departmental meeting is usually the best approach) for monitoring the status of every acquisition prospect currently in the house (by virtue of having survived Step 3), and for confirming that there are *enough* such prospects to meet the impending demands of the strategy model. When the number of plausible projects in the pipeline lags—it's time for the editor-in-chief to earn her lofty status (and, we hope, pay) by taking appropriate corrective action. Otherwise, the vitality of the entire publishing program is likely to wane in the not-too-distant future.

Chapter 14
Creating Your Basic Author Contract

The property rights of authors, and of the creators of other artistic and intellectual works, are established and governed in the United States by the Copyright Act of 1976. This act, which became effective 1 January 1978, asserts that ownership of such a property derives from the act of *creation,* not (as with the previous copyright law) from the act of copyright registration. Only in a limited number of specific instances (called "works made for hire") is this creativity—and thus basic ownership of the result—attributed to the publishing organization; anthologics, multi-level curriculum units, statistical database reproductions, and books written by paid staff members on company time are the major examples.

Initial property rights to all other manuscripts are clearly vested in the author(s) of those works—and publishers can only reproduce and distribute them after negotiating permission to do so from the author(s). A negotiated author contract spells out the specific uses a publisher is authorized to make of a specified manuscript, and reserves all other property rights for the writer (or subsequent licensees).

The U.S. Copyright Act of 1976 confirms an author's property rights for life plus 50 years (or a publisher's rights in a "work made for hire" for 75 years after publication). It allows the author an opportunity to renegotiate any contracted transfer of those rights after 35 years. But otherwise, *it does not interfere with the basic right of two parties to contract.* Essentially, then, as long as you negotiate honestly, you can contract with an author on whatever terms you mutually desire, for the right to publish a specific manuscript.

In actual practice, however, most of the American publishing industry (as with most of its counterparts in other countries) follows a traditional pattern in its agreements with writers. This pattern calls for both a territorial and a linguistic definition of the extent of the rights transferred; it distinguishes between the publisher's right to reproduce and distribute its own edition of the work, and subsidiary rights for additional uses or adaptations (which may or may not be put under the publisher's control); it usually specifies compensation of the author by a royalty based on either the eventual sales price or the publisher's net receipts, plus a share of any subsidiary rights income received by the publisher—though the compensation may be in the form of a flat fee instead of a royalty.

How you apply and elaborate on this pattern will have a great deal to do with the eventual success of your publishing program. Authors typically receive between 8 and 12 percent of the revenue generated by a publisher. Those whose books succeed represent the long-term worth of the publishing house, a worth created at substantial cost and risk. That worth is only as secure as the contractual agreements the publishing house has made with its authors.

Some COOs or CEOs of publishing houses reserve for themselves the authority to negotiate all author contracts, on the assumption that the task is too important to be delegated. But it is the series acquisition editor who will eventually have to get the author to deliver as contracted. Disciplining authors is difficult at best, and the series editor needs all available clout to do it. Allowing those series editors to negotiate and sign contracts—with the implication that they'll have the same powerful role regarding the author's next book—is one of the best ways to give them that clout.

So publishers are well advised to leave the contracting to the series editors. But how can editors be expected to deal with all of the legal and financial implications of such agreements, without spending more time than they can afford at the task? The answer lies in your development of a good basic contract—which can be refined as appropriate from case to case.

A publisher's basic contract has two major purposes. First, it provides a plausible starting point for negotiation with an author regarding a specific manuscript. Second, it provides a basis for control over the bargaining process, to prevent an unwary editor from committing you to a perpetually unprofitable deal.

When a series editor sets out to select or recruit authors to fill the blank slots on a future season's editorial planning model (as much as 2½ years before anticipated publication), it is too early to complicate matters by proposing specific contract terms. But eventually—if a given work survives the screening process—the negotiating editor must finally (usually 12-24 months before publication) broach all of the mundane details of mutual obligation, and of the division of the proceeds, with the author.

The least awkward way of doing this is simply to inform a new author that you would like to publish her/his book if a satisfactory agreement can be reached, state that you have enclosed the basic contract you normally offer, and invite her/him to either propose specific amendments, or just countersign it to conclude the deal. Most first-time authors will sign without quibbling; those who don't have at least assumed the burden of getting specific about what they want.

In the case of an author who's published with you before, it is normal to offer the terms of her/his most recent contract as your opening proposal for the new agreement.

In those instances in which an author (new or repeat) does take exception to this initial offer, insist on an explicit counter-proposal. Such counter-proposals should then be subjected to the scrutiny of the core management group (or at the very least, the publisher), for a determination as to how far the editor can go in meeting the author's requests.

To retain control over this bargaining process between editor and author, then, a publisher must develop a sound basic contract. As noted elsewhere, the chief finance officer should periodically review this basic contract to make sure its terms do not undermine the profitability of the program; at the same time, he should stipulate (with the publisher's approval) the *maximum* royalties and advances that can be tolerated if warranted by circumstances. By thrashing out such limits in a basic contract that will be the heart of every commitment to an author, the finance officer can safeguard profitability without being directly involved in the negotiations. Requiring that all exceptions to the basic contract be approved by the publisher gives the finance officer a reasonable opportunity to see that necessary discipline is consistently practiced.

If you'll put your basic contract on a word processor, it will be easy to respond to authors' counter-proposals by rewording the agreement to whatever extent you're willing, and then sending a proposed new document for the author's approval or amendment. Just keep repeating the process until everybody (including your business manager) is satisfied. Only rarely will you have to break it off because of irreconcilable differences. A competent series editor should always have in the pipeline enough alternative prospects to be undaunted by that possibility.

Developing a basic contract requires that you take a position on a number of issues on which publishers are divided. The most important of these issues are reflected in the twelve numbered sections of the sample contract that appears here as Figure 14a.

Figure 14a—Sample Author Contract

Date _____

To Whom It May Concern:

This letter constitutes a binding contract between_____,
hereinafter referred to as the Author, and _____,
hereinafter referred to as the Publisher, whereby said Author grants to said Publisher exclusive rights to publish or adapt, and/or license others to publish or adapt, a manuscript created by said Author which is tentatively titled
"_____," hereinafter referred to as the Work.

1. The Author hereby certifies that the language and contents of this Work are not plagiarized from any other source, and do not libel or slander any other

party. Said Author assumes full responsibility for any damages resulting from claims to the contrary.

2. The Author hereby conveys to the Publisher exclusive rights to reproduce and/or publish (in book or other form), to adapt to other media, to license other parties to publish in whole or in part or adapt to other media, and to distribute and sell or license other parties to distribute and sell, this Work and all the contents thereof. This exclusive right to publish, adapt, license, distribute, and sell shall be applicable to the original English language version of the manuscript, and to any translations into any other languages—and shall extend to all nations and territories of the World without exception.

3. The above grant of subsidiary rights to the Publisher to license other parties to publish and/or adapt said Work is exclusive and without exception. It includes the right to license translation, serialization, excerption, condensation, inclusion of all or part of the work in another book, reprinting, adaptation to radio, television, cinema, stage, audio-visual or electronic media, utilization by a book club, and all other uses of the Work or its contents. The Author shall in no way infringe upon this exclusive right of the Publisher by authorizing other parties to utilize any portion of the Work in any form.

4. In compensation for this grant of rights, the Publisher hereby agrees to pay the author a royalty of twelve and a half percent (12.5%) of net receipts (after refunds or credits for return of merchandise are deducted) from the sale of its own edition(s) of said work. The Publisher furthermore agrees to pay the Author fifty percent (50%) of any royalties received by said Publisher from other parties licensed to utilize this Work in written (printed or electronically reproduced) form, and eighty percent (80%) of any royalties received from other parties licensed to adapt all or part of the Work to another medium.

5. The Publisher agrees to pay the Author a cash advance of fifteen hundred U.S. dollars ($1,500.00), to be deducted from subsequent royalties earned by the Work. Five hundred dollars ($500.00) of this advance shall be paid when the Author returns a signed copy of this contract to the Publisher, a second five hundred dollars ($500.00) shall be paid when the Author delivers a completed first-draft manuscript of the Work to the Publisher, and the final five hundred dollars ($500.00) shall be paid when the Author has completed final revisions of said manuscript in a manner satisfactory to the Publisher. No portion of this advance will be refundable in the event that this contract is legally and properly abrogated by the Publisher, or in the event that the advance is never equaled by future royalty earnings.

6. If this Work is not published in book form, and offered for sale to the public, or licensed for publication and/or adaptation by another party, within two (2) years following submission of the completed first-draft manuscript to the Publisher, all rights herein conveyed shall revert to the Author.

7. It shall be the responsibility of the Author to obtain written permission(s) from the owner(s) of any copyrighted material or illustrations to be included in this book, and to furnish copies of said permission(s) to the Publisher along with the manuscript. It shall also be the responsibility of the Author to prepare

and provide any appendices or indexes to be incorporated into the Work, or to compensate other parties for preparing and providing said materials.

8. The author will provide the publisher with both a hard (words on paper) copy of the manuscript, and an electronic disk utilizing a compatible word processing program. If a complete first draft of the manuscript of this Work, covering the subject matter previously agreed upon by the Author and the Publisher, consisting of no less than _____ words and no more than _____ words, together with all agreed illustrations, appendices, and permissions, is not delivered by said Author to said Publisher no later than Midnight, _____ (date), this agreement may be revoked by written notice of the Publisher, if the Publisher so desires.

9. The Author shall be entitled to an accurate accounting of receipts from sales and licensing of this Work by the Publisher at any time more than thirty (30) days after the previous such accounting. The publisher will pay all royalties due the author, less a reserve of not more than ten percent (10%) of royalties earned in the most recent twelve (12) months to cover credits and refunds for subsequent merchandise returns, no more than six (6) months after initial publication of the work, and no more than every six (6) months thereafter. In the event that additional works by the same author(s) are currently being marketed by the Publisher, royalty accounts from all such titles shall be combined with that for this title, for the purpose of calculating recovery of royalty advances, reserves against returns, amounts due the author, etc.

10. In the event the Publisher decides manuscript updating or revision is appropriate for a subsequent edition of this work, the Author agrees to either accomplish that updating/revision within 180 days of the Publisher's request, or to forego up to 50 percent (at the Publisher's discretion) of royalties from the revised edition for purposes of compensating another author selected by the Publisher to accomplish said updating/revising.

11. Legal interpretation of this agreement shall be governed by the laws of the State of [insert state].

12. This Letter of Agreement constitutes the only and entire legally binding agreement between the Author and the Publisher with respect to the Work herein identified.

Signed:

For the Publisher:_____
            Date: _____
Witness: _____

For the Author: _____
Social Security No.: _____
            Date: _____
Witness: _____

Before patterning your own basic contract on this sample, you should definitely submit your version to your corporate general counsel (lawyer) to make certain it is soundly applicable to your circumstances. The author is not a lawyer, and offers no assurance that your needs are covered by such a generic sample. However, Figure 14a will serve to focus your thoughts about 12 critical issues:

(1) *Legal Liability:* It is usual for publishers' contracts to require the author to assume liability for libel, slander, plagiarism, etc. However, writers' groups object—and court precedent suggests that such contracts may not shield the publisher from damages if a book does violate a third party's rights. But at least (as with Clause 1 above), this is one issue on which you should state your preference, and let the author argue if he/she is so inclined. (You might learn something useful about the credibility of the book from that argument.)

(2) *Geographic and Linguistic Limits:* The North American English language community is a sufficiently cohesive audience that most publishers insist on exclusive rights in that language, in both the United States and Canada, as a bare minimum. Beyond that, how far you're willing to forego the export and translation possibilities of a book may differ from situation to situation. Again, the sample below puts it in the best possible terms for the publisher (all languages, all countries), and leaves it to the author to take the initiative if he/she objects. Certainly your marketing department should be consulted before you accept amendments here.

(3) *Subsidiary Rights:* The importance of subsidiary rights differs from publisher to publisher (depending on marketing capability for selling licenses) and from book to book (depending on adaptability to other uses). This (as well as territorial and language limits) is an area in which publishers are often able to yield to authors as a bargaining maneuver. But until you deliberately decide to yield, make sure you've stated clearly each *specific* subsidiary right you consider a valuable part of your acquisition; since "subsidiary right" is an imprecise legality, you may not be able to make generalities stand up should the author ever want to make a side deal without you.

(4) *Royalty Basis:* About three-fourths of independent publishers base the royalties they pay authors on their *net receipts* (after discounts and returns) from sales of their edition(s) of books. The other fourth follow the traditional pattern of the big trade houses (mainly because that's the practice that's gotten the most publicity), and base royalties on the list prices of their books. Whereas the latter are traditionally very standard—at 10 percent of list price (often cut in half on the publisher's direct sales to consumers), the former only average about 11 percent (obviously a better deal for publishers).

However, most publishers paying on the basis of net receipts can actually, normally, afford 12-13 percent—and editors-in-chief usually campaign for such norms, to improve the odds of impressing quality writers. There is little solid evidence that increasing net receipt royalties *beyond* 13 percent (or list price royalties beyond 10 percent) will tempt competent writers to choose a publisher they might not otherwise have chosen—but on this score, every publishing house gets to "call 'em as it sees 'em" and take the consequences.

(5) *Cash Advances:* Advance payments to help support authors as they write are normally deducted from the first royalties a book earns. A third of independent publishers manage to acquire books without offering such advances. For the other two-thirds, typical advances (as of 1991) are in the $1,500-$2,500 range. Under normal circumstances, a cash advance should never exceed the anticipated first-year royalties a book is expected to earn. Within those limits, most finance officers will agree that it's safer to mollify reluctant authors with bigger advances (eventually recoverable from royalties) than with higher royalties. But beyond those limits—you're courting expensive future write-offs!

(6) *Must You Publish?* Most publishers believe that they should not be required to publish a disappointing or untimely manuscript just because the author delivers it as specified. Clause 6 of the sample contract in Figure 14a gives the publisher an "out"—recognizing the right *not* to publish by specifying what will happen (return of all rights to the author—without a refund of any advance) in such a situation.

(7) *Permissions and Supplements:* Authors sometimes argue that elaborations of their basic manuscript are not their responsibility. Clause 7 disagrees—by making clear the author's responsibility for getting written permission for use of any attributed material, and for providing such supplementary material as an index or an appendix. (Editors often arrange with free-lancers for these supplements, on agreement that the costs will be charged against future author royalties.)

(8) *Deadlines and Length Limits:* A major portion of the crises that arise in publishing houses are related to the failure of authors to (a) deliver contracted manuscripts on time, or (b) edit their work to the previously anticipated length (which has a bearing on both marketing prospects and production costs). By including these requirements in their contracts, publishers can give editors more leverage in disciplining writers to perform as agreed (without actually canceling many books in the process). In recent years, it has also become common for publishers to stipulate in their *preferred* basic contract that the manuscript is to be submitted in both paper ("hard copy") and electronic form—though that requirement may certainly be waived if it stands between you and a masterpiece!

(9) *Accounting Credibility:* Sadly, there's been some merit to author's suspicions about the integrity of a few publishers' royalty accounting practices. Assuming you've nothing to hide, the best way to overcome this suspicion is to offer any writer who demands it her/his line from your monthly accounting feedback. The sample contract in Figure 14a also stipulates that royalties will be paid every 6 months instead of the traditional 12; some publishers even prefer to settle accounts quarterly. Thus, the contract reduces the temptation to get too far behind the eight ball by "borrowing" from the royalty reserve.

And note that the sample contract prevents you from having to pay an author royalties on one book while still trying to recover royalty advances from another.

(10) *Future Revisions:* If you see long-range potential in a book (especially one that contains current data), the importance of the wording in Clause 10 of the sample is self-evident.

(11) *Legal Interpretation:* Many contracts specify that any dispute between author and publisher about interpretations of the terms will be settled under the procedures of the American Arbitration Association. But since that's unfamiliar ground to most people, the sample contract below leaves disputes to the due course of the laws of the publisher's state.

(12) *Eliminating "Implied Contract" Terms:* Authors will sometimes contend that because an acquisition editor was sympathetic to certain ideas they expressed about marketing, design, etc.—those were part of an "implied" oral contract. The last clause of the sample above is important for prevention of any such misunderstandings.

As publishers' contracts go, the sample in Figure 14a is relatively simplified and brief. Near the other extreme, the trade book contract suggested by The Authors Guild contains 29 clauses—with numerous sub-clauses—governing a much more detailed list of contingencies. Interested publishers can learn how to obtain a copy of that contract (with supporting explanation) by writing to The Authors Guild, Inc., 330 West 42nd Street, New York, NY 10036.

Very few publishers pay their lawyers to examine every author contract. And those who hire attorneys actually to write their basic contracts tend to end up with unnecessarily complicated documents that may scare authors away. But certainly, once you have drafted this basic document, you should subject it to initial scrutiny by your general counsel to make sure none of the wording seriously compromises your position.

CHAPTER 15
Author Pool Development and Promotion

In days gone by, acquisition editors were prone to insist that "networking" among their personal contacts was the most effective way to generate an adequate flow of usable book proposals; this made for great job security ... you couldn't be an acquisition editor unless/until you had a "network." But in the author's experience with several hundred acquisition programs, this is simply no longer a valid approach—if it ever was. However diffident acquisition editors might be about "hustling," it's those who make an aggressive effort to solicit proposals from a broad base of author contacts (far beyond any personal network) who most regularly meet their strategy model goals.

At the heart of such an aggressive acquisition effort lies the "author pool"—a name-and-address database of potential authors who might write a future book appropriate to your acquisition strategy or editorial niche. A good author pool is an accumulative process—and it starts with the simple act of creating a list-building mechanism. Most editors-in-chief find that their basic computer network (or any unlinked PC with database software) provides all the necessary technology. It's merely a matter of setting up a file, with an entry form something like this:

Figure 15a—Sample Author Pool Data-Form

```
 12-07-1992              Author Pool DataForm                    15:02
Series[         ]   Source[              ]
Enty Date[       ]  Last Contact[        ]
Name[                                        ]
Addr1[                                      ]
Addr2[                                      ]
C/S[                        ] Zip[        ]
Off Ph[                     ] Home Ph[        ]
CONTACTS:
[                                                               ]
[                                                               ]
[                                                               ]
[                                                               ]
[                                                               ]
[                                                               ]
[                                                               ]
NOTES:
[                                                               ]
[                                                               ]
[                                                               ]
```

While every series editor should be asked to give high priority to adding names specific to *their* series needs to this file, the actual database should be *centralized* to include all series on the acquisition strategy model. This keeps the publishing house from becoming vulnerable to unethical editors who treat their author contacts as "personal property"—which they hope to take with them (and deny to their predecessor) if they leave the organization. It also makes it much easier to promote actual proposals from the pool—by combining such promotion for all series in a single, routinized program.

(Incidentally, it's a very good idea to use the same database—simply by assigning special category-codes for the "series" blank—to accumulate names/ addresses of illustrators, indexers, translators, ghost writers, and similar specialists whose help you might eventually need. For initial contacts, you'll find their professional associations listed in Bowker's *Literary Market Place*— see Appendix 2.)

If you'll brainstorm with all members of your acquisition department— plus the publisher, the marketing manager, and anyone else who might be familiar with the sources described below—you'll find that six traditional sources will give you a substantial head start on the quick identification of an author pool. They include:

(1) *Previous Authors:* The first names on any publisher's list of potential future authors should be the people who have satisfactorily written for the house in the past. Include notations about previous contract terms, since they will probably be the starting point for any future negotiation.

(2) *Authors' Recommendations:* Because they are usually heavily involved in the field of interest that they share with your editorial program, present and previous authors often know other people who would be qualified to write about other aspects of the subject. An occasional personalized, word-processed letter to the author list inviting such recommendations should be a steady source of new names.

(3) *Organization Leaders:* Enterprising series editors are usually involved with associations and similar organizations concerned with their editorial subject areas. Periodic surveying (by personalized form letters) of leaders in such organizations, requesting suggestions as to potential authors, will not only help build your list; it will make those leaders more aware of who you are—for other networking purposes.

(4) *Advisory Committees:* If you've organized an editorial advisory group or peer review panel, it should consist of knowledgeable people who've already made a modest commitment to help you. A questionnaire survey of such a group, asking for addresses of potential authors with background notes, would be appropriate once or twice a year.

(5) *University Faculty:* Senior faculty members at the universities that are strongest in your chosen subject area usually advise graduate students—and those graduate students are often eager for opportunities to publish. Circulating your catalog and mission statement to such a faculty list, with a cover

letter requesting recommendations of potential authors, can be a very productive pool-building tactic.

(6) *Periodical Writers:* Conscientious series editors regularly scan all of the major periodicals concentrating on their subject areas. Among other things, this enables them to identify people who are writing useful, provocative articles which might be expanded into books. While journal editors may be reluctant to give you the addresses of their writers, by-lines usually identify their institutional affiliations; you'll find addresses of those institutions readily available in appropriate directories.

But ultimately, the best way to create a good author pool is to *advertise your needs.* Quite a few small publishers have gone from only a score of known manuscript sources to several hundred in a year or less by overcoming their diffidence about "acquisition promotion"—and following this simple two-step procedure:

First, they've created a brief, straight-forward "author guidelines" brochure telling prospective writers just how to go about submitting book proposals to their acquisition editors. Then they've advertised the availability of this *free* brochure in the classified sections (or even small display ads) in periodicals that share their subject-specializations. Requests for the free brochure provide addresses of a constant stream of would-be authors who share their subject-interests.

Thus it becomes important that you *never* give intermediate contacts quantities of that brochure for pass-along to others. You want more than the initial brochure communication with individual authors—you want their actual names and addresses!

An author guidelines brochure may be an elaborate booklet with fancy graphics, containing an extensive essay on your mission, your editorial series, and your publishing processes—complete with photos of key staff members to create a friendly impression. But many of the best ones are nothing more than single-sheet folders, generated on a word processor and reproduced on a photocopier. At this stage of the game, content is much more important than graphic image.

The first critical ingredient of such a brochure is its title. Use a caption that quickly suggests that the brochure offers a significant opportunity to the aspiring writer. Titles like "How to Submit Your Book Idea to (name of publisher)" ... or "Improving Your Chances of Getting a Book Published" ... or "What Every First-Time Book Author Should Know" will catch the attention of the audience you're trying to reach.

Start the text with a brief description of the kinds of books (subject area, style, etc.) you're prepared to consider. Summarize your mission statement and your editorial series categories as clearly as you can. Discourage authors from submitting proposals that don't fit this description. This can save you and those authors valuable time.

Next, describe the form in which you prefer that book proposals be initially submitted. Most publishers are wise to insist on nothing but 2-to-4 page outlines, including all chapter headings and itemized lists of the major topics or contents of each chapter. Specify that significant illustrations or appendices should be described as part of such an outline. You might invite authors to give a brief summary of their experience with the subject matter, and their previous publishing accomplishments, in a cover letter—but assure them that you'll send a questionnaire (such as Figure 15b below) to elicit background data at the appropriate time. Discourage people from sending manuscripts (or even sample chapters) until you've decided whether the project fits into your editorial strategy.

Give assurances in the brochure that all proposals will receive prompt attention and frank response. It's reasonable to say that if the proposal is clearly not appropriate to your current needs and plans, you'll respond to that effect within 2 weeks; it only takes a couple of minutes of screening to reach this conclusion. Indicate that you'll acknowledge your *potential* positive interest in any proposal, and ask clarifying questions, within a month or so—but make it clear that another 2 or 3 months will probably then be needed to reach your decision on any seriously-considered project.

Then describe the general process by which you evaluate a book, making clear the involvement of your colleagues in other publishing functions (marketing, pre-press, finance) beyond the acquisition department. (This helps explain why you need the outline first; obviously, all of these people can't read the complete manuscript.) Describe the roles these other functions will play in the future development of the book, if you agree to publish it. But emphasize that the author should communicate solely with the specifically assigned series editor whose signature appears on your acknowledgment of the proposal; don't encourage even your best authors (let alone your untested prospects) to distract your entire staff.

Explain briefly the form in which you'll eventually prefer that a manuscript be submitted: whether an electronic disk is required, which word processing programs you can most easily convert, whether accompanying hard copy is expected, etc. Be especially diligent about begging authors *not* to do any more word processor formatting of their manuscripts (centering heads, indenting text, etc.) than is absolutely necessary for clarity. Otherwise, your copy editors may eventually have to wade through such manuscripts line-by-line to *remove* this coding so it won't confuse your desktop system.

Finally, briefly describe the terms of your basic author contract (such as illustrated by Figure 14a). You may want to indicate that these terms are negotiable, but don't belabor the point; you'll find unsigned and first-time authors much less concerned with the details than veterans. Some small publishers spell out their normal, modest royalty advances—to ward off authors they won't be able to afford *before* they've spent time evaluating proposals.

When you've created this author guide, send a copy to every periodical you can identify that shares your general editorial interests—along with a news release announcing that the guide is available free to interested parties. Then prepare classified ads for the most important of those periodicals, and continue to promote the availability of the brochure on a regular schedule. Code all return addresses in your news releases and ads so you can trace the sources of requests for the brochure. Keep the classified ads (or small spot ads) running continuously in those journals from which you get the best responses.

Create posters promoting the free brochure, for display in your conference exhibit booths (along with request cards). Send your news release, and more request cards, to schools or organizations that share your editorial focus. (But don't send pass-along copies of the brochure itself; remember, you want potential authors to request that directly from you, so you'll have their addresses.) Offer the brochure in your mail order catalogs or flyers. Some specialized publishers have even gone so far as to mention their author guideline brochures on the backs or jackets of books.

Whether or not a potential author has given serious thought to writing a specific book in the near future, a news item or ad offering such a brochure will incite curiosity about what is actually involved. By responding before the writer finds another publisher, you should be able to multiply the size of your author pool almost at will, at the same time you're training those writers to do things your way.

Such aggressive author identification makes it easy for a small publishing house to function as an effective talent scout within its subject area. Because many of the contacts made are first-time authors (who never thought of themselves as such before), they tend to be more imaginative (less inhibited) with their proposals—and this leads to intellectual innovation (and thus those "compellingly unique" book features so vital to the marketing team). Even when some authors you discover desert you for the conglomerates after they "hit the big time" with several successful books—you may find it more profitable to scout for new talent than to try to outbid the competition.

But an author pool is only as good as the flow of book proposals you can persuade it to submit. Publishers use a variety of devices to encourage their accumulated address lists to submit outline proposals—giving their acquisition editors a head-start over competition—and frequently, an opportunity to help authors reshape their books before their energies and egos are overly-invested in actual manuscripts.

Some add the author pool to their mailing list for seasonal catalogs and new title announcement news releases. Some personalize periodic form letters (on the word processor) to inquire whether each author is working on (or contemplating) any book that might be appropriate to the publisher. Some actually circulate lists of relevant book-ideas authors might want to adopt—though this runs the risk of generating good proposals for your competition.

But by far the most effective device this author has seen for stimulating a steady flow of author proposals is the informal acquisition department newsletter. As with those guideline brochures, fancy graphics is of questionable value here. Many of the best newsletters of this type come straight off the word processor (or at most, the desktop page generator)—utilizing a paste-on masthead and colored paper for short-run reproduction on the office copying machine. They seem to work just as well as two-color printing on rag stock, or more elaborate productions.

Such author pool newsletters are usually two-to-four pages; it's better to send them out more frequently than to use all your ammunition in a single blast. In their editorial content, the best ones simply tempt prospective writers to "live vicariously" through the experiences of other authors. They announce new contracts the publisher has recently signed. They boast gently about promising levels of publicity contact (reviewer, talk show) interest in forthcoming titles—as measured by requests for advance review copies. They crow when books go back to press for reprints—and wax even more eloquently about subsidiary rights deals (with book clubs, mass market houses, overseas translators, etc.)

But above all, they quote reviews. They announce any-and-all bookstore autographing parties, or association speaking dates, arranged for their authors. And they cite talk show appearances—even those remote, no-cost radio interviews publicists find so easy to arrange. This not only reiterates the kinds of books you're seeking (because you've succeeded with them in the past); it assures would-be authors that—despite your modest size and budget—you do know how to get attention for your new titles.

And interspersed among all of this reportage, you should constantly offer new copies of your guidelines brochure to any who've lost them—and constantly remind this audience that you want chapter outlines with cover letters *before* they send manuscripts—and constantly review the subject areas and book types represented by your acquisition series. The typical result is a new flurry of proposals after each newsletter mailing. Some will be recirculated proposals you've seen before—but it takes only a few minutes to reject them again while you're sifting the rare-but-precious jewels from the acquisition mailbag.

The most common interval for mailing such a newsletter is quarterly (every 3 months). Because the cost is negligible, mailing one every-other-month (or even monthly) is usually effective if you have enough to report. Mailing *less* frequently than quarterly runs the risk of dropping below the list's "horizon of awareness."

Note that space on the author pool dataform illustrated above (Figure 15a) which is labeled "Last Contact." Use this to enter the current date *every time* you have any kind of contact (from a proposal to a change of address) that indicates a given writer is still interested in being on your list. Then periodically send personalized form letters—with pre-stamped postal reply cards—to authors whose last contact dates are more than a year old; ask them to return the card if they want to remain on your list. (It might be well to send a follow-up copy of this letter a month later, before actually deleting an author address.)

Some series editors also send brief questionnaires whenever new author addresses are added to the list—soliciting some indication of the kinds of projects that writer contemplates. Responses can be followed by personal letters of encouragement whenever the editor spots particularly appealing book ideas.

In promoting dialogue with potential authors, an acquisition editor must give reasonable care to preventing those writers from claiming proprietary rights to generic ideas—simply because they've once proposed them. Let common sense be your guide. But when you get strikingly unique proposals that are indeed appropriate to your subject area, make sure you file all the correspondence and phone notes for a reasonable period—and compare it with any similar ideas from other authors, to make sure you can't be accused of future piracy.

CHAPTER 16
Alternate Product Sources and Media Options

As we've suggested before, series editors should be prepared for the possibility that newsletters and other reminders to their author pool list may not always inspire enough good book proposals to meet their strategic goals. Therefore, every acquisition editor should be simultaneously monitoring and tapping alternate sources of manuscripts.

The most widespread alternate approach is for each series editor to maintain an "idea file" of brief, hypothetical one-line descriptions of non-existent books (or other media products) which they'd *like* to make available to their audience—and systematically invite appropriate authors to adopt those ideas, and submit outline proposals for executing them. This runs the risk of handing good ideas to writers who may end up contracting with the competition—but if it's done judiciously, that is a risk well worth taking.

If the editor systematically prints out a list of all of these accumulated one-line ideas every quarter, deletes from that list any which no longer seem appealing or unique, and scans the rest (it should only take a few minutes) to match the best ones with appropriate, *potential* authors from their pool—it should be a fairly simple matter to write each selected author and ask if she'd be interested in submitting an outline proposal for creating such a book. A telephone follow-up of each such author invitation a couple of weeks later will enable the editor to move on to a second prospective author if no interest is indicated. Systematically pursued, this process should provide a healthy supplement to the flow of spontaneous proposals originated by the authors themselves.

Where, then, does a series editor get such home-grown book ideas? Periodic brainstorming sessions within the acquisition function itself (with the publisher, and appropriate people from the marketing department, invited to participate) will be the easiest source to tap. But you might also use word processed letters (at least annually) to solicit suggestions from your Board of Directors or Editorial Advisory Committee. Not-for-profit publishers find that surveys of their membership (or officers) can yield useful suggestions; publishers who also own magazines or journals use subscriber surveys for the same purpose. Classroom adoption publishers might include brief product-idea questionnaires with all complimentary examination books sent to educators. And additional suggestions can be solicited through conference exhibit booths.

It is, of course, not always necessary to have an "author"—in the usual sense of the word—to carry out a book idea. You might, instead, simply identify people who have first-hand knowledge of appropriate subjects (especially in the area of historical recollection) ... or who are "prime movers" in an appropriate cause or industry or discipline; then use staff personnel or on-site free-lancers to record intensive interviews with them. Once transcribed and edited, those "oral history" and "personal insight" interviews can become fascinating manuscripts.

If those "prime movers"—or celebrities whom you believe have appeal to your audience—aren't articulate enough (or willing) to give you what you want as an oral recording, you might accumulate a pool of prospective "ghost writers" who'll do the tough work for them—on the basis of accumulated notes, correspondence and documents, supplemented by face-to-face and phone interviews. Under normal circumstances, a ghost writer (who gets, at most, modest second billing on the title page) will expect about half of the total royalties (beginning with *all* of the contracted advance)—or a lump-sum payment of around $50 an hour (which should be charged against the contracted author's future royalties) when the manuscript is delivered.

A careful series editor may also be able to assemble good manuscripts from collections of speeches, conference papers, or periodical articles—or to convince an author to expand on a single such kernel to develop a book. Assembling your own roomful of talkative experts—each of whom has signed a publication release for a fraction of the total royalty—and recording their discussion of (and later written comments on) a timely topic can produce a powerful book-length manuscript in a hurry. Teachers' course notes and informal syllabi may be convertible into superb adoption books or classroom supplements.

Sequels to, or continuations of, the most successful books in your backlist (utilizing the same authors, or different ones), and updated new editions of appropriate backlist titles, are equally-promising possibilities. Repackaging databases (from membership lists to survey results) maintained within your organization—or collections of graphic materials (from charts to pictures) accumulated through other projects—can also lead to salable new books.

Anytime a series editor decides to propose a book from any of these alternate sources, that editor should (unless someone else has already done so) prepare a project summary and chapter outline that can be subjected (as needed) to the same verification and interdepartmental evaluation processes you've established for routine author proposals. Such a project then becomes simply one more candidate to fill one of those blank lines on the acquisition planning model.

If you develop a strong rapport with the devotees of your chosen subject area, and a good customer list, you may well find that your highly specialized audience has never heard of some very good books published by others who lacked such contacts. On the other hand, if you create a good trade distribution program or a large consumer mail order catalog and customer list, you might be able to offer this general constituency your own editions of books the original publishers were too specialized, or too impoverished, to make widely known and available.

In either case, it's appropriate to make offers for reprint rights to other publishers whose books of several seasons past have never been properly presented to *your* constituency. To monitor this possibility, every series editor should attempt to arrange catalog exchanges with competing publishers— both domestically and overseas.

The most common format for such reprints is the "trade paperback"—a full-sized version of a traditional hardcover, but without the original case binding. Trade paperback reprint rights to books that were not widely circulated in the original edition can normally be obtained for royalties of about 7 percent of your anticipated list price, or 10 percent of your net receipts; advances are typically similar to those offered original authors: $1,000-$3,000. Such rights are usually licensed for 7 years, with renewal options.

By offering a similar royalty, you may be able to get reprint rights to good titles other publishers have let go "out of print," translation rights to books from other countries, or co-publishing rights to books published overseas in English, with even smaller advances.

When buying reprint rights, it is customary to pay the original publisher an "offset fee" if you intend to photograph their pages rather than resetting the type. The traditional offset fee is $3 a page—considerably less than most publishers pay to regenerate those pages. And look at all the proof-reading you save!

Some acquisition editors get a steady stream of appropriate new books by identifying publishers in other countries whose interests are similar, and studying their advance announcements and new catalogs carefully to identify English language titles they might reproduce (with or without editing for regional idioms), or foreign language titles they might translate. Such transactions can easily be negotiated by mail or phone, especially if the publishers involved have done business with each other before.

But most of the exchange of publication rights across national borders takes place at a dozen or so international book fairs (in Europe, the Middle East, Canada, and Mexico). You'll find the most important dates, locations, sponsors, etc., listed in *The Bowker Annual of Library and Book Trade Information* (see Appendix 2).

The granddaddy of all these gatherings is the Frankfurt Book Fair, held in Germany each October. Hundreds of publishers, from almost a hundred countries, display their latest titles and announce forthcoming ones at the Frankfurt Fair Grounds each year. Some come to buy rights, some come to sell, and most are open to either possibility.

Frankly, for most small publishers, a trip to Frankfurt is little more than a tax-exempt vacation. Unless you're really geared to acquire and subsequently publish three or four translated or English language titles each year, you'll probably never recover the expense of the trip.

But if your publishing niche is international in scope, and you really are able to use a significant infusion of imported creativity, an annual trip to one or more of the better book fairs could become a vital part of your acquisition strategy. And you might even earn back part of your expenses on the spot—by renting a booth and offering translation or co-publishing rights to your own books.

Literary agents are also a good source of manuscript proposals. These agents are sales representatives who specialize in negotiating with publishers and other media, on behalf of the writers who are their clients. You'll find an extensive listing of the best agents in Bowker's *Literary Market Place* (Appendix 2). Most of these agents develop and nourish personal contacts in the acquisition departments of the major publishing houses, as well as among small publishers whose special editorial niches correspond to the interests of their clients. Because of the breadth of those contacts, an experienced agent is usually better informed about current trends in royalty scales, advances, and subsidiary rights terms than most editors. So small publishers often get nervous when approached by these "hired guns." But when an agent approaches a small publisher, it is almost always because he couldn't sell the project at hand to one of the bigger houses; given their druthers, agents go where the money is.

So take the ball away from them; start by asking why the project wasn't sold to a bigger publisher. You won't get many frank confessions of rejection, but the plausibility of the response may help you decide whether you're being offered badly flawed goods. Then treat the proposal just as you would if you were talking directly to the author. Make a quick judgment as to whether it fits your acquisition strategy. If it does, explain the procedure (and time frame) through which you evaluate such projects. Unless an available table of contents serves the same purpose, insist on a chapter outline prior to (or along with) any complete manuscript the agent may already have in hand. You might give the agent a copy of your basic contract for perusal while you're making that evaluation, and even a copy of your author brochure and catalog to help her evaluate your relevance to other clients.

If you subsequently decide you are interested in the proposal, you're likely to find an agent more willing to challenge your standard contract terms than most individual authors are. Agents get substantial portions of their income from subsidiary rights, and thus are inclined to want those rights reserved for the author, rather than ceded to the publisher. And because they're more realistic than authors about bestseller prospects, agents usually push for larger advances. So it is important that you determine *in advance* just how far you're prepared to amend your basic contract—and then stand your ground by insisting on those terms.

Far from finding the prospect of such negotiations intimidating, some small publishers enjoy them enough to encourage agent proposals. If you're game for that, send your author brochure and catalog to the list in *Literary Market Place* and let the cards fall where they may.

From video-cassette players to home computers to automobile audiotape decks, expanding use of new consumer communications media offers exciting opportunities to those publishers who are flexible enough to seize them. But these opportunities are dependent upon having a pre-press department that can convert book manuscripts into finished reproduction masters for those other media.

The first requirement is the development of script formats into which manuscripts must be converted, for each of the new media you desire to produce. If neither your acquisition nor your pre-press personnel are familiar with such format requirements, turn to the production vendors you expect to use for guidance. Ask them what kind of modification of the text is needed from the author for any project; they may even be able to steer you to freelancers adept in preparing such scripts.

The next thing you need is a procedure for dealing with those production vendors. Most pre-press and business managers have already established such a procedure in their bidding process for buying printing. Starting with a vendor pool such as you can identify from Bowker's *A-V Market Place* directory (see Appendix 2) of multi-media consultants, production services, and others who can help you cope with the peculiarities of any likely electronic or photo-graphic medium—it's basically a matter of asking at least three vendors for price bids. As with strange printers, it is wise to ask each bidder for names of several recent clients so you can check references (especially if you aren't familiar with the technology).

Finally, there remains the possibility of adding *other publisher's* books—or information packages in other media—to your catalog to "flesh out" the resources you're making available to your chosen audience. This can be a good method for getting a new publishing venture off-the-ground (by making it more credible with customers) in a hurry.

Essentially, this makes a "distributor" of you. As we said in Chapter 1, it's basically an insult to insist to another publisher that your distribution efforts (from catalog promotion to order processing) are worth *more* than the combined efforts of the author, the real publisher, the paper-maker and the printer—so 50 percent discounts are the most you can expect from self-respecting sources. (And the merchandise available from those who *aren't* self-respecting is usually junk!)

Because they can generate their own books—and pay author royalties—for considerably less than that 50 percent, most small publishers find such "distribution" to be much less profitable than original publishing itself. Eventually, the start-up that goes this route discovers that the "distributed" items are dragging down their operating margin—and should be phased out.

CHAPTER 17
Screening and Shaping Book/Project Proposals

In a properly functioning acquisition department, each series editor's in-box accumulates a steady flow of project proposals from authors, agents, other publishers who want to sell rights, and even the editor himself—tossing plausible book ideas from such other sources as oral histories, conference papers, collections of articles, symposia, or ghost-written celebrity memoirs into the stack for comparison and consideration. The first task of the series editor is to quick-screen this stack to eliminate the *obviously inappropriate* projects—and that's likely to be more than 80 percent of them. With relatively little experience, a series editor who understands the target-definitions implicit in the acquisition strategy model (or even the house's general "publishing niche" as summarized in the corporate mission statement) should be able to identify inappropriate or clearly-inept proposals (whether in outline form or complete manuscript) with no more than five minutes of careful scanning. In fact, this is the kind of job frequently assigned college interns who work on a department-wide basis (under the editor-in-chief), whittling down the flow of incoming mail before it even gets to the series editors.

The rejection process is poorly handled by a surprising percentage of series (acquisition) editors. While it is humane to be both gentle and helpful, you cannot afford to let your acquisition staff get bogged down with excessive and unnecessary hand-holding at this point. A polite, personalized word-processed letter (only the crass still cling to pre-printed "rejection slips"), simply explaining that the proposal does not currently fit your needs—with an enclosed copy of your author guideline brochure (Chapter 15)—is really all that is appropriate in most cases. If the editor thinks the project is plausible for *another publisher,* and knows one or two names that (with quick reference to Bowker's *Literary Market Place* addresses) might be useful, suggesting those alternate contacts to the author is certainly a reasonable investment in goodwill. But *don't* make a research project of it; the series editor's time should be saved for proposals that have real potential for your publishing house.

If a proposal which has survived this initial quick-screening has arrived in a form with which you'll have difficulty working, the series editor should take the initiative in contacting the potential author and asking that it be appropriately reshaped. Essentially, what the series editor should have at the beginning of the process is (1) a 2-4 page *chapter outline,* clearly indicating the basic contents and organization of the proposed book, and (2) a cover letter explaining why the author thinks it will be useful and/or salable. If, instead, you receive a complete manuscript—or a proposal in any other format that does *not* include such a chapter outline and overview—you should use a personalized word-processed form letter to explain that before a decision can be reached, the proposal must be evaluated by a number of people—most of whom will not have time to read a manuscript. The author should be reminded that the one person most qualified to prepare a summary which does justice to the project is *that author;* you'll usually find them eager to comply. (Meanwhile, offer assurances that the manuscript or other material they've sent will indeed be safeguarded until it is needed—or returned.)

The next things you'll need after the chapter outline and overview cover letter will be (3) answers to the initial questions which come to mind during that initial screening (such as the author's willingness to change a bad title, or a more explicit description of anticipated illustrations or appendices), and (4) comprehensive background data on the author and the topic/project. You can combine requests for these two items with the above-mentioned request for reshaping a proposal (to outline and cover letter) if such reshaping is required.

The best way to develop the clarifying questions you'll want answered (Item 3 above) is for the editor-in-chief to schedule weekly one-on-one meetings with each series editor, in which the latter can briefly describe each of that week's proposals which has survived initial screening—and which the editor would like to investigate. If a project got past that first screening (as "plausible"), but has failed to truly interest the series editor as a candidate for a *specific* slot on the planning model, the editor-in-chief should be invited to express an opinion before the series editor decides between immediate rejection or a second-round query for more information.

The best way to get comprehensive background information on both the author and the topic (Item 4) is to send that writer your own "background questionnaire"—and emphasize that its careful and prompt completion is essential to your decision process. *Make sure* that background questionnaire asks the author for a good general summary of the subject and scope of the proposed work (100-200 words) *and* an explicit statement (another 50 words) of the *unique compelling features* that will prompt people who already have libraries in the subject area to want to purchase this one more book. Point out to the potential author that the summary and unique-features description they include in the questionnaire may well become *the basic promotional copy* for the future book—so they'll want to give it their "best shot."

Use the sample on the next page as a starting point for development (or improvement) of a questionnaire keyed to your particular situation.

Figure 17a—Sample Author Background Questionnaire

1. Author's Name (as it should appear on any eventual contract and/or title page: _____

2. Author's Mailing Address: _____

_____

Office Phone _____ Home Phone _____
Social Security No. (for potential contract) _____

3. Working Title of Proposed Book: _____

_____

Suggested Subtitle:_____

4. Description of contents and style (100-200 words) which author believes would make good promotional presentation: _____

_____

_____

_____

_____

_____

_____

_____

_____

_____

_____

_____

_____

5. Unique features compelling enough to persuade readers who already have books on the subject to purchase this one more (about 50 words that author believes will make good promotional material):_____

_____

_____

6. Author's present employment (organization, position, time-span):

_____

_____

7. Significant past employment positions or other affiliations:

_____

_____

8. Previous books by this author (including year, title, publisher):

_____

_____

_____

9. Periodicals in which author's work has been published (with years):

_____

_____

_____

10. Review media author believes will be especially interested in this proposed book (with addresses if known):

_____
_____
_____
_____

11. Other contacts (with addresses) which author believes would be important in promoting or selling this book (and why):

_____
_____
_____
_____

12. Other comments by author:

_____
_____
_____
_____

Please enclose several good, sharp, recent photos of author—including at least one full-face shot and one action shot—and return this questionnaire promptly to:

Attn: _____ (Editor)

[STRIP IN YOUR PUBLISHING HOUSE'S NAME & ADDRESS HERE]

If the proposed book is to be a collaboration between two or more authors (or major illustrators), each of them should complete a separate questionnaire. You'll be surprised what jewels one will offer which the other(s) considered insignificant!

Along with the blank questionnaire, your (series editor's) letter exhorting the candidate to be especially diligent about Questions 4 and 5 should also—after consultation with the editor-in-chief—raise any other issues on which you wish clarification ... and/or an indication of the author's willingness to utilize good suggestions from you and your colleagues.

Only after the series editor has assembled these first four components of the presentation (cover/overview letter, chapter outline, author background questionnaire, responses to editor's initial queries) does the project (which we can now call an incomplete "proposal package") warrant any significant investment of editorial time.

To this point, then, we've only dealt with the screening and assembly of potential projects which a series editor should accomplish *prior* to serious time commitment. But with those four basic presentation components in hand (and any pre-submitted manuscript safely stored for potential future use), it is now time for the series editor to do what is necessary in order to certify that the project is deserving of some commitment from other members of the publishing team. Basically, there are six things to which the series editor should eventually certify before others give it serious attention:

(1) *Strategic Appropriateness:* The easy (and perhaps only proper) way for the series editor to certify that the project is indeed compatible with the purposes and strategy of the publishing house is to identify the *exact blank line* on the acquisition strategy model (Chapter 12) for which it is being proposed as a candidate.

(2) *Competitive Uniqueness:* The bare minimum a series editor should offer by way of assurance that the proposed book wouldn't be bucking head-on competition is an analysis of similar titles from Bowker's *Subject Guide to Books in Print* (Appendix 2). Examination of the catalogs of competing publishers, field tours of major local bookstores, and consultation with good subject-area bibliographies can provide additional assurance. If similar books are already on the market, the series editor owes all concerned a convincing explanation why this one will nevertheless be welcomed by readers.

(3) *Literary Competence:* If you've previously published anything by this author—and were satisfied—this one's moot. But otherwise, the series editor should certify to the rest of the team that said editor has personally read a reasonable sample of the author's writing (from earlier books published elsewhere, journal articles, or one or two sample chapters of the impending manuscript), and is satisfied that the author writes well enough to provide an appealing manuscript that won't require excessive stylistic reworking. (*Don't* simply pass the samples around to others—marketing personnel, peer reviewers, etc.—for stylistic appraisal; a series editor who can't tell good writing from bad, without coaching, is professionally unqualified anyhow!)

(4) *Author Credibility:* Here the series editor must provide assurance to all concerned that the author knows the subject—and can be trusted not to mislead the reader or embarrass the publisher due to ignorance, errors, or chicanery. The editor who does not feel qualified (via specialized subject-knowledge) to certify an author's competence should have access to a *peer review panel* of experts willing to give a quick opinion after examining the author's cover letter, chapter outline, and background questionnaire.

If a series subject area is at all arcane or technical or highly specialized, it behooves the series editor to brainstorm with others (the editor-in-chief, the publisher, previous authors, etc.) to accumulate names and addresses of experts who might be willing to offer quick opinions of the credibility of authors and their approaches on the basis of outlines and questionnaires. While commercial publishers usually pay a modest honorarium (typically $50-$100) for each such opinion, not-for-profit publishers can usually get their members to provide this service at no cost—for "the good of the cause." All it takes is a form letter (personalized via word processor) explaining what you want—and asking if the candidate would be available for several such opinions a year.

It's generally considered adequate to request three such "peer review" opinions (from the three most appropriate panel members you haven't bothered recently) when the editor needs help assessing a project. Unless that editor intends to track each reviewer down for a phone conversation, it's a good idea to enclose a quick-response questionnaire (with *stamped* reply envelope) which simply gives the reviewer ample opportunity to warn you if anything seems amiss. Realistically, that's about all you're going to get out of such a remote reviewer anyhow.

(5) *Legal Invulnerability:* Obviously, you can't expect series editors to be legal experts. But as each proposal unfolds, it is incumbent upon the editor to be alert for possible plagiarism (over-dependence on the works of other writers), slander or libel (insupportable allegations against others), or product liability (misleading assertions that might cause damage to readers). If the editor has any suspicions on any of these scores—that concern should be clearly stated as part of the proposal package. The publisher (in consultation with the core managers) bears the burden of deciding—if/after the project has been otherwise approved—whether it's worth paying a lawyer for an opinion before proceeding.

(6)*The Editor's Commitment:* Finally, each series editor should be required to certify that, after all the evidence developed to this point, *he/she still really believes* the project should be adopted/contracted to fill the indicated slot on the planning model (or future editorial schedule)—before other staff members are asked to spend time evaluating it. It is not appropriate for series editors to circulate proposals about which they're unsure—in hopes somebody else in the house will lend them courage or commitment. Those other people have their own work to do—and should not be used as substitutes for a series editor's deficient "courage of commitment."

When the original "proposal package" (cover letter, chapter outline, background questionnaire, author response to initial queries) has been supplemented by these six certifications from the series editor, it is ready to be presented (through the editor-in-chief) to the rest of the publishing team for (1) inter functional evaluation and suggestions, and (2) a decision-to-contract (or reject).

Thus, a series editor's working life should consist primarily of (1) seeking out (by communicating with an accumulative author pool) a constant flow of proposals appropriate to the series, (2) quick-screening to reject the obviously inappropriate or unacceptable submissions, and (3) nursing the remainder through the above steps ("the acquisition pipeline"), to develop a complete "proposal package" for submission (with sincere commitment) to the editor-in-chief. In the next chapter, we'll see how that editor-in-chief involves the rest of the publishing house in deciding whether to go forward with the project.

CHAPTER 18
Feasibility Evaluation and the Decision to Publish

Given a reasonable flow of well-screened, sincerely-endorsed project proposals from series editors, it should be the responsibility of the editor-in-chief to engage the rest of the publishing house in their further consideration and (hopefully) eventual acceptance; a wise publisher will not give permission to contract until this is done. How much of the mechanics of this interface with other functions is delegated to the individual series editors should be left to the discretion of the editor-in-chief.

The first step in achieving inter-departmental involvement is to make four copies of the complete proposal package—for the marketing, pre-press and business managers, and for the publisher. Then the editor-in-chief or series editor should deliver those copies (one-by-one), along with a financial feasibility assessment form somewhat like Figure 18a on the next page (with the acquisition section completed by the series editor), to each of those core managers *in the order just listed.* Whether it's best to hand-carry proposals from office to office, or to route them through the corporate message system, will depend on the size and style of your organization.

The first evaluator, the marketing manager, should simply be asked to record on the form how many units (copies) of the proposed book he feels *reasonably confident* his marketing team/program would be able to sell in the first 12 months after publication (perhaps 18-24 months for slower-starting classroom-adoption books)—assuming a reasonable (but as yet unspecified) price. While marketing managers are frequently reluctant to admit it, the major determinant of this quantity is *the accumulated ability of the marketing team* to present this type of book to the appropriate audience (as suggested by their first-year sales of similar recent books)—not nuances of price or literary quality. However, their estimate of any book will also be seriously (and properly) influenced by their (marketing's) assessment of the "compelling unique features" spelled out in the author questionnaire, and the appeal of the "working title" indicated in the proposal.

This specific point-of-interchange between acquisition and marketing is one of the most critical moments in the career of any proposal—and perhaps in that of the resulting book as well. Here is marketing's opportunity to make the voice of the "real world" (their customers) heard in the inner sanctum.

Figure 18a—Sample Feasibility Evaluation Form

ACQUISITION INPUT
Author/Title _____

Ms-Ready Date _____ Approx Ms-Word Count _____

No. Illustrations _____ Type Illustrations _____

Special Graphics Requirements _____

Signed (Acquiring Editor) _____

Date evaluation initiated _____

MARKETING INPUT
Optimal Publn Date _____ Suggested Binding _____

Assumed Cover Style (graphics, colors, etc.) _____

Estimated first-12-months unit sales (assuming a reasonable price):
_____ Initialed: _____

PRE-PRESS INPUT
Estimated unit inventory cost for marketing's estimated first-year quantity (above) plus 10 percent promotional overage, based on our recent $_____ average pre-press page cost, and our recent $_____ average per-page-impression paper/printing/binding cost, both marked up ___ percent for infla-tion hedge:

$_____ pre-press + $_____ p/p/b = $_____ total   Initialed: _____

FINANCE INPUT
Unit inventory cost times our calculated (x____) pricing multiplier (to support financial strategy model) yields a suggested cover (pre-discount) *minimum* price of $_____, which we propose to round to $_____.
Initialed: _____

Price accepted as reasonable by:

_____ (For Acquisitions)

_____ (For Marketing)

Does Marketing believe price could be higher? [] Yes   [] No

Permission to contract is [] granted   [] denied:

_____ (Publisher)

Effective Date: _____

FINANCE OFFICER'S TRANSMITTAL REVIEW
Cover price confirmed/adjusted as $_____

Initial print quantity (+/– 10%) set at _____

Review date: _____ Initialed: _____

The marketing manager should, of course, consult any/all members of the department whose input is appropriate. If any of them have questions or suggestions that might significantly influence the sales estimate, the marketing manager should communicate with the series editor to request any further information (regarding end-paper supplements, etc.) his team desires, and/or to propose improvements (in title wording, etc.) before completing the estimate.

Bear in mind that marketing's quantity estimate is a *hypothetical* number— not an automatic print-buying quantity. This estimate should not restrict the business office in its eventual decision as to how much inventory capital and warehouse space should be tied up by the project.

Next, the pre-press managing editor should be asked to estimate how much pre-press (copy-editing, design, typesetting) money will be required to get the book ready for printing— and (based on recent printing-bill data, or a query to the print-buyer in the business office) how much more it will cost to put marketing's first-year quantity estimate (plus reasonable overage for complimentary promotional copies) into the warehouse. Dividing these combined costs by the estimated first-year sales quantity will produce an estimated *unit cost* for adding the new title to the inventory.

Don't get hung up trying to make this unit cost correspond exactly with the business office's eventual "cost-of-goods" tax-accounting. That's an off-line affair which finance should be free to manipulate later, for the house's greatest tax advantage.

Now the business manager (finance officer) should be asked what *pre-discount cover price the book must bear* in order to support the house's approved financial strategy model (see Figure 9a). The process by which a finance officer converts this strategy into a "pricing multiplier" that can be applied to the estimated unit cost, to indicate a minimum feasible price, is further explained in Chapter 37.

Once these estimates are all recorded on the form, it should be re-routed to the series editor for (signature) certification that she (speaking for the author) does not object to this price—and then to the marketing manager for his acceptance of the price as "reasonable." If either of these parties declines to sign at this point—the proposal has flunked the feasibility analysis and must either be rejected or appropriately revised.

When this process yields a suggested price that marketing (or even the series editor) won't accept as "reasonable," the subsequent interaction of the various functions can often make further important contributions to the shaping of the proposed book. While it is very important that no function change its estimate simply to make the editor happy, it certainly is legitimate for that editor to offer further explanations, solicit (and negotiate with the author, if necessary) marketing or design suggestions for making the book more salable or more economical, and attempt to persuade those other functions to change their estimates accordingly.

Each department should photocopy, and retain for future reference, relevant portions of each proposal package to which it contributes an estimate. This is especially important in three cases:

(1) *The publisher* should keep a file of all finished evaluation sheets—and should systematically review the estimates on each published book a year after it goes on sale, to see how accurately the various functions had projected sales and costs. This is particularly necessary to guard against over-timidity in the marketing function; their persistent under-estimating to "play it safe" can be disastrous by killing potentially good books.

(2) *The marketing function* (specifically, its promotion coordinator or copy-writer) should retain copies of all author background questionnaires—since they contain most of the raw material that will eventually be needed to prepare cover, catalog, and other promotional copy.

(3) *The business office* should use copies of each evaluation form as a basis (and reminder) for rechecking actual lengths, costs, etc., just before the book goes to press (see line 30 in Figure 9d). If the facts suggest a last-minute price increase, a prompt meeting of the core management group should confirm that finance recommendation. And in this final review (recorded at the bottom of the form in Figure 18a—if-and-after the book has been accepted and gone into pre-press production), the finance officer should assess the current cash and inventory situations of the enterprise, and finally (by sending each manager a photocopy of the now-completed form—including this transmittal review) inform all concerned of the actual initial print-purchase quantity.

When the inter-departmental feasibility evaluation has been completed, and a summary document like Figure 18a (without that mid-production trans-mittal review data) has been added to the proposal package, you're now ready for the "decision-to-publish"—perhaps the most critical recurring phenome-non in the life of a publishing house. At this point, responsibility shifts to the publisher. As the editor-in-chief turns over each completed proposal package—with a recommendation that a contract be offered—it is the pre-rogative of the publisher to submit the proposal to whatever decision-making process she feels is appropriate—or which the owners/sponsors may require to assure their input. Such input is especially appropriate in not-for-profit publishing programs—where the non-financial purposes of the sponsors are often more important than a book's financial feasibility.

The publisher should not complete the "permission to contract" section of the evaluation form until the prescribed decision-making procedure has been completed—and the acquisition function must be constantly and clearly aware that *no* commitment can be made to an author until that permission is formally granted.

In some publishing houses (particularly commercial ventures largely owned by the person in the publisher's chair), all that may be required is the submission of the competed proposal package to that publisher—with appropriate response to any questions he may wish to ask the editor-in-chief or acquiring series editor. But it is more common (and more prudent) for commercial publishers to assemble the entire core management group (publisher, editor-in-chief, pre-press development, and marketing and business managers) to discuss each package—perhaps calling in the sponsoring series editor to "testify"—before the publisher decides whether or not to give permission to contract.

In not-for-profit publishing houses, it is fairly common (and not unreasonable, wherever feasible) to invite a group representing the membership (and usually appointed by the trustees) to study each proposal package, sit in on the final presentation and discussion, and either advise the publisher or *actually make the decision themselves* by voting on the project.

By requiring disciplined execution of both the inter-functional feasibility evaluation and the decision-to-publish procedures described above, then, the publisher can enforce both the corporate mission statement and the prevailing financial strategy (as translated into finance's pre-pricing "multiplier") without unduly interfering in the intricate work of the acquisition function.

Chapter 19
Contract Negotiation and Substantive Editing

Finally, in the work of the series editor, we come once again to the question of how much bargaining leeway should be allowed in contract negotiations. We've said before, and will say again, that not only the terms of the basic contract, but the ground rules for amending that contract, should be subject to financial discipline. Liabilities for future royalties cannot be reduced by the whims of budget-makers; they are solid legal obligations.

Publishers are caught between a double pressure for lower prices on the one hand, and the resulting lower revenue (to cover their investment, operating costs, and profit goals) after discounts and royalties on the other. As they negotiate with authors, acquiring editors are not usually in a position to keep those interacting pressures in sharp focus. They must, therefore, accept the more detached guidance of the business/finance function to avoid putting the house into no-win situations.

These editors will find that if they *use* the remoteness of such financial judgments in their negotiation with authors—by simply insisting that they're required to refer *any* change in the proposed contract to top management for review— much of the awkwardness of negotiating contract details evaporates. It's reasonable for the editor-in-chief or publisher to make an on-the-spot decision about any truly insignificant departure from the basic (or most recent) contract which an author or agent requests—but significant changes should always be run through a core management group meeting, assuring that all functions will be properly forewarned of anything that affects them.

So the series editor does not face a very complicated negotiating process. It's largely a matter of offering first-timers the basic contract, and established authors the same terms as their last contract, and then referring any exceptions they may propose "up the ladder" to the publisher and the core management group.

After the contract is signed, it is foolhardy for an acquisition editor to simply sit and wait for the manuscript to turn up. The very letter that formally acknowledges the deal should confirm the target publication season (which one assumes has already been discussed during the negotiations—after the series editor identified which strategy model blank the project was nominated to fill). Along with that reminder, the editor should specify to the author a target date (within the delivery terms of the contract) necessary to get the project onto the pre-press development schedule (Figure 9d) at a timely point. And this is a good time to re-iterate your plea that the author not include any unnecessary formatting on the word processed manuscript disk—since you'll just have to take most of it out, to avoid confusing your desktop system. Finally, this letter should routinely conclude with a request by the editor for a rough schedule of the writer's intentions.

Then, sometime about 6 months before the target manuscript delivery date, the editor should phone the author (or at the very least, write) to inquire how things are progressing—and offer any feasible help or encouragement. At that 6-months-prior point, unless the author seems to have the project well in hand, the editor should start calling more often (perhaps every month)— making reference both to the contract delivery date, and to the likelihood of a publication delay of a season or more if the target date is not met.

Editors should make sure writers understand (and are occasionally reminded) that these delivery dates refer not only to the basic manuscript—but to any supplements/appendices, illustrations and permissions for use of other writers' words. The acquisition editor who considers persistent nagging of a reluctant author to be "beneath his dignity" is probably doing an injustice to both the writer and the publishing house.

Along with that manuscript, the author normally has the responsibility (under the contract) for documenting the written permission of confirmed copyright holders for any use of copyright-protected material in the prospective new book. Sponsoring editors must be careful to see that such documentation, as it arrives, is preserved in the permanent file for that book.

But the publishing house then finds itself on the other end of this process—as other writers for other publishers seek permission to use material from its books in their manuscripts. Since income from such permissions is normally negligible, responsibility for processing routine "rights and permissions" requests—whose main impact is to *protect* your rights from abuse—is usually left in the acquisition function (the negotiators and "keepers" of the contracts). A well-organized acquisition department assigns specific responsibility to someone (usually an administrative assistant, or each series editor) for screening all such requests, making routine responses when established policy applies (including requirements for nominal payment), referring exceptional cases to the editor-in-chief for special handling (*including transfer of serious subsidiary rights negotiations to the marketing department*), and maintaining a permanent file of all permissions granted to others. This permanent file can become invaluable in demonstrating that one has diligently defended a copyright which others contend has (by unchallenged misuse) slipped into the public domain.

"Permissions" are not normally requested if the author believes the intended usage is covered by the somewhat ambiguous "Fair Use Doctrine" set forth in Section 107 of the U. S. Copyright Act of 1976. This established the right of others to quote from a work—within reason—in appropriate critical reviews, news reports, legislative proceedings, etc., or for the purpose of illustrating the views of an author being discussed by another writer. Custom suggests that such "fair use" should never exceed 200 words—and some lawyers think that's stretching it; after that, we're talking about serious subsidiary rights.

The marketing and negotiation of subsidiary rights deals for serious re-use of book materials in other editions or media is properly a marketing function (see Chapter 32). But the "Rights and Permissions" administrator in the acquisition department is often given responsibility not only for permitting free use of materials (with appropriate credits) within established policy limits, but for completing routine transactions for nominal usage at a modest fee. Something on the order of 5¢ per word for the first half-million estimated readership (thus, an absolute minimum of $15 a page), plus 1¢ per 100,000 additional anticipated readers, is appropriate.

When the raw manuscript with necessary permissions is finally in hand, the series editor's focus shifts to helping the author improve that manuscript by changes in its organization and/or contents. It should *not* be necessary to rewrite major portions for an unliterary author; any professional series/acquisition editor should have spotted that problem in the screening process—and suggested (and helped find) a ghost writer if the project merited such assistance.

To help them sort the substantive editing forest from the copy editing trees, experienced sponsoring editors subject each incoming manuscript to the fastest initial reading they can accomplish (only bothering to correct obvious grammatical errors that don't slow them down). They make brief notes after each chapter as to what was accomplished in that segment, and what problems they are experiencing (as a reader) at that point. Then they go back over those notes when they've finished, and ask themselves whether the manuscript could be improved by presenting the material in a different sequence. They consider the impact of adding or deleting information at critical points. They consult reference books or telephone available advisors if (despite the preliminary screening) they now question the reliability of any of the text.

Then the substantive changes they believe would improve the book are itemized in a memo to the author—keyed to manuscript page numbers. The editor should give the author only a few days to ponder those suggestions (not enough time to descend into a "blue funk" writing block!), and then telephone (or make a face-to-face appointment) for discussion of each point. While listening carefully to the author's defenses, the editor must stand her ground if she thinks real weaknesses of the manuscript are being ignored or denied. Remember, if your contract is properly prepared, the author can't force you to go to press without satisfactory revisions.

Only after these substantive issues have been thrashed out, and the actual changes have been made in the physical manuscript, should anybody worry about the spelling and punctuation. Certainly the series editor should make corrections (on hard copy or the computer) when he sees obvious errors—but the basic work of correcting spelling, punctuation, grammar and syntax belongs not in acquisition, but with the copy editing perfectionists of the pre-press development function.

But—beyond proposal solicitation and screening, negotiation of contracts with authors, and recommendation to authors of substantive revisions in their manuscripts—the series editor's responsibility still does not end when the book is turned over to pre-press for final polishing. Throughout the process—before contracting, and even after formal publication, as long as the book remains on the active list—the acquiring editor (or that editor's successor) should function as the author's bridge to (and spokesperson with) the other functions of the publishing house.

It is seldom a good idea to give authors direct access to these other functions (even the pre-press copy editors), since they're often inclined to pressure those functions (especially marketing) for expenditures of time and money that cannot be justified on the basis of probable results. Dealing with the sensitive diplomacy of such situations is best left to the person who knows each author best—his sponsoring acquisition editor.

Once substantive changes in the raw manuscript are completed, the most essential role of the sponsoring series editor is to keep the author informed. In the post-manuscript, *pre-publication* period, writers are somewhat like new fathers in old-fashioned maternity wards: they know they had a major role in the act of creation, but nobody has much use for them at the moment. The pre-press managing editor rushing toward a bound book date, the marketing manager intent on getting the new title off to a fast start, the business manager buried in a hundred other royalty accounts, will only be disrupted and irritated by authors' "great ideas" or pleas for information. So it is the series editor (who has a major stake in keeping the author happy until the next book is contracted) who must find time to keep track of vital information about the progress of each book, and relay that information to the writer.

Editors (as well as authors) can seriously disrupt other segments of the publishing team by inappropriate interference. In the most effective publishing houses, publishers (aided by editors-in-chief) work to engender mutual respect by each function for the professionalism of all other functions. When this happens, editors learn to trust their colleagues to provide the non-acquisition support each book needs *without* their (or the author's) nagging. The result is usually an improvement in both morale and performance.

But there is a place for editorial nagging! Few things disrupt publishing houses as frequently or as frustratingly as authors who misbehave when they get proofs of their forthcoming books. Most of the disruptions stem from two problems: failure of an author to return those proofs with corrections by the stated deadline (to which the rest of the complex production schedule is geared), and the tendency of authors to second-guess themselves by engaging in extensive rewriting (rather than simply and properly correcting typographic errors) during the proofreading process. The series editor owes it to the rest of the publishing team to prevent these disruptions, insofar as possible. It is one of the most difficult tasks that confront such editors.

The first thing editors must do to reduce this problem to manageable proportions is to establish a climate of respect for deadlines among their authors. (This will help get manuscripts completed, as well as proofs returned.) Begin with the author guidelines brochure, and all other forms of prepared instructions for contracted writers. State clearly that failure to abide by deadlines may mean necessary removal of the book from its place on the production schedule—and thus a substantial delay in publication. Point out that this can have a serious negative impact on the marketing program—which cannot aggressively promote books unless it is sure of their timely availability.

It is customary in most publishing houses to show proofs of initial type-setting (those "rough pages" referred to on line 22 of Figure 9d) to authors, so they can assure themselves that the finished product will be correct. (And publishers get a lot of good, free proofreading of those rough pages by doing so!) But series editors must make sure that all proofs that go to authors are accompanied by firm deadlines—and by a stern reminder that non-compliance (or excessive rewriting) can delay (or even prevent) publication. Editors-in-chief should make sure their series editors have the backing (and disciplined insistence) of the publisher for such statements.

The fact of the matter is that disciplining authors is not really as difficult as the editorial community has made it appear. Many editors simply *never try;* their proper concern with keeping those authors happy (for the next book!) makes them more willing to risk upsetting the copy editor or marketing manager than the writer. But such an attitude displays an unprofessional lack of respect for ones colleagues, which no publisher can tolerate without serious consequences.

So what does the series editor do with an author after those proofs do come back—and the presses are rolling? No time is as excruciating for the creative personality as this. Nervous writers are frequently paranoid writers, and editor-author relationships can suffer lasting damage at this stage unless the editor creates a new focus of mutual attention.

Veteran acquisition editors believe that this is the appropriate time to start talking about the author's next book. They let all that author second-guessing they discouraged during proofreading come to the fore now—and redirect the nervous energy a writer might use to disrupt your marketing department into creating an outline proposal for another book.

In fact, at this time when author and editor have reached the peak of a significant mutual experience, it is often easy to go beyond the next book and lay the foundations for a long-term publishing relationship. The most effective basis for that relationship is the expressed interest of the publisher (via the series editor) in the writing *career* of the author. The editor need only inquire, now that there's time for reflection, whether the writer has a long range agenda of other prospective books. She might even point out that such an agenda can be a useful focus for the author's professional development and career enhancement.

We won't belabor the point. But consider making it routine procedure for each series editor to conclude each author's work on a book (after the proofs are cleared) by such an inquiry into long range literary aspirations. Point out (without guaranteeing!) ways the publishing house might help showcase the evolution of that writer's works—assuming, of course, that they continue to have relevance to your acquisition strategy—by promoting book reviews, speaking engagements, magazine excerpts, etc.

Getting involved this way in the career aspirations of the author pool is one of the best things a small, independent publisher can do to impede the efforts of the big houses to lure away its best, hard-won writers.

PART IV
Pre-Press Development

CHAPTER 20
Anticipating a Basic Production Strategy

Managers of small publishing houses are sometimes uncomfortable talking about strategies for each of their basic functions—because they instinctively feel that "strategy" is complicated stuff only appropriate to the big publishing combines, but unnecessary in their own seat-of-the-pants managerial environment. But as we've said before, strategy—which essentially means simplifying the big picture so you can understand, communicate, and more-easily manipulate its components—is more important to small organizations (with their narrow margins for error) than to big ones.

Perhaps no place in the publishing process can small but on-going errors of judgment cost you as much as in the basic pattern by which you convert raw manuscripts into bound books (invoking a total cost-stream likely to consume a third of the house's total cash flow!). So before you set the structure and basic procedures of your pre-press development function into concrete, it behooves you to think through the sequence of major steps as well as the physical nature of the end products—which you envision for this conversion process.

We might as well be up-front about saying that, in the current "state of the art" of normal book publishing, most independent publishers make a grave mistake if they don't *insist* that the person primarily responsible for pre-press development learn the ins-and-outs of "desktop publishing"—really desktop *page-generation* from special PC software that combines typographics and page layout. A total installation (computer plus software plus basic peripherals) for utilizing this new technology can be leased for under $500 monthly—so if you're publishing at least three or four books a year, it'll more than pay for itself in composition savings. And it gives you much better control of pre-press projects than when manuscripts have to be "sent out" for design or typesetting—or when cumbersome paste-up is required.

The rest of this chapter will assume you agree. But even if you don't, the necessity (and the procedure) we're proposing for the definition of a coherent "production strategy" will still be applicable to the organization of your pre-press development function.

When you think about what has to happen, between the author's commitment of words to paper (or disk) and the printer's shipment of finished-goods inventory, your answers to 12 questions will, in effect, shape that basic "production strategy." Those questions are:

1) Who'll do most of that necessary, laborious key-punching?
2) How will we minimize redundancies while assuring reasonable accuracy in correcting the manuscript?
3) How will we introduce the necessary graphic design into the manuscript?
4) Who will do the actual typesetting?
5) What kind(s) of reproduction masters will we turn over to the printer?
6) What kind(s) of binding will best suit our needs?
7) Who will do the printing and binding?
8) Who will provide the paper?
9) How will we assure printing quality and timeliness?
10) In what manner should the finished books be delivered to us?
11) What range of print quantities will we normally assume?
12) How will we anticipate needs for reprinting?

There is certainly more than one good combination of right answers to these questions—depending on the size of your program, the end-usage envisioned for your books, and even the experience and technical know-how of your staff. But the majority of independent publishing houses getting good results at low costs tend to answer them somewhat as follows:

(1) *Who will do most of that necessary, laborious key-punching?* This was as much as half of the typesetting cost—and perhaps a fourth of all pre-press costs—in the traditional way of "making books" before the era of the electronic manuscript. Now, for a major portion of the books published each year, there is *no* cost to the publisher—because it's done by the author, on his word processor. It's not inappropriate to suggest in your author guidelines brochure that, all other things being equal, you're more receptive to manuscripts that will be delivered on a disk (using some popular word processing program that can easily be converted to the one you use) than you are to projects that don't have this "production head start." Some publishers even offer authors a modest royalty increase (say half-a-percent) if their manuscripts conform.

Obviously, then, it behooves your pre-press managing editor to investigate available software programs (which sometimes cost less than $100) for converting other popular word processing texts to the program you use. At the same time, you should explore optical scanners—peripheral equipment that will copy a typed or computer-printout manuscript (and any line art) right into your desktop files.

(2) *How will we minimize redundancies while assuring reasonable accuracy in correcting the manuscript?* The key lies in plotting a sequence of changes-of-responsibility that moves the manuscript from raw (though substantively-correct) form to whatever the printer will need in as few steps as feasible. The sequence small publishing houses that are adept at desktop page generation usually find most effective (without running unrealistic copy editing perfectionism into the ground) goes something like this:

a) As soon as the manuscript arrives, get it onto the basic word processing system (by conversion, scanning, or even re-keying), so that all substantive-editing changes can be incorporated as they are decided. (If extensive rewriting is in order, this might wait until the author can send a revised disk.)

b) Enter the project on the pre-press development schedule (see Figure 9d) only when such a complete raw manuscript (whether or not substantively edited) is available for input.

c) Use a formal transmittal or "launch" meeting between acquiring editor and copy editor (plus any kibitzers who'll find it useful) as soon as all substantive-editing changes have been input—to exchange necessary art, locate its best position in the manuscript, obtain the acquiring editor's choices for all basic design (page layout and type-choice) options, and answer questions about the specifics of the project.

d) Complete a fast copy-edit on the word processor (with a little help from the spell-checker!)—while also inserting such generic codes and art-locations as will be helpful to the desktop page-generating operator, so the interpretation of those codes can be checked during subsequent editing.

e) Import the word processing manuscript file into the desktop page-generating computer/system, and provide "roughly paged" print-outs to the copy editor (project manager) and to the acquiring editor (usually for forwarding to the author). Specify the scheduled deadline for any corrections from the acquiring editor or author. (Conventional acquisition editors may be horrified at showing the author something no more final than this, as his last look at the manuscript, which he's already had months to perfect. But that author's natural anxieties will give you some good—free—help with the copy editing and proof reading at this stage ... and it's better to get that *now* than at the last minute. A wise publisher will support the managing editor who contends that assuring the author he's had the *very last say* on minute details by waiting until later to show proofs—or needlessly repeating the process—is neither practical, nor a proper encumbrance on the pre-press drive for economy and on-time completion.)

f) Now perform a very careful "slow" copy edit (while the author is independently "doing his thing" with his set of rough pages)—not only making additional corrections, but appropriately adjusting positions of illustration

g) Prepare end-product printing specs (in consultation with, or subject to the approval of, the pre-press manager), and request bids from at least three appropriate printers.

h) Use another meeting of the acquiring editor and the copy editor (project manager) to review (via their marked-up "rough page" hard copies) all corrections proposed by the author or either editor—with the acquiring editor as the final arbiter of which proposed changes/corrections will be accepted.

i) Input agreed changes/corrections into the desktop file, and print out final pages for (quick!) inspection by acquiring and copy editors. (Since that nervous author has already had a shot at it—verifying agreed changes from the "Step h" hard copy should constitute all of the proof-reading normally needed with a desktop system.)

j) Obtain cover graphics from marketing (or another specified source), and order any necessary color separations.

k) Generate final repro material (disk copy or laser page print-out) on desktop system.

l) Deliver final repro materials (including art) and printers' bids to the print buyer for use in her inventory purchase procedure.

(3) *How will we introduce the necessary graphic design into the manuscript for text formatting?* We've recommended elsewhere that responsibility for cover graphics (really an "ad") be delegated to the marketing function; they'll do it better than anyone else! Fundamentally, the design of the *interior* pages is largely a matter of (1) telling the computer, through the desktop program, exactly when and how to change specifications (size, font, etc.) of the type it is currently, electronically "setting"—every time one letter in the manuscript (including headings) bears a different specification than the one before it, and (2) telling the computer how much blank space to leave—at what point in the manuscript—for each illustration. We'll examine a detailed process for accomplishing all of this in Chapter 23.

(4) *Who will do the actual typesetting?* It will come as no surprise by this point that this author believes *your own desktop operator* should do most of the typesetting, for most books, for most publishers. Fairly inexpensive laser printers now produce pages of such high resolution that only a super-critic with a magnifying glass can find rough edges—and readers don't care anyhow! But if you do insist on using external vendors (for distinct type selections,

etc.), bargain with them first about how much money you can save by coding word processed manuscripts to instruct their computers.

(5) *What kind(s) of reproduction masters will we turn over to the printer?* The traditional standard for the industry has been to give the printer *camera-ready pages* (from your laser printer, an external image-setter, or paste-up), plus illustration halftones or color separations to be striped into designated locations. But today, most major book manufacturers (printers) can prepare their plates from disk-copies of your desktop files. It certainly behooves you to investigate which printers can do this—and include several in your bidding pool—to determine whether you can save steps (and money) by using the finished laser print-out pages only for your final internal check, and sending the printer a copy of the desktop disk.

(6) *What kind(s) of binding will best suit our needs?* An overwhelming proportion (better than 80 percent) of independent publishers' books are produced as "trade paperbacks"—roughly 5⅝ x 8 inches. But metropolitan newspaper book reviewers, and a few libraries, are still gun-shy about paperbacks—so a few publishers do modest hardcover first editions (followed 6 months later by paperbacks), or separately bind 500 sets of sheets as hardcovers (with or without dust jackets) just for the reviewers and picky libraries. However, expensive reference books, or "coffee-table" volumes with four-color interiors, are frequently done in hard covers only—to help justify their price tags. Classroom and field-reference materials are sometimes more usable with wire bindings or looseleaf covers. Determine what your normal pattern will be *before* you start identifying your potential printer-pool, developing printing specs, making cost estimates, etc.

(7) *Who will do the printing and binding?* In Chapter 38, we'll get more specific about procedures for buying printing. But in your basic strategy, it should be assumed (and decreed) that you *won't tie yourself to any one printer (no matter how good) as a "captive account"*—but will systematically and openly solicit competitive bids to make sure that even the most satisfactory of vendors don't start taking you for granted.

(8) *Who will provide the paper?* Every reputable book manufacturer maintains a basic inventory of popular paper stocks appropriate to most books. And no matter how much you expect to buy, they're always buying in much larger quantities—which means that even after they mark it up, their paper usually costs you less than any you buy direct from the paper-maker. But even more importantly, when you buy your own paper and something goes wrong— or the printer wastes an unusual amount—it's almost inevitably *your* paper (not covered by the printer's price) that is blamed for the problem. Unless you're *very* sure of what you're doing, follow the lead of 95 percent of other independent publishers and *let the printer supply the paper.*

(9) *How will we assure printing quality and timeliness?* The most important thing you can do is to specify any delivery dates or particular quality issues that concern you, in a letter acknowledging acceptance of the winning printer's

bid, and insist that his rep initial those conditions before getting the job. (More about that in Chapter 38.) But you can also assure better quality by making sure you've built into your schedule time to check the printer's "blues" showing exactly what's going on each page; this may cost you a week and perhaps $50—but it's good insurance *unless* you're very familiar with and sure of the chosen printer. Since book covers are the source of most quality problems, you should also be insistent on seeing color proofs of all covers before the run is printed ... and you should consider spending an extra nickel or dime a book for cover lamination or extra-tough stock. (Recently, printers have been especially enthusiastic about a new "lay-flat" lamination process for paperback covers.) And you should build into your procedures for accepting deliveries from printers a random spot-check of representative cartons or skid-sections, before you approve the bill. As long as you haven't paid for the job (and refuse to), you'll get cooperation in adjusting for printer errors; after you've paid—satisfaction comes much harder.

(10) *In what form should the finished books be delivered to us?* For ease of handling in small storage areas, and minimum damage as stock is moved from truck to warehouse to picking line, most independent publishers prefer to have the printer deliver books in stencil-marked cartons. But if your normal print runs are large enough, and your warehouse handling equipment is adequate, you may be able to save money and handling time by eliminating the cartons in favor of large skids. In either case, you can prevent wear-and-tear on books (especially those with sensitive covers) by spending a few extra cents per unit to have them separately shrink-wrapped in transparent film. If you're marketing supplemental bulk-use items (such as student handouts, or tests) with your books, it's especially advantageous to have those shrink-wrapped in various quantity-selections (10, 25, etc.) to save laborious counting when orders are filled.

(11) *What range of print quantities will we normally assume?* Your pre-press preparations and total production process will function most smoothly if you generally anticipate working within a pool of familiar printers (though you should always leave a true competitive opening for newcomers to break into that pool). But before you select candidates for that pool, you should match not only their favorite press dimensions, but their interest in jobs of a given size (such as 1000-1500 book "real short runs") to your needs and preferences. That means making some preliminary assessment of the probable quantities you're most likely to be ordering.

(12) *How will we anticipate needs for reprinting?* Does the printer who manufactured each initial run of a book automatically get all orders for reprints of that title? When it's as simple as recopying a desktop disk (or making sure each printer returns your camera-ready laser pages as soon as he's "shot" them), you're in a position to realistically solicit competitive bids on reprints as well as initial runs. If the original printer saved plates (because you warned him of a potential quick reprint) or film, he's got an advantage in

such bidding. However, if you "gang" reprints for several books initially manufactured by several different printers—you may be able to save enough to more than offset that advantage.

CHAPTER 21
Organizing and Managing On-Time Pre-Press Development

With those 12 leading questions from the previous chapter well-aired, you're ready to begin organizing (or re-organizing) another of the four basic functions of the publishing process—pre-press development of such books as have been contracted and substantively-shaped by the acquisition function. General responsibility for organizing this function is commonly vested in the pre-press managing editor—one of the members of the core management group (publisher, acquisition editor-in-chief, managing editor, marketing manager, business/finance manager) who essentially "run" the publishing house. In well organized book publishing enterprises, that individual's responsibilities look something Figure 21a on the next page.

In small publishing houses, the managing editors usually function more than half-time as the star copy editors (and project managers), in addition to managing the over-all function; sometimes they operate the desktop system as well. Their principal managerial chores consist of making and monitoring new title development schedules for each book, preparing printing specifications and obtaining printing bids prior to handing finished projects over to the print-buyer, assigning and supervising copy editors (project managers) and desktop operators in the execution of the 12-step pre-press sequence outlined (under Question 2) in the previous chapter, and recruiting and training new copy editors and desktop operators as needed.

How many copy editors and desktop operators the department will need depends on the number of book projects envisioned for the year ahead. If the managing editor is insistent about developing a smooth, non-redundant pre-press sequence like our 12-step example, and defending the department from having to do acquisition's author-tending chores, a good copy editor (and project manager) can keep up with two series (acquisition) editors—and that means delivering some 5,000 finished pages per year (about two books a month) to the print buyer. A good desk-top operator can probably keep up with two copy editors—cranking out up to 10,000 pages per year. Having sprung from pre-cybernetic times, this author has been absolutely amazed at

Figure 21a—Sample Job Description: Pre-Press Manager

TITLE: Managing Editor
Salary Grade: E
Reports to: Publisher
Coordinates with:
>Other Core Managers
>Series Editors

Directly supervises:
>Copy Editors
>Desktop Operators
>Administrative Assistant

Budget line responsibilities: Line 422-435 (Pre-Press Dept.)
Accountability Indices:
>Average Days Camera-Ready Delay
>Average Total Pre-Press Cost per Camera-Ready Page

GENERAL RESPONSIBILITY

To arrange and supervise the timely, cost-effective transformation of all substantively-edited manuscripts into camera-ready pages, with necessary art and color separations.

SPECIFIC OPERATING RESPONSIBILITIES

a) To provide accurate cost estimates for copy-editing and pre-press page production of proposed books;

b) To initiate, monitor, and execute the New Title Development Schedule for each forthcoming product;

c) To recruit and train copy-editors and desktop operators, and perform periodic performance and pay reviews of same;

d) To maintain an adequate pool of free-lance copy editing, proof-reading, illustration, indexing, and similar contacts;

e) To establish a selection of typographic styles for interior formatting and composition of all forthcoming books;

f) To supervise any necessary external typesetting and color separation;

g) To provide printing specifications to an appropriate selection of vendors, and solicit manufacturing bids, for utilization by the print buyer;

h) To forward camera-ready pages or completed disk-files for the printers to the print buyer.

i) To arrange for an adequate reference library, and circulate appropriate periodical subscriptions, to assure staff familiarity with significant trends, developments, and new technology relative to pre-press manuscript processing and page production;

j) To personally attend, and encourage staff participation in, an appropriate schedule of industry seminars, association activities, and other forums for the enhancement of professional knowledge, skills, and productivity;

k) To propose budgets for pre-press staffing and related expenses;

l) To become sufficiently familiar with the responsibilities and procedures of the Publisher to be able to function in that capacity should the need arise;

m) To represent the concerns of the pre-press development function in the core management group.

the page-generating capacity of the two- and three-person pre-press departments of some of the best-organized desktop-era publishing houses with whom he works.

But the department should only staff to a level for which it is absolutely assured it will have full-time work. This suggests that if you're doing less than ten books a year, the managing editor should be able (with occasional freelance help) to handle virtually all of the pre-press development work alone. And not until about 20 books a year will you probably have *full time* pre-press work for both a managing editor and a copy editor. It may take 30 books a year to justify adding a full-time desktop operator (by which time you may also need another copy editor); until then, if you can't find a part-timer, the copy editor(s) may have to handle the keyboard. For the interim levels— between new staff additions—enterprising managing editors accumulate (and budget for) pools of freelancers to supply in-house capacity on an as-needed, part-time basis.

Because the two types of basic pre-press page-generators (copy editors and desktop operators) are in steady demand in all kinds of offices—and because these are not the star strategic roles in most publishing houses—there is considerable turnover in these positions. For that reason, managing editors need to equip themselves with quick-start recruiting programs (pre-written classified ads, second-round screening application forms, skill tests, interview outlines) and be prepared to run ads and screen applicants as often as necessary (with as little redundant planning as feasible). And they need to be able to get the recruits into productivity as quickly as possible.

Within the context of small publishing houses, these are both good entry-level positions; managing editors who are willing to do some basic training often have more luck (and spend less money!) recruiting on that basis— seeking inexperienced people with good grammatical/linguistic skills (copy editors) or graphic sense and dexterity (desktop operators ... who are probably also great computer game players) who "want to break into book publishing," and training them from the beginning in the "new technology" of the electronic manuscript.

Some publishers insist that their copy editors must have significant insight into the subject matter of the house's "editorial niche" in order to know whether words are being correctly used, spelled, etc. But that can become a very expensive proposition. Usually, it makes more sense for a highly technical publisher to transfer this burden to the series editor (by asking for a higher level of refinement of the "substantively edited" raw manuscript)—thus leaving the pre-press manager free to recruit their basic (high-turnover) "page generators" from the general population.

To get the new copy editors and desktop operators into productive work as quickly as possible, the managing editor must also develop simple orientation and training procedures—requiring a minimum of the supervisor's time.

The best training seems to be on-the-job familiarization work in some of the simpler aspects of the program. A rookie copy editor might be asked to spend several days just cranking raw manuscripts onto the system (by conversion disk, optical scanner, etc.), and then several weeks doing those first "quick edits" on a number of projects (so a veteran copy editor can judge, on that careful second edit, how well they performed). A beginning desktop operator might simply be assigned to handle the importing of word processor files into the desktop, or monitoring the laser print-out of "rough pages" for the second edit—until they're familiar enough with the system to start translating generic codes into graphic options.

Assigning copy editors as project managers, and allocating sufficient desktop support to each of them, is largely a matter of keeping a running tally of the number of projects in each department member's hands at any given time. Supervising their performances goes hand-in-glove with the managing editor's continuous responsibility for monitoring the New Title Development Schedule (which originally appeared as Figure 9d, but is repeated on the next page as Figure 21b to save wear-and-tear on the book's binding) and negotiating necessary adjustments with the other members of the core management team.

As (and only when) the managing editor is presented with a raw *complete* manuscript (whether or not it's yet substantively edited) does she give the book a place on the development schedule (by adding a new right-hand column to the spreadsheet). In a well-disciplined publishing house, no one is authorized to make any commitments concerning availability dates, prices, etc., until a book is on this schedule.

Then, using the numbers in the second column (which represent the number of days prior to the book's formal publication date by which each step should be completed), the managing editor creates an arbitrary target schedule for that project. The abbreviation before each target-number indicates the department (function) that is responsible for each step. For this exercise, managing editors usually keep 3-year calendars posted somewhere near their desks—but even when arbitrary date-plotting lands some deadlines on Sundays or holidays, those details are easy to adjust as the project nears the relevant point.

Week-by-week, then, the managing editor checks the status of all projects *before* attending the routine core management (department head or "executive committee") meeting. All other core managers should know the status of their departments' assignments on books currently "in the works." Unless routine review of an integrated deadline schedule (see Chapter 8) has already identified problems, the managing editor should use the spreadsheet during the meeting, as a basis for adjusting any dates that have slipped. That means the core managers must, on the spot, agree as to how the lost time will be made up—or acknowledge a change in the targeted (line 46) "bound book" date. Marketing, then, may or may not find it necessary to change the formal

Figure 21b—Sample New Title Development Scheduling Model

	1	2	3	4	5	6	7	8
1	AUTHOR CODE >>>>>	Who/When	Melb	Sinc	Will	Dunb	2nd Sprg	3rd Sprg
2								
3	Raw Ms. Delivered	Acqu-250	1217	0107	0214	0610	0710	0810
4	Dev Schedule Entered	PrPr-245	1222	0112	0219	0615		
5	Input to Word Processor	PrPr-240	1227	0117	0224	0620		
6	Subst Edg Transmitted	Acqu-180	0227	0317	0424	0820		
7	Launch Meeting	Acqu-180	0227	0317	0424	0820		
8	Special Publicity Inputs	Acqu-175	0304	0322	0429	0825		
9	Info/Photo File to Promo	Acqu-175	0304	0322	0504	0830		
10	Interior Art Transmitted	Acqu-170	0309	0327	0509	0904		
11	Title Finalized	Acqu-170	0309	0327	0509	0904		
12	CIP Data Sent	PrPr-165	0314	0401	0514	0909		
13	ABI Data Sent	PrPr-165	0314	0401	0514	0909		
14	Promo Copy Pkg Done	Mark-165	0314	0401	0514	0909		
15	Pre-Page Offer to SubRts	Mark-160	0319	0406	0519	0914		
16	Special Marketing Queries	Mark-160	0319	0406	0519	0914		
17	Author Brochures Offered	Acqu-160	0319	0406	0519	0914		
18	Cover Concept Approved	Mark-160	0319	0406	0519	0914		
19	First Copy-Edit Done	PrPr-160	0319	0406	0519	0914		
20	Page Format Set	PrPr-155	0324	0411	0524	0919		
21	Cover Art Arranged	Mark-155	0324	0411	0524	0919		
22	Rough Pages Ready	PrPr-140	0408	0426	0509	1004		
23	End Papers Inserted	Mark-130	0418	0506	0519	1014		
24	Print Specs Ready	PrPr-125	0423	0511	0524	1019		
25	Printing Bids Invited	PrPr-120	0428	0516	0529	1024		
26	Cover Art Ready	Mark-120	0428	0516	0529	1024		
27	Ads (if any) Placed	Mark-115	0503	0521	0603	1029		
28	Second Edit Completed	PrPr-115	0503	0521	0603	1029		
29	Author/Ed Changes Input	PrPr-110	0508	0526	0608	1104		
30	Price/Quantity Check	Bus-105	0523	0611	0623	1119		
31	Final Pages Approved	PrPr-100	0518	0606	0618	1114		
32	Printer Confirmed	Bus-100	0518	0606	0618	1114		
33	Pages to SubRts, Pre-Revs	Mark-95	0523	0611	0623	1119		
34	Repro Disk Ready	PrPr-95	0523	0611	0623	1119		
35	Print Order Sent	Bus-90	0528	0617	0628	1124		
36	Announcement NR#1	Mark-90	0528	0617	0628	1124		
37	ABI Data Updated	Mark-90	0528	0617	0628	1124		
38	Local Store/TV Letters	Mark-85	0603	0622	0703	1129		
39	Blues, Cover Proofs OK	PrPr-75	0613	0702	0713	1209		
40	Announcement NR#2	Mark-75	0613	0702	0713	1209		
41	Inventory File Initiated	Bus-75	0613	0702	0713	1209		
42	Product File Input	Bus-70	0618	0707	0718	1214		
43	Printer Shipments Set	Bus-65	0623	0712	0723	1219		
44	Warehouse Alerted	Bus-60	0628	0717	0728	1224		
45	Comp Labels Ready	Mark-55	0703	0722	0803	1229		
46	Bound Bks Checked In	Bus-50	0708	0727	0808	0103	0201	0301
47	Comps Shipped	Bus-48	0710	0729	0810	0105		
48	Advance Orders Shipped	Bus-45	0713	0801	0813	0108		
49	Editorial Comps Shipped	Bus-40	0718	0806	0818	0113		
50	Copyright Registered	PrPr-25	0803	0821	0902	0128		
51	Printer Art Recovered	PrPr-25	0803	0821	0902	0128		
52	Permanent File Opened	PrPr-20	0808	0826	0907	0203		
53	Store Phoning Finished	Mark-20	0808	0826	0907	0203		
54	Formal Publication Date	Mark-0	0828	0915	0922	0223	0320	0420

publication date (line 54), to give it adequate time to work with "advance copies" (for reviewers, wholesaler stocking, etc.).

Note in Figure 21b (a very small publishing house currently doing only six books a year) how the managing editor has apparently used the spreadsheet to warn acquisition that—if it is to deliver two additional spring titles at the monthly intervals marketing wants—it should have raw manuscripts to input 250 days earlier. These are probably one-person departments, talking to each other very effectively through the New Title Development Schedule.

For the solicitation of printing bids for each book (line 25 on the model schedule), the managing editor (or the business office, if it's assigned to collect its own bids) should maintain a database of approved printers, each of whom is reasonably compatible with the house's "basic production strategy" (Chapter 20). To begin the development of such a pool, you should send a word-processed letter to 20-30 book manufacturers identified from such sources as Bowker's *Literary Market Place* (Appendix 2) and/or Ad-Lib's *Directory of Book Printers* (Appendix 1). Describe your anticipated range of print-quantities, your normal trim (page) sizes and binding requirements, and any special concerns you may have about printers—and ask those who are interested to tell you who (in their organization) should receive your future "invitations to bid" on forthcoming books ... and what you'll have to do to establish credit. (Some will ask for one-third or one-half advance payment on the first job.) Only after any given printer has submitted a potentially-winning bid on one of your book projects need you go to the additional trouble of requesting references and phoning other publishers for whom they've worked.

New printers will seek a place in your pool as they discover you. The process for each of these subsequent additions is the same; they add new horizons to the process. But also keep *eliminating* from this database any printer about whom you get bad reference reports, or with whom you have a bad experience, or from whom you receive out-of-reach quotations on several projects in a row.

For the actual solicitation of bids, add to your word processor file of form letters one that recapitulates your normal printing specifications—telling the manufacturer all he needs to know to give you a quote. Essentially, this means quantities, sizes, paper and ink requirements, binding style, and method of packaging-for-delivery—along with accurate information about how and when you'll deliver to the chosen printer the necessary raw materials: camera-ready pages or computer disk, plus additional art.

You're free to adapt the sample in Figure 21c if you wish.

Figure 21c—Sample Printing-Bid Solicitation

[ON YOUR LETTERHEAD]

8 January 1993

Mr. James James
James Printing Company
4444 James Boulevard
Jamestown, Ohio 44444

Dear Jim:

We are now soliciting bids (for three alternative quantities) on the following book manufacturing job. If you would like to be considered in our selection of a printer for this assignment, we would appreciate receiving your quote and terms by 29 January 1993.

TITLE:	Qnty	Qnty	Qnty
Mars: Duty of a Teacher (208 pgs + cover)	2000	3000	5000

MATERIAL WE'LL PROVIDE:
Camera-ready interior pages (minor line art in place)
2-color line separations for cover

APPROXIMATE DATE MATERIAL WILL BE READY: 25 Feb 1993

BINDING: Perfect-bound paperback

TRIM SIZE: 5⅜" x 8"

INK: Black interior throughout / Two PMS colors each cover

INTERIOR PAPER DESIRED: Your stock groundwood
(Please attach sample to bid)

COVER MATERIAL DESIRED: Your choice two-color, laminated perfect-binding   (Please attach sample to bid)

SPECIAL COVER TREATMENTS: Reverse plate bleed; laminated

PROOFS NEEDED: Pre-press blues of text, plus 50 color cover-proofs

PACKAGING: In marked cartons

Along with your price quote, please give us (1) the approximate number of working days required in your plant for this job, and (2) your non-binding estimate of freight cost for delivery to our warehouse in Fitchburg, MA.

Thank you,

Robert Roberts
Publisher
r/j

Note that the bid request seeks to provide your print buyer with a reasonable range of quantity unit-prices for his eventual press-run decision. It is also feasible (especially with reprints—for which reproduction materials are immediately available) to gang several books into a single bid-request, inviting a lump sum figure for each per-title quantity indicated, to make the job more enticing for the bidders (and its supervision less taxing for the print buyer).

But long before that, with the schedule in place, an effective managing editor delegates pre-press development of each forthcoming book to a copy editor (assuming the house is big enough to have any such delegatees). How that pure soul should best proceed is the focus of the next chapter.

CHAPTER 22
The Copy Editor as Project Manager

As the acquisition function informs the pre-press managing editor that each new, raw manuscript (whether or not substantively edited) is ready to be input to the word processor, responsibility for accomplishing that input, and subsequently steering the book through pre-press development, should be clearly delegated to a specific individual. Among those who'll necessarily be involved, the copy editor is in the best position to serve as a responsible bridge from raw manuscript to camera-ready pages (or finished desktop disk).

Therefore, the wise managing editor assigns a specific copy editor not only to correct spelling, punctuation, grammar and syntax, but to serve as the pre-press project manager for each book. That copy editor's job looks something like Figure 22a on the next page.

Because copy editors are usually out-ranked by acquisition's series editors, there's a tendency in many publishing houses to let the latter unload author hand-holding "dirty work" (getting illustrations and permissions, clearing proofs, etc.) on the former. In this writer's opinion, that is a big mistake which must be prevented by the managing editor—with consistent support by the publisher—if you expect to maximize finished-page productivity (and thus hold down per-page costs) in your pre-press department. And because those costs are properly factored into prices (see Chapter 37)—and projected prices sometimes determine the feasibility of publishing specific books in the first place—it behooves those acquisition editors to stay out of the way (and keep their authors out of the way) of the copy editors (and the desktop operators) once books have moved into their domain.

To generate those approximate 5,000 finished pages a year which we referred to earlier as a plausible (though admittedly ambitious) target for one full-time copy editor (supported by half-a-desktop-operator), the copy editor will have to spend about half of his working hours concentrating hard on those careful "second edits" of each project (assuming six pages an hour). Most of the other half of his time will be divided between fast "first edits," consultation with series editors, clarifying instructions for the desktop operator, and communing with the managing editor about printing specifications, etc.

Figure 22a—Sample Job Description: Copy Editor

TITLE: Copy Editor
Salary Grade: C
Reports to: Managing Editor
Coordinates with:
      Series Editors
      Desktop Operators
Accountability Index:
      Number of first-pass and second-pass pages copy-edited per working hour

GENERAL RESPONSIBILITIES

To serve as pre-press project manager for, and accomplish correction and formatting of, such specific books as are assigned by the Managing Editor.

SPECIFIC OPERATING RESPONSIBILITIES

a) To coordinate with series editors on transmittal of specific manuscripts as assigned by the Managing Editor;

b) To act as general project manager for such assigned manuscripts;

c) To correct syntax, spelling, grammar, and punctuation of assigned manuscripts in first-pass quick-edit (with spell-checker);

d) To query unclear or non-credible passages from such manuscripts to appropriate series editors;

e) To translate series editor's typographical and layout choices into appropriate page-generation codes;

f) To consult with the Managing Editor on the development of printing specifications and solicitation of printing bids on all assigned projects;

g) To accomplish thorough second-pass copy editing of such assigned manuscripts on rough page print-outs—possibly with freelance help;

h) To provide rough page print-outs of all such manuscripts to the appropriate series editors—with deadlines for editorial or author corrections;

i) To review all proposed manuscript corrections, changes and queries with the appropriate series editor;

j) To arrange input of changes approved by said series editor into the electronic manuscript file;

k) To arrange final proof-checking and blues-checking of assigned projects as scheduled;

l) To deliver final and complete reproduction materials on assigned projects to the Managing Editor as scheduled;

m) To establish permanent, consolidated files on all assigned books;

n) To propose appropriate updates of house appendix to officially designated stylebook and graphics options.

Each copy editor will, of course, have a copy of the managing editor's New Title Development Schedule (Figure 21b). Three additional tools will be essential to quality copy editing at reasonable speed: an automated spell-checker component in the basic word processing program, a good reference dictionary (preferably, the one your spell-checker is based on), and a stylebook.

A well-organized pre-press department will officially adopt one of the numerous manuscript stylebooks currently in print as its copy editors' definitive authority on nuances of word usage and structure—both to achieve consistency (especially when using freelance help), and to save hours of supervisory time instructing new editors. (Among other things, it will provide those near-universal correction marks/symbols that copy editors and proof readers use to convey their wishes precisely.) The stylebook most widely adopted by U.S. independent publishers is *The Chicago Manual of Style,* now in its thirteenth edition from the University of Chicago Press, 5801 Ellis Avenue, Chicago, IL 60637.

You should then append to *every copy* of this stylebook in your pre-press department an additional section of guidelines specific to *your* publishing house (peculiarities of capitalization that you prefer, checklists of esoteric symbols important in your subject-area, etc.) You should also append (or keep nearby) looseleaf samples of all the graphic options for finished-page components (text type, subheads, etc.) from which you'll invite sponsoring acquisition editors to pick-and-choose.

In a well-disciplined publishing process, the copy editor only actually performs half of those 12 steps in the development sequence we outlined in Chapter 20. However, as the project manager for a given book, she's also responsible for nagging other people (with support from the managing editor) to see that the other steps are accomplished in a timely manner.

Her first task is to see that the raw manuscript gets onto the word processor (Step 1), while the managing editor is simultaneously working out the scheduling details (Step 2). Inputting the manuscript to the computer system can be as simple as a few seconds of disk-copying, or as complicated as nurse-maiding an optical scanner (or even pounding a keyboard) for several hours. You might also make this the point at which you check for, and remove, any unnecessary formatting codes that may eventually confuse your desktop system. It is for these latter eventualities that some pre-press departments have clerical aides—and others use these as opportunities to give any brand-new copy editing recruits some "system familiarization."

Perhaps the most critical moment in the pre-press phase of each book project is the "launch meeting" (Step 3)—when the acquisition editor finally admits that he and the author are through making substantive changes, and the manuscript is ready for refinement. It is fundamental to sound publishing that no serious copy editing be attempted before this point; otherwise, you'll lose track of "which changes have been copy edited, and which haven't." Many of the typos that eventually get into books are "errors in late copy changes."

A foresighted copy editor will use the launch meeting to make certain whoever is creating the cover art (with positioned type) comes to general agreement with the acquisition editor as to what is appropriate—and formally accepts the New Title Development Schedule deadline (line 26 in Figure 21b) for delivering that art. At the same time, he should anticipate any need for color separations—and be ready to coordinate arrangements for them at Step 12. He must also review the manuscript elements (with the acquisition editor) until he knows everything necessary both to instruct the desktop operator on layout, and to advise the managing editor on printing specifications.

The fast edit (Step 4) of the word processor manuscript file, after the launch meeting, will require some uninterrupted concentration—but the copy editor can get valuable assistance by running the manuscript through the spell-checker program, and this can be done simultaneously with other work (such as a "slow edit" of a different book)—since the computer will only require the editor's intervention when it finds (and stops at) a possible error. Since the fast edit involves basic formatting, it is best done internally rather than by a freelancer. Most contemporary copy editors do it right on the computer screen, without using a hard-copy manuscript.

Importing the file into the desktop page-generation system (Step 5), and using the keyboard to "kick it into rough pages" (with approximate spaces for illustrations) for the author's and copy editor's "slow edits," is properly the responsibility of the desktop operator. But (unless the same individual is performing both functions), it behooves the copy editor to be sociable with that desktop operator—so they can develop their own shorthand to simplify and clarify coding, layout instructions, etc., in keeping with the peculiarities of their specific desktop software.

We won't belabor the critical nature of Step 6—the careful, slow "second edit" of the rough-paged manuscript that is conducted by the copy editor, or parceled out to a dependable freelancer, while the author and acquisition editor are taking their last shot at the same material. As we said earlier, this step alone probably consumes half of the working life of a conscientious, project-managing copy editor—*unless* you pay extra for freelance assistance (in which case, you're entitled to expect considerably *more* than those 5,000 finished pages a year from said project-managing copy editor). These careful second edits are almost always performed on a hard copy of the "rough page" print-outs, since that enables the copy editor to compare notes with the acquiring editor (Step 8) before making definite changes.

Because serious money is at stake in the cost of translating each book into properly-margined, properly-bound book pages (with good reproduction of illustrations, and an effective cover), the managing editor normally plays a major role in preparing the actual printing specifications (see Figure 21c) for each book (Step 7); at any rate, it's an essential collaboration between the project manager (copy editor) and said managing editor. Which of them arranges the simple mechanics of getting word processed bid-invitations out to the pool of printing vendors—so the business office's print buyer won't have to worry about communicating unfamiliar nuances—is not an issue of great importance.

The last point at which the copy editor need devote any significant time to each project is the reconciliation of proposed corrections (and other changes if—tsk!, tsk!—the author insists) with the formatted electronic manuscript in the desktop system (Step 8). This is most effectively accomplished by sitting with the acquiring editor and comparing—page by page—the rough copy print-outs on which both the copy editor and the author (or acquiring editor) worked. The acquiring editor (as the author's representative) should have the "last say" on which changes are actually made—but should be required to make all such decisions "on the spot"; no fair delaying the project at this stage for further consultations with the author.

Then the copy editor only need communicate those changes to the desktop operator for input (Step 9), and see that the final pages (run out on the laser printer, whether or not you intend to actually print from those "camera-ready" pages) are circulated back to the acquiring editor for a quick check. Simultaneously, the copy editor should check those final pages against the marked-up rough pages on which the desktop operator was given the final corrections. (In most publishing houses, this is all of the formal "proof reading" needed.)

The copy editor's only role in Step 10 is to nag the assigned party (hopefully, marketing) to deliver the cover art on time. Step 11—generating actual reproduction materials (high-resolution laser print-out, or a computer disk) for the printer is a technical process fully within the desktop operator's domain.

Finally, in Step 12, the copy editor (as project manager) need only gather up those basic reproduction materials, along with all related art (including the cover), and the printing bids (unless the managing editor took care of those)—and deliver the package to the managing editor—who'll put them into the hands of her colleague the business manager. If color separations are required (and you don't choose to leave that detail to the printer), clear responsibility for ordering them should also be determined at this point. And then the copy editor "wraps up" the project by establishing a "permanent file" for the book—though the New Title Development Schedule may provide subsequent reminders for a few minor chores like registering the copyright.

Publishing houses differ in assigning responsibility for putting each book "on the record" by obtaining for it an identifying International Standard Book Number (ISBN), Cataloging-in-Publication (CIP) data for the verso page, and formal copyright registration. Whether these steps are to be performed by the acquisition editor or the copy editor is an issue that must be thrashed out (by the publisher, editor-in-chief, and managing editor) during preparation of the New Title Development Scheduling Model (Figure 21b). Whoever does it, the basic mechanics of these three tasks are:

(1) *ISBN Registration:* Assuming you've already registered your publishing program with the International Standard Book Numbering Agency (which for U.S. publishers is maintained by R. R. Bowker Company, at 121 Chanlon Road, New Providence, NJ 07974), the responsible individual must see that each book is assigned a permanent identification number under the ISBN system (so it can always be identified and tracked to its source by bibliographers, booksellers, etc.). These numbers are actually assigned by the ISBN agency, which must calculate a control digit (to be added to your publisher prefix and the book's identifying number) that aids computerized systems in discovering processing errors. When you obtain your publisher-identifying prefix on original registration with the system, and periodically thereafter, the agency will give you a sequence of such numbers for use on your near-future books (even before they're titled); then you need only report back to them the actual titles you've assigned to each number in the sequence.

(2) *Cataloguing in Publication:* The Cataloguing in Publication Division of the Library of Congress (Washington, DC 20540) was once eager to not only preassign an LC subject/author code number to each of your forthcoming new books, but to provide the bibliographic information needed for library card files so that you can print it on the verso (back) of the title page. This enables libraries to enter the book into their index system so readers can find it— without their having to spend time (or use a processing service) to develop the indexing data. Any publishing house with serious ambitions to sell to libraries that does not take advantage of this opportunity, is thumbing its nose at the library market. Unfortunately, the Library of Congress now contends it's too understaffed to offer such service to additional new small publishers— so you may have to ask them for suggestions as to where else you can get it done.

(3) *Copyright Registration:* Under the Copyright Act of 1976, books do not slip into the public domain because of failure to register copyrights, as they previously did. But persistent failure to include a copyright notice on the verso of the title page certainly undermines the rights of author and publisher. And failure to follow through by registering that copyright with the Library of Congress makes it virtually impossible to recover prior damages when a copyright infringement is discovered. So for the very modest fee involved, prompt registration of the copyright as soon as each book comes off the press (with due notice of that copyright on the back of the title page) should be an automatic routine in any publishing house. You can get the forms and instructions you need from the Register of Copyrights, Library of Congress, Washington, DC 20559.

Chapter 23
Desktops, Designers, and Outside Typesetters

A very few years back, it was not uncommon for a small publisher to pay a freelance designer or studio $1,000 or more to create typesetting specifications, and paste up the finished type for a typical book—while paying an external typesetter perhaps $2,000 to set that type (even when it was delivered on a word processed disk). This meant per-page costs of $10-15 just to produce the image-masters (camera-ready pages) from which the printer would work—in addition to copy-editing costs for correcting and "marking up" the manuscript.

Today, a single in-house "desktop operator" (working full time—with two adjacent work stations so she can move back and forth between two projects simultaneously) can crank out the finished pages and reproduction disks for 40-50 books a year, at a total cost (including salary and equipment lease) of about $1,000 a book—often under $5 per page! While you can find a wide range of software for accomplishing this (on either DOS-based computers or "Macs"), the two programs that have proven most popular with small publishing houses over the past few years have been *Pagemaker* (for its simplicity) and *Ventura Publisher* (for its versatility).

Since design specifications in a well-organized pre-press department come from the "graphics option samples" appendage to the style book—all worked out in advance by the managing editor, for book-by-book choices by the acquiring editors, and code-translation by the copy editors (project managers)—there simply will be *no book designer* needed in the pre-press development of the vast majority of books published this year. And because good basic desktop systems provide ample type variety ... and relatively inexpensive laser printers now generate finished pages with a resolution of 600 dots-per-square-inch ... and more-and-more printing plants can make their plates directly from disk-copies of your desktop files instead of "camera-ready" pages—the external typesetting vendor is also rapidly becoming unnecessary to most small publishing houses.

Essentially replacing them (at much less cost) is that amazing "new kid on the block" in the pre-press department, the desktop operator. This author suspects that the best ones developed their skills as whiz-kids in computer game competitions; the dexterity with which they change images on a computer screen with keyboard or "mouse" can be downright disconcerting to an old veteran of conventional page preparation. And as they become adept at importing images from their optical scanners and associated "graphics packages"—new horizons open before you. Many are able to create fantastic cover designs right there on their PCs—and the folks who should know assure us they'll be routinely incorporating halftones and color separations *right into the desktop files* in a very few years!

Essentially, their work on each manuscript project imported into their desktop system from the word processor resolves itself down to two challenges: (1) telling the computer when/how to change type specifications as the manuscript proceeds from one coded element to another (basic text to caption to chapter heading, and back to basic text, etc.), and (2) leaving the right amount of blank space in the right location for each of the illustrations (some of which will eventually be "scanned" right into the file, others separately stripped into the blank spots by the printer, on his pre-plate film).

Some pre-press managers still insist on pasting up pages one-by-one, from repros of galley type, so they can have random placement of artwork in relation to type. That's a high price to pay for a relatively unimportant result! In such cases, it behooves the publisher to re-inquire periodically: "Haven't you folks learned yet how to tell your desktop operator where to leave the blank spaces?" But if you're still in that old-fashioned mode, most of what we'll say below about communicating type and layout specifications to a desktop operator is applicable to instructing an external typesetting vendor. You'll find numerous such vendors listed in Bowker's *Literary Market Place* (Appendix 2), and building a competitive pool of them is similar to building your printer pool (see Chapter 38).

It's really not all that complicated. The key to both of the above challenges is a good system of generic codes that signal the desktop operator, or an external typesetter's computer, when to change from one type specification to another—and where to leave how much blank space. Figure 23a, on the next page, covers most of the graphics options you'll need for most books.

The graphics coordinator (usually the pre-press managing editor) who developed this set of codes chose double-reverse-slashes to signal the computer, typesetter, or whomever that "here comes a change in your instructions"; don't set these (coding) keystrokes as type until after next (code-ending) double-reverse-slash." (It's important that you use, for this signal, some keyboard element or combination that you never expect to have appear as a normal part of manuscript text—so the computer will *always* know it's a change-signal.) Some desktop software packages, and most external typesetting vendors, have generic codes of their own for many elements—and those should be incorporated into or consolidated with your basic codes, to save some steps. And some desktop or vendor computers will translate any codes you give them automatically, and follow the instructions (using the type faces and sizes, line-lengths, leadings, etc., which the operator has indicated for each code). Most small publishers, however, simply depend on the desktop operator to read-and-follow, and then remove, these instructions as they occur.

Figure 23a—Sample Checklist of Generic Codes

IN BASIC TEXT-PAGE FORMAT:

\\00\\ = leave 1 page blank
\\01\\ = leave 1 line blank
\\02\\ = leave 2 lines blank
\\03 .. 09\\ = leave indicated number of lines blank
\\10\\ = switch to specified main-text type
\\11\\ = switch to specified secondary-text type
\\12\\ = switch to specified appendix type
\\13\\ = switch to specified index type
\\14\\ = switch to specified caption type
\\15\\ = switch to italics in same font/size
\\16\\ = switch to boldface in same font/size
\\17\\ = underline
\\20\\ = switch to specified chapter-title type
\\21\\ = switch to specified subhead type
\\22\\ = switch to specified header type
\\23\\ = switch to specified footer type

IN 2-COLUMN FORMAT:

\\30\\ = switch to specified 2-column main text type
\\31\\ = switch to specified 2-column secondary text type
\\32\\ = switch to specified 2-column appendix type
\\33\\ = switch to specified 2-column index type
\\34\\ = switch to specified 2-column caption type
\\35\\ = switch to specified 2-column subhead type

**SET TITLE AND VERSO PAGES AND END-PAPER INSERTS
AS SEPARATE ART TO BE INSERTED ON BLANK PAGES**

In places where the copy editor and desktop operator are the same person, that editor may even choose to skip the coding and simply format the pages right on the computer, following an agreed pattern, after the text has been imported from the word processor. But it's still important to develop the code-chart, in order to identify the "menu" of typographic options necessary to create pages in your preferred style(s). It actually takes fewer such options than most editors assume.

Those codes that simply instruct the computer to leave so many blank lines (or pages) for illustrations can be used in various combinations to create an appropriate hole for almost any piece of art. In those rare cases where it won't work, just cut out and re-paste the type for *that specific page,* make a sharp stat of it, replace that text with a blank page in the electronic manuscript, and deliver the stat to the printer to be stripped in as just another separate piece of (full-page) line art.

Don't worry that some illustrations will begin low on one page, and finish at the top of the next page, on that first roughly paged print-out. It may scare authors (if that's what you send as proofs)—but it's a simple matter for the copy editor (in that second, slow edit) to move any illustration up or down to a logical single-page location (remembering to change such text-reference words as "above" or "below" accordingly).

By pasting up a stylebook sample of each acceptable typographic option your desktop system and design sense allow (as to type faces and sizes, line lengths, etc.) for each typographic element on the menu, you make it fairly easy for the copy editor (pre-press project manager) to show the sponsoring series editor his choices—and let the latter's preferences constitute the book's interior "design."

In most cases, that's really all that's needed. Except for cover art (which we've suggested you delegate to marketing), most of that money publishers have traditionally paid outsiders for page-by-page design, paste-up, and type-setting itself is *no longer needed.*

In a well-organized system, then, the desktop operator doesn't get into the act until Step 5 of the 12-step pre-press development sequence we outlined in Chapter 20. When instructed by the copy editor that all is in readiness (and the first fast edit is completed), the operator electronically "imports" the manuscript from the word processor into the desktop system. Then the operator quickly "kicks it into pages" by feeding the copy editor's specifications (as to the number of lines on each page, the location of headers and footers and/or page numbers, and the specific translation of each element from the generic code chart—Figure 23a) into the system, and then flipping through the sequential pages (on the computer screen) to complete translating (and remove, if necessary) the codes—and provide adequate space for each illustration. (Here the stylebook may also dictate that he insert blank pages to keep new chapters from starting on the left-hand side of a spread.)

Once he reproduces "rough pages" of the result on the laser printer (for the copy editor, with a photocopy for the acquiring editor and/or author), he can then sit tight as far as that manuscript is concerned until the copy editor reappears with corrections and changes. He may, meanwhile, be asked to do additional work on cover graphics, or the layout of charts that will eventually be incorporated as though they were illustrations. Otherwise, he just bangs ahead with the next book in line.

He then re-engages with each book when corrections and changes are finalized. He inputs these, and makes other necessary adjustments, as instructed by the copy editor (project manager)—and then produces a set of "final pages" on the laser printer. These are reviewed quickly by all concerned, last-minute refinements are made, and the operator generates either camera-ready pages (on a high-resolution laser printer) or a disk-copy of the file—for the chosen printer to use in preparing plates. And that's essentially it.

Keeping the process that simple is what it takes to get 10,000 pages a year from one desktop operator!

PART V
Marketing

CHAPTER 24
Organizing Your Marketing Department and Strategy

Book marketing is that part of the publishing process that has the basic responsibility for generating *customer orders* for your books (and related products and/or services). Its constituents are both the eventual readers (not the authors!), and the intermediaries who help readers learn about and obtain those books—book reviewers, author-oriented "talk show" producers, bookstores and wholesale dealers, librarians, educators, subsidiary rights buyers, etc. The marketing function's essential objective is the maximization of total net sales volume (after discounts and returns).

The healthy interaction of key players in a publishing house is somewhat like that in a courtroom: you don't get the best results unless every critical interest is vigorously represented; nobody should pull their punches. Many publishers' aspirations to sell more books are undermined because their marketing functions (and budgets) are diverted and diluted to "keep authors happy" (an acquisition concern) or "make the stockholders proud" (the publisher's job) or "concentrate on the most profitable deals" (a business/finance goal). Some marketing managers even like these diversions—because they provide alibis when sales volume lags. But this is the only function in the publishing house capable of *stimulating enough cash flow* to keep the place afloat—and if we divert 'em, they can't do it!

So, as the job description in Figure 24a on the next page illustrates, it behooves the publisher to make sure the marketing manager accepts maximizing *sales volume* (regardless of how profitable it turns out to be) as her particular, over-riding goal. While the publisher may occasionally (and properly) be persuaded to refine the ground rules under which that goal is pursued (for example, by mandating basic sales terms that are more profitable, or requiring some arbitrary commitment to a new product line that "hasn't caught on yet"), the marketing manager's own obsession should always (within the limits of such rules) be to bring home as many sales dollars as possible for every marketing dollar (including payroll) she spends.

In most book publishing houses, she accomplishes this by the carefully-strategized and professionally-executed orchestration of two sub-functions: promotion and sales.

Figure 24a—Sample Job Description: Marketing Manager

TITLE: Marketing Manager
Reports to: Publisher (General Manager)
Directly Supervises:
     Sales Coordinator
     Promotion Coordinator
     Administrative Assistant
Budget Line Responsibility:
     Net book sales revenue
     Subsidiary rights revenue
     All marketing expense lines
Accountability Index:
     Month-to-month growth in annualized sales volume
     as a percentage of the previous year

GENERAL OPERATING RESPONSIBILITIES:
To plan and supervise all activities concerned with generating orders for the books, other products, subsidiary rights, and/or services offered by this publishing house.

SPECIFIC OPERATING RESPONSIBILITIES:
a) To plan, update, and communicate an explicit model of all anticipated marketing campaigns, continuously updated to project the next 15 months;
b) To recruit, train and supervise all personnel reporting directly to the Marketing Manager;
c) To pre-screen and periodically review any/all contracts or similar agreements with any external agents and/or representatives retained to assist in the marketing program;
d) To pre-screen all public statements regarding the publishing program and its books, to insure their compatibility with and contribution to fulfillment of the mission statement;
e) To propose and administer consistent business terms (as authorized by the Publisher) compatible with the standards of the industry, and the financial goals of the publishing house;
f) To obtain and maintain realistic measurements of the effectiveness of all on-going marketing campaigns, as well as individual promotion and sales presentations, to document appropriate allocation of marketing effort and budget to the most effective approaches;
g) To provide estimates of the sales potential of proposed future products, and of the year-ahead sales volume growth rate, as requested by other core managers;
h) To represent the concerns of the marketing function and staff in deliberations of the core management group.

Generally speaking, there are only two ways to sell books: (1) singling out potential customers important enough for special effort, and persuading them one-on-one (face-to-face in their own offices or your exhibit booths, by phone, or by mail) that selected components of your product list (most often, individual new titles) meet their particular needs, or (2) communicating through mass media (direct mail, book covers, book review or talk show publicity, "piggyback" inserts, periodical print-ads, broadcast commercials, point-of-contact displays, phone canvassing, etc.) with entire categories of prospective customers on an impersonal basis (usually in support of *all* of the books in your list that even vaguely relate to each category's needs or interests).

We call one-on-one selling to select prospects the "sales" function, and selling to entire audience categories by mass media the "promotion" function. In the typical small publishing house, the over-all marketing manager also doubles as coordinator of one of these secondary functions (sales or promotion), and the assistant marketing manager handles the other. However, for clarity's sake, the sample job description in Figure 24a assumes that assistants are available to coordinate both subordinate functions.

Until net annual sales are in excess of $1 million, the typical profitably-streamlined publishing house functions with a single promotion person—who plans all mailing pieces, ads, etc., designs and writes (or obtains from free-lancers) all promotional material (book covers—including art, news release announcements, catalogs, mailing and cross-sell or "piggyback" insertion brochures, print ads, broadcast commercials, telephone canvassing ["cold turkey"] scripts, crowd-stopping visual displays, etc.), and handles the distribution of complimentary books to publicity intermediaries (book reviewers, talk show producers, etc.). By the time a promotional assistant is feasible, either the complexities of the house's own accumulated promotional mailing list will demand some administrative help, or the expanding flow of new titles will justify an additional copywriter. But since it buys mass duplication/circulation of each of its precious messages, the *promotion* function seldom requires much staff; it prospers by spending its money on greater "outreach" (media exposure) rather than payroll.

The formal job description of the promotion coordinator in a general-interest publishing house looks something like Figure 24b, on the next page.

The *sales* function, on the other hand, is labor-intensive—because its constant goal is to get "one-on-one" with selected customers or prospects, and custom-interpret the book/product list to best serve each of their individual needs or interests. It meets these customers face-to-face either in their offices, or in the publisher's exhibit booths; it responds to their specific inquiries and other leads both by telephone (outbound telemarketing) and by personalized mail—often using the two in combination. It intercepts customers placing orders by phone with carefully-crafted "upsell" scripts, whereby order-takers suggest related additions to the initial order. And (in conjunction with its promotion partners) it occasionally merchandises "point-of-purchase" materials (from complete floor displays to posters to hand-outs) and cooperative advertising programs to intermediate buyers (especially bookstores), to help deliver its sales messages to remote shoppers.

Figure 24b—Sample Job Description: Promotion Coordinator

TITLE: Promotion Coordinator
Reports to: Marketing Manager
Directly Supervises: Administrative Assistant
Budget Line Responsibility:
      Promotional Media
      Promotional Postage
      Promotional Production
      Co-Op Ad Credits/Rebates
      Complimentary Book Distribution
      Bulk Mail Processing
Accountability Indices:
      Promotional costs as percentage of trade sales;
      Promotional costs as percentage of direct sales;
      Average promotional cost per new additional to direct-customer list;
      Average promotional cost per valid teacher-exam request;
      Average promotional cost per bookstore comp-request.

GENERAL RESPONSIBILITIES:
To accomplish and/or arrange creation and distribution of media presentations that generate (1) bookstore and classroom sales leads and (2) direct-from-reader orders at the lowest feasible per-unit or per-sales-dollar cost.

SPECIFIC OPERATING RESPONSIBILITIES:
a) To create and/or update basic promotional copy for all books currently in, or scheduled for addition to, the catalog;
b) To organize and maintain accurate mailing lists of all recent customers, prime prospects, and publicity contacts;
c) To advise the Marketing Manager on promotional aspects of each review, update or extension of the marketing strategy model;
d) To write, and arrange appropriate illustration and production of, promotional materials, displays, etc., needed to execute the marketing plan;
e) To refine and execute an on-going program for systematic and effective introduction of new titles to major publicity outlets, key trade accounts, and other appropriate contacts;
f) To generate high-quality prospect-leads for sales follow-up in the development of new bookstore accounts;
g) To promote valid requests for, and arrange distribution of, appropriate samples to educators wishing to consider them for classroom adoption;
h) To create and execute a profitable, on-going program for direct sales to individuals and libraries who share the publisher's subject-interests;
i) To create appropriate telemarketing scripts as requested by the Sales Coordinator;
j) To create appropriate exhibit and point-of-purchase display materials as requested by the Sales Coordinator;
k) To create appropriate promotional inserts for use by authors and other supportive parties.

Here is a typical job description for the sales coordinator in a trade-oriented publishing house (where the sales function is most significant):

Figure 24c—Sample Job Description: Sales Coordinator

TITLE: Sales Coordinator
Reports to: Marketing Manager
Directly Supervises: Customer Service Supervisor
                     Administrative Assistant
Budget Line Responsibility: Sales Commissions
                     Sales Travel and Entertainment
                     Exhibit Costs
                     Telemarketing Costs
                     Sales Support Materials and Supplies
                     Sales Department Overhead
Accountability Indices: Month-to-month annualized sales volume trend from
            (a) accounts directly handled by sales manager,
            (b) commissioned rep accounts,
            (c) order processing upgrades,
            (d) outbound telemarketing, and
            (d) exhibits.

GENERAL RESPONSIBILITIES:

To plan and arrange targeted selling of our publications via staff sales trips, commissioned sales reps, order-entry cross-sell and up-sell, outbound tele-marketing, and exhibiting—to achieve maximum sales per dollar spent.

SPECIFIC OPERATING RESPONSIBILITIES:

a) To personally service the publishing house's twenty largest accounts;

b) To arrange and supervise systematic on-site representation by commis-sioned sales reps covering bookstores/library wholesalers in most states;

c) To integrate effective order processing, plus customer service cross-sell and up-sell tactics, into the marketing strategy;

d) To plan, arrange and supervise systematic outbound telemarketing to open new bookstore accounts;

e) To develop a test program of staff sales visits to selected accounts, as a means of evaluating the possible future replacement of commissioned reps with staff personnel;

f) To identify two marginal states, and monitor them as exclusive test territo ries for (d) and (e), to facilitate over-all cost-result comparisons with (b);

g) To plan, schedule, arrange, supervise participation in appropriate trade and library exhibits in a manner that effectively supports marketing objectives;

h) To administer systematic response to all product inquiries and sales leads, from all sources, by one or more of the above selling activities;

i) To coordinate with the Promotion Coordinator the preparation of all sales-support materials essential to success in all of the above sales activities;

j) To provide such budget-proposal, book cover, and sales-estimate input as may be requested by the Marketing Manager.

Some publishers "farm out" most of their sales function (especially in the bookstore trade) to "distributors"—who warehouse "consignment" inventories of their books (i.e., the distributor doesn't pay for them until it collects from the bookstore), and take 55-65 percent of the list price of each book (in some combination of discounts and commissions—much of which each distributor passes on to its customers) for this service. (The publisher also normally has to pay shipping costs for moving its inventory to the distributor.)

But since publishers surrender most (often all!) of their profit margin to the distributor whenever they sell their books at discounts of more than 50 percent, and since the actual *selling* attention the distributor (primarily just an "order taker") can devote to any specific book in its inventory, except for a very few top-sellers (divided between a number of publishers), is very small—this does not normally prove to be a healthy, profitable marketing tactic for publishers. The large number who still do it generally reflect a reluctance on the part of small publishers to accept responsibility for getting one-on-one with the "real world" challenges presented by customers.

(Contrary to frequent defensive assertions, such a distribution arrangement usually does not even help a start-up publisher build a customer base—since the distributor seldom tells the publisher who's buying the books. It is primarily useful for the single-book "self-publisher" who has *no* marketing function, and is willing to bribe a distributor with most of the normal publisher's profit margin—either for egotistical reasons, or just to get the author's cut for himself.)

Others attempt to reach bookstore, library and school markets by retaining "commissioned reps"—independent agents who cover specific territories on behalf of a number of publishers, for commissions that range from 10 percent (sometimes less for major wholesale accounts) to 25 percent (for school or special-market selling) of the publisher's net receipts from the territory. Once again, each rep must offer so many new titles every time he calls on a bookstore or other customer (usually two to four times a year) that he can do little more for most of those new titles than "scan the order form"—and even less for the backlist. Furthermore, most commissioned rep contracts require the publisher to pay commissions on *all sales* it makes to the rep's customer-category in the rep's territory—whether that rep had anything to do with the sale or not; a major portion of a rep's commissions often come from single-copy orders entirely generated by the publisher's promotion.

So the majority of thriving, growing, profitable independent publishers eventually choose (and learn) to handle their own sales function. They usually accomplish this in two ways. Certain qualified individuals (either specialized staff sales reps, or such heavy-hitters as the marketing manager, the editor-in-chief, and even the publisher herself) periodically travel out into the world to meet customers—calling directly on major accounts in their places of business (usually to introduce the forthcoming season's list of new titles), and interfacing with more modest customer contacts at book exhibits associated with subject-area, professional, or trade conferences. Most of the remaining one-on-one selling is accomplished either by personal mail, or (probably more effectively) by telephone—either by the people who respond when customers call, or by trained telereps who initiate their own calls to promising leads. More about that in Chapter 27.

A typical marketing department in a million-dollar publishing house, then, might consist of the marketing manager, who not only plans strategy and represents the function in core management deliberations, but *doubles* as sales coordinator (traveling to visit key accounts several times a year, staffing exhibit booths—sometimes with colleagues from the acquisition function, following up complimentary samples with phone calls to major accounts, and negotiating subsidiary rights deals) ... plus a promotion coordinator (the assistant marketing manager) ... a customer service supervisor (the "assistant sales coordinator") ... customer service "telereps" (who not only take incoming phone orders, but input mail orders to the computer between phone calls—and even do some script-guided, outbound telemarketing) ... and an administrative assistant (who maintains mailing lists and provides clerical back-up as needed).

Customer service was traditionally part of a separate order-processing function in the business office. However, the improvement of order processing software and the sales-potential of on-line contact with customers—for either "upsell" telephone intervention, or automatic "cross-sell" promotional insertions in mail orders—are increasingly persuading publishers to move *all* such contacts into marketing's sales sub-function—as amplified in Chapter 27.

However it is staffed, effective book marketing is usually a careful orchestration of the interplay between the sales and promotion sub-functions. Strategizing that orchestration (planning its general pattern) is the most important single activity of the marketing manager. The best way to get all of book marketing's complexities into focus and under control is to display a well-brainstormed, prioritized list of the *audiences you most need to reach* on a spreadsheet like that in Figure 9b—and then plot on it a sequence of appropriate, usually-repetitive exposures to each of those audiences. Optimally, the spreadsheet should extend over the next 15 months (though you may not be able to print it all out at one time), so it summarizes not only the relatively-unchangeable quarter immediately ahead, but (for review and adjustment) the following 12-month annual cycle of a complete and seasonally-varied sales year. The two biggest mistakes marketing managers tend to make in laying out these strategy models are:

(1) Too many of them try to spread a limited budget too widely—hitting all plausible audiences spasmodically, rather than concentrating repetitively on the most responsive few. The typical amateur book-marketer feels guilty unless he's "taking every feasible shot at every possible customer." But more

experienced (and successful) marketing strategists saturate their best audiences before they spend *any* time or money on less-responsive ones. As a result, their marketing staffs are, at any given time, only responsible for updating and executing a fairly limited number of on-going campaigns. Because they're not dashing blindly in too many directions at once, they have the time and composure to give real *quality thought* to refining the general strategy, and the limited number of individual presentations on which it rests.

(2) Insecure strategists are afraid to promote to a given (good) audience more than three or four times a year—although only about 10 percent of any audience is "listening" each time, and a different segment will pay attention (and buy at the same rate) a couple of weeks later. Marketers who know better communicate with their best audiences every 2-to-4 weeks—in preference to diluting their impact into infrequent shots at more marginal audiences.

There are six basic steps to creating a sound marketing strategy model. First, the marketing manager must brainstorm audiences and selective sub-components of audiences—and then re-arrange all of those identified into priority order (according to their documented or assumed responsiveness to the book/product list). Second, he must ascertain what *initial response* he hopes to stimulate from each such audience-segment to qualify appropriate prospects for intensified sales follow-up (face-to-face, by phone, or by mail)— or otherwise set in motion a sequence of interactions that will result in sales. Third, he must frame some suitably attractive offer that will maximize those qualifying responses, *within the established sales terms of the house* (i.e., without violating limits approved by the publisher, after analysis by the finance function, to assure eventual profitability).

Fourth, he must then determine the sequence of promotional presentations (direct mail, print ad, broadcast commercial, telephone canvassing, cross-sell insertion, review and talk show publicity) and sales follow-ups (by field visit, exhibit, telemarketing—outbound or "upsell," or personal mail) that he believes will maximize both the percentage of each audience-segment that will respond to (accept) that initial qualifying offer—and the total resulting dollar-volume from the sales follow-up of those initial responses. And fifth, he must estimate the maximum frequency with which he can repeat each pre-qualifying offer to each audience-segment to maintain a constant stream of sales (or sales leads) without experiencing diminishing returns (a decline in the relationship between marketing expense and resulting sales dollars). Then he simply starts plotting those exposures to those audiences, at those intervals, on the spreadsheet.

Finally (sixth), he must determine how far down his list of prioritized audience-segments his budget will stretch—giving maximum effective exposure (without diminishing returns) to each audience in priority sequence. We repeat (!): the prime rule of sound marketing strategy is *not to dilute the payback by spreading money over any secondary audience until you've done all you effectively can to each higher-priority audience.*

The result of these six steps, then, will be a finite number of on-going "exposure campaigns" repetitively concentrating on the audiences from which the marketing manager believes she'll get the maximum eventual sales volume payback for each marketing budget dollar (payroll as well as other costs) spent. Each of these campaigns, then, can be further broken down into one or more "presentations"—the actual, individual promotional exposures of the initial offer and/or the sales follow-ups that make the campaign work. An on-going direct-marketing campaign may have only *one* presentation—such as a basic mailing piece that is constantly refined and updated—which does the *entire job* when it makes contact with a vulnerable customer, and requires no sales follow-up. But most trade and school-adoption campaigns include both a continuously-repeated "initial offer" presentation (such as the news release that offers interested bookstores or curriculum planners complimentary advance copies of a forthcoming book—and must be changed from book-to-book) and the sales follow-up telemarketing script or personalized closure letter that will be directed to each individual responding to that initial order (after the complimentary book is delivered).

An analysis of the 1991 marketing strategies of 165 independent publishers (average sales $2.2 million) found direct mail to be by far their favorite promotional tactic—with 82.8 percent rating it among their top-three marketing approaches, compared to 20.3 percent for print advertising, 19.9 percent for book review publicity, and 3.3 percent for talk show publicity. When it came to one-on-one sales tactics, 52.3 percent rated distributors among their top three approaches (despite those profit-eating bonus discounts!), compared to 35.1 percent for conference exhibits, 33.1 percent for commissioned reps, 27.8 percent for telemarketing (rising rapidly year by year), 11.9 percent for staff sales trips, and 5.3 percent for representation by a bigger publisher.

In summary, then, there are four major tasks in managing an effective book-marketing program: (1) prioritizing audiences, (2) outlining (strategizing) on-going campaigns to each audience, (3) planning and executing the individual presentations (promotional exposures or sales follow-ups) needed for each campaign, and (4) constantly refining those campaigns and presentations in the light of actual results.

Once begun, the development of a good marketing strategy model is an evolutionary affair. At the end of every quarter, the marketing manager should extend the model another 3 months into the future (so that it again projects the next 15 months—an immediate quarter which is more-or-less fixed, and four following quarters [an annual cycle] which are still eligible for on-going adjustment).

By working with the computer system or the business manager to analyze sales results by audience category, and by tactics (direct mail vs. exhibits vs. telemarketing, etc.)—and by constantly moving future money from those tactics that pay worst (in sales/cost ratios) to those that pay best—a marketing manager can virtually guarantee a gradually improving sales result from each marketing budget dollar!

Finding ways to track the impact of various segments of the marketing program—from computer tallies of source-of-sales codes (as they appear on order forms, or are queried-and-reported by customer service telereps), comparison of month-by-month trends in designated test states (or zip-regions), sales report break-downs by customer categories, etc.—is a major (and often slighted) responsibility of the marketing manager. Those who brush off this responsibility with alibis about inadequate computer systems or inefficient order processors are simply reflecting their own incompetence as managers. Because the marketing budget is usually second only to the printing bill in the cost-categories of a publishing house, it is essential that publishers demand documentation that marketing money is used in the most effective way.

So even though the computer system is normally part of the basic "office facility" maintained by the business function, the marketing manager has a major stake in the order processing software that is utilized by that system. At the very least, he should insist that it (1) function fast enough to enable order-takers (customer service "telereps"—as described in Chapter 27) to find customer files, open new accounts, and enter orders "on-line"—while the customer is on the phone, (2) record both "source of sales" codes (identifying specific order forms, promotion campaigns, etc.) and "type-of-account" codes (distinguishing between the various, prioritized audience-segments targeted on the marketing strategy model)—to enable the marketing manager to determine what is working, and what isn't … and adjust the strategy accordingly, (3) retain enough historical data to allow sales people to analyze individual accounts over several years, (4) automatically build an accumulative mailing list, coded by audience categories, and (5) keep track of all *complimentary* book distribution—by treating publicity contacts as "100 percent-discount customers" (and automatically maintaining mailing lists of them).

As noted earlier, each presentation and anticipated response in the on-going marketing program must abide by the sales terms previously approved by the publisher (after consultation with the business manager), to assure eventual profitability. In most publishing houses, the initiative in proposing establishment or amendment of such sales terms rests with the marketing manager (who thus has an opportunity to make them *palatable* to customers, as well as profitable to the house).

Generally speaking, publishers' sales terms offer a trade-off between size-of-order and discount-from-list-price. But within the range of pricing mark-ups, budgetary ratios, and margin expectations normal in American book publishing, it is very seldom profitable for any publisher to sell books at discounts larger than 50 percent of the list price—or give discounts on orders for less than five books (single or assorted titles); at the same time, middleman-dealers can seldom make money unless they receive discounts of at least 40 percent—though most acknowledge their obligation to order-in-bulk to earn that margin.

Unfortunately, some desperate publishers still accept (from distributors, book clubs, special religious "ministries," etc.) the insulting proposition that what happens *after a book leaves the publisher's warehouse* (just in the process of moving it through the distribution pipeline) deserves a larger share of the reader's money (the list price) than do the *combined* efforts of the *author,* the *printer,* the *paper-maker,* and the *publisher*! Sadly, those who accept that ridiculous proposition inevitably undermine other publishers' efforts to resist it.

The most straight-forward and logical publisher discount schedules distinguish (by the *book-title,* not the customer—to avoid entanglement in FTC regulations on discriminatory discounting) between "trade" (bookstore, general-consumer-interest), and "non-trade" (classroom, vocational/reference) titles. Within those categories, they discount *only* on the basis of the quantity (units—single or assorted titles) purchased at a given time—in a single purchase-order. (Professional and reference books are usually treated as "non-trade" because their higher prices normally inhibit trade middlemen from bulk-stocking and aggressively displaying them, yet those middlemen are tempted to combine single-copy orders for them with bulk orders for less expensive titles to obtain substantial price mark-downs.)

For general-interest "trade" titles (regardless of who buys them—wholesalers, so-called "distributors," bookstores, interested organizations, authors, even libraries or individual consumers), it's generally wise to offer *no discount* on any purchase of less than five books (except for occasional pre-pub direct-to-reader promotions limited to specific titles and specific time-periods). On 1-to-4 book orders, processing costs usually eat up all of the publisher's margin, even without discounts. Offering a 40 percent discount on 5-or-more—or sometimes 10-or-more—books ordered at one time gives bookstores and other middlemen the minimum margin they need to make a profit.. Trade discounts then typically escalate (by units ordered) upward a couple of percentage points at a step, to a large-quantity (anything from 25 to 100+ books) top of 50 percent. This gets the publisher entirely out of the business of discriminating between various categories of customers—and bases everything on *the actual benefit* (via economies of scale) of bulk ordering to that publisher.

For "non-trade" classroom or professional/reference titles, it's equally unwise to offer *any* discount on less than five books. Typically, publishers of such books offer the traditional 20 percent "short discount" for five-or-more books (because schools and some libraries expect it), and a flat "dealer" discount of around 35 percent on substantial quantities (say, 100-or-more)—to enable wholesalers servicing contract accounts with schools or libraries to get into the act.

These discount guidelines are, obviously, generalities. There are occasional reasons for taking exception to any of them. But *don't kid yourself* about the financial realities when you do. The flimsy rationalizations (such as pretending there are few costs associated with high-volume, bonus-discount "add-on" sales—or that you're going to be repaid for losses by vague "future goodwill") used to justify most over-50 percent discounts are usually deceptive.

It is reasonable to offer middlemen buying-for-resale some compromise concessions on a couple of other points. First, there is clearly a trend (over the past 5 years) toward attempting to induce more direct-from-bookstore sales (circumventing the high-discount wholesaler and higher-discount distributor) by offering "free freight" (whereby the publisher pays the shipping costs) to book dealers ordering in substantial quantities (or on a pre-pub basis) for resale. Publishers normally spend about 3.5 percent of net receipts from book orders on outbound transportation costs. Frankly, it's probably not profitable for the publisher to "swallow" that as an across-the-board policy—but it can be used as a reasonable bonus reward for high-quantity, pre-pub, or first-time orders. Otherwise, you're probably wise to stick with the traditional terms—adding actual shipping/postage amounts to credit orders, and charging specified shipping/handling amounts on prepaid (or credit card) direct consumer orders.

Any publisher who is serious about selling through trade (bookstore, wholesaler) channels will find it virtually mandatory to offer credits (toward future purchases) or refunds for the return of unsold, undamaged merchandise. But you have every right to—and should—insist that such returns be truly undamaged and resalable, and that the returner prepay shipping costs. Some publishers offer "bonus" discounts when resale buyers (whether wholesalers, stores, or other organizations) order on an agreed *non-returnable* basis. Since independent trade publishers normally experience returns (for refund or credit) of 7-to-8 percent of their sales volume, the typical 2-to-3 percent non-returnable bonus is a reasonable trade-off.

Some publishers also assess penalties for returns—though general experience suggests that if you're seriously involved in *trade* selling (to bookstores or wholesalers), this will scare off quite a few dealers. The most common penalties either deduct a modest percentage (like 10 percent) from the return credit for administrative costs, or limit return credits within a year to a certain portion (like 10 percent) of the dealer's total purchases. This policy makes most sense when selling into the college bookstore market (where sloppy buying habits by the stores often lead to excessive returns).

Finally, there is the issue of *credit terms* and *consignments*. Because *financing* (for working and inventory capital) is a major problem of most independent publishers, it seldom makes sense for them to finance other people's businesses—by selling to anyone on "extended" payment terms, or by shipping "distributors" consignment inventories that won't be paid for until the distributor collects from its eventual customer. The industry convention is "30 days E/O/M" (i.e., they should pay you within 30 days of your end-of-the-month statement). The reality is that in 1991, the average receivable owed to independent publishers was paid after 54.2 days. Even if you state your formal terms as "30 days E/O/M," you'll have your work cut out for you actually collecting within 50 days. You only encourage further delays by formally extending longer terms. And be very leery of those "distributor" deals whereby you're required not only to ship (usually freight-free) on consignment (i.e., they don't owe you until they sell the books)—but also to give them 90 days *after their sale* to pay you. That's really financing somebody else's inventory—which is not publishing, but unprofitable (interest-free!) banking ... hardly a small publisher's proper business!

Offering credit accounts (bookstores, etc.) 2 percent discounts for immediate payment has proven a disappointing tactic for most publishers. The customers tend to pay late, but deduct that bonus discount anyhow—creating a lot of expensive, extra computer work and bruised goodwill if you try to collect the difference.

The marketing function should also be called on as needed to estimate the sales potential of proposed future books (by reflecting on its *own past performance* in the selling of similar books to the intended audience-category), and to counsel the publisher on revenue budget projections. While some marketing managers cling to conservative estimates to reduce the risk of missing goals, wise publishers know that such estimates are really marketing's truest self-assessment of *its own capability*, rather than legitimate "literary criticism" of the nuances of specific books; in those publishing houses, marketing managers who consistently "guess low" don't last long.

So once you've established a good marketing structure (the right combination of sales and promotion people), prioritized your audiences, modeled a strategy for orchestrating the interplay of promotion and sales through a limited set of on-going campaigns, and defined the terms on which you're prepared to sell books—it's time to start telling the world what those books are all about. And that, as we'll see in the next chapter, is what the *promotion* section of the marketing team does for a living.

CHAPTER 25
Creating Effective Promotional Formats and Copy

However much the promotion coordinator may or may not be involved (doubling as either marketing manager or assistant marketing manager) in shaping and refining the combination of on-going campaigns to prioritized audiences that constitute the over-all marketing strategy, this individual's specialized focus is on the design, copy/art creation, and production/circulation of all reproducible promotional presentations (book covers, news release announcements, complimentary samples, catalogs, mailing and cross-sell and "piggyback" brochures, end-paper promotions on the blank pages left in the last signature of any subject-related book, print ads, broadcast commercials, telephone canvassing scripts, crowd-stopping visual displays, etc.), which inform the reading public and important intermediaries (trade buyers, educational course-planners, book reviewers, talk show producers, subsidiary rights buyers, etc.) about the publisher's product line.

Because single-book direct-selling presentations usually give the buyer too little choice to generate a profitable statistical probability of response (since each such presentation has only that single-book chance of coincidentally relating to the buyer's motivating needs and interests at the time of each fleeting promotional contact), most of a publisher's non-salary promotional budget is best devoted to updating, reproducing, and mass-circulating a *limited number* of comprehensive *multi-book* presentations (catalogs, subject-area brochures, multi-title print ads, etc.) required for the combination of on-going campaigns specified in the marketing strategy model. (This constant updating and re-issuing of previously-proven presentations has led more than one good promotion coordinator to describe her work as "something like a magazine editor's.")

Nevertheless, much of the typical promotion coordinator's *time* (as opposed to non-payroll money) is actually devoted to introducing *individual* new titles to key contacts in the marketplace (largely by writing and circulating news releases offering complimentary samples—for subsequent sales follow-up). We'll see how such single-title key contact promotion is best accomplished in the next chapter. And the raw material for all of those on-going promotional exposures listed two paragraphs above—even though largely used in multi-book promotions—is most easily and effectively created *one book at a time,* before each new title is published—by assembling a basic promotional "copy package" for each title. A well-organized promotion coordinator usually maintains a word-processing file of such copy packages for all titles currently in (or soon to be added to) the publisher's list—so that various components can be updated (with recent review commentary, etc.) and/or re-used (in numerous combinations with other books) as appropriate.

The fundamental time-saving idea behind the "copy package" approach is that—as all experienced copy writers know—a major part of the work of creating promotional copy is invested in (1) rounding up the necessary background information, and (2) getting into the right mind-set to empathize with the probable, remote audience for each separate book. Since the promotional copy writer has to do both of those things to generate the very first description needed for *any* book (usually a news release announcement for sub-rights buyers and other key contacts—but sometimes the copy for the book cover, or the new title's page in the seasonal catalog), smart copy writers (usually the promotion coordinators themselves) immediately adapt (at the same sitting) that first description into additional versions for every distinct type of presentation the marketing program is ever likely to need.

Thus, having created the initial news release, they simply make a word-processed copy of it re-labeled as "book cover copy" ... and another re-labeled "catalog copy," etc., etc... and immediately move around or delete sentences, and rearrange the format, to fit the normal style and length of each kind of presentation. By making sure they start (as is usually necessary) with one of the longer presentations (the news release announcement, or cover or catalog copy), they find that most of the shorter presentations (for subject-area brochures, print ads, exhibit or point-of-purchase displays, etc.) can be created simply by deleting most of the initial words and sentences.

The range of presentations routinely utilized by any given publisher's marketing strategy may-or-may-not include news release announcements, book covers, catalogs, mailing and cross-sell or "piggyback" brochures (for your own, middleman, or author circulation), print ads or similar card-pack inserts (for publisher sponsorship, or co op programs merchandised by the sales function), broadcast commercials, telephone canvassing ("cold turkey") scripts, crowd-stopping visual displays, and even "up-sell" or "call-back" scripts for the sales function's telereps (if/as requested).

Seasoned book promotion copy writers eventually learn that five good paragraphs will usually tell virtually anybody outside the publishing house (and the author's proud, immediate family) all they'll ever want to know about most books before they decide whether-or-not to buy them. Envision those five paragraphs in the sequence most effective for the initial new release announcement of a book's forthcoming publication:

Paragraph 1 is a journalistic-style lead that proclaims both the fact of impending publication, and the compelling unique features of the forthcoming book ... why a reader who already has a library on the subject will find it worthwhile to buy this one more title. (If your program is properly organized, the writer—or project-organizing editor—was required to summarize this information in a background questionnaire *before* your acquisition function decided to publish the book; it is probably the single most important statement relevant to either the decision-to-publish, or the eventual marketing of the title.)

Paragraph 2 reports the basic bibliographic facts that both readers and intermediaries will eventually want to know—the exact title, the author's name(s), the publication (availability) date, the price, the ISBNumber, the binding (hardcover, trade paperback, etc.), and the address and/or order-phone number of the publishing house.

Paragraph 3 summarizes the book's contents, scope, style and nature. This summary, too, should be quickly adapted from the author's pre-acquisition background questionnaire—which, obviously, should be routinely forwarded to the promotion function the moment each new title is contracted.

Paragraph 4 describes special auxiliary features of the book which may enhance its perceived value. This includes the nature and number of illustrations, a listing of appendices, reference to any significant foreword, a description of associated study/discussion guides or exercises or tests, etc.

Paragraph 5 tells the reader why the author(s) should be believed—by presenting biographical credentials and referring to previous publications (periodical or book-length).

Most promotion coordinators find that such an initial announcement news release can be quickly copied-and-amended into five additional formats which will provide (at one sitting) most of the copy ever likely to be needed to incorporate the book fully into their on-going marketing strategy. Certain special aspects of each of these six basic copy package components should be kept in mind:

News release copy will be greatly enhanced by the careful development of a newspaper-type headline that dramatizes that "compelling unique feature" hopefully identified in the first paragraph. Even the insider book-experts who get such releases are prone to quick-scanning—and quickly consigning everything that doesn't either "seduce" or "threaten" them to the wastebasket!

Book cover copy (and subsequent lay-out and art) should take into account the anticipated setting in which most *undecided* buyers will first see it. That means trade book covers must be eye-catching and readable to bookstore shelf-browsers (whether face-out or spine-out); direct-response (mail order) book covers must communicate effectively when reduced (in catalogs, ads, etc.) to postage-stamp size; classroom covers must carefully avoid embarrassing the conservative political sensitivities of most educational institutions. And remember that hardcover or paperback covers can often be made more effective by incorporating (even on the *front* cover) advance quotes from experts, and (on the back panel) "bar codes" for automated inventory-scanning in distribution centers. (For services that will inexpensively convert your ISBN and price into bar code art for the cover mechanical, consult Marie Kiefer's *Book Publishing Resource Guide*—as per Appendix 1.)

Catalog copy for a book's first-season introduction in the publishing house's formal, comprehensive active-title catalog can be dressed up by incorporating (line-scanning into the desktop typesetter) a reproduction of the book cover.

Pass-along brochures that can be offered to the author (for "piggyback" insertions in their own correspondence, newsletters of their organizations, etc. ... telling potential readers how to direct-order by phoning your toll-free number) can easily be adapted (with order coupon) from your catalog copy—and produced in limited quantities (on colored stock) on your office photocopier. This is a very good way to deal with an author's pre-publication anxieties—by giving her something constructive she can do to help sell the book without meanwhile disrupting your marketing department with naive, unwanted advice.

Annotation paragraphs that condense the entire presentation into 50-100 words can be recombined with other books for a wide variety of mailing and piggyback-insertion brochures—and may even be appropriate for some large-space, multi-title display ads or card-pack inserts. They'll also eventually be useful for the backlist section of the catalog, for end-paper booklists on the otherwise-blank pages of the last signature of another subject-related book, and as quick-reference guides for your telereps. These entries should be periodically updated to incorporate useful comments from book reviewers.

Six-to-ten-word condensations of scope, unique features, and price are the copy-package components you'll need for most book ads, display posters, and quick-script "handles" for field sales reps or your phone order-takers. Again, a few words from a rave review may later say it better than you can—so update these entries periodically!

Assuming it takes no more than an hour (given availability of a good author background questionnaire) to write that initial announcement news release, a competent copy writer should be able to develop the other five versions in no more than another hour. Because their expertise is supposed to be in *empathizing with the audience* (rather than second-guessing the author), it is seldom necessary for copy writers to read actual books (or manuscripts) themselves; they should depend on those author background questionnaires instead. Thus, no more than 2 hours per title—supplemented by periodic file-updates to replace your own "hype" with subsequent review raves and hard sales data—should provide virtually all of the promotional copy about specific books you'll ever need.

All of the various kinds of promotional presentations that have been identified above require a collaboration of copywriting skill (which provides not only the copy package components, but additional headline, order form, and other supplementary wording) and graphic design/art talent (which illustrates and physically locates those precious words in the available presentation space—or presentation time, in the case of telemarketing and broadcast scripts—in a manner calculated to best seize the audience's very fleeting attention, engage its positive interest, and lead it through the presentation via a persuasive route). This collaboration may be accomplished by a single individual (a promotion coordinator) who learns to handle both (copy and graphics) sides, or by an effective working relationship between the promotion coordinator (as info-organizing copy writer) and a good graphic artist. When two individuals are involved, publishers often find it better to use an artist from an advertising or mail agency (rather than their own pre-press department) for such promotional graphics—because the split-second requirement of good promotional art/design is different from the orderly, economical style of good interior book design.

Both the copy and the layout/art of each finished presentation required by the marketing strategy should be subjected to six basic tests. To succeed, the presentation must earn an honest "yes" answer to each of these questions:

(1) *Does it establish relevance FAST?* The typical reader is subjected to perhaps 1,500 appeals for attention every day (from bumper stickers, telephone calls, ads, mail, broadcast commercials, crying babies, visiting salesmen, calls of nature, etc.). To preserve our sanity, we learn to dismiss such appeals very quickly—unless they communicate strong relevance to our immediate and personal needs or interests in *split seconds.*

(2) *Does it DRAMATIZE benefits or dangers early?* Once our fleeting attention is engaged, our brains are very adept at sorting out "hype" from messages that offer us real benefits, or pose real threats. Unless we're quickly convinced that reading a message will actually help us—or that failing to do so may harm us—we're unlikely to invest precious minutes in absorbing the "meat" of any promotion.

(3) *Is it keyed to the audience's FRAME-OF-REFERENCE?* Inexperienced book promoters tend to forget that the audience doesn't really care about the "insider" drama of your publication schedule—and isn't impressed by publishing-house jargon. You have to talk to teachers, preachers, gardeners, parents, scientists, and even little kids (studying the covers of children's books) in their own languages, and in terms of *their* needs, activity-cycles, possibilities, and heroes—not yours!

(4) *Does it clearly offer something UNIQUE?* The person most likely to buy any book is a fellow-devotee of your subject-niche and the author's topic. That means he probably already has a few dozen similar books. Unless you can tell him *specifically* what he'll get from yours that isn't in any of those similar books—and that will be of enough value to him to justify an additional purchase—you're not too likely to make a sale.

(5) *Does it document author-credentials that inspire CONFIDENCE?* In a time when virtually every food may give us cancer, and every politician is a self-proclaimed messiah, skeptical readers are quick to demand: "Who says

so?" Effective promotion must engender confidence that your guy knows what he's talking about, and can be trusted.

(6) *Does it elicit an easy, obvious, SPECIFIC RESPONSE?* Okay—so you convinced me. But having sat through your promotion, I'm not likely to invest a lot more of my precious time in doing what you want me to do (call your toll-free number, fax back an order form, go pester my bookstore, examine your free sample as a potential classroom resource, etc.) unless you've made it easy for me to do so. So boil it right down to 1-2-3 ... and make those instructions so obvious I don't have to hunt for 'em!

(7) *Is it a PALATABLE demand on the reader's time?* From the very beginning, most readers are not likely to dive into the process of deciphering your promotion if it looks like it'll tax their patience. So if it takes more than seconds to absorb—organize the presentation with sub-heads, calculated paper-folds, second-color highlighting, fast-summary order forms, and other devices that enable the reader to quick-scan for relevance without committing himself to a research project.

The first question you should ask, when planning any promotional presentation from a mailing piece to an exhibit-booth display, is: *What do you want it to accomplish?* If it is expected to do the total marketing job alone (i.e., generate direct orders on a profitable basis without further sales follow-up), you will find that this is only likely to work with a highly pre-qualified audience—usually people who've bought similar books from you before. So you may need to adopt a more complex intermediate strategy to *accumulate that direct-response customer list,* by achieving an initial sale to an acceptable percentage of a rented list or magazine ad audience, in conjunction with your on-going campaign for exploiting the customer list. While list-building promotion can be justified with considerably less than the $3-for-$1 ratio between resulting sales and promotion costs which is ultimately required for most profitable direct-response selling, it still must "prove itself" by demonstrating an acceptable per-name cost for each such customer-list addition. Few marketers can accomplish this with responses of less than 1 percent from external (rented) lists—compared to the 3-7 percent responses they'll expect from later, repetitive exploitation mailings to their accumulated buyer lists.

In any case, the effectiveness of each promotion should be measured by the actual responses it generates. Ineffective promotion managers tend to plead the difficulty of making such measurements as a way to avoid accountability for results. Others rationalize away poor responses by claiming "echo effects" (untraceable orders they assume the promotion is generating through indirect channels) or public-image "goodwill." Frankly, in this author's quarter-century of experience kibitzing the efforts of several hundred publishing houses, these alibis have almost always proven self-deceptive. If you can't justify the money spent by the short-term results (either in actual dollar volume, or in acceptably-low unit costs of such specifically-targeted responses as new mailing list additions, valid teacher-examination requests, exhibit booth interviews, etc.) that you can trace—you should consider the promotional presentation a failure, and discontinue it in favor of a better candidate.

Finding ways to trace results (both in terms of numbers-of-responses and dollar-volume) is a primary indicator of professionalism and competence in book promotion and marketing management. This has become much easier since book marketers have begun to rely heavily on (and readers have become accustomed to using) highly promoted direct-order phone numbers (whether toll-free or not). It's largely a matter of (1) training everyone who takes orders or information requests by phone to *always* ask: "Would you mind telling me how you learned about this book?" (or brochure, or special offer), at an appropriate point in the procedure, and (2) making sure any phone stations which *aren't* immediately inputting data on-line to the computer are supplied with "call report" forms, so that such source-of-sales information (as well as the order or request itself) can be easily recorded for later evaluation of the effectiveness of each campaign or presentation.

Because of the growing inclination of the American consumer and the American bookstore to order-by-phone, publishers who *dramatically repeat* their direct-order numbers in all promotions usually find that this not only generates more orders (by simplifying the mechanics for the customer), but reroutes those orders from the mail to the phone—thus making possible faster and less expensive on-line processing, with easier source-of-sales tracking. (Altogether, over 70 percent of established publishers now have toll-free order lines, and over a third of their total sales volume now arrives by phone. That later percentage will almost certainly increase as publishers learn to promote this option more effectively.)

A major portion of publishers' orders or inquiries which don't come by phone are from major accounts (such as wholesalers) whose response is indeed some sort of "echo effect" from your total marketing effort—but which should seldom be attributed to *specific* promotions. By eliminating these key-account results from individual-promotion tallies (when comparing one promotion with another), but still including their volume in your over-all assessment of marketing results in relation to costs, you may well find that you need less response to make your on-going promotions to direct-buyer lists profitable than you have previously assumed.

A great deal of mail response which doesn't come from such middlemen as wholesalers can be traced to specific promotions by distinctively coding the order form or response address ("Dept XX") of each promotion. To trace buyers who use their own purchase order forms (especially bookstores or libraries), some publishers even offer modest "preferred customer" discounts (a bonus 2-or-3 percent on selected promotions) to those who address those forms to such a coded "department"—or specify a valid "bonus discount code."

It is, then, not prohibitively difficult to trace and measure the approximate results you get from specific promotions, and relate them to costs (either as sales dollars resulting from each dollar spent, or by calculating the unit cost of each response). The goal is not simply to reach some "acceptable" benchmark (such as those minimum $3-for-$1 paybacks from repetitive consumer-list exploitation, or the $5-for-$1 payback that most publishers need on trade-discounted direct-to-bookstore campaigns)—but rather to *compare* the results of different promotional offers and presentations, and different media or lists, so you can constantly shift promotional dollars from those campaigns, offers, presentations, and lists that do *worst* to those that do *best*.

The same logic applies when the goal of a specific promotion is not to generate the ultimate sale, but rather to produce a properly qualified lead for more expensive, customized follow-up contacts from your *sales* function. By tracking the source of each lead (information-query or comp-copy request) that such ice-breaking promotion generates, you can determine the promotional cost of qualifying a bookstore for a telemarketing follow-up, an educator or book reviewer for an appropriate complimentary sample, or any appropriate middleman for a full-blown presentation of your catalog and trade terms or "dealer plan." Being able to assign a dollar-cost to each such lead not only helps you relate that cost to its eventual value, but tells you which promotions, and which basic tactics (direct mail, print ads, exhibit booths, etc.) are doing the most cost-effective job of generating each type of lead your over-all marketing strategy requires. From that point on, promotion has done its part; subsequent conversion ratios (usually about 1-in-5) are the responsibility of the sales function.

There are probably more alibis for promotions that can't be justified in terms of the comparative direct-sales dollar-payback, or the comparative cost of producing each new customer or qualified sales lead, than for any other single failure in book marketing. We won't belabor the point that it's very dangerous to tolerate such alibis! But for that substantial part of book promotion dedicated to generating sales leads, just "getting response" doesn't automatically justify a campaign. Such two-stage strategies (in which promotion generates a lead for sales to follow up) are never successful unless that "other shoe" eventually drops into place; the promotional responses must be worth what they cost you.

So along with measuring the cost of generating each bookstore request for a reading sample of your next new book, you need to maintain a constant tally of the percentage of those requests that eventually result in a sale. The same can be said of catalog inquiries, teacher examination requests, exhibit booth interviews, etc. If closure rates are consistently low, any experienced marketing manager will recognize this as a symptom of ineffective *sales follow-up* (or be reminded of it by a politically-astute promotion coordinator). But when closure rates for individual campaigns differ from the house's norm—some rethinking of the audience selection, the chosen media, the "come-on" character of the offer, etc., is in order.

Some useful generalities about the different media-formats available to book promoters can be made. By far the independent publisher's over-all favorite among media choices is *direct mail.* (There is a difference between *direct mail* promotion and *mail order* marketing. Direct mail means that the postman carries your message to the audience; mail order [more accurately called "direct response"] means you use the postman [or UPS] rather than the bookstore to deliver the books to readers—whether the orders came via mail, phone, fax, or whatever.)

Most U.S. direct mail promotions are distributed as "third class bulk rate" mail, by publishers who've obtained special permits from their local post offices. This means their postage for most promotions is reduced to two-thirds (or even half, if they're not-for-profit) of the usual first-class rate for a single piece, and they can include several ounces in that piece without additional postage. (Because the precise weights-and-rates keep changing, you should consult your postmaster for current details.) In return for these special rates, you're required to presort and bundle bulk mail according to postal regions; you can get an additional rate reduction by further sorting it down to individual mail routes.

The post office will also provide you a permit for postage-free reply envelopes and cards (for which you pay bonus-postage when they're returned to you). Since the cost of this service has skyrocketed in recent years, mailers who were once enthusiastic now seem ambiguous as to whether it is a cost-effective device, or whether it's better to let customers use their own stamps. (The new era's more-preferred method for stimulating impulse-response is the toll-free phone number, used in conjunction with credit card charges.) Mailers are also divided about the value of a postal service that will send back undeliverable "dead letters" and furnish any known forwarding addresses when bulk rate mail does not reach the addressee; you get this service by imprinting the words "Address Correction Requested" on the address panel of your bulk rate mailing pieces. Again, as the per-piece charge goes up, some mailers conclude it's less expensive just to automatically remove from the lists everybody who doesn't reorder within 2 or 3 years—or use occasional first-class mailings to clean the list—and take your chances in the meantime.

Direct mail has a very distinct advantage over other media, in that it can usually accommodate much more copy (and thus, almost any number of separate books/titles) in a single promotion without adding much to the total cost. So while broadcast, print media, and telephone canvassing promotions are much more likely to be focused on single books (with their lower statistical probabilities of profitable response), direct mail is generally more profitable when it exploits *every penetration of the attention barrier* by exposing the reader to *everything you have* specifically relevant to that reader's known or suspected interests. New titles and bestsellers may be highlighted as features of such promotions, but the odds favoring response go up dramatically when everyone who doesn't buy those headliners still has an opportunity to consider other enticing books.

Direct mail promotions are a designer's dream. Not only do they let you employ options of type, pictures, blank space, and color; they also give the designer relatively unlimited space, and an extra dimension—the folds or separation-of-pieces in the mailing package—to manipulate the presentation's impact on the reader. A majority of bulk rate book promotion designs make the most of this last dimension by presenting everything on a single, multi-fold, self-covering piece of paper rather than sticking unconnected components into an envelope. Publishers are more-or-less evenly divided about the relative merits of these "self-mailers" (with their lower costs) and traditional envelope-letter-enclosures packages. However, when you can use one envelope to "share postage" for a number of separate and self-contained promotions going to *different people* or serving different needs at a single address—such as when presenting several diverse books to the staff of a library or a college department or a business office—you begin to see why the envelope-versus-self-mailer decision should be made on a case-by-case basis.

For valid reasons, perhaps a majority of all books published today are *never* the subject of a single-title *print ad*—and many never appear in *any* periodical print-ad display. Until a generation ago, when direct mail exploded into prominence with the advent of computer-maintained address lists of marvelous selectivity, newspapers and magazines were the main media of book promotion. As many of the national magazines fell apart and newspaper empires declined from the competition of direct mail selectivity and television consumer-saturation, the print media had to change focus to survive.

Now print-ads offer you two primary ingredients for your promotional mix—(1) geographic selectivity on a localized basis (via metropolitan newspaper ads), for regional consumer saturation campaigns at considerably less expense than television commercials, and (2) subject-interest selectivity (either professional or consumer) on a regional, national, or even international scale through magazines keyed to well-defined special-interest audiences. If the many selections offered in Standard Rate & Data Service's newspaper and magazine directories (see Appendix 6) don't get quite as specialized as you want them, take a look at *Ulrich's International Periodicals Directory* (Appendix 2) for a world-wide index of what's available to deliver an audience sharing virtually any special interest you can name.

It is generally assumed that American readers scan the pages of those newspapers and magazines from left to right, across two-page spreads, with their eyes making exploratory sweeps about a third of the way down from the top of the page (or any set-apart block of ad copy they decide to investigate). So once you've selected appropriate print media, the copywriter and designer must conspire imaginatively to intercept those eye-paths with something that will conquer natural attention barriers, and stop eye-movements, in split seconds.

One way to improve the odds is with placement of your ads—in the publication and on the page. Most advertisers prefer right-hand pages in magazines, since it is along the right margin of the spread that one's eyes must pause before a reader turns the page. Many journals and magazines will also allow you to specify placement on one of their covers (front or back, inside or outside) for an extra charge.

A wide range of space-units in print media can be utilized to play effective, specific roles in a promotional strategy. The basic unit is the full page; it gives you complete control of a distinct block of space, while utilizing the editorial matter on the facing page (if any) to help stop the reader long enough for your claim-for-attention. Mechanicals prepared for standard 7"x10" magazine pages can be modestly photo-reduced or enlarged to accommodate most other magazine pages; they'll also dominate a tabloid-size page (because no larger ad can be fitted onto the page with them), and—especially when slightly photo-enlarged—give you a reasonable shot at attention on a full-size newspaper page (when purchasing the entire page-space would be too expensive).

If your ads are confined entirely to magazines, sometimes you can make a given budget go a lot farther with "island half-pages" (two columns by three-fourths of a page, on a three-column page), which dominate the page without requiring you to buy all of it.

The "spot ad" that dramatically displays a quick message (often little more than a cover-photo of a book with a self-explanatory title—plus a price and order-phone number) in a sixth or even a twelfth of a magazine page (or even in a "classified ad" section) can get you a lot of exposure for a single book (or a single special offer) for a modest space budget—especially if repeated in over-lapping media over a period of time. Such ads are primarily used to tap *very-specialized* sub-components of the audience for a given book who are not part of the publisher's normal "constituency." But you have to be very good at copywriting and (especially!) design to pull it off. Because they're small and over-shadowed by bigger ads, most spot ads go virtually unseen, for lack of imaginative (visual or verbal) drama.

Don't overlook multiple-page possibilities in print media. If you publish in a well-defined special interest area and don't have a good, universal mailing list of those who share that interest, anything from a two-page spread to a centerfold insert might be used to deliver your *entire (condensed) catalog* to virtually your *entire potential audience* at less cost than a hit-or-miss mailing schedule might require.

And in comparing potential ad media in your area of interest, find out if they offer reader-service "bingo-card" inquiry referrals, from subscribers who circle appropriate code numbers to ask for more information about a specified ad. Also learn what it costs to have your own reply card or self-sealing order form bound in, so that it tears off at the page carrying your ad.

Print advertising is also the most important (but not only) medium used in "co-op ad" programs, which trade sales forces often merchandise to their bookstore accounts. A cooperative advertising program, as the term is used in the book trade, means something quite different from the "co-op mailings" a number of small publishers have advertised to share postage and list costs (by inserting several compatible houses' promotions in a single envelope to libraries, stores, etc.). It refers to a joint endeavor between you and your resale accounts (especially bookstores), whereby instead of spending all of your mass promotion money yourself, you turn some of it over to them to help finance their local promotions of your books. To make sure those retailers actually have your books on hand to service the results of that promotion, the amount of money you make available should be tied directly to the bookseller's recent (or pre-publication) purchases of the title(s) being promoted.

A typical cooperative advertising arrangement will offer booksellers credits (against purchases from the publisher) amounting to a set percentage (usually 5 percent to 10 percent) of the publisher's *net* (after discount) receipts from each participating bookseller's purchases of a specific new title, within a specified period. The percentage represents most of the money the publisher could normally afford to spend on promotional support of any major new title—so cooperative advertising programs are usually only offered for choice trade titles, and frequently (wisely) limited to pre-publication or other early purchases (when the title most needs help getting launched).

Usually, any participating bookseller is required to submit plans and copy for the publisher's advance approval, and is later required to submit actual copies of advertising bills and tear-sheets before a reimbursement credit is issued. Credits are normally limited to some portion (usually 50 percent or 75 percent) of the bookseller's documented expense. Often the publisher gets an extra bonus because of the lower rates many newspapers and broadcasters charge local businesses such as bookstores.

Publishers often create good ads for the books they've selected for cooperative campaigns, and include glossy proofs in their sales rep's kits. But most do not require the bookseller to use their ad to earn co-op rebates, if the retailer has a different concept that seems plausible. Many also make co-op money as easily available for other bookstore promotions (mailing out "flyers," inclusion in "Christmas Catalogs," etc.) as for print ads.

You can waste a lot of money and create customer ill-will by embarking on poorly conceived cooperative advertising programs that will primarily be exploited by trade accounts to squeeze you for a "bonus discount" without really providing any effective promotion for your book(s). You should be very disciplined about requiring advance approval of ad plans, and documentation of the bills. Insisting that the bookseller pay part of the bill is an important aspect of this approach; it prevents indifferent mishandling on the local end. And always remember that co-op ad programs are the exception rather than the norm among small trade publishers; if you're not convinced it'll make you money—don't do it!

Cooperative advertising programs are one of the areas of potential discrimination between competing customers that the U.S. Fair Trade Commission tends to watch with great interest. The fair trade guidelines say you must do business with all of a competing group of customers on equal terms; if one is eligible for a cooperative allowance, so are the others. You can establish reasonable regional limitations for testing purposes, but you must be careful booksellers aren't competing across those boundaries. To get a clear idea of the nuances you must observe, call the nearest metropolitan field office, or the Washington headquarters, of the FTC.

Because it can be tied directly to actual bookstore orders (though you may be undermined later if those books are returned), and because it spreads advertising risks over a range of different bookseller approaches, and because it benefits by local insights and local media rates—investing a percentage of prepublication sales in cooperative dealer advertising can not only give your sales team a better shot at getting stores to stock a given new title; it may well result in better advertising at less cost than you'd achieve using the money yourself.

As postage costs have climbed steadily in recent years, mass promoters in many industries (especially those seeking direct-response sales) have found various ways of getting their appropriate promotional brochures inserted into *other people's* envelopes or shipping cartons. Four such methods which have won special favor with book publishers are cooperative mailings, carton stuffers, card packs, and single-title author-pass-along flyers. Companies providing insertion media of the first three types are cataloged in appropriate sections or supplements of the media directories published by Standard Rate & Data Service (Appendix 6). Your own acquisition department should be responsible for offering the last type to each author.

(1) *Cooperative mailings* are simply large bulk rate envelopes that contain multiple brochures or other promotional pieces from a number of different marketers seeking to appeal to the same audience. A few of these have been organized from time to time exclusively for book publishers, to reduce postage costs of reaching schools and libraries and bookstores, but none have caught on as established "staples" of book marketing. Many other cooperative programs have shown more staying power, by including book promotions in mailings packages featuring a variety of interest-related non-book products (from seeds to camping equipment).

(2) *Carton stuffers* are promotional pieces that are inserted into the packages containing merchandise previously ordered by the addressee (for example, a promotion for gardening books, inserted in the cartons in which a seed company or nursery fulfills its mail orders). Sometimes publishers are able to negotiate reciprocal carton-stuffing arrangements with marketers of

other merchandise related to the same audience needs/interests as their editorial topics; a tentmaker and a publisher of camping and woodcraft books would be typical partners in such an undertaking. Some compatible publishers have also negotiated profitable deals with *each other,* in which they exchange inserts and gain exposure to each others' captive audiences.

The most obvious carton stuffing tactic is to make sure brochures and catalogs about your full book list go into your *own* shipping containers; individual needs and interests change enough in a few weeks that people who've just ordered from your catalog are reasonably likely to find something else they want there by the time the first order is delivered. The post office agrees that a typically thin publishers catalog is an "incidental" enclosure in a book-rate package, which does not require first class postage. By stocking your warehouse with a selection of such materials and cross-referencing them with related book titles on your order-processing computer, you can achieve automatic "cross-selling" of additional books every time a customer reveals an interest by ordering anything from you.

(3) *Card packs* are an increasingly popular hybrid between direct mail and print ads, by which sponsoring media (most often those with periodical circulation lists) mail entire decks of postcard-sized promotions for different books and/or other products to audiences (gardeners, clergymen, physicians, curriculum supervisors, etc.) sharing a relevant interest. The card pack format requires each participating promoter to compress each presentation (including order form and/or order phone number) into that two-sided postcard size. You pay a cost-share proportional to (and usually supply finished inserts for) only as many cards as you wish to include in each pack.

(4) *Author pass-along flyers* may be the biggest single bargain in book-promotion media—because they not only sell books ... they help keep nervous authors occupied during that painful time between finishing-their-manuscript and the publication date. These are simply quick adaptations of the "copy package" presentation (complete with direct-order coupon and/or phone number), typeset on the desktop unit, reproduced on the photocopier, and provided to the author in *whatever quantity he'll agree to circulate* prior to publication (as insertions in his own correspondence, his organization's newsletter, etc.)—to help get the book off to a good start. Very little cost—and often surprisingly good results!

Television and radio commercials are less-used than direct mail or print ads, and may soon be surpassed by telephone canvassing, in the tactics of American book promoters. Their audiences are too unselective for all but trade and consumer mail order publishers; others have to buy too much wasted circulation to justify the rates. Furthermore, initial production of a good television commercial usually requires a lot of up-front-money.

However, as the fastest-acting and widest-reaching of the mass promotion channels, broadcast advertising does have a demonstrated capability for selling books. Since it must work very fast (for reasons of both attention spans and media rates), it is best at presenting selected single books with broad popular appeal, in quest of a simple result (either a visit to a bookstore, or a direct order). It is up to you, then, to plan the rest of your strategy (adequate bookstore stocking and displays, mail order follow-ups, continuity series of related books, etc.) so that this simple initial action will ultimately pay off. (Since using your most enticing books to lure people into stores through television commercials does your *competitors*—whose books are also there—just about as much good as it does you, it's no wonder that the book marketers using widespread broadcast advertising most effectively are not the publishers, but the larger retail bookstore chains.)

If broadcast advertising fits into your strategy (and it doesn't always require a lot of money, as anyone who has used well-timed radio spots to introduce regional books can tell you), you should give very serious thought (at least the first time around) to obtaining the help of a good advertising agency experienced in these media. This is especially true where television production is involved; it's expensive and complicated, and can become much more of both when you don't really know what you're doing. Amateurism can easily sap away most of the impact of a commercial, by confusing the reader only momentarily. Furthermore, *time placement* of your commercial (in the right period of the day, or in conjunction with programming content that will help attract the right audience) is often very crucial to results—and practiced ad agency procedures for specifying appropriate placement and confirming that it was delivered can be very useful to book promoters without broadcast ad experience.

Don't overlook the possibilities of "p/i" arrangements (which can stand for either "per inquiry" or "percent-of-income") with radio and/or television stations—in which you provide audio or video tapes into which they can incorporate their address codes, and they forward you all the orders in exchange for a share of the results (rather than their usual time-rates). If you can develop a commercial that works well enough in this respect to stay on the air in various parts of the country for some time, you'll find it an excellent way to build a customer mailing list for repetitive consumer direct mail exploitation. If you can't find an ad agency experienced and interested in this approach, try contacting individual stations that run a lot of inexpensive mail-order-merchandise promotions and asking them to suggest agencies with which they've worked effectively.

The telephone is becoming increasingly useful to book marketers not only as a substitute for face-to-face sales calls, but as a very selective, very intensive mass promotion medium—through which you can reach an entire category-audience by giving a names-and-numbers list and a carefully scripted message to one or more well-coached phoners, and having them deliver that message to every prospect they can contact. This technique is called "canvassing." (Because it is an unsolicited intrusion into the life of its audience, the term "cold turkey telemarketing" is also used to distinguish it from phone sales follow-ups of qualified leads).

Telephone canvassing is available from service bureaus in most major metropolitan markets. However, most publishers have found such services so expensive (in relation to results) that they've preferred to develop their own canvassing teams—often using part-timers and/or temporary help.

Such extensive use of long-distance phoning will only be practical if you make arrangements for special rates. Most of the long-distance phone carriers now offer such rates—and the competition is fierce enough that they're easy to find. Your phone company will also be more-than-eager to tell you about special equipment it can provide to make telephone canvassing more efficient, and training services for the personnel you plan to use.

Personnel requirements are considerably different from those for other kinds of marketing work. Obviously, a pleasing and durable voice is a considerable asset. And canvassers must be mentally-agile enough to field a wide variety of questions and responses. But above all, they must possess a psychological tolerance for constant one-on-one exposure to a steady stream of strangers, and for the (often irritable) rejection that the odds dictate they'll encounter about 80 percent of the time. Only psychological tolerance will enable them to break an unsuccessful connection and move right on to the next call—number after number, at a rate of a-dozen-or-so an hour (only a third of whom will be available-to-listen). Even when promotion managers recruit and screen specifically for such psychological tolerance, the turn-over rate among telephone canvassers (where they're used) is probably higher than for any other job in a publishing house.

While more subtle talents may be needed for the kinds of one-on-one selling by phone we'll describe in Chapter 27, for mass telephone canvassing of entire categories of prospects the key is to find people who'll effectively deliver a pre-scripted message time after time, with a minimum of ad-libbing or freelancing. Your best copywriter and sequence-designer should then hone that script so the listener has already heard the most compelling and vital parts of the message *before* he/she could normally interrupt or hang up. This means jam-packing 20 to 30 seconds with information, before you get the listener conversationally involved with a carefully-focused question.

Rather than trying to recruit and train your phone canvassers to handle all of the questions and options that are likely to be thrown back at them during such calls, it's usually more practical to have a supervisor in the area (whether working on the canvassing project, or working on something else except when needed by the canvassers) to whom all such questions can be transferred. This means providing that supervisor with a phone that can break into any of the lines on which your canvassers are working. And the supervisor should have, at hand, a comprehensive library of (or on-line access to) data on books, prices, terms, customer status, and whatever else might come up.

The most cost-effective canvassing programs provide each telemarketer with a computer key-board for direct and immediate order-input. If that's not feasible, you should prepare a well-thought-out recording form—on which names and numbers can be listed for the canvasser's guidance, and orders or inquiries or complaints or other comments can be referred to appropriate parties. While it's easier to put the names-and-numbers on if you design a sheet that can record the results of a number of contacts—it's easier to refer the results to the right place if you use pads of smaller forms, with only one contact to each sheet. "You pays your money and takes your choice."

Telephone canvassing is an effective way to get renewal orders for the latest edition of a yearbook, to offer an appropriately specialized list the introductory volume of a continuity series, to solicit new bookstore accounts by pushing a special offer on your current bestseller, to screen teachers who've asked about similar books in the past when offering samples of a new text or supplement, or simply to sell a practical book whose contents and value can be easily described to a properly-qualified list of confirmed mail order buyers—professional or consumer. The best medium of exchange for canvasser transactions is a valid credit card number; otherwise, your profit margin may well be dissolved by billing costs and uncollectable debts.

CHAPTER 26
Introducing New Titles to Your
Key Publicity Contacts and Major Accounts

As noted in the previous chapter, (1) because single-book promotions offer such low statistical probability of intercepting the attention of any given reader/buyer at a time when he's susceptible to that *particular, limited* subject-appeal, and therefore (2) most books should *never* become the focus of extensive single-title mailings or print ads, it would seem that we're being fairly callous about denying new titles and their authors a real "moment in the sun." But that is not our intention.

It's simply a fact that realistic small publishers usually find that their most effective way of supporting single new titles is by highly selective, *labor-intensive* (not media-intensive) work by both their promotion and sales teams to introduce those titles to the "cream of the audience" in search of big initial orders and important free publicity-exposure (which will then initiate momentum, on a broader scale, for many smaller orders)—rather than scattering their limited promotion money over vast, loosely-targeted audiences.

So most of the single-title work of effective small marketing departments is concentrated on introducing each new title (well *before* its formal publication date) to their *most important* purchasing and publicity contacts—making virtually certain that each of those contacts who might have a real interest in the book is fully aware of its arrival on the scene.

The first requirement for accomplishing this is the accumulation of a good "key contact" list of major publicity sources (book reviewers, talk show producers, influential "friends of the house," relevant organizational newsletters, etc.) and sales prospects (wholesalers, chain buyers, your biggest bookstore accounts, large-system library examination centers, appropriate curriculum planners, subsidiary rights buyers, etc.). Developing this list by routine accumulation, plus special research in such directories as Ad-Lib's *Book Publishing Resource Guide* (see Appendix 1) and Bowker's *Literary Marketing Place* (see Appendix 2) should be a major responsibility of the promotion coordinator.

In a trade publishing house, this key contact promotion list should include the appropriate buyer for every bookstore or wholesale account that (in the past 12 months) has produced 2 percent or more of the publisher's total annual sales volume; this will normally be 20-30 names at most. It should also include any library examination centers with which the publisher has established sampling arrangements, and all bookstores who've enrolled in any special "dealer plans" the publisher may have offered. The sales coordinator should have the option of including additional accounts she believes have special potential; some like to include *all* active, bulk-buying bookstore accounts.

A classroom-adoption publisher should accumulate a similar list of all seemingly-qualified curriculum planners and other educators who have demonstrated (either by adoptions, or by sincere examination-sample requests) a valid interest in that publisher's books within the last 2 years—subject-coded so that appropriately selective prospect lists can be generated for each forthcoming new book.

All types of publishers (even those confined to direct-response books ... who will subsequently try to inform their entire past-customer list directly of each appropriate new title, as outlined in Chapter 30) should also include in their key contact lists (1) book reviewers (by name or title) of periodicals that share a strong interest in their subject-niche(s)—specialized or regional journals, and specialty-page editors of major metropolitan newspapers, (2) producers of radio and TV talk shows who've been receptive to their authors in the past, and (3) *all* buyers of major subsidiary (mass market reprint, book club, first-serial, translation) rights who've shown recent interest in their books. Again, your own contacts can be supplemented by selected names from *Book Publishing Resource Guide* and *Literary Market Place.*

Before most promotion coordinators got their own computer terminals, it was common to limit key contact lists to 100-or-so names, so they could be hand-sorted for each new title. But now, most promotion coordinators find it feasible to accumulate and manipulate category-coded lists of a thousand or more contacts—using appropriate selection criteria to sort special introductory-campaign lists for each new title.

To help you pin-point appropriate customer or publicity prospects for specific forthcoming books, the database form on which you maintain this key contact list should include one field for entering individual book codes designating who should receive advance promotion on the title, and another designating those who should receive (automatically, or as a result of their own requests) complimentary samples or review copies of the book itself. A good form (usable with any normal database software) will look something like Figure 26a, on the next page.

The "category" blank is available for whatever internal organization the promotion coordinator feels would be useful (for identifying book reviewers and talk show producers and major accounts and sub-rights contacts and teachers and others you may want to approach differently from time to time). "Last activity" simply confirms (by year and month) the last date you had evidence the contact was still there—and potentially interested in your books.

"Annual volume" gives you a frame-of-reference when talking with actual buyers from your major accounts. "Call-back" gives you a reminder of promised or appropriate follow-up dates.

Figure 26a—Sample Key Contact Data-Form

```
┌────────────────────────────────────────────────────────────────────┐
│  05-13-1991                Key Contact File                  16:42   │
│ ORGANIZATION[_____] CATEGORY[_____] │
│ ADDRESS[_____] LAST ACTIVITY[_____]  │
│ CITY/STATE[_____] ZIP/COUNTRY[_____]          │
│ INDIVIDUAL[_____] ANNUAL VOLUME $[_____] │
│    PHONE[_____] BEST HRS[_____] CALL-BACK[_____]  │
│ PROMO[_____] │
│ COMPS[_____] │
│ NOTE1[_____] │
│ NOTE2[_____] │
│ NOTE3[_____] │
│    RESULT1[_____] │
│    RESULT2[_____] │
│    RESULT3[_____] │
│    RESULT4[_____] │
│    RESULT5[_____] │
│ TITLE SLUG1[_____] │
│ TITLE SLUG2[_____] │
│ TITLE SLUG3[_____] │
│                                                           page= 1    │
└────────────────────────────────────────────────────────────────────┘
F1=EXIT  F2=DUPE FIELD NO.   F4=DICTIONARY     F5=RESTORE PAGE  F9=UPDATE
```

Those lines captioned "promo" and "comps" are particularly important. They are used to record (by category or individual selection) the stock or project numbers of each forthcoming book that should be called to the attention of each entry on the list. Some database software is capable of adding a book's code (two or three digits) to all appropriate lines by category-selection; nevertheless, promotion coordinators frequently choose to flip through the list name-by-name, and designate targets at the beginning of each individual new title introduction campaign. The "promo" line should be coded to indicate which contacts are to receive advance news releases and other announcements on a given title, and the "comps" line should indicate which (as a result of the promotion coordinator's decision, or the contact's subsequent request) are to receive complimentary advance copies of the book itself, as soon as it becomes available. The computer can then simply select all those with a given code on the appropriate line, and print out mailing or shipping labels at each appropriate stage of the campaign, to introduce or actually deliver any given book.

Fairly early in the pre-publication campaign to introduce each new title, the appropriate acquisition editor should be invited to add to the list (with "promo" and/or "comps" coding for that title) the names of specialized reviewers, influential acquaintances of the author, etc., who could help get the book off to a good start. (See "P-8" entries in Figure 26b, on the next page.) As with the promotion coordinator's own entries into the list, however, these should be limited to people whose influence is deemed to be *worth a complimentary advance copy*. (Don't make the "key contact list" a direct-selling list of potential individual customers; those should be accumulated elsewhere, or incorporated into your computerized customer file, for use as discussed in Chapter 30.) And *after* each new title campaign, the promotion coordinator should call up all names coded for that particular book and *remove* any editor-or-author entries that are not deemed generally appropriate for other, future titles.

Figure 26b—Sample Pre-Publication Introductory Sequence

[P = months-before-formal-publication]
P-8 Plan Title Insertion into General Marketing Program
P-8 Editors Add Specialized Contacts to Promo List
P-8 Author-Editor Special Marketing Interview
P-7 Code Title into Promo List
P-7 Reply Card Announcement NR to Sub-Rights Contacts
P-7 Coupon Announcement Flyers to Author
P-7 Plan/Distribute Piggybacks
P-6 Sub-Rights "Ms. Ready" Letter
P-6 Query Letters to Special Marketing Contacts
P-6 Pre-inform Reps, Distributors
P-6 Pre-print Add-On Letter to Select Accounts
P-6 Initial ABI Input
P-5 Phone Follow-Up of Special Market Inquirers
P-5 Photocopies to Sub-Rights Requesters
P-4 Phone Follow-Ups of Sub-Rights Requesters
P-4 "Pages Ready" Letter to Other Sub-Rights Contacts
P-4 "Pages Ready" Follow-Up to Special Marketing Contacts
P-4 Reply Card Announcement NR #1 to Qualified Dealers
P-3 Final Sub-Rights, Special Marketing Phone Follow-Up
P-3 Page Photocopies to Pre-Reviewers
P-3 Updating the ABI Data
P-3 Reply Card Announcement NR to Coded Reviewers
P-3 Reply Card Announcement NR to Coded Broadcasters
P-3 Reply Card Announcement NR #2 to Qualified Dealers
P-3 Exam Offers to Major Library Systems
P-2 Complimentary Book Distribution
P-1 Bookstore Phone Follow-Ups
P-0 The Launching Party!

Once the key contact list is established and developed, it should also be the promotion coordinator's responsibility (using the "copy package" material created as each new title moves into the pre-publication development pipeline—as per the previous chapter) to make sure that each of these contacts (unless hand-picked as "inappropriate" for a given book) is effectively informed of every forthcoming title's unique qualities, and whatever else might help convince that influential individual to help it get off to a good start (by either publicizing it, or purchasing it). To keep important prospects from "dropping through cracks," experienced promotion coordinators find it useful to develop a basic checklist of routines for accomplishing this. Such a checklist for introducing new trade and general-interest titles (and developing qualified leads for the sales function) should look something like Figure 26b above.

This general strategy/schedule should, of course, coincide with (and be incorporated into) the basic "new title development schedule" created by the managing editor as per Figure 21b. Thus, sometime around 8 months prior to formal publication (see first P-8 entry in Figure 26b above), the promotion coordinator should review the basic marketing strategy model—and locate every on-going campaign and anticipated multi-title presentation into which each specific new title should be incorporated—including its systematic listing in "end paper" promotional lists in the last signatures of related titles that will be introduced or reprinted in the future. Then, utilizing the existing "copy package" (Chapter 25), she must make specific arrangements for seeing that it *is* incorporated.

The formal "publication date" (essentially, "P-0" in Figure 26b), incidentally, is whenever your marketing function says it should be; it's the earliest date on which it's kosher for book reviewers to publish their opinions of the work. Most marketing managers like to set these 30-to-60 days after they expect to have bound books (advance samples)—to give them some time to drum up publicity, complete sales follow-ups, and deliver advance orders to key accounts *before* the public "launching." This helps "peak" the attention book experts are giving each title around a given date—thus hopefully generating maximum momentum.

Between those two terminals of the introductory sequence, then, a typical well-planned introductory program in a trade-oriented publishing house, such as that illustrated in Figure 26b, will have the promotion coordinator (see P-8) interviewing authors (by phone) or editors to identify "special marketing" contacts (organizations outside the book trade that might buy in bulk for various uses or resale programs), determining (P-7) which categories or single entries in the key contact list should be coded to receive promotion and/or automatic comp-copies of the title, getting off an early announcement news release to sub-rights buyers (P-7), with a reply card offering a comp copy of preliminary page-proofs, offering letter-insert direct-order brochures for authors to distribute to personal contacts (P-7), and arranging similar circulation (P-7) of such "piggyback" insert-brochures by others (including the publishing house itself).

In the sixth month before publication, this strategy anticipates taking another shot at all the sub-rights prospects—using a personalized word-processed letter to inform them when advance page-proofs will actually be available, getting off similarly-personalized letters offering more information, bulk discount terms, and eventual complimentary copies (on request) to those "special marketing" prospects identified earlier, telling any commissioned reps or distributors with whom the publisher might be working what they'll want to know about the new title, possibly contacting large wholesale accounts with a special bonus-discount offer for very-early, large-quantity orders that might increase ("add on to") the initial print run, and providing R. R. Bowker Company (the major bibliographer of new books for stores, libraries, and others) of the basic facts about the forthcoming publication on the "Advance Book Information" (ABI) forms its ABI Department (see Appendix 2) will provide on request.

In the fifth month before publication, the promotion coordinator turns over any special marketing leads to the sales coordinator, who'll query (by phone) the plans of anyone who asked for more information as a result of the P-6 "special marketing" letter—and sends off any advance page-proofs sub-rights buyers may have requested.

In the fourth month, the promotion coordinator reports all sub-rights leads to sales, for one-on-one follow-up. Meanwhile, he takes another shot at all sub-rights and special marketing names that *haven't* expressed interest to date, with letters reminding them again that advance page-proofs are now available. And the more general pre-publication promotion begins, with a news release announcement to key trade accounts offering (via reply card) a complimentary advance copy.

In the third month before publication, while the sales function is making a final telephone sweep or sub-rights and special marketing leads, the promotion coordinator gets off page-proofs to the major book-industry "pre-reviewers" (*Publishers' Weekly, Library Journal, ALA Booklist,* and possibly others) who alert bookstores and libraries to "what's coming"—while also providing any late-change data (re: page counts, prices, publication dates, etc.) to Bowker's ABI system. At the same time, a second news release with comp-copy offer goes out to the key trade contacts (many of whom will have overlooked the previous month's announcement), and to all book reviewers and broadcast talk shows coded (P-7) for promotion about this book. A similar offer of complimentary examination copies might be sent to any large-system library examination centers on the key contact list.

Finally, then, in the second month before formal publication, the strategy envisioned in Figure 26b anticipates receipt of the first printed copies of the book—which are promptly dispatched to all who have requested, or been automatically coded to receive, complimentary copies. And a few weeks later, the sales function follows up all of the comp-requests from bookstores by phoning to solicit specific stocking orders. Then it's marketing's turn to celebrate the formal publication date of the book (knowing it's been given a conscientious send-off) by throwing a party!

As is reflected in Figure 26b, the principal tools used by veteran promotion coordinators in such campaigns—to initiate free publicity from the reviewers and talk shows, and generate highly-qualified sales leads from trade accounts, sub-rights buyers, curriculum planners, big library systems, etc.—are (1) those advance news release announcements of the forthcoming publication of each new title described as part of the basic "copy package" in Chapter 25, and (2) automatic complimentary copies (except in special cases where they might be inappropriate or offensive) to all of the key contact categories relevant to each book.

All of those news releases should offer complimentary advance copies on request—just to see who's *especially* interested—but it's additionally normal (and wise) to send *automatic* complimentary copies to large portions of the list as soon they're available—regardless of who's asked and who hasn't. (Many are routinely offered so many free samples that they simply don't bother to request more, even when a title piques their interest.) Remember— anybody whose potential influence or purchase isn't worth a free advance sample of any appropriate new title *shouldn't be on your "key contact" list* in the first place. And don't worry that bookstores might put those free samples on display and sell them; that's exactly what you want! A fast-selling sample is the best sales pitch for a bulk stocking order that you could possibly engineer!

Follow-up responsibility for handling responses from those contacts you're hoping will give you free publicity (reviewers, talk shows, etc.) also normally falls to the promotion coordinator. But follow-ups of complimentary books or other materials sent to actual or prospective *buyers* on the list (major accounts, subsidiary rights buyers, etc.) should normally be assigned to the *sales coordinator*—your top "one-on-one" specialist in "bringing home the bacon."

A classroom-adoption publisher would, of course, skip all the announcements to book dealers, and direct them instead to their educator contacts. And a direct-response vocational/reference book publisher would probably limit dealer promotions to wholesalers, skip the libraries (who should, instead, be included in their direct-response customer list for exploitation as per Chapter 30), and concentrate only on book reviewers and subsidiary rights contacts (with library examination centers as possible secondary targets).

Book reviewers who respond to your announcements normally require no follow-up except the complimentary review copy. But it's a good idea to include with that book another copy of the news release that pre-announced its publication—to help them round up background facts for their eventual review. It is also customary to include a formal data-slip specifying the exact, official title and price and ISBNumber, the proper spelling of the author's name, the binding (hardcover, trade paperback, etc.), and the formal publication date. This data-slip should remind the reviewer of the two tearsheet copies of any resulting review that publishers are entitled to expect (though seldom actually receive). Some publishers combine the data-slip (as a tab-insert folding over the top of the title page) with a reply form, on which the reviewing medium is asked to tell you whether/when it expects to publish a review.

In recent years, it has also become common to include the publisher's toll-free direct-order phone number in such news releases and data-slips. An increasing number of periodicals include such numbers in their reviews—thus helping their readers obtain books that local stores don't stock.

Broadcast talk shows are voracious in their appetite for guest-authors—and very good about including your toll-free order numbers in their scripts! While television shows outside the author's home area may raise travel-expense complications (since only the national network shows normally promote enough sales to make such expenses worthwhile—and such network shows often pay their guests honoraria that cover such expenses anyhow), radio talk shows have become the favorite broadcast-publicity medium of independent publishing houses; it is not unusual for a small publisher to book even a relatively unknown author on several dozen such shows. You can buy a mailing list of these radio outlets from Ad-Lib Publications (Appendix 1). Because most of them connect their audiences and guest-authors via remote phone hook-ups, no travel expenses are involved.

Incidentally, when they respond to your advance sample copies by requesting interview arrangements with a given author, you can avoid having to track down that author to negotiate a mutually-acceptable date—by getting the author's permission to pre-print his/her phone number on a gummed label, with instructions for the broadcaster to call it to arrange an interview. Just stick that label right onto the cover of the complimentary book before you send it.

When you send advance announcements to subsidiary rights buyers, you may find that they don't want to wait until the book comes off the printing press to see how it might fit into their plans. (This is especially true of book clubs, who may want to "join" your printing by having your printer run off the interior pages of their edition while he's doing yours. More about this in Chapter 32.) So the early news release (or an accompanying cover letter) should offer to provide *advance page proofs* (photocopies of your first-round desktop print-outs) to any who wish to read the book prior to the initial printing. If you confine this offer to major sub-rights prospects (mass market reprinters, first-serial syndicates, and book clubs or translation prospects specializing in your subject area—generally the only sub-rights categories that belong on your key contact list anyhow), it should be worth your while to make an extra set of preliminary text-page photocopies for any such contact who shows enough interest to ask for them.

Once again, follow-up of such interest by major sub-rights buyers is properly a *sales* function (not a promotional chore). As is true of a large portion of any good contemporary book-marketing strategy, *"promotion* generates high-quality leads for *sales* to close."

But the surest pay-off comes from those actual-buyer names you've included (from all accounts that produce at least 2 percent of your total sales) as a top-priority category of your key contact list. As complimentary copies of each book are sent out to all names in this portion of the list, the sales manager should be immediately informed of the shipping date—and of any prior indication of interest by any/each account as a result of the (often repeated two-or-three times) news release announcements.

A well-managed sales function will then create a basic telemarketing script that will be used 2 or 3 weeks later—in personalized phone follow-ups "just to make sure you got the complimentary book we sent"—always tying in the prompt question: "So how many copies do you think you'd like to try for openers?"

Such systematic announcement and sample-copy distribution of each new title is the heart and soul of effective, on-going communication with your key contacts—and the most useful *single-book* campaign you can initiate to support any given new title. Don't worry that you'll irritate those key contacts by sending too much mail. Most of them are on hundreds of other "key contact lists" as well—so they're used to sorting through tall stacks of mail to separate the "wheat" from the "chaff." In fact, it'll occasionally be worthwhile to amplify this stream of promotion by adding special news releases reporting important commentary by other reviewers, successful sub-rights negotiations, and other developments that make it obvious that any given book is "a winner" they won't want to overlook.

But the tall mail-stacks on those contacts' desks put a premium on writing great headlines for your news releases, brain-storming great titles for your books, and designing envelopes and labels that dramatically signal *relevance* to their concerns in the split seconds before they're otherwise consigned to the waste basket!

CHAPTER 27
Organizing Customer Service's
Response to Phone or Mail

In times gone by, incoming orders were routinely punched into publishers' invoicing computers by specialized "order entry clerks" in the business office—working off-line from written order forms, purchase orders, and scribbled notations of phone messages. Generally speaking, this was traditionally one of the dullest jobs in book publishing—and boredom generated a high level of employee turnover. But things are changing!

Partially to alleviate that boredom, many publishers promoted the best of their order entry clerks to the role of "customer service representative"— putting them "on line" with real live customers via phone and mail ... to trace missing orders, answer invoicing questions, approve merchandise returns, or field complaints. Along about then, it started becoming obvious that as these customer service reps talked to their accounts (often developing first-name relationships with important repeat-buyers), they were perfectly capable of making appropriate (and helpful) purchasing suggestions to those customers.

But business managers rightly contended that since these people were on *their* payrolls, doing *marketing's* work as a sideline was a very low priority. And in too many publishing houses, marketing was sloppy about encouraging the customer service reps—by making sure they got early and adequate information about new books and special offers, and credit for the sales they made. So the rich sales opportunities of "customer service" long remained largely hypothetical.

And then, better order processing software and the steady increase of phone orders (as the direct marketing industry began retraining the American consumer to "dial-800" rather than "send back the order form") led more and more publishers to explore on-line order entry ... whereby order clerks (by momentarily setting aside the mail orders they were inputting before the phone rang) could punch new-account customer files, book purchases, changes of address, and even financial corrections into their keyboards *while they were talking with customers* by phone.

Publishers quickly discovered that old fears of "losing the paper trail" if orders weren't backed up by written documentation were largely unjustified; clerks actually made *fewer* errors key-punching while they listened than they did trying after-the-fact to decipher other people's scribbled phone-order notes. And astute business managers realized that they'd been spending more money laboriously matching and filing and recovering documentation than it would have cost simply to replace (duplicate) most challenged orders.

Prudent order entry programs still file the paperwork on small numbers of very large or very suspicious orders. Everything else, these days, is likely to go into a temporary "holding stack"—and get dumped a few weeks later if there are no repercussions. Hours and hours of dull paper-shuffling are thus eliminated. And only the very dense go to the trouble of creating paper documentation of phone orders just so they'll have something for that temporary stack; most of us have finally conceded that the computer record is usually more reliable than our scrawling.

At any rate, as those traditional order clerks went "on line" to enter purchases from the phone, two things happened. First—most customers couldn't tell the difference between the "order clerk" who answered the 800-number, and the "customer service rep" to whom they were transferred when problems arose ... so the better order clerks began learning to solve those problems themselves. Second—quite a few order clerks who'd been recruited for unharrassed paper-shuffling and calm, off-line key-punching of mail orders proved psychologically ill-suited to the faster-paced, often-pressurized, personality-challenging work of simultaneous on-line interaction with both a live customer and an unforgiving piece of fairly complex computer software.

What followed was a steady re integration of the roles of the order processor and the customer service representative. Sad as it may seem in personal terms, computerization really has obsoleted that traditional, unhurried, off-line "order clerk." Those who can't make the transition from off-line data processing to on-line customer service (with the mail-order inputting as a between-calls fill-in) tend to look for other jobs. Recruiting criteria for their replacements generally include people who don't mind pressure, think fast on their feet, and like personal one-on-one interaction with strangers.

Old-style, off-line order-entry personnel (and sometimes, supervisors scared by change) almost inevitably resist this transition by insisting that their order processing software won't find a file—or allow a new entry—fast enough to avoid awkwardness with the phone-in customer. In actual practice, this has almost always been proved a flimsy alibi. While it may take a little ingenuity with the procedure guide (for instance, asking a promotion-tracking question to keep the caller usefully occupied while the computer searches), virtually all of the publishing-specific order entry software widely used today *will* accommodate on-line input.

But why are we discussing this in a chapter on "marketing"—rather than under "business management"? Well, this gradual transformation (in "state of the art" publishing houses) of the old-time "order entry clerk" into an on-line customer service "telerep" has created a new breed of publishing personnel fully capable of cashing in on the sales potential of that rising volume of live phone interactions with customers that almost all publishers (and especially those who aggressively promote their toll-free numbers) are experiencing. As a result, marketing managers are increasingly more-than-willing to assume responsibility for recruiting, training, supervising and paying the "customer service reps"—as long as sales opportunities are very high on their priority lists, and appropriate budget-share adjustments are made. Since sales potential is threatened whenever orders aren't handled right, there's been no decline in order processing diligence as this function has moved (in more and more publishing houses every year) from the business office to the marketing department.

In effect, the customer-service telereps have become the sales coordinator's "field sales force." Some are even retitled as "account representatives"—and assigned specific territories or customer categories. They're increasingly proving just as effective as—and far less expensive than—traveling sales people (whether staff or commissioned). In the twenty-first century, it seems obvious that these one-time "order entry clerks" will be the predominant (and often only) component of most independent publishers' *sales* staffs.

And in the process, the one-time "order processing supervisor" has, in many marketing departments, become the assistant (or sometimes even principal) sales coordinator. Because of the inevitable pressures of the lively role of the telereps, a major aspect of this supervisor's job may be continuous recruiting. The job looks something like Figure 27a, on the next page.

Meanwhile, the mass promotion (direct mail, advertising, publicity) half of marketing's one-two punch has been refocusing on *making that 800-number ring*. Many publishers (wisely) make this a *dedicated order line* that only connects to the marketing department; callers who use it for other traffic are politely given another number. To direct the results of their promotion to the (customer service) sales telereps for immediate follow-up, this order-phone number is prominently and frequently repeated in all catalogs, order forms, mail promotions, exhibit displays, end-paper promos, ads, news releases and carton stuffers—and on all customer invoices, statements, packing slips, and other documents that might prompt customer service calls.

So when a customer or potential customer—or a buying influencer such as a book reviewer or curriculum decision-maker—calls that highly publicized number today, the customer service rep (now frequently called a "telerep") who answers is often prepared to do anything from processing a credit card purchase to authorizing a book return or comp-copy shipment—or even opening a new account. (In the marketing departments of many not-for-profit member-service organizations, they even renew memberships or journal subscriptions, or take conference registrations—in addition to handling book orders.) They're well-informed about all promotions, and persistent about asking customers: "Where did you see this 800-number?"—so they can enter source codes for virtually all orders (and even for the complimentary-sample requests stimulated by publicity news releases), to give the marketing manager reliable feedback about which sales and promotion tactics are working—and which aren't.

Figure 27a—Sample Job Description: Customer Service Supervisor

---

TITLE: Customer Service Supervisor
Reports to: Sales Coordinator
Directly Supervises: All Customer Service Telereps
Budget Line Responsibility: Marketing Expense Lines 102-107
Accountability Indices:

> Transactions completed per 100 staff hours
> Invoice lines per 100 staff hours
> Staff errors per 1000 transactions
> Upsell contribution to phone-order volume

GENERAL RESPONSIBILITY:

To maintain an effective system for responding to all orders for, inquiries about, or claims-adjustments concerning books, other products, and services of this publishing house—and to recruit, train and supervise telereps who can make those responses in a sales-maximizing yet cost-effective manner.

SPECIFIC RESPONSIBILITIES.

a) Ongoing supervision of daily order-entry operations;

b) Continuous refinement of the organizational structure and resulting job descriptions of the customer service section;

c) Continuous refinement and documentation of procedural checklists for responding to all recurring customer service situations, queries, orders and claims;

d) Recruitment, orientation, and periodic performance review of all authorized customer service personnel;

e) Updating and circulation of useful work-station quick-reference materials on products and terms;

f) Continuous skill-enrichment training of the telereps;

g) Regular feedback of workload and performance indices to the sales coordinator, and to individual telereps;

h) Implementation of cross-sell and upsell programs initiated by the promotion and sales coordinators.

It is important that both the order processing software *and* business office policy accommodate the *immediate* opening of new accounts, often while the customer is on the phone, if the telereps are to follow up effectively on the leads promotion generates. This means that whenever the telerep types a finder code (based on the zip code and the customer's name) into the keyboard, and learns that there is no existing account for that bookstore, that telerep must be pre-authorized to tell the customer: "I'm going to set up an account for you with an initial credit allowance of $100 (or $50, or whatever your business manager insists); our invoices are payable within 30 days of your end-of-the-month statement"—and the software must accommodate that immediate action. (You can still check against such a near-universal reference as Bowker's *American Book Trade Directory* [see Appendix 2] for verification that the bookstore actually exists, before you ship.) That modest credit limit will protect you from losing much on the occasional deadbeat you encounter—and the few small amounts you can't collect will cost you much less than it would to *actually check references* on every small new bookstore account. By the time most bookstores exceed that modest limit on a subsequent order, you may already have enough payment history on them to avoid ever having to check references. Meanwhile, this ability to *proceed immediately* with the initial order enhances the telerep's chances of establishing a positive relationship between your publishing house and the new customer.

If that automatic credit limit doesn't cover that initial order, the telerep must then ask for prepayment, or send a pro forma invoice (which must be paid before you ship)—or (explaining the delay) ask for credit references for checking before shipment. And all *bad debt* accounts must be kept on the computer—and clearly flagged by it—so that new accounts *won't* be automatically opened for them when they call again.

Thus, good telereps become not only the principal sales force, but the customers' (or publicity contacts') agents within the publishing house. Tell 'em the problem and they'll solve it—or quickly find someone who can. For the reader who has no specific book in mind, but only knows what kind of information they're seeking—the telerep becomes a live index to the catalog. If other departments have to be consulted—the rep does the legwork (usually by inter-office phone) and calls the customer back.

And once they're clearly identified as *marketing* people, telereps become the key players in a (usually highly effective) new component of many publishers' sales tactics—on-line "up-sell." This is the term used to describe a routine whereby the telerep inserts into each incoming phone-order conversation a suggestion for adding one or more additional, interest-related books to the customer's original request. The scripts they use to achieve this (at "Step 13" in the sample phone-answering procedure guide displayed earlier as Figure 11c) are carefully crafted (as needed—at the sales coordinator's request) by the promotional copywriter. Disciplined, automatic repetition of such upsell scripts has increased the *average* phone-order unit-of-sale (from both bookstores and individual readers) by as much as 20 percent in some publishing houses!

You'd think those phone duties would give telereps more than enough to do—but it's surprising how much extra time the good ones in small marketing departments find for other work. Veterans can usually handle 50-or-more phone calls a day—and that's more than are normally experienced by the typical single-rep publishing house. So regardless of staff size, there are always slow periods—when even the best efforts of the promotion people won't keep that 800-number busy. For those times, in a well-organized order processing program, each telerep has a pre-sorted stack of written orders from the morning mail to get into the computer. These will go much, much faster than open-ended phone conversations.

To help them switch back-and-forth from the phone to paper orders, properly equipped telereps wear headphones so they can respond to the order-line without removing their hands from the keyboard. When a new call buzzes in their ear (if there's more than one telerep, the switchboard will search for the first open work-station), they answer: "One moment, please," and finish the paper order they're presently inputting. Then they ask: "May I help you?"—and they're off-and-running with another personalized, on-line transaction.

The ability of phone-switching equipment to search for that first unbusy work-station is one key to organizing your telerep sales staff. If you have one telerep who's a superb sales-person, and another who's much better as a key-puncher—put the former at the work-station that is first-in-line in the phone's search-sequence. That means incoming calls are most likely to go to that star sales rep—leaving the star key-puncher to handle most of the mail orders. Nevertheless, each knows how to do both things—so they're both able to adjust to a changing ratio between phone orders and mail orders.

This phone-searching capacity also plays a very helpful part in training new telereps. For those first few nervous days, the newcomer should always sit in the last work-station in the phone-search sequence and be given a pre-sorted stack of very simple written orders (such as prepaid orders from individuals) to enter—just to get used to the process and the software. After several days of such unharried interaction with the computer, a reasonably qualified newcomer will almost inevitably learn enough to "move up the line" into greater proximity with those incoming phone orders and live customers.

But perhaps the most dramatic contribution telereps are making to publishers' sales efforts is in *outbound telemarketing*. Essentially this means calling selected customer-prospects *before* they call you, to make a sales "pitch"—just as a traveling sales rep would call on a potential trade buyer or classroom adopter in the latter's office.

Intruding on prospective customers with unsolicited sales calls often creates negative irritation and backlash. At any rate, most good telereps are too busy (and too valuable) to fritter away time on low-probability "cold turkey" canvassing.

But the publishing house that gears its mass promotion to providing *qualified leads* for these sales telereps (information queries, complimentary book requests, agreed dealer-plan restocking schedules, etc.) can use its most effective telereps to open new accounts, negotiate "dealer plan" agreements, follow up complimentary samples to solicit initial stocking orders for new titles from established accounts, etc.—using predictable (early morning, etc.) slow periods to contact those leads, while junior reps or the main switchboard cover the order phone for an hour.

As more telereps learn to do more and more of this—publishers are finding them a cost-effective improvement over buying plane tickets for field sales people, paying commissions on promotion-generated "special orders" that commissioned reps had no hand in generating, or giving 55 percent-plus discounts to middleman distributors.

CHAPTER 28
Selling to the Book Trade and Comparable Retailers

There are some 22,000 retail bookstores operating in the U.S., and another 2,000 serving Canada with much of the same merchandise. Of these, about one-fourth (with perhaps half the total sales volume) are chain or franchise operations—mostly buying through central offices or contracting inventory selection (for smaller chains) through wholesalers. We'll say more about dealing with both the chains and the wholesalers later in this chapter.

Of the remaining 75 percent, less than half keep as many as 1,000 different titles in stock at any given time. However, since some of these specialize in subject-niches, just as most small publishers do, such smaller stores can be very good accounts for independent publishing houses with parallel specialties. So—after eliminating the chain outlets (approaching those, instead, through key contacts in their central buying offices)—the most sensible targeting strategy for independent publishers who wish to sell through bookstores is to concentrate on retailers who devote significant shelf space to the subject-categories reflected in the publishers' individual acquisition planning models (see Figure 9c).

Before we get too involved with the mechanics of doing this, however, let's consider for a moment the *self-selection* process each publisher should undergo before deciding whether such efforts are really worth the time and money they'll cost. In recent years, many independent publishers of all sizes have convincingly demonstrated that they can reach relatively specialized audiences more effectively and more profitably through targeted *direct response* marketing than through the book trade. (If they include appropriate libraries in such direct response marketing—as suggested by Chapter 30—they'll inevitably find that this also stimulates purchases from trade *wholesalers* who serve bookstores as well as libraries; but that's a fringe benefit for which they do not have to make any special efforts or concessions.)

So unless you're publishing books with truly *broad* appeal to the general public, and unless you plan to publish enough (at least six each year) to have new titles that will attract bookstore attention *throughout* the year (because it's only when you're introducing new titles that you're likely to get qualified sales leads from which on-going bookstore accounts can be developed)—you really shouldn't be diverting your attention and your budget from other opportunities to pursue trade marketing (through bookstores) very seriously. Instead, concentrate on direct sales to actual readers—and accept the occasional bookstore order that meets *your* terms as a nice bonus for which you are probably overdue!

If trade marketing *truly is* a realistic strategy for you, however, you can rent good mailing lists of bookstores—selected by the subject-areas they favor—from either Ad-Lib Publications (see Appendix 1) or Cahners Direct Mail Services (see Appendix 2). We'll examine some special nuances of selling through four sub-segments of this market (mass market book racks, college bookstores, religious bookstores, and those chain outlets) below. But most *independent* trade bookstores—where independent publishers of general interest titles are most welcomed—select, procure, and resell their merchandise in more-or-less the same way, regardless of its subject matter. (And most multi-media outlets handle calendars and posters and compact disks and software packages and video-cassettes in much the same way they do books.)

So successful trade marketing is largely a matter of targeting the right segments of the bookstore market—by matching your acquisition subject-categories with the store interest-categories reflected in the Ad-Lib or Cahners breakdowns—and developing a program for accumulatively converting promotionally-generated leads (publicity-inspired "special orders," sample copy requests, catalog requests, etc.) into solid accounts and continuous outlets.

One set of said outlets that requires moderately-specialized handling is the thousand-or-so stores (both secular and religious) that handle a significant volume of *children's books.* It's not that they operate differently with respect to the terms they seek, or the processes by which they select and resell merchandise. But you certainly have to give extra emphasis to marketing's impact on book *covers*—and to offering complimentary pre-publication samples to the store merchandise buyers—to introduce new children's books to them effectively. This is because the *literary* merits of children's books are often overshadowed by their *graphic* merits.

Bookstore "exit polls" have indicated that perhaps half of adult-book sales are instigated by the publisher's promotion and publicity (i.e., the reader went into the store looking for a *specific* title)—but that's not true in the case of children's books. Because babies aren't going to read book reviews or watch talk shows, it is the actual *display* of a children's book that generates most of the bookstore sales. So the *cover graphics* of children's books must not only attract the right kind of "browser" attention (child or adult) to succeed in bookstore shelf-displays—they must convince the *store managers/buyers* that they will do so *in advance,* in order to ever get on those shelves. And the books themselves must be *durable* enough to survive (unblemished) a lot of preliminary fondling—as youngsters (or their parents) examine the merchandise before making a choice. These factors make *advance samples* of new children's books—with aggressive one-on-one sales follow-ups (face-to-face or by phone)—more-or-less essential to their successful trade introduction.

You'll also find that *endorsements* can be especially useful when/if you make any educational claims for such a book—since what is-or-isn't good for very young children is complex, specialized business. And, since its own decision-to-display is usually the decisive factor (with respect to the many product options it has), the children's book store is in a better position than most to shop around for good deals. So bonus pre-publication discounts, free shipping, etc., may be more important here than elsewhere.

Altogether, bookstores spend about $4.5 billion a year (after their substantial discounts) to stock their shelves with publishers' books. About a third of this constitutes purchases of *mass market* paperbacks (low priced, rack-sized reprints). This segment of the market is dominated by a dozen-or-so major imprints—mostly owned by the large publishing conglomerates, and accounting for perhaps 90 percent of mass market sales. Their principal distribution pipeline flows through a small handful of "national distributors," who serve about a thousand local "independent distributors" or "rack jobbers."

The latter have a relatively free hand in moving merchandise onto, and off of, book racks in airports, news stands, and similar highly-trafficked locations—and they do it largely on the basis of "what's sold since the last shelf-check, and what hasn't." When they conclude a book isn't selling well enough to justify its shelf space, they remove it and substitute another. Then, following the generally-accepted conventions of mass market distribution, they simply rip off the covers of the books they've removed, and send *those covers only* back to the publisher—for full "returns" credit for the unsold (and presumably discarded) inventory.

Frankly, this is not a game many small, independent publishers can afford to play. It requires huge press runs (50,000 print-quantities are considered modest), expensive mass-promotion support (often built around celebrity authors who've collected six-digit advances), and the financial ability to take large risks and absorb occasional large losses. Consequently, virtually all under-$30-million publishing houses are well-advised to focus their mass market aspirations on *selling reprint rights* (see Chapter 32) to those dozen-or-so mass market giants—and settling for a royalty split (with the author) that requires no inventory or distribution investment.

The $3-billion that bookstores spend on other (hardcover, full-sized "trade" paperback, children's) books, however, is reasonably accessible to small and mid-sized publishers—though, even here, the conglomerates enjoy great competitive advantages because of the reluctance of many stores (especially the chain organizations) to deal directly with small vendor accounts—and because of routine discrimination against those same small accounts by some wholesale middlemen (see Chapter 1).

Nevertheless, a small publishing house with a well-defined subject niche that yields books with *truly* broad popular appeal (from gardening to self-help, philosophy to fiction) ... and with enough patience and persistence to spend several years building an account base ... has a good chance of establishing solid, repeat-buying accounts with several hundred stores that share that publisher's interests, and will stock its books. And once such a bridgehead is established, competitive pressures tend to bring other stores, the chains, and reluctant wholesalers into the picture *on terms acceptable to the publisher.*

Many start-up publishers attempt to "steal a march" on this patient process of building a viable, accumulative base of bookstore accounts by contracting with "distributors" or "commissioned reps" to ramrod their initial titles into the latter's existing store (and wholesale) accounts at the very beginning of the enterprise. In this writer's experience coaching scores of start-ups, that has seldom worked well. Conventional distributors' terms (55-65 percent discounts/commissions, free freight, publishers' consignment-financing of the distributor's inventory, and delayed payments) generally make whatever volume is achieved *unprofitable* for the publisher—who then finds it difficult to break out of this captive relationship, because the customer contacts all remain in the hands of the distributor.

And because commissioned reps usually have so many new books (for so many different publishers) to present in each sales call, they are usually helpful in launching a new publishing house *only* if the entrepreneur has enough capital to bring out *numerous* attractive new titles at the very beginning—and keep the flow moving fast enough to claim a major part of each rep's presentations every season. Those are not the capital circumstances of the typical book publishing start-up.

Thus, most publishers entering the bookstore market are best off doing it on their own—by patiently stalking those initial (usually modest) sales to a growing list of stores, and then concentrating on systematically upgrading these accumulated accounts into a network of effective distribution outlets. More about how to do that later in this chapter.

But while we're generalizing about the bookstore market, we should first note that in addition to the divisions of this market between chains and independents, and between basic "trade" bookstores and "mass market" paperback racks, there are two other sub-divisions that require some special marketing twists: college bookstores, and religious bookstores.

Just as general bookstores are represented by their own trade association (the American Booksellers Association, 137 West 25th St., New York, NY 10001), many of America's 3,000 college bookstores pursue common interests through the National Association of College Stores (500 East Lorain St., Oberlin, OH 44074), and perhaps half of the U.S.'s approximately-4,000 religious bookstores (primarily evangelical Protestant) are represented by the Christian Booksellers Association (2620 Venetucci Blvd., Colorado Springs, CO 80901). Anyone with special interest in any of these retail segments of the book trade will do well to inquire of those associations about the informative publications, exhibit opportunities, and associate-member programs they offer to publishers.

College stores traditionally buy-and-sell books in two distinctly different ways. They serve as textbook procurement-and-distribution agencies for the schools with which they are associated—stocking the titles the educators adopt for their classrooms (see Chapter 29), usually buying them on "short discount" terms (20 percent off for five-or-more). When several commercial enterprises compete with the resident college store, all are likely to over-stock any given title in overlapping anticipation of estimated demand—so merchandise returns are a particularly burdensome problem in this sector of the market.

The very same college stores also (usually) function additionally as general bookstores—though their title selections lean toward academic subjects and trade paperbacks. For this part of their merchandise, they expect normal trade (40-50 percent) discounts. To avoid "fair trade" violations, publishers should identify specific *books* (not customer accounts) with their separate "trade" (general interest) and "text/reference" (short discount) schedules. Play fair with the college stores, and you're likely to find them better outlets for many specialized, esoteric, literary, and/or academic titles than are most commercial trade bookstores.

Religious bookstores are as varied as American religion itself—but a major portion tend to be oriented toward either evangelical Protestantism (the mainstream of the Christian Bookseller Association constituency), or Catholic constituencies. The Cahners lists (Appendix 2) will help you target either sub-set. Non-evangelical Protestants, and both Jewish and non-traditional religious publishers, essentially have to continue promotionally sweeping all stores that handle religious books to sift out an accumulative list of sympathetic accounts—just as specialized secular-interest publishers do. But within those parameters, selling religious books to religious bookstores is very much like all other trade book marketing.

One significant difference does exist, however, in the evangelical market. Evangelical publishers—inspired by the success of the most experienced evangelical distributor, Spring Arbor (which deserves more credit than it gets for pioneering telemarketing to bookstores)—have been much less bashful than others about using uninvited "cold turkey" telephone canvassing to get their books into CBA-type stores. For that reason, such stores have become more conditioned to buying in this manner than have secular trade stores. Yet as more and more evangelical publishers have tried it, there is evidence that overkill is beginning to generate resentment. So a significant number of evangelical trade houses are now shifting tactics—and joining their secular counterparts in seeking qualified leads (complimentary book, dealer plan brochure, or catalog requests) before they phone.

Independent publishers' experiences with the secular bookstore chains (representing about a fourth of all trade outlets, and half the money) as trade distribution accounts have not generally been happy. The major chains (three of which do at least three-fourths of all chain business) are primarily geared to dealing with less-than-50 very large trade publishers—who can provide them with large inventories of hundreds of new titles each year, in quantities that earn top trade discounts and minimize unit shipping costs ... *without* consuming a lot of selection and purchasing time (or expertise—which many chain buyers seem to lack), and with fairly easy computer-to-computer adjustments of (often substantial) return credits and co-op promotional allowances. Those large trade publishers are able to insist on their normal trade terms (you seldom see one of them selling anybody its books for less than 50 percent of the cover price!), because they (being able to afford six-digit advances) own virtually all of those "celebrity author" titles that dominate the best-seller lists—and the chains can't afford to be deprived of those best-sellers as the magnets that draw crowds into their display areas.

Modest-sized independent publishers, on the other hand, don't have that huge, steady new-title flow or many of those celebrity authors—so they've largely been forced to come hat-in-hand to the chains, which have frequently required them (if they want to be able to tell prospective authors that "we can get your book into the chains") to accept unreasonable merchandise-return practices (for example, returning books damaged-beyond-resale, and arbitrarily deducting credit for them from the chain's payables to the publisher), very slow payment (often exceeding 90 days—sometimes with belated documentation demands that are obvious delaying tactics), and often-questionable co-op promotion schemes (really disguised bonus discounts).

But because, even on those terms, most independent publishers represent such a tiny potential trickle in a big chain's cash flow that it's hardly worth the necessary purchase-interview or accounting time—and because they have a legitimate concern with the inability of many small publishers to provide either adequate promotional/publicity support or eventual return-refund guarantees—most chain buyers simply decline to deal directly with most small publishers. Instead, they require those publishers to have their new titles presented through a "distributor"—an extra middleman who will (of necessity, since he too must eat) rake approximately 10 percent of the eventual reader's dollar out of the publisher's share. That represents all of the profit most small publishers could have expected, before the distributor came into the picture!

We've belabored this point elsewhere, so we'll restrain ourselves here. Chapter 26 explains how you can (after you've identified them) add the appropriate central-office buyers of the significant chains to your key contact list, and make certain they're exposed to each of your new titles as it approaches publication—for whatever interest they may choose to demonstrate. But whether this will result in sales on terms that are really worth any small publisher's time and energy is an open question. Once again, "you pays your money and takes your chances."

A significant portion of independent publishers simply elect to "write off" that half of trade bookstore dollar-volume represented by the chain outlets— and concentrate their promotional money on accumulating a list of independent store accounts attuned to their particular acquisition niches, with whom they can pursue the other half of the market on healthier terms.

One group of intermediate middlemen—linking small/independent publishers with many of their bookstore (and especially, library) customers —which has proved more useful (on terms publishers can more reasonably afford) has been the traditional book wholesalers. In accurate terminology (often deliberately or accidentally confused by those with a stake in the game), a "wholesaler" is different from a "distributor" in that the former is a *real customer* of the publisher—actually buying books, and paying for them (usually plus actual shipping costs) "up front" ... though often after the 60-90 day delays also characteristic of many bookstores and libraries. Reputable wholesalers seldom condition purchases on publisher acceptance of their internal "co-op" promotion programs, and accept the publisher's normal trade discount schedule on a take-it-or-leave-it basis (though they must eventually get 46-50 percent on bulk purchases, if the wholesaler is to profit from handling a publisher's books).

The "distributor," on the other hand, contends that he "works for" his publisher-clients—so he buys nothing "up front" (insisting on a consignment inventory for which he won't pay until 60-90 days after each book is sold)—and expects the publisher to pay all of the shipping costs. Trade distributors argue that they provide an extra value—field sales representation—which the wholesalers can't match; but most of them accomplish this through already-overloaded commissioned reps (not their own people), and it tends to be ineffective.

Consult *Literary Market Place* (Appendix 2) for a concise listing of the major trade (store/library) wholesalers now functioning as reputable components of the U.S. book industry. Then approach the appropriate wholesalers one-to-one, by contacting each (by mail or phone) to ask which member of their organization you should place on your key contact list (as per Chapter 26) for the purpose of keeping them informed about your forthcoming new titles. If you're at all relevant to their constituencies, most will be eager to get on that list—and they'll guide you as to what general information (about terms, your backlist, etc.) they need, when-and-if it becomes appropriate.

Being able to inform bookstores (via both your mail promotions and your telereps) that your books are available through specific wholesalers will help you get books into some stores who are reluctant to "buy direct" from small, unknown publishing houses. But even more importantly, wholesalers are the *predominant* suppliers of books to public and school libraries—who (stimulated by publisher promotion and publicity) buy two-thirds of their needs from such "one-stop-shopping" intermediaries, simply because (as public agencies) they can't realistically handle the bureaucratic paperwork required to purchase separately from several thousand independent book-vendor (publisher) accounts.

But the principal avenue independent publishers must pursue to make their books accessible to large audiences through bookstores on a profitable basis is, as we've said before, the gradual accumulation of a viable number of accounts with individual bookstores (or chains, if those happen to sign on at acceptable trade terms, via key-contact selling) who will be reasonably susceptible to stocking subsequent new titles as the publisher brings them forth. The most likely bookstores to buy your next new title are those who bought from you before—so the larger your accumulated account list, the easier it gets.

Remember that the critical element in successful trade marketing (though bookstores) is *that initial order for each new title.* Once each title is in a number of stores, whether or not it succeeds will depend far more on the previously-exercised skill of your *acquisition* function than on anything a distributor, field rep, or telerep can do. Stores tend to *re-order* a title only on evidence that an initial stock has been exhausted (by their customers) within a reasonable time. For that reason, they're relatively unimpressed by backlist promotions; they usually assume that if a book was any good for them, they've already got it.

Very, very rarely has a publisher found it effective to pursue this entire task of systematically placing new titles in an accumulative network of compatible bookstores by media *promotion* (direct mail, print ads, cold-turkey telemarketing scripts) alone. Because bookstores are used to serious one-on-one attention from the field sales forces of the large trade houses, they expect one-on-one attention (not impersonal media-category treatment) from smaller publishers as well.

Many very-traditional trade publishers delegate the entire task of selling to the stores to field sales representatives—their own, or somebody else's (through one of those distributor or commissioned rep arrangements about which we've expressed so much skepticism). To put the trade selling challenge into perspective, let's examine how such a traditional face-to-face field-selling program works. Once you've planned itineraries that get your house sales reps (or key staff people pressed into temporary field selling service) into the vicinity of each of your significant bookstore or wholesale accounts (or prospects) two-to-four times a year, there are seven basic steps each of those field reps should take in performing each customer visit for which they're scheduled. They are:

(1)*Confirming Each Appointment:* Wherever your sales rep is, she/he should find time to phone ahead 2 or 3 days before each appointment to remind the buyer of the forthcoming visit, and prevent surprises by people who don't take their appointment calendars as seriously as they should. (If your reps are maintaining frequent contacts with the home office, a marketing department secretary might make these calls for them.) If you're having particular success with a specific book at the time, this will also be an opportunity to "prime" the buyer for the substantial order-quantity you'll be suggesting when you arrive. These advance confirmation calls will be much easier if you've made certain that the personal names of all buyers, and their phone numbers, have been listed on the itinerary outline.

(2) *Pre-Checking the Accounts:* Before each day's calls, a sales rep should (from routine sales reports regularly duplicated and distributed to all concerned) check the status of each account that will be visited, noting any credit problems or recent complaints and making brief notes as to how to handle them. Any significant recent orders (or returns) of specific titles should also be noted for comparison with a subsequent inventory check (below). Such information (along with any special assignments relevant to that account delegated by the sales coordinator) might be listed on the "call report" form (also see below) that the sales rep will use to record what actually happens; this will make it easy to use that sheet of paper as a guide for the interview, as well as a recording device. In addition, your rep should pre-mark a comprehensive order form with suggested quantities for each new title (being careful not to overstock the account and cause embarrassing returns).

Preparing these notations (i.e., pre-planning each sales call) is a routine chore that can fill some of those lonely evenings in motels that are the bane of a traveling rep's existence. Or it's work that can be done back at the home office, by the sales coordinator, and forwarded to each traveling rep on a weekly basis.

(3) *Checking the Customer's Inventory:* Unless a bookstore or wholesaler objects (as some will), the first thing you or your rep should do on arriving for a scheduled visit with a book dealer is to *physically examine that customer's inventory* of your books. Actually count the stock of each title (whether on the shelves or in a back storeroom), and compare the results with those recent order-quantities noted on your preliminary checklist, or monthly sales reports. Then add to the pre-marked order form whatever backlist replenishment quantities you feel the dealer should have—in order to service a hopefully-continuing demand until your next visit.

(4) *Highlighting Selected New Titles:* During the process of pre-checking each account (above), the field sales rep should select and list one or more (very few) new titles that seem to have the greatest potential for profitable turnover in each store, and plan to concentrate the actual interview with the store's buyer on those books. These selected titles will normally be more-or-less the same for most stores (depending on the character of each season's list). However, some modification might be suggested by what you learn about a store's clientele and sales patterns during your pre-interview inventory examination. At any rate, you'll do better concentrating your sales talk on

getting the store to take those best-chance titles seriously, than by attempting to give "equal time" to every new title on the list.

Give the buyer a very brief description of the nature and contents of each such book, suggesting as succinctly and strongly as you can why the store's patrons are likely to buy it. (This quick presentation is referred to by veteran sales people as the "handle"—the thing that enables the buyer to grasp the book idea/project easily.) Also describe any advertising or publicity efforts you have planned that should bring readers into the store asking for the book (with particular attention to co-op and dealer-listing ads in which the store can participate). Show samples of, and take orders for, any point-of-purchase display materials you may have available in conjunction with the book. And by all means (since your travel kit probably won't have room for enough actual book samples) present a color proof or some other demonstration of the effectiveness of the book's cover as a point-of-purchase display. Be specific in your own recommendation of a reasonable advance stocking quantity for the store, but be careful not to overload them and generate the disillusionment of extensive and early returns (meanwhile tying up the store's shelf space and capital).

(5) *Presenting the Rest of the List:* Once you've described those key titles and taken orders for the agreed quantities, you should quickly go over your comprehensive order form, using it as a checklist. Offering your brief "handle" and the suggested quantity you noted during your pre-check for each of your new titles that didn't make that "select" list, and pointing out any backlist titles that deserve restocking because of past performance or forthcoming publicity, should only take a few minutes. Now ask the buyer to sign the resulting order if it is to be initiated by you, or to take a copy of your order form (with your address and trade terms) for guidance if a purchase order must be initiated within the store and mailed or faxed later. But make sure you're using carbon paper, so that you also retain a copy for your own reference and follow-up (or can give the customer a duplicate, if you're handling the paperwork).

(6) *Dealing with Service Problems:* At any point in your visit at which you identify any type of service problem in your organization's handling of the store's account, you should demonstrate eagerness to solve that problem without delay. Hear the customer's side of the problem, ask for a phone, and place a collect call back to your own marketing or business department if the problem seems serious enough to warrant that; you'll impress the customer, even if you do have to report back later with a delayed answer. Try your best to leave each account "in good standing"—and in a good mood!

(7) *Completing a "Call Report":* Most competent sales coordinators develop some sort of written checklist or memo-form on which appropriate notations about each sales visit can be recorded on a single sheet. Whatever form you use, insist that each field rep document the results of each interview (and note appropriate follow-up actions) while the visit is still fresh in mind. You might

use the same form for your advance "pre-check" of each account and your after-the-fact "call report." If a rep is going to be traveling for several weeks, call reports should be mailed in at the end of each week so that others can begin the appropriate analysis and follow-up actions.

Make no bones about it, though ... most independent publishers are finding such face-to-face, on-the-road servicing of bookstores (except for a very few, very major accounts that can be covered by the marketing manager and/or sales coordinator) no longer practical—as travel costs have gone up, and telephone rates have gone down. The best method most of them have found for establishing and servicing bookstore accounts is the continuous orchestration of (1) promotional lead-generating and (2) systematic mail/phone sales follow-ups—directed toward those select portions of (Ad-Lib, Cahners, Christian Bookseller Association, etc.) bookstore lists that match the publisher's subject-interests—and especially the bookstores that have already established accounts through previous purchases.

Generally speaking, most such campaigns progressively expose appropriate bookstore accounts to the publisher's list by capitalizing on seven recurring circumstances:

(1) *Opening New Accounts:* An account is automatically opened for every bookstore, on the publisher's computerized order-entry system, when the first formal contact occurs. This may be a single-book "special order" (responding to a bookstore patron's demand, stimulated by a book review or other publicity); it may be only a request for a catalog, or a complimentary copy of a forthcoming book as offered by the promotional lead-generating program; or it may be a substantial order stimulated by some third-party action (such as a teacher's or an author's). At any rate, your customer service telereps should have the ability to open an account for the bookstore immediately (whether talking with them by phone, processing mail inquiries and orders, or following up the orders-or-requests collected in an exhibit booth), as previously described in Chapter 27. This should happen even if they're only requesting information or a free sample—so they'll automatically move up a notch in your mailing list priorities, and you'll be ready-and-waiting when they come back with that first order.

Unfortunately, too many publishers simply open that new account (perhaps having told the customer by phone that they were doing so), and let it go at that. You should *almost always* seize this golden opportunity to send a (word-processed) personalized form letter telling the customer what you've done, indicating their account number and credit allowance/limit, enclosing your catalog and sales terms, and inviting subsequent calls on your order line (perhaps even asking for a specific telerep—*their* account representative). Go through this process even for catalog and comp-copy requesters; it'll make them feel a lot more comfortable about calling with their initial order.

(2) *Upgrading "Special Orders"*: The second recurring situation for which you should prepare an automatic response is the bookstore "special order"— trade terminology for those single-book orders many stores will send you when *your promotion* stimulates *their patron* to ask them for one of your books that they haven't chosen to stock. As we've noted before, you'll lose money trying to fill-and-bill such orders at a *discounted* price—so it doesn't make much sense to give bookstores discounts on orders of less than five books. You should, however, have a well-thought-out letter on the word processor with which your telereps can follow up each single-copy shipment (with its no-discount invoice) with a strong pitch for *ordering four more of the same title*—or four copies of your currently-most-popular bookstore title, even if it's a different title—to qualify for a trade discount. In the letter, the rep should offer to issue a credit wiping out the single-book invoice, and incorporating it into the new (now five-book) invoice at the discounted price. The idea is not just to sell four more books—but to *make that bookstore aware of your terms,* and of your more popular titles.

Some publishers have their telereps follow all those "upgrade" offers (a week later) with a phone call encouraging the customer to accept the deal. Others leave it up to the letter itself to make it so easy for the customer to accept ("To accept this offer, just phone 1-800-xxx-xxxx and ask for Joan") that no phone follow-up is deemed necessary or appropriate. The choice is yours.

(3) *Periodic Restocking:* Every time you fill a bulk (5+ copies) order for any specific title from any bookstore, you have an automatic opportunity to schedule an effective follow-up that may well sell more of the same book, and will at least increase the store's awareness of you and your other books. Do this by preparing a word-processed form letter (for personalization) that can be sent *3 months later*—reminding the store's book-buyer of that bulk order, and suggesting they check to see if any are still in stock. If the original amount is seriously depleted—this is clear evidence that the title is selling in that store, and that a replenishment order would thus be a good investment for them. A week after you send each such letter, your telerep should then phone and ask whether the store would like to place a re-order. Or, if you've scheduled a face-to-face field visit to the account, make sure the follow-up restocking query is on the agenda.

If you *don't* get the re-order, make an additional effort by telling the store (by phone, mail, or face-to-face) about very similar books on your list, which might also appeal to their patrons.

(4) *Re-engaging with Each New Title:* While your promotion coordinator is sending out news release announcements of forthcoming new titles, and inviting interested bookstores to request complimentary samples, you might *unilaterally* send such samples to all of your established bulk-buying accounts (say, every store that has ordered five-or-more books at least twice during the past 2 years), with a personalized word-processed letter stating that you plan to call and ask how they liked it a couple of weeks hence. Then—unless an

account has clearly warned you that they don't want such calls—put your telereps (or your sales coordinator) to work making those follow-up contacts and soliciting initial stocking orders of each new title from each bulk-buying account.

(5) *Merchandising Co-op Promotions or Point-of-Purchase Displays:* If you've decided to use part of your promotion budget on co-op ads or mail-promotion allowances, or if you've prepared posters, counter-dumps (shipping cartons that open up as displays), title-promoting bookmarks which stores can use as statement-stuffers, etc.—these represent another reasonable opportunity to enrich your personal contacts with your established bulk-buying accounts. Get out personalized word-processor letters from your telereps to their assigned accounts describing any such offer—and then phone 10 days later to ask if the store would like to participate. At the very least, it gives you another opportunity to stress the virtues of the specific new title around which the offer or material revolves.

(6) *Merchandising Publicity Breaks:* By maintaining close liaison between your promotion and sales coordinators—and the editors sponsoring specific new titles—you should be able to identify a number of opportunities for helping your bulk-buying bookstore accounts take advantage of forthcoming (or recent) publicity for your books. Photocopy particularly impressive book reviews; fax (or mail) memos about broadcast talk show appearances scheduled for an author, or news releases about major speaking engagements, to store accounts in impacted areas—and then have your telereps follow up by phone to offer to expedite book shipments if those stores want to take advantage of such publicity.

(7) *Dealer Plans:* Once you've established a nucleus of repeat buyers, you might be able to intensify this distribution exposure by offering *bonus discounts* (*e.g.,* an extra 5 percent—or a flat 50 percent) to those who agree to stock a minimum number (say five copies) of a specified variety (say ten titles) from your list, and *automatically* accept and display that minimum amount of each *new* title (subsequently deciding whether to add it to the list, or let it replace one of the older titles). Such a plan should commit the dealer to checking his inventory of those titles every quarter—with the understanding that your telerep will be calling to ask what replenishment books are needed. These replenishment calls, then, provide an ideal opportunity to talk about forthcoming new titles, or otherwise enhance your working relationship with that store.

Because bookstores succeed or fail on the *margin* they achieve between what they pay for books and what they sell them to their patrons for, your sales terms will be especially critical to any program like those described above for developing a solid base of bookstore accounts. For a review of the terms sought by this segment of the market, we'll refer you back to Chapter 24. Bookstores need at least 40 percent discounts on their merchandise to operate profitably. Publishers seldom make money if they give discounts of more than 50 percent. Thus, healthy book trade marketing is largely confined to that 40-50 percent discount range.

Bookstores will argue that publishers should give them discounts on single-copy (or 2-to-4 copy) orders simply because *they can't make money* handling such "special orders" for their patrons without that discount. But there is no good reason why *you* (who also can't make money processing such orders at discounted prices) should pay a penalty because a bookstore neglected to *stock* your title in sufficient quantity to meet demand. So wise publishers simply stick by their guns: "no discounts on fewer than five books."

The *least wise* publishers around are those who succumb to pressure, and let bookstores dictate sales terms to them. If an account is going to be good for you, it'll have to operate within terms you've reasonably established. If it won't—it's *not going to be good for you.* And that means there's no sensible reason for catering to that account.

One category of trade accounts that many publishers have found to be more hospitable to healthy trade terms than bookstores themselves are *non-bookstore retailers*—speciality outlets dealing in sporting goods, garden suppliers, personal computers, vacation tickets, gifts, supplementary classroom supplies, etc. Virtually all such retailers operate on margin requirements no tougher than those faced by the bookstores—so they've generally proven receptive to publishers' normal trade terms. (In fact, some publishers are convinced they're much less merchandise-returns-oriented than are bookstores.)

It's easiest to sell your books to such outlets when you offer very specific, single-carton quantity-selections—either a carton combining a modest inventory of several of your most-appropriate titles for that retail speciality, or an on-going sequence of promotions offering single-title cartons or interest-related best-sellers or new books. If you can arrange with a carton-supplier to pre-print promotional copy on the exteriors so that those cartons become self-contained displays—so much the better. Make sure that the *bottom* of the carton (or the last book) is "salted" with a dramatically-visible reminder that all of the books have sold—and a new stock should be ordered from you (simply by calling your toll-free order line) promptly.

Then you just pepper the trade journals covering your targeted retail specialty with spot ads—or mail a brochure to appropriate lists—offering more information ("without cost or obligation") about this attractive impulse-purchase sideline that you can provide to interested stores who'll call that toll-free number. Have a good mail follow-up ready for each inquirer, and back it up a couple of weeks later with a call from one of your telereps soliciting the carton-display order.

Once you've established such non-book dealer accounts, they should be regularly and routinely followed-up as if they were bookstores.

CHAPTER 29
Selling to Classroom Educators

Three categories of educators, between them, make decisions about classroom resources that result in about $4 billion in purchases from U.S. publishers each year. To get your share of this money, you have to learn to practice an unusual art—one which trade and "mail order" marketers often find baffling, and which business managers more-or-less constitutionally mistrust. It's called "giving away books profitably."

Though there are a few exceptions (and we'll deal with them separately, at the end of this chapter), most classroom adoption purchases (to obtain a specific textbook or other learning aide for the participants in a specific educational adventure) are initiated by a knowledgeable educator who *has a sample* of each strong candidate-product in hand. While some publishers go to considerable lengths to get these educators to *pay for* or *subsequently return* those samples—most veteran educational marketers agree that such efforts cause too much hesitation, confusion and ill-will (and, in fact, cost too much paper-shuffling money) to be worthwhile. So most simply (1) offer free samples to qualified decision-makers, (2) limit that offer to short-discounted books intended *primarily for the classroom*—excluding titles many teachers would want *for themselves* as professional resources, and (3) screen the requests to eliminate (and ignore) unqualified decision-makers, as suspected "free-loaders."

Where very extensive, expensive samples would be involved (as is frequently the case with multi-media el-high or religious curriculum kits), publishers sometimes find it more economical (and convincing) to prepare demonstration samples (commonly known as "samplers") combining a modest selection of representative materials from the program—or video-cassettes on which good teachers both demonstrate and talk about the materials and related pedagogy—and offer those instead of actual product samples.

Books that could be used *either* as potential classroom adoption resources or simply as handy additions to the teacher's personal library are usually (and properly) *not* routinely offered as free samples. However, if a teacher cares enough to be willing to make the case—by phone or mail—for a potential classroom adoption, the marketing department frequently decides to send the sample anyhow.

But don't kid yourself about books that are written *primarily* for adults and subject-experts; people who tell you they're considering classroom adoptions of those (even for college courses) are usually simply building a library at your expense. On the other hand, you *don't* want to get into petty arguments with educators about their eligibility for samples; this only creates ill-will. Classify the books (as classroom materials or professional references) your own way, only include those for which you're offering samples in your "adoption promotion" mailings or ads, and *arbitrarily* pass judgment (by whatever criteria you consider reasonable) on the qualifications of those who make requests. Many publishers don't even acknowledge unacceptable requests; they simply discard then—trusting the teacher (and presumed "free-loader") will eventually forget, without starting an argument.

Books intended primarily for *the teachers* should be separately promoted and sold as *professional reference materials*—following the techniques described in the next chapter.

For your true classroom adoption materials, then, the key to effective marketing is to get samples (or samplers) into the hands of the right educators *before* they make each semester's decisions.

In the secular el-high (elementary/high school) market, a further distinction must be made between *basal* and *supplementary* materials. A "basal text" is the core resource for one of the basic (language arts, math, history, social studies, etc.) courses, at a given age-or-grade level. It usually must be compatible with other texts used in the same subject-area at other age levels. Developing an integrated "core curriculum" series for an appropriate span of age-levels is a long-term, capital-intensive project; for this reason, most basal texts (though there are exceptions) are the products of the "school divisions" of very large publishing enterprises.

About half of the U.S. states require public el-high schools to select their "basal" texts from approved lists of books that have been examined and endorsed by professional committees. (In some cases the educators are given a range of choices; in some they're not.)

If your books are geared to this basal text market, you've probably already sent forms letters to all state departments of education asking for their current rules. To get on the approved lists in such states, you normally must submit samples—along with price data, assurances of long-term availability (they usually "adopt" materials for 5-8 years), etc.—in advance of each statewide subject-committee (drawn from the ranks of public educators) meeting to review and update the appropriate list. The big basal text publishers also court the members of these committees (when they can identify them) with more extensive promotion—and sometimes more questionable tactics.

So basal text marketing is pretty complex stuff. You have to develop "key contact" lists of state selection-committee members, and promote to them somewhat as Chapter 26 describes trade publishers introducing new titles to their market. In some cases, simplified versions of these tactics may even be worthwhile in getting supplementary materials added to state approval lists.

Outside the central-adoption states (in the other half of the country), basal texts can be marketed very much as are supplementary classroom materials.

As we said earlier, the key to marketing these supplementary materials (and basal texts in that half of the country not bound by central adoption lists) is to get the right sample (or "sampler") into the right educator's hands at the right time. This is true whether you're marketing el-high, religious curriculum (church school), or college classroom resources.

Overwhelmingly, independent publishers find *direct mail* to be the most effective promotional medium for accomplishing this. A 1991 sampling of educational publishers found 100 percent of el-high houses, 100 percent of religious curriculum programs, and 95 percent of college-oriented publishers citing direct mail as one of their three most important marketing tactics. Its strongest competitor was academic exhibits—similarly cited by 55 percent of el-high publishers, 80 percent of religious curriculum publishers, and 45 percent of college publishers. In third place came print advertising (in appropriate educational or academic journals)—scoring 27 percent among el-high publishers, 40 percent in the religious curriculum market, and only 15 percent at the college level.

In most cases, the central strategy of adoption promotion mailings is to encourage educators to ask for samples of books they believe might be appropriate texts (basal or supplementary) for near-future courses for which they are charged with selecting resources. Some publishers do this by including sample-request forms (instead of order forms) in their promotions—and asking enough questions (such as the starting date and approximate registration of the course, or the name of the text currently being used against which yours is competing—and even, at the college level, names of department chairs, or office hours) to intimidate or help screen out possible "free-loaders." (Some publishers spend the necessary postage to send such forms back to all unidentified requesters—on the theory that if they really have a potential use for the book, they won't mind making this second request.)

But let's not dwell too long on out-foxing the "deadbeats." A certain amount of unethical library-building is an inevitable result of applying the sampling principal—but the principal is worth that extra, hidden cost. The people selecting classroom materials—be they in el-high, religious, or college programs—are the most informed (and generally most responsible) audience book marketers encounter. They take their work seriously (often—even in the secular schools—"religiously"), and they'll never buy "a pig in a poke."

So before you can sell them a book or other classroom resource—they've got to have enough of the material in hand to evaluate it thoughtfully. Some publishers believe this can happen (without giving away a sample) at an academic conference exhibit booth—where teachers can actually browse through your collection. But they don't make such important decisions on the spot; if you really want to be considered, you must accept the fact that *your sales representative* must be there when they decide—and for virtually all independent publishers, the best (and perhaps only feasible) on-the-spot sales representative is the sample product (or "sampler") itself.

In the religious curriculum market, the best sources of mailing lists of exhibit opportunities are the headquarters of the denominations to whom you hope to sell. If those won't cooperate (by offering list rentals), you'll find that most major mailing list rental companies have access to similar lists.

The best source of el-high public school adoption-promotion lists in America is Market Data Retrieval (see Appendix 5). On the college level, MDR competes head-on with CMG Information Services (see Appendix 3). The catalogs of both of these companies are very instructive introductions to the demographics (head counts by subject and age level, etc.) of the classroom adoption book market. Standard Rate & Data Service's *Direct Mail Lists* directory of available rentals (see Appendix 6) also recapitulates most of the same data.

But no educational publisher should too quickly dismiss print advertising (in appropriate educational journals) as a third alternative (to direct mail and exhibits)—especially when materials are appropriate on such a wide scale as to require too large a direct mail investment, or when they relate to inter-disciplinary or non-traditional courses.

Just as with direct selling (see the next chapter), every time you get a positive response (a sample request that you judge to be legitimate) from a classroom adoption decision-maker, you should add that person's name, address, and relevant data (subject, grade-level, etc.) to an accumulative mailing list. Use appropriate subject-category selections from this permanent list to amplify (in fact, lead the way for) future promotion.

Just as with direct selling, you'll probably find your mailings (and even journal ads) to external audiences other than your own accumulative list more effective when they promote *all* of the books you have available in the appropriate subject area(s)—rather than just one new title. But you certainly should highlight those new titles—since well-informed educators are already likely to be somewhat familiar with your backlist.

Once an educator has a sample in hand, the majority of classroom adoption publishers simply "accept the odds" that the sample will do its job, and attempt no additional sales follow-up. But an increasing number (especially in religious curriculum marketing, where non-professional volunteers often make the decisions) find that well-scripted phone follow-ups by their sales telereps can tip the scales in enough cases to make this extra effort profitable.

Just as with direct selling, this is a marketing arena in which it's fairly easy to compile and compare unit costs for generating a "valid sample request" by each alternative medium (direct mail, exhibits, print ads, review publicity, etc.)—and even to go a step farther by comparing the percentages of samplers from each medium who *eventually decide to buy.* (That latter calculation simply requires hand-matching the limited number of bulk-size adoption orders you'll receive during any period with sample requests from the same institutions or areas.) Thus, a well-organized marketing department is almost certain to get progressively better results by shifting its focus from those things that work worst to those that work best.

As we noted earlier, some marketers take exception to the general belief that offering (and perhaps following-up by phone) free samples to appropriate educators is the best way for a modest-sized publisher to sell classroom adoption materials. The three most common alternative approaches they use are field (face-to-face) sales reps visiting educators in their own school offices, representation by distributors (especially in the college market)—whose own catalogs and reps provide (for a healthy fee) more-or-less "cooperative" marketing for a number of small publishers, and trade-style marketing through "teacher supply stores."

In this author's experience, commissioned field reps and distributors work even less effectively (and often cost even more) in this arena than they do in bookstore-oriented trade marketing. Repeating that (Chapter 24) discussion here would only bore you. Certainly, if it works for you—don't fix what ain't broke. But if you're a newcomer to the market—beware of wooden nickels!

The "teacher supply store," on the other hand, has proved to be a profitable outlet for some mid-sized marketers of supplementary classroom materials. These should be approached essentially the same way as the other non-book retail outlets discussed at the end of Chapter 28.

In addition, religious curriculum marketers have an alternative (and usually well-paying) alternative tactical opportunity to sell *repeat* orders, by focusing special promotion for forthcoming years (or quarters) on their existing customers. Since the often-volunteer church school organizations now using your basic curriculum must undergo significant, often-difficult re-orientation if they change to another curriculum, fairly routine efforts (occasional user-friendly newsletters about program modifications and additions, plus personalized word-processed letters actually soliciting confirmation orders for the next year) to keep in touch with current customers usually result in a big pay-back for relatively little expense.

CHAPTER 30
Selling Directly to Readers and Libraries

More books are now sold in direct transactions between publishers and actual readers (whether professionals at work, or consumers pursuing private interests) than are sold through bookstores (not counting mass market racks). And because each publishing house can scale its direct-response marketing efforts to whatever amount of working capital it has available (instead of "going for broke" to crash through trade distribution barriers), this is generally a more practical, profitable way for a non-conglomerated independent publisher (especially if tightly focused on a specialized professional or consumer-interest niche) to market books than by concentrating on traditional trade channels.

For the vast majority of publishers, there is only one basic direct response marketing strategy that works: (a) find an inexpensive way to screen likely audiences to generate initial orders (with mailing addresses) from appropriate readers; (b) then re-contact that accumulating address-list of first-time buyers at regular intervals (the most successful direct response publishers do it 10-20 times a year) to repetitively offer this audience a variety of other books of related subject-interest. (The exceptions to this basic strategy are those *very few* specialty publishers with access to an institutional membership list or journal ad-audience that so exactly parallels their book-topic interests that they never need build their own customer list—and may even be able to "piggyback" on institutional communications rather than paying postage for their own mailings.)

Of course, before you can screen prospective buyers for first-time book purchases, you have to identify audiences that will give you those new customers at a reasonable cost. That means *testing* audiences available through various media—mailing lists, print ad media, radio stations or television channels, conference exhibits, phone-canvassing lists, "piggyback" inserts in other people's cartons and mail, etc. Publishers generally find that any external media audience that returns *the entire promotion cost* plus the cost of the books (including shipping/handling) in a test large enough to yield at least 35 orders (to reduce probabilities of statistical "flukes") is a reasonable screening audience for further, extensive list-building promotions. Achieving this usually requires a minimum 1 percent response from the most widely-used medium—direct mail.

In analyzing the results of diverse publishing clients' campaigns to build and exploit accumulative direct response customer lists over the years, the Huenefeld Publishing Consultants have concluded that the most profitable programs—once established—devote at least 70 percent of the total promotion budget (not counting staff payroll) to repetitive exposure of the *entire book list* to the *entire previous-buyer list* 10-20 times a year. They devote an additional 10 percent of the promotion budget to testing new external, rented lists or other media for acceptable response rates (using mailers, ads, etc., that have worked acceptably before), and the remaining 20 percent to systematically canvassing the *best* external lists or media-audiences they've successfully tested (repeating such screening contacts only at intervals of three months or more)—for the purpose of adding new first-time names to their buyer list.

Of course, a new ("start-up") program must first devote 100 percent to audience tests—but it should very quickly shift 90 percent of its promotion money to screening of acceptable external audiences *just as fast as it can identify them through those tests,* and then start transferring money (up to 70 percent of the total) from such screening to repetitive exploitation of the customer list *just as fast as it accumulates enough names on that list to use that much money.*

A majority of all new audience tests fail; even those 1 percent responses from test lists deemed "acceptable" are not immediately profitable (since that usually only pays for the promotion and the books themselves). True profitability during any given accounting period requires—and publishers who've done it right usually get—*3-to-7 percent responses* from those repetitive mailings to previous buyers. (It's all those tests that fail, and those marginal "screening" results, that drive *average* direct mail responses down to that conventionally-cited 2 percent norm.)

Though mail is the principal medium independent publishers use for direct response marketing, it is, as we've pointed out, by no means the only one (especially for achieving those first-time purchases from which you build your own customer list). Customer names can come from ad coupons, from television or radio commercials, or from telephone canvassing solicitations; they can be stimulated by carton-stuffers inserted in other people's shipping containers; they can come from flyers distributed at conferences, or by eager authors. The trick is to find the one (or combination) approach that will add qualified first-time buyers to *your* customer list, for repetitive exploitation, at the lowest cost-per-name. Over the long run, the maximum acceptable promotion cost for acquiring each such new customer *by any method* is around $3.50.

Instead of mailing in their direct orders, readers are more-and-more-frequently telephoning, and using credit cards to make payments. An analysis of 55 direct-marketing publishers of professional books found that, in 1991, they averaged getting 27.7 percent of their orders by phone; 20 direct-marketing consumer interest publishers got 35.5 percent by phone. And because phone orders are less expensive to process (and offer such other marketing advantages as up-sell opportunities and easier source-of-sales tracking), publishers are increasingly encouraging them by installing *and promoting* toll-free numbers; 58.2 percent of those 55 professional book publishers just cited, and 75 percent of the 20 consumer marketers, had toll-free order lines in 1991.

Small publishers find direct marketing particularly appealing because—assuming they handle the creative aspects of design and copy professionally—they encounter each potential customer on *an equal footing* with those conglomerated giants of the publishing industry who've tended to drown out smaller voices in the bookstores; people simply don't tend to think about your most-famous competitors while they're looking at *your* attractive ad or mailer. And since your own promotion budget determines how extensive your market outreach will be at any given time, you have more-or-less full control over the pace of investment, inventory depletion, fulfillment, and the other capital requirements or workloads stimulated at any given time. You're in a position to start modestly, test results, and plow back proceeds on a "pay as you go" basis.

Because mailing lists and ad media keyed to almost any conceivable consumer interest, or professional/vocational specialty, are readily available to publishers, direct response marketing can be used to achieve distribution of almost all kinds of books. (Textbooks are a special case, as described in Chapter 29; however, even there basic direct response logic is the key; you're simply concentrating on *giving away samples effectively* by getting the right people to ask for them—rather than making an actual initial sale to identify a new customer.)

One limiting factor (primarily applicable to consumer books) is the unit-of-sale (the potential dollar-size of the resulting orders). Most publishers find it difficult to make money processing orders totaling less than $20 (though some small houses truly geared to on-line phone-order entry actually manage to show a profit on orders under $10). So some publishers only include books priced at $20 or more in their direct response promotions; others specify a minimum order amount (suggesting that smaller-quantity buyers go pester their bookstores or libraries). Most, however, simply include enough books in each promotion that the *typical* order will be for more than one book ... and don't worry about the marginal exceptions.

In any case, for reasons both of (1) achieving acceptable order-sizes and (2) giving the reader enough choice to create a statistical probability that the required percentage will find something they can't resist, publishers generally find that they need *at least 35* good books or other products—all related to the basic interest(s) shared by the main audience (the past customer list)—to conduct a successful, long-term direct response marketing program.

Until they have 35 titles, many "start-up" direct marketers arrange with other (even competing) publishers to buy small lots (say, 25 at a time) of their compatible books (or such other media packages as video-cassettes or software disks) for inclusion in their direct marketing promotions and inventory—to increase the statistical probability of both responses and acceptable order-sizes. This is not as profitable as promoting your own books—since the cost of that inventory (after the discounts you can negotiate) is usually 50 percent or more of the selling price—whereas that of your own books (inventory plus royalty) is usually (if you're doing it right) only 40 percent or less. So this tactic (which will indeed dilute the attention any one of your own titles gets—even while increasing the over-all response) is usually only wise *until* you can build your own book list to offer your audience 35-or-more choices.

Because it is so important that the accumulating customer list share a well-defined interest (or related set of interests), direct response marketing is very dependent on the *discipline* exercised by the publisher's acquisition function. When acquisition editors forget discipline—and acquire books that "don't really fit the niche"—the direct response campaign is probably well-advised to *leave those off-target books out* of all mailing pieces, print ads, exhibit displays, etc., which are primarily intended to *add new names* to the customer list (promoting them only as "incidentals," to the already-confirmed previous-buyer list). People who get on your list by buying an *uncharacteristic* book eventually cost you a lot of money, by persistently ignoring your repetitive future efforts to sell them non-related books in which they have little interest.

Publishers of professional/vocational books should be aware that *people in institutions* buy books just about the same way people at home do. Religious publishers of clergy-level theological works, pastoral counseling or church leadership resources, etc. ... educational publishers of pedagogical aids, professional reference books, or *reproducible* (as opposed to bulk-purchased) classroom materials ... business-oriented publishers of anything from training materials to top-level strategy guides ... all find that multi-title mailers or ads directed to *individuals* in their target industries or institutions are just as profitable as those tightly-targeted promotions so dear to the hearts of law and medical book publishers.

And while two-thirds of public and el-high school librarians, and perhaps half of college and corporate librarians, buy most of their books through wholesalers (for the administrative advantages of "one stop shopping"), direct marketers find that librarians who *do buy directly* on one occasion are more-than-normally likely to do so again. So they include appropriate library lists in their direct response screening campaigns (perhaps tallying them separately—since they know two-thirds of the orders won't come direct), and they add every librarian who sends a *direct* order to that previous-customer list for top-priority, repetitive saturation.

Surveys of librarians indicate that *collection-area supervisors*—of children's book, young-adult, adult fiction, adult non-fiction, reference book, etc., departments—are the major book-purchasing decision-makers in this market. The "acquisition librarian"—target of so much mail—is often just a purchasing administrator; the head librarian may be more concerned with personnel policy than book selection. And after book reviews (see Chapter 26) and specific patron requests (usually stimulated by those book reviews), the surveys indicate that *direct mail from publishers* is the next-strongest influencer of those book-selecting supervisors. Furthermore, librarians have generally abandoned their old prejudices against the independent publisher's favorite format—the paperback book. So clearly, librarians deserve a serious place in your direct response marketing strategy (even if much of the resulting response is *indirect*).

Adding direct response promotion/selling to your marketing strategy, then, is a fairly straight-forward process. First you prioritize your prospective audiences. Then you sort those audiences into sub-categories (if any) that need to be talked to in a certain way. Each such category which needs to be *specially addressed* must be the object of a separate on-going, three-part "campaign" like the first four lines under "Direct Buyers" on the sample strategy model in Figure 9b—and a separate code-category in your accumulative mailing list.

For most of that accumulative customer list (first "direct buyer" line on that model), you simply keep repeating your best presentation every 2-4 weeks. Meanwhile, you use that same proven basic mailer you're sending the customer list—or the most effective previous ad you've tested—to continue devoting about 20 percent of your promotion budget to screening new customer names out of the most-responsive outside audiences (mailing lists, ad media, etc.) you've previously identified by testing. And you use either that same presentation, or a less-expensive condensation of it, to test *new* audiences with 10 percent of your promotion money.

After you've (1) identified a target audience (or sub-audience), there are six more basic steps in the development of each on-going direct response campaign for selling to that audience: (2) organizing your "offer"; (3) choosing basic offer-delivery tactics; (4) choosing *specific* media; (5) arranging and scheduling execution; (6) creating your presentation; and (7) guaranteeing fulfillment. Some observations about each of these seven steps:

(1) *The Audience:* As in the planning of any marketing strategy (see Chapter 24), the first step in developing a profitable direct response program is *identifying and prioritizing target audiences*—whether for professional or consumer-interest books ... and whether at home or in institutional settings. You do it the same way you do with any other marketing tactic—simply brainstorming what kinds of people might directly purchase your books, and consulting your order-processing computer for any helpful analyses of existing direct response customers it might offer. But since you'll be communicating

directly with those audiences (through media that give you access without distribution middlemen)—once you've identified such an audience, you're much closer to paydirt than at this stage of a less-direct (trade, classroom adoption, special marketing) strategy.

(2) *The Offer:* Once you have a target audience clearly in mind, the next step is to determine *what you'll offer* that audience. In direct response book marketing, your offer will normally consist of a combination of (a) an assortment of books with stated prices, and (b) the terms on which you're willing to sell those books (or even give some away, as premiums and/or samples). Generally speaking, the most effective assortment of books is *everything you've got* that's relevant to the known or assumed interests of the audience. Highlight (by location, typography, and art) the best-sellers, call attention to new titles— but give readers *every possible chance* of finding something they want, by including *all of your relevant titles* (unless embarrassingly obsolete).

As for sales terms, experienced direct marketers quickly learn that *if they really have unique books,* and *if they do a good job of presenting them,* prices aren't as much of a hurdle (and gimmicks aren't as much help) as the amateurs usually think they are. So the "norm" in sales terms, for direct response presentations, includes both the full stated price *plus* a reasonable shipping/ handling charge. Trade and library accounts will complain if this exceeds actual postage or parcel-delivery charges; direct response buyers, on the other hand, generally *expect* that it will include extra money for handling the transaction. Such charges generally range between $1.00 and $3.00. But since each additional book after the first one achieves various economics of scale, a major portion of direct response marketers only make *one basic charge* to cover the first book—though some do require additional shipping/handling payments for additional units. The idea is to make the transaction as simple as feasible.

But other publishers insist they've done well offering bonuses (quantity discounts or premium books) for larger orders. Again—"you pays your money and takes your choice."

Sales terms must also include arrangements for payment. You have to decide *in advance* whether you'll (1) bill those customers who wish, and trust them to make reasonably prompt payments, (2) arrange with a bank for a credit card "merchant account," or (3) insist on actual payment with each order (thereby ruling out telephone orders). Virtually all direct response marketers agree that one-or-the-other of those first two options is essential to the tactic; sales barriers evaporate when you can keep reminding the audience (on every two-page spread of your promotion) that all they need to do to get a book is to phone the designated number. But small publishers are divided on the question of whether credit card services are worth the 3 percent-or-so of total sales that they cost; with bad debt losses for independent publishers only averaging about 1 percent of sales, many would just as soon bill-with-shipment, and wait a month or so for their money.

(3) *The Tactic:* The combination of things you're offering *might* effect your choice of tactics for delivering that offer. Another reason direct marketers like direct mail so much is that normal formats (catalogs, multi-page folders, card decks, etc.) put few limits on the number of titles they can include; print ads are more restrictive; broadcast commercials are almost-inevitably limited to single titles (with their low statistical probability of success).

(4) *Specific Media:* The best medium for most of your direct response promotion (that 70 percent suggested above for repetitive exploitation of an accumulated customer list) is almost certainly direct mail; you own the list, and it would be wasteful not to make use of it. But for seeking (testing) new audiences, and skimming those first-time orders from them to enlarge your own list, you should systematically review directories of rental mailing lists (see Appendix 6), print media (Appendix 6), book exhibits (Appendices 4 and 6), and/or—especially for regional books—radio or television stations (Appendix 6).

(5) *Arranging/Scheduling Execution:* Now that you know precisely how you're going to deliver which offer to which specific mailing list, ad audience, etc.—it's time to go back to the Marketing Strategy Model (see Figure 9b) and relate each planned exposure (repetition) to the appropriate "window" (time-column). Experienced promotion planners usually do this on a quarterly basis—since marketing plans and budgets that get too far ahead are very likely to change before they happen. Now back up from each exposure you've scheduled (each mailing, each ad, etc.) to identify and deadline (date) every significant step *anyone* must take to make it happen. Enter each date, event, and the initials of the responsible party in a database (similar to that scheduling form in Figure 8c), and you'll end up with a detailed, itemized task list and schedule for the quarter's promotion. (This works for *all* kinds of marketing strategies—not just "direct response.") Then you're ready to call all of those people whose initials you've entered together—to compare notes and clarify assignments for that quarter's program.

(6) *Presentation:* Since we've already discussed the creation of direct mail, ad, and other presentations in Chapter 25 ... we'll just refer you back there at this point. Essentially, the presentation is an appropriate combination of copy (hopefully derived from those "copy packages" described in Chapter 25) and design (which will be a graphic layout of type and art for mail and print promotions—or well-sequenced copy within a strictly-choreographed time-frame for broadcast promotions or tele-canvassing scripts).

(7) *Guaranteeing Fulfillment:* Even while the campaign is being created (Step 6), you should make a clear list of all books involved, all codes to be utilized in the promotions, any special prices or other terms, and estimated sales quantities for each title—and provide copies to your inventory monitor/ buyer, order processing supervisor, and anyone else whose work is likely to be impacted by the promotion. Here again (especially when launching major

new promotional campaigns), it may be worthwhile to get all concerned together for a few minutes to make sure all signals are clear and understood. Once you've done enough direct response marketing to develop "base line" expectations—norms for response percentages, average order-size, unit costs, after-cost gross margins, etc.—it's easy to get "in a rut," complacently continuing to do the same thing month after month and year after year as long as it's keeping you afloat. But the publishers who get rich at direct response marketing are a more restless breed; they're *constantly* challenging the basic components of their program with tests they hope might reveal an *even better* approach.

Among the aspects of the program you should be constantly reviewing and periodically challenging (by testing other options and comparing cost/result ratios) are your basic target-audience identifications, your accumulation of approved "screening lists" for adding new customer names, the frequency at which you repeat exposures to your basic customer list, your offers—combinations of books and terms, your tactics for seeking first-time customers—direct mail vs. ads vs. exhibits, etc., and your presentations—specific copy and design options.

To test anything effectively, you have to compare results with a "control"—a previously-proven alternative. For most publishers, the "control" with which any test is compared is *a repetition of their most effective, similar previous promotion.* You must test *only one significant element* at a time; if you try a new presentation to a new audience, you'll never know which variable was responsible for any failure. This means you test new audiences (through mailing lists or ads) with your best previously proven promotion piece, and new presentations (mailing pieces, ads, exhibit displays, etc.) to your previously-most-responsive audiences. The prime test audience for most publishers is a sample (1,500-2,500 names) from their accumulated past-buyer list; if they're testing a print ad rather than a mailing piece, they simply create a newsletter for the sample audience and insert the ad therein.

Whatever you're testing, it's axiomatic that you can't draw conclusions (except that you've failed) from less than 35 responses; fewer would pose too great a risk of "statistical fluke" to allow you to safely assume you could get the same results on a larger scale. So you start any test by determining what you can afford to spend to get at least 35 responses of the order-size or other qualifying characteristics that you're seeking. That's the *minimum* amount you should plan to spend on the test; however many mailing pieces or ad column-inches or broadcast seconds that'll buy you is your minimum test arena. (At the same time, since most tests fail, it's usually foolhardy to try something new on a scale larger than whatever you could afford to spend to produce 50-or-so responses; if that doesn't get you the 35 you need, the promotion you're testing is *ex officio* a failure.)

The basic question all tests should ask is: "How does the cost-per-response (or per resulting sales dollar—if that's what you're going after) compare with the simultaneous control promotion?" But some veterans who have their marketing models and their past result-data really well organized learn to *by-pass the control* by simply asking: "Does this approach (on the basis of 35-or-more responses) offer me a *lower* cost per response—or a *higher* sales volume per dollar spent—than I've been getting from my basic approach?"

Marketing planners—and *especially* direct response planners—who claim they can't really track results for comparison with their best previous efforts simply mustn't be tolerated in this era of easy-and-inexpensive computerization. *Finding ways* to prove the value of every type of exposure, every category of customer, and every specific presentation is *part of their job.* The real pros won't give you alibis; they'll eventually give you explicit comparisons (cost-per-response or cost-per-sales-dollar) between each of the campaigns on the marketing model—and then they'll challenge those results by testing explicitly-tracked alternatives.

CHAPTER 31
Special Market, Export, and Remainder Selling

Enterprising publishers are often able to supplement their primary revenue streams by developing low-cost programs to make four types of sales outside their traditional trade, classroom, and/or direct response markets. These four major supplementary sales opportunities are "special marketing" (through non-traditional middlemen), exporting, "remainder marketing" (of surplus or obsolete stock), and subsidiary rights selling. We'll save that last category for its own (next) chapter.

"Special Marketing" essentially means selling your books through channels other than those normal and basic to the book industry (the bookstore/library trade, classrooms, or direct-to-readers). Generally speaking, publishers have found four kinds of special marketing opportunities to be most lucrative: (1) selling through retail speciality outlets other than bookstores, (2) selling through organizations that share their subject-interests, (3) selling "premium editions" to companies that can use large quantities in their own promotional efforts, and (4) selling to-or-through the author's personal contacts.

Selling through retail specialties other than bookstores (garden shops, sporting goods outlets, travel agencies, gourmet shops, or what-not) is especially attractive to modest-sized publishers because most of the conglomerated giants who dominate the bookstore world are too clumsy and inflexible to go elsewhere. But you have to keep remembering that these non-bookstore merchants aren't likely to have the time (or interest) to learn an entire new merchandising style or approach—so you have to make sideline bookselling easy and automatic for them.

The simplest way to do this is to assemble a "starter selection" of a few (3-to-5) copies of each of your several (5-to-10) most popular and most appropriate (to the retailer's speciality) titles, shop around for a custom-vendor of shipping cartons that will open up as counter-top displays (with point-of-purchase posters, labels or "flip-ups" included), create a brochure explaining how the package works (and how the stock that sells can be quickly replaced) ... and then either (1) try to sell this package "cold turkey" through mailings to appropriate lists of retailers or ads in appropriate trade journals (see Appendix 6), or (2) probably more effectively—offer such merchants (via such mailings or ads) a complimentary sample of your most-appealing title closely related to their retail specialty, along with that how-to-display brochure, as a premium to solicit leads—and then follow up those leads with hard-hitting direct mail and/or telemarketing.

You should build into the package, and explain in the brochure, a mechanism for restocking the display as certain titles "sell out." One good way to do this is a place a re-order card in front of the next-to-last copy of each title-stack. Another is to mail each participating merchant a monthly checklist of the titles and quantities, inviting them to check the display and order such replacements as are needed (giving them a phone/fax option if they prefer) ... and then follow up with your own phone queries to all who haven't re-ordered within 2 or 3 weeks.

Price the original "starter kit" attractively (you should be able to include enough titles to justify a 50 percent discount and free freight), and then apply your normal trade discount schedule to restocking orders. In your original promotion, clarify the discount basis by citing the total discounted cost of the package, and then the *total retail price* they'll get back from their customers when all those books are sold. Offering normal return privileges will also help you overcome initial sales resistance.

After you've placed such displays in a significant number of stores, it's a good idea to develop a larger selection (perhaps even offering a free bookrack) as an upgrade opportunity for those merchants who are most successful with the program. You might also incorporate into this larger display an automatic order plan for a modest test quantity of each appropriate, forthcoming new title. New titles might also be added to existing displays when you're phone-checking inventory replenishments monthly or quarterly; suggest that any slow-selling titles be returned and replaced by these new candidates.

If your editorial concerns parallel those of specific not-for-profit organizations or institutions, there should also be "special marketing" opportunities to sell them—or their local chapter or congregations—bulk quantities of your books for use in their own fundraising, educational, public opinion, group discussion, training, or other programs. Many churches run informal bookshops for their members, and add the discount-margins to their operating budgets; libraries sponsor book-discussion groups in which all participants buy the books under discussion; school projects are sometimes financed by book fairs at which parents enrich their children's bookshelves; service organizations use good books to instruct the public how to do helpful activities.

To encourage such local organizations as churches to establish their own informal bookshops—both for convenience to their members, and for fundraising (from the margins they retain after your discounts)—follow a procedure similar to that described above for special marketing to non-book retail specialties. However, you'll probably need to add a "how-to" booklet to the kit (or combine it with the initial brochure), to help them with such things as keeping inventory and sales records, promoting sales, and possibly even ordering books from other publishers to make the venture more viable.

Creating discussion guides for use with particularly-topical special interest books as a means of promoting their use in group programs is also an effective way to tap the sales potential of local chapters of organizations (or religious denominations) that share your concerns and point-of-view. Combine the discussion guide with a quantity order form (with whatever discounts and shipping-charge terms you consider appropriate)—and promote the guide itself as a *free* offering (to specialized lists or in organizational journal ads) to identify leads. Then keep pounding away with repetitive direct mail to convert those leads into quantity orders.

In the pre-publication development of each new title, there should be one routine point at which marketing's key contact developer interviews the editor (and even the author) about other possibilities for *large-quantity* usage of the book in national or regional programs of sympathetic organizations. Use news release announcements with cover letters (see line 16 of Figure 21b) to solicit requests for complimentary examination copies—and then follow up as you would with any other important pre-publication sales lead. Again, it should be feasible to offer kindred-spirit organizations the same quantity discounts and other terms you offer bookstores.

Just as it's often feasible to sell large quantities to organizations for use in their own programs, you may occasionally be able to make even bigger deals to sell commercial enterprises *their own editions* of appropriate titles—for use as goodwill or lead-qualifying premiums, or even as "how-to" bonuses in the cartons in which they ship expensive equipment, materials, etc. Once again, the easiest way to effect such sales of premium editions is to brainstorm (with or without the author) a prospect list, offer those prospects examination samples (via news releases and cover letters), and follow up any who respond with sales-closure letters and phone calls.

Such premium editions typically replace the publisher's book cover copy with promotional copy provided by the sponsoring buyer; sometimes, the premium buyer will even want its own name (in conjunction with yours) on the title page. Thus, the minimum quantities you offer should be large enough (usually 1,000+) to make these press changes cost-effective. Since such merchandise will not be resalable to others, you should offer *no* return privileges; in fact, you may want a one-third "advance" before you start printing to avoid being left "holding the bag" when somebody gets last-minute cold feet. And because the freight bills on such quantities are substantial, state in your offer that it's FOB directly from the printer (i.e., you'll add the freight to their bill).

Sadly, publishers who go to all of the trouble necessary to sell and negotiate such large-quantity premium editions sometimes literally "give them away" by treating them as "add-on" sales. *I.e.,* they convince themselves that there's no real expense except the printing bill—since they had to do all of the acquisition, editing, and typesetting anyhow—to produce their own edition. And since the premium edition usually increases their own press run for the inside pages, the printer's unit cost often comes down. So some publishers feel that anything they get from such sales over-and-above printing costs is 100 percent-profit—so they only need "add-on" some modest mark-up far below the normal price level.

Unfortunately, many such modestly-priced "add-on" deals, with their low-percentage profit margins, leave the publisher's own basic edition saddled with such a large share of those normal staff and inventory costs that the total profit margin of the publishing house shrinks. And stockholders and auditors are usually unimpressed with the explanation that it happened because you gave somebody else (the premium buyer) free copy-editing, typesetting, etc.

Once you exclude general marketing, warehousing/fulfillment, and order processing costs, which don't really contribute to such premium editions, from the financial models of under-$30-million publishing houses that operated "in the black" in 1991, paper/printing/binding costs were still *only one-third* of the remaining total (for management and acquisition, royalties, pre-press development, financial administration, office facilities, and a normal margin). This suggests that appropriate pricing for add-on deals (such as "premium" editions) calls for multiplying the printer's unit price by at least three. That should still leave the premium buyer with an attractive unit cost.

Another "special marketing" channel too-often overlooked by publishers is the author herself. People working inside publishing houses quickly learn to classify authors as either "non-promoters" or "self-promoters." Some are so diffident about selling that they even object to superlatives in promotional copy about their books. Others are so aggressive that they'll attempt to dictate your marketing strategy and copy. Marketing people tend to prefer the former; at least they don't get in the way. But while authors should be prevented from interfering in your basic marketing activity (and it's the acquiring editor's responsibility to make this clear to them), smart marketing managers recognize that extra sales can indeed be made by moderate catering to the aggressive writer's urge to promote herself and her book.

After reading the background questionnaire submitted by any new author who has signed a book contract with you, the marketing manager (in consultation with the editor) should decide whether further conversation with that writer is in order. During a follow-up interview (which can be done by phone almost as easily as in person), the marketing manager can not only pick the author's brains about special sales possibilities, but can enlist the writer in the actual selling process in a way that won't interfere with other marketing efforts.

Every writer of a forthcoming book is hounded by personal contacts who want to know where/when/how they can get a copy. Few can have such confidence in their publisher's distribution system to assure people that it will be in every bookstore after publication date. Often (if the contacts are important), this puts the author on the spot to take the initiative in getting the contact a book—and sometimes it's awkward not to make it complimentary.

You can solve all these problems for your authors by routinely generating as part of your basic "copy package" (see Chapter 25) a reformatting of the basic promotional copy (with a routine order coupon) as a direct-order brochure that the author can insert in personal correspondence, offer as newsletter inserts to organizations that want to help him promote his book, pass around whenever he has speaking engagements, etc. Use your desktop system to produce the "master," and colored paper in your photocopier to run off whatever quantity the author will agree to circulate effectively.

Among other benefits, such brochures give you a way to divert (and utilize) authors whose egos and energies might otherwise cause disruption of your routine marketing program. And when you have a real self-promoter on your hands, you may find that the resulting sales volume is surprisingly substantial.

Another opportunity to increase your income without publishing more books is to export them to other countries. But before too many sugar plum fairies dance through your dreams of riches from overseas, stop and ponder that *it'll be much harder to sell overseas than at home*—so don't divert much time or money to it until you're satisfied you're adequately covering your domestic opportunities.

Many publishers manage to avoid the inevitable pitfalls (and much of the work) of communicating with unfamiliar cultures by *selling rights* to compatible foreign publishers—for either English-language editions or translations of their books—or working out more elaborate co-publishing deals. We'll explore those options in the next (subsidiary rights) chapter. Nevertheless, if the subject-matter that dominates your acquisition strategy is truly appropriate for foreign audiences, English is now read by educated people in enough of the world to make the exporting of your own editions a realistic book marketing strategy.

Exporting is sometimes accomplished by direct selling—using international mailing lists, or advertising in internationally-circulated special interest journals. However, currency and credit problems, plus the high cost and slow speed of delivering books to many parts of the world, make this only marginally profitable (at best) for most. Others attempt to reach major distributor outlets by signing up with U.S.-based "export reps" who call on selected wholesalers, bookstores, universities, large library systems, etc., throughout the world. You'll find such reps listed in *Literary Market Place* (see Appendix 2) and *Resources for Book Publishers* (see Appendix 1).

Generally speaking, however, the export tactic that has worked best for most of the independent houses who've pursued such sales seriously and successfully has been the contracting of exclusive regional distributors in each major overseas market-area (Canada, Australia/New Zealand, Britain—sometimes with other Commonwealth countries, western Europe, Slavic Europe, the Arab world, Southeast Asia, Japan/East Asia, etc.). You'll find a number of potential distributors listed in *Literary Market Place* and *International Literary Market Place* (Appendix 2). The best way to start recruiting your export combination is to personalize a word processed form letter for each likely-looking prospect, and send it with your catalog to solicit expressions of interest. Then you should treat each response as a "key contact" sales lead—to be personally and seriously followed up by the marketing manager herself.

Don't overlook compatible foreign publishers (especially in countries not covered by the major regional distributors). Many will be amenable to including books from North American publishers in their catalogs "if the price is right."

So what price *is* right?

As we've said a number of times before, you seldom make money selling anybody your books for less than half of the cover price. A 50 percent discount does, however, still leave you enough money to promote those books—and you must do such promotion, if you expect to sell effectively through domestic wholesalers, distributors, etc. They each handle *too many publishers* to provide very effective supporting promotion for the individual books of any of those clients. On the other hand, your promotional efforts will seldom be very effective overseas—so if a foreign distributor truly convinces you that *it will effective introduce your titles* to its society, it's not unreasonable to throw in another 5 percent (for a maximum 55 percent export discount).

In the case of short-discounted text, reference, or professional books (for which your own large-quantity dealer discount should normally be only 30-35 percent), you'll only be able to afford 40 percent for the overseas distributor if you hope to make the same profit you would at home. However, foreign distributors who specialize in such books (especially in scientific and technical fields) are often amenable to such a discount level.

Overseas distributor terms should (and normally do) specify that shipments are FOB the publisher's warehouse, or the distributor's U.S. consolidation/shipping point—and that all transportation beyond that point is to be arranged and/or paid for by the distributor. Payment terms are usually 90-days-after-shipping/invoicing—to give the distributor plenty of time to receive and verify each shipment.

Recruiting the distributor network is then a major task of key contact marketing. Each successful contact developed will eventually be important enough to you that it's worth checking individual credit references and learning individual customs-declaration rules appropriate to each potential distributor. And remember that you can get burned on currency exchanges unless you've negotiated for payment in U.S. dollars—or at least for their equivalent *at the time* and *in the place* of the eventual currency conversion.

When a publishing house can't sell all the copies it has printed of a given book before the world forgets about them or their subject, the traditional way of disposing of the surplus is called "remaindering." Essentially, this means selling the remaining inventory to a wholesaler who specializes in supplying discount outlets, at a salvage price usually at-or-below the original manufacturing cost of the books. You'll find the leading "remainder dealers" listed in *Literary Market Place* (Appendix 2).

Systematic remaindering of excess inventory can not only supplement your sales volume, but also reduce your storage costs. And if you do end up selling books at less than the inventory cost, you're then entitled to write off the difference as a legitimate tax deduction.

Generally, trade publishers find that it is unwise to remainder stock unless they are prepared to declare a title out-of-print and discontinue it; its appearance on the remainder market will undermine future restocking by stores and wholesalers, and alienate those who discover their own inventories of the book have been undercut. Publishers marketing primarily by mail order must decide themselves whether a title's appearance in discount lists will destroy its effectiveness in their own program; often such direct-marketing publishers do decide it is feasible to remainder most of the stock of a title they've over-printed, while maintaining a few hundred books for their own customers and future library and specialist demand.

Conventional book remaindering is a fairly simple process. The first step is to prepare a description of each title you want to include in the sale. Usually, the easiest way to do this is to cut out old catalog entries (including publication dates and prices), paste them up as a reference sheet or folder, and run off enough photocopies for your remainder dealer list. Add notations indicating how many copies of each title you have available for sale. Send these photocopies to your list of dealers, with a cover letter offering to send complimentary samples of any titles that interest them. Solicit (by cover letter when you send the samples, and subsequent phone follow-ups) unit-price bids (FOB your warehouse, with the buyer paying shipping costs—on 30-day terms). Make it clear that you'll sell to the first acceptable bidder after a specified (near future) date.

Then treat each response as a key contact sales lead. But bear in mind that "remaindering" is never as profitable as the selling of your better books at normal terms—so don't devote a lot of time (or any appreciable amount of money) to this activity. And when you're offered only a few cents per unit for certain titles, consider seriously that it's probably more economical to grind them up for packing material than to pack and ship them as remainders. The idea is to make the entire remaindering process incidental and automatic. If it converts yesterday's mistakes into a little extra cash, well and good. But don't throw good money after bad by taking it too seriously!

CHAPTER 32
Selling Subsidiary Rights

"Subsidiary rights" are the licenses a publisher (or agent) sells others to allow them to adapt a manuscript to some secondary use that does not compete seriously with the original book edition, but provides (through royalties or fees) additional income for both author and originating publisher (or the author's agent, if such rights were withheld from the originating publisher). Income from subsidiary "print" rights (for use of all or part of the actual text in another book or a periodical) are usually split 50/50 between author and publisher (who handles the marketing of such rights). Traditionally, rights to adapt a book (or portions thereof) into another medium have been split 90/10 in the author's favor—making it hardly profitable for the publisher to spend time and money marketing most such licenses. However, many independent publishers specify a better split (from 80/20 up to 50/50) in their author contracts—thus giving their own key contact developers more incentive to go after audio- and video-cassette, stage and movie adaptation, and other non-print adaptation deals.

The important thing to remember here is that *there's nothing automatic about subsidiary rights.* Copyright law makes it clear that *all rights* originate in the act of creation—and thus belong *to the author* until and unless that author contracts to transfer them to a publisher or some other party. So when you contract to publish a book, you (the publisher) only acquire such subsidiary rights as are specified in the written contract document. Furthermore, such generalizations as "all subsidiary rights" may be considered by a judge to be so "pointlessly vague" that they can later be ignored by an author or agent.

So in your author contracts, it's important (as illustrated by paragraph 3 of Figure 14a) to list all of the specific rights you consider important—as well as making a general claim. If an author or agent balks, you then must simply decide whether their withholding of certain rights is significant enough to make you reconsider the project.

There are seven basic categories of subsidiary rights that should be considered in evaluating, contracting, and marketing most books. These indicate the kinds of people you should be accumulatively adding (initially from *Literary Market Place*—as per Appendix 2) to your key contact list for pre-publication publicity, and subsequent follow-up of any expressions of interest. In virtually all situations, effective rights-selling strategies start with news release announcements and/or personalized letters to any of these seven categories of buyers appropriate to the project—offering to send them a complimentary copy (or a photocopy of the rough pages or manuscript, if they're in a hurry), if they think it *might* be of interest to them. From there on, it's simply a matter of one-to-one key contact sales follow-up (by mail and phone) to elicit specific offers from those buyers, and negotiate a deal around the best offer you get for each/any category of rights.

A license to allow another publisher to utilize any specific subsidiary right, with respect to any manuscript, usually takes the form of a "letter of agreement" spelling out the exact terms and specifying what (if any) advance payment is due on acceptance of the deal. Since it is customarily the *buyer* who makes the first offer, over a period of time any aggressive subsidiary rights promoter will get to see a wide sampling of such documents.

The seven basic rights categories are:

(1) *Co-Publishing Rights:* These license another book publisher to manufacture (from your film, disk, or camera-ready pages ... usually with both your names on the title page) and sell (on an exclusive basis, in specified major segments of the book market) its own edition of a book you've acquired, edited, and type-set—*simultaneously* (and in potential competition) with your edition of the book. (Often, either the originating publisher or the co-publisher handles all of the manufacturing for both parties, and sells the other sufficient copies to serve its needs.)

Co-publishing agreements are usually made when a publisher used to operating in only one of the major segments of the book market (trade, classroom, direct-response to a special constituency) comes into possession of a manuscript with strong secondary (or even primary) potential in another segment—where it has few contacts, little experience, and little future interest. Thus a direct-marketing association press, for example, might occasionally have a title that also has major trade or classroom possibilities; the association (the "originating publisher") might then seek co-publishing inquiries from selected trade or classroom publishers whose distribution would not seriously impinge on its own direct sales to its constituency.

The most common co-publishing agreements are 7-year licenses granted by the originating publisher to the co-publisher, clearly specifying the market segments reserved to each party, and obligating the originating publisher to provide edited, formatted disks, film, or camera-ready pages of the interior— plus its own cover design and title page for modification by the co-publisher. The latter then handles its own printing, marketing, fulfillment, and collections—and pays the originating publisher 35 percent of all receipts from its sales of its edition. From this, the originating publisher must pay the author (usually about 10 of those 35 percentage points—since the royalty is properly based on the co-publisher's sales volume, not the originating publisher's reduced share), and cover all acquisition, editing, and pre-press (design, type-setting) costs. Whatever's left from its 35 percent will be the originating publisher's profit. Meanwhile, the co-publisher uses its 65 percent to cover the printing, marketing, fulfillment, etc.—and its fair share of the profits.

Co-publishing deals are often made by large publishing houses to fill blanks in their acquisition schedules for which their editors have not been able to find suitable manuscripts. Sometimes (particularly with comprehensive reference works) they pay substantial up-front "advances" against the originating publisher's anticipated future share—in the $10-25,000 range.

Aggressive co-publishing negotiators frequently try to persuade smaller, less-experienced originating publishers that what they're really buying is "reprint rights"—as described immediately below—because these royalties are so much lower. (Not-for-profit publishing programs are particularly prone to buy such "wooden nickels" from large commercial operators.) But reprint rights are properly for *later* publication of a book the originating publisher has already substantially exploited for its own purposes. If the rights buyer gets in on the original edition—with exclusive distribution privileges for one of the major book markets—it's *co-publishing,* and you deserve 35 percent.

(2) *Reprint Rights:* These license another publisher to print its own edition from edited text *after* your edition has had its moment in the sun—for distribution only within a prescribed market and/or format. The most common reprint rights are (1) for "mass market" (news stand) editions that the licensees are also authorized to sell throughout the book trade (to bookstores and library wholesalers), and (2) for overseas English-language editions (in Great Britain, Australia/New Zealand, etc. ... with U.S./Canadian rights reserved to the original publisher).

Reprint editions are usually licensed for 7 years. At the end of that time, all rights revert to the originating publisher. Royalties are usually based on the reprinting publisher's list price for each unit sold—and average 7 percent (though they often escalate from 6 percent up to 8 percent based on the accumulative number of units sold). All royalties (including any advance) are usually split 50/50 with authors (though that depends on the originating publisher's contract with the author). Advances range from a "not very interested" $1,000 through a $3-10,000 "normal range" to $100,000 or more for sure-fire celebrity books or hardcover-proven best sellers.

It is not uncommon for an originating publisher to continue marketing its own trade paperback or hardcover edition even after a competing mass market reprint edition hits the newsstands—but sales of the latter usually decline rapidly once the lower-priced mass market book is available.

Sometimes, reprint rights to formats other than mass market paperbacks (such as a hardcover library edition—or a fancy leather-bound gift edition—of a book originally published as a trade paperback) are sold within the domestic (U.S./Canadian) market. Terms are usually the same as for mass market paperbacks—but advances tend to be considerably lower.

When English-language reprint rights for other parts of the world (Great Britain, Australia/New Zealand, etc.) are sold, customary terms are the same as for domestic mass market reprints—though the book will often be reproduced in a trade paperback (larger size) or hardcover format rather than as a (small) mass market paperback.

In addition to the royalty advance, it is customary for reprint rights buyers to pay a $3-per-page "offset fee" for using the originating publisher's edited camera-ready pages, film, or disks to produce its edition.

(3) *Electronic Adaptation Rights:* With contemporary technology, it is fairly simple to make books available on computer disks, or directly onto a reader's computer screen (via modem access to the publisher's files). The latter approach is primarily used by bibliographers and researchers to seek out specific kinds of data from a wide variety of remote databases. The former approach has been coupled with fast-developing "cd-rom" (compact disk—read-only memory) technology to generate the "electronic book." As formatting techniques improve, and inexpensive cd-rom disk-reading equipment becomes more available (since you can only read, and thus don't need a keyboard), this format is often preferred over the book itself when libraries, researchers, and others consult lengthy reference works or such database publications as directories, sets of regulations, and statistical compilations.

Both of these common electronic adaptations (cd-rom and on-line access through modems) are too-often purchased (by aggressive electronic database distributors) from unwary, inexperienced, insecure, or cash-desperate publishers for a fraction of what those publishers should actually receive. In this case, the rights buyer has very little inventory production expense; it's simply a matter of doing a little formatting and disk-copying. When you sell such rights, you should consider cd-rom adaptations as the equivalent of co-publishing (and demand 35 percent of the "take"); don't kid yourself that cd-rom disks won't cut significantly into sales of your own books. On-line access to your database (i.e., the right to sell the phone number of your modem) should be viewed as the equivalent of wholesale distribution—which means you should hold out for 50 percent of resulting revenues.

In both cases, your author contract may give most of this money to the author *unless* (recognizing a reference or database book as a "natural" for such electronic adaptation) you've wisely altered the conventional subsidiary rights terms to specify a 50/50 (as with "print rights") split for electronic adaptations and distribution—rather than settling for the normal 10-20 percent share the publisher usually gets on non-print adaptations.

(4) *Translation Rights:* Licenses to translate books into other languages are sold on the basis of a specific language *and* territory—though most buyers will insist on "world rights" for any language except Spanish (where you may be able to negotiate separately for such heavily-populated countries as Spain itself, Argentina, or Mexico). The terms are similar to basic reprint rights—except that contracts are usually "for the life of the copyright" (since the buyer

must finance an expensive translation), and the advances are usually lower (in the $500-$1,500 range, because the buyer must put most of his "front money" into the translation rather than the advance).

As with other print rights, author contracts usually split translation income 50/50 between writer and originating publisher.

(5) *Book Club Rights:* In the proper sense, a book club license authorizes the club to publish a single printing of its own edition, for distribution only to its members. Customary royalties are 10 percent of the club's *member price* for its edition—which is usually about 80 percent of your price for your own edition. Half of the royalty is normally paid when the club prints its edition, and the other half when it completes its distribution to its members. Again, typical author contracts split this money 50/50 between writer and original publisher.

If they make a deal early enough, book clubs often seek to "join your printing" by contracting with your printer (using your plates—with your permission) to print their edition at the same time he prints yours. In such circumstances (i.e., when you give that permission), it is customary for the printer to reduce the unit price he's quoted you—because of the larger interior-page press run. You should insist on it!

Some book clubs also make offers to buy some portion of a publisher's existing (or forthcoming) inventory of its own edition of a book—for presentation in the club's catalog as an "alternate selection." This is simply a disguised form of catalog distribution—and should properly earn the book club no more than the 50 percent maximum discount you can afford to give cataloguers and wholesalers. When a club asks you for larger discounts (with the claim that these are "add-on" sales which you wouldn't get otherwise, which don't compete with your own marketing, and which don't cost you anything)—you're on the short end of a Brooklyn Bridge sale! You can no more afford to accept such deals than you can the 55 percent-plus bonus-discount distributor terms we've warned against a number of times in this book.

(6) *Serial Rights:* These are one-time licenses to periodical publishers (from magazines to newspaper feature syndicates) to use part or all of your manuscript as articles or serialized installments. They come in two conventional categories: "first serial rights"—for *exclusive* pre-publication excerption or serialization, and "second serial rights"—for non-exclusive serialization or (more commonly) excerption *after* you've published your book.

The economics of book publishing and journalism suggest that you should get about one cent per word, per 100,000 anticipated reader-circulation of the serial usage, for such rights. However, when exclusive pre-publication *first serial rights* are involved—or when part of your book is to be used in another, potentially competing book—you should insist on a *minimum* of five cents per word (plus an additional cent for each 100,000 anticipated readers over 500,000).

Some of the best serial rights deals are with newspaper feature syndicates that have their own rates for the multiple newspapers that decide to run the materials they offer. In such cases, it's customary for the syndicate to offer you half of all proceeds from their serialization. This usually turns out to be as good (for you) as the formula outlined above.

Once again, as print license income, serial rights fees are customarily split (by contract) 50/50 with the author.

(7) *Non-Print/Non-Electronic Adaptations:* All non-print adaptations other than the two electronic media (cd-rom, on-line modem access) discussed earlier are generally considered non-competitive with—and often promotionally supportive of—the publisher's book edition. For this reason, publishers have traditionally taken only 10 percent (though we recommend you insist on 20 percent) of the royalties, fees and advances paid by other media (audio- and video-cassette packagers, movie and stage play and radio and television producers, etc.) for licenses to adapt their books into appropriate scripts. The offers differ—but you should be seeking (mostly on behalf of your authors) something like 10 percent-of-net-receipts from the adapter ... roughly equivalent to the 7 percent of list price you'd receive from a reprinter. In many cases (especially the movies), producers will offer a down payment roughly equivalent to a mass market advance ($3,000+) for an "option"—which means you hold the rights for them for a specified time (2-4 years), and then recover those rights if the media production has not been completed.

When a forthcoming or recently-published new title shows definite signs of turning into a bestseller, the value of the subsidiary rights (for exploitation of the work by others) escalates dramatically. But since those values are always highly speculative anyhow, it is difficult to determine just what you (in your behalf and the author's) should hold out for. So the "rights auction" has evolved as the industry's customary mechanism for determining such values through competitive bidding.

It is probably wisest to limit any single auction to a specific *one* of the major subsidiary rights—reprint, translation, or first-serial. And an auction is probably not appropriate unless at least three potential buyers in one of those rights categories have indicated real interest in the property during your early key contact promotion—and have asked for advance reading copies. You should be very realistic about determining that enough interest exists to assure you some competition for the rights. Nothing can undermine your credibility (for future auctions) as fast as declaring a race that nobody enters!

When you do have at least three legitimate potential contenders for one of the major categories of rights, you can set an auction in motion by dispatching personal letters to all of your key contacts in that category, advising them that you plan to open bids and implement a telephone auction on a given future date (at least 6 weeks away, so there'll be plenty of time for advance reading). Offer to establish a "floor" for the auction, by accepting a commit-ment from the first buyer willing to guarantee purchase at an acceptable minimum asking price (or advance)—usually in five digits, if the property really merits an auction. (This means that the publisher guaranteeing such minimum terms is assured-in-return of the right to top any final bid by 10 percent and thereby take the rights from the top-bidder if it wants them that badly). Make sure you spell out these ground rules in your letter soliciting floor bids and/or opening-round bids, even though it's assumed all of the rights buyers you'll be dealing with understand them.

Once you've got a "floor" for each category of rights being offered, you should then solicit written, sealed opening bids prior to your announced deadline. On the appointed date, open all of the bids and telephone all buyers who were interested enough to make a bid (except the floor)—telling each in turn the high bid at the moment, and asking if they wish to top it. Call those who bid back (in the same order) with news of any subsequent higher bids during the day; if they're still raising their offers at the end of the day, inform them all that you'll keep going tomorrow.

When everybody has dropped out except the high bidder, inform your "floor" bidder of the final offer and ask if he wishes to exercise his "topping" option, before you confirm the high bid.

When it's over, summarize the deal in a "letter of agreement" and get the winner to countersign promptly. Meanwhile, keep all your notes, in the un-likely event that a snag or misunderstanding arises, and the next-highest bidder needs to be contacted.

PART VI

Business Operations

CHAPTER 33
Organizing and Managing the Business Office

While computers, telemarketing and desktop composition have dramatically altered the way book publishing is done, perhaps none of the changes the industry has experienced in the past generation has been as significant as the changed status of the business manager. In the 1950s (when publishers and editors were just beginning to learn to speak cordially to their marketing colleagues, and had hardly discovered the operational people "in the back room"), the typical business manager was little more than a bookkeeper who watched over the order clerks in his (then inevitably masculine!) spare time. Today, in well-organized publishing houses, the business manager joins the publisher, acquisition editor-in-chief, pre-press managing editor, and marketing manager as one of the core managers of the publishing process. In fact, because business/operations assumes a relatively neutral stance in the inevitable strategic competition between the acquisition and marketing functions, she is frequently designated as the "associate publisher"—who chairs that core management group (and referees the strategic prima donnas) when the publisher is away.

The business manager is the leader of the operational team whose job it is to administer the fiscal and physical assets (the receivables and cash, the inventory, the office space and equipment) of the publishing house. This manager is in a natural position to exert direct control over the cost-effectiveness of a major portion of the day-to-day operations; she controls the flow of data that points the way to profitability in the rest of the house. For this reason, the principal "accountability index" for measuring the business manager's performance is the over-all operating margin (income less expenses). And because of this monetary focus, the business manager usually doubles as the "chief finance officer" of the enterprise—though sometimes, in personally-entrepreneured small companies, the publisher choses to retain this particular responsibility.

To accomplish this sweeping mission, the business manager must be both a *systems designer*—incorporating the diverse inventory administration (print buying, warehousing, shipping), financial administration, and facilities administration (office, computers and phones, other equipment, routine supplies) operations into one smooth, non-redundant workflow—and a *master politician* (persuading each of these operational functions that it is succeeding ... by helping improve the operating margin ... every time it manages to cut its own budget.)

In the typical well-run publishing house, then, the business manager is likely to function more-or-less as suggested by Figure 33a, on the next page.

The acquisition, pre-press development and marketing managers can achieve their major objectives largely within their own departments, by the nature of the new manuscripts or development schedules or sales/promotion campaigns they initiate. But the business manager's principal objective, maximizing the operating (profit) margin, requires that manager to exert influence not only in the logistical "support" functions of the business office, but in those other functions beyond her direct control. Yet it is important to the proper functioning of a sensitive, creative organization such as a publishing house that core managers interact on a peer level as much as possible; they should function as equals. So the business manager must influence those acquisition and pre-press and marketing peers with well-analyzed financial data and insight, not with the clumsy financial intimidation too often associated with stereotypes of the role.

Perhaps the most essential contribution a good business manager makes to the other members of the core management group is a constant flow of background data, giving them a clear perspective on the current functioning of the entire operation. This can be accomplished both through periodic (monthly, quarterly, annual) financial feedback (as described in Chapter 36), and through constant monitoring of the actual workflow of the organization (by assisting in, and—if necessary—taking responsibility for, such scorecards as illustrated by Figures 7b and 8b).

In addition to providing such perspective on the current workflow, the business manager should exert constant pressure for profitability in the planning and decision making of the core management group. This means calling on the finance coordinator ("controller"), if that is a different individual than the business manager, for periodic analyses of all aspects of the business that have a significant impact on that profitability (the "bottom line"). As far as feasible, the business manager should anticipate profitability issues that will arise in core management meetings, and be ready with hard data to make certain that group does not unknowingly lock the enterprise into unprofitable, or excessively risky, situations.

As you'll see in Chapter 37, it is even possible for the business manager to "stack the deck" diplomatically on her acquisition and marketing colleagues, by campaigning for pricing procedures and sales terms and basic author contracts and pre-contract evaluation procedures that are deliberately calculated to help insure profitability.

Figure 33a—Sample Job Description: Business/Operations Manager

TITLE: Business Manager (Operations Manager)
Reports to: Publisher (General Manager)
Directly Supervises:
> Finance Administrator (Bookkeeper)
> Inventory Administrator (Shipper)
> Facilities Administrator (Office Manager)
> Administrative Assistant

Budget Line Responsibility:
> Miscellaneous (non-sales) income
> Total Finance/Inventory/Facilities expenses
> The operating margin
> P/P/B inventory investment

Accountability Indices:
> Trend of operating margin as percent of sales
> Trend of inventory Investment as percent of sales
> Trend of P/P/B per-page-impression unit cost

GENERAL OPERATING RESPONSIBILITIES:

To manage the principal physical and fiscal assets of the publishing house (inventory, office space and equipment, financial records, bank accounts) so as to provide adequate logistical support for general management, editorial acquisition, pre-press development, and marketing at the lowest feasible cost, while maximizing the before-tax operating margin.

SPECIFIC OPERATING RESPONSIBILITIES:

a) To recruit and supervise a support management group for day-to-day coordination of financial administration, Inventory maintenance and shipping, and administration of the enterprise's physical facilities;

b) To serve as the chief financial officer of the enterprise;

c) To monitor and appropriately adjust the cash flow of the enterprise so as to meet current needs without disrupting the timing of strategic operations;

d) To establish and refine an integrated sequence of procedures for purchasing and replenishing book inventory to meet customer demand promptly, while utilizing the smallest feasible accumulative capital investment;

e) To monitor key operating indices so as to alert the Core Management Group to situations requiring their intervention;

f) To advise the Publisher and the Core Management Group regarding the impact of major management and strategic decisions on profitability;

g) To represent the concerns of the operations (finance, print-buying, shipping, facilities) staff in core management deliberations.

Because this focus on profitability normally gives the business manager a sharper perspective on the financial implications of major decisions than the other members of the core group, this individual is also in a position to take a leading role in management's handling of corporate risk. The first rule of sound risk management is that an organization should virtually *never* take a gamble it cannot afford to lose. Any decision that could potentially wipe out the enterprise is a wrong decision—unless said enterprise is already on the verge of collapse anyway, and can only be saved by accepting and beating long odds. The business manager's role, then, includes recognizing such situations and issues as they arise, and documenting the risks involved so clearly that the other core managers (including the publisher) cannot fail to see them.

The business manager's dedication to profitability (rather than marketing's thirst for growth, or acquisition's concern for direction, or pre-press's obsession with time) usually makes this person the natural financial conservative of the core management group. Many business managers complain that they often have to play the "heavy"—by criticizing unrealistic proposals from other functions—simply because their bosses (the publishers) are not strong enough to stand up to the strategic "prima donnas" of aggressive marketing and acquisitions departments. But in fact, it is usually better for the on-going dynamics of the core management group for the business manager to play this critical "nay sayer" role than for the publisher to do it.

When the publisher undermines a marketing or acquisition proposal with criticism, the sponsor of the idea is very likely to drop it entirely (and maybe even become reluctant to advance other new ideas) because "the boss won't buy it" or "I'm sticking my neck out and getting too much flack." But if the criticism comes from a peer, the business manager, those acquisition and marketing managers are more likely to shake it off, go back to the drawing board, resolve the weaknesses that the business manager identified, and come back to the core group for another shot at the idea. Thus a weak plan or a dangerous temptation is sidetracked *without* inhibiting the future imagination and creativity of the core group.

Yet most of the business manager's life is spent not in core management group deliberations, but in directing the day-to-day operations of inventory maintenance (print purchasing) and warehousing and shipping, financial administration, and facilities administration. In the typical small publishing house, the business manager also serves not only as chief finance officer, but as the eventual print buyer. The pre-press managing editors, project managers, and/or production managers usually (and properly) write the print specifications—and may even be responsible for obtaining competitive bids from an accumulative pool of acceptable vendors—but it should be the business manager/finance officer who *makes the final decisions* on print purchases (the most expensive and potentially vulnerable financial commitments characteristic of the enterprise). We'll see how this inventory-maintenance responsibility can be organized for easy accomplishment in Chapter 38.

But once a publishing house passes that first million dollars in annual sales, the business manager will also inevitably need competent assistants to supervise and/or administer the day-to-day financial recording and updating and feedback, the actual storage of inventory and shipment of orders (from computer packing slips initiated by marketing's order-input), and routine office administration (from covering the switchboard to buying paper clips to getting busted equipment fixed fast). We'll look at the work of these key subordinates in Chapter 36 (financial administration), Chapter 39 (storage/ shipping), and Chapter 40 (facilities).

As spokesperson for all of these business/support functions in the organization's top management deliberations, the business manager should take special care to see that none of these distinct sub-functions suffers isolation or alienation because of remoteness from the core management team and the publisher. This means not only maintaining a steady flow of information from the core group to the support-function administrators, but also giving the concerns of each support section strong representation in core management deliberations. (When all of their clout is pooled in the hands of the business manager, shippers and bookkeepers and office managers frequently have greater policy impact than if each specialized function were separately represented by its own supervisor.)

But to lead these diverse functions effectively, the business manager must proclaim and enforce one of the most difficult principles in logistical management—that of the supremacy of cost effectiveness over non-essential quality. It is the task of each support function to perform on an *adequate* basis at the lowest feasible cost. Little is gained (in terms of the publishing organization's true objectives) by better-than-adequate performances, if they cost extra money. People seldom buy (or decline to buy) your books because of such production nuances as paper-shades. How fast you fill orders, or collect your receivables, or pay your bills—or how impressive are the quarters within which you perform this work—has little or no impact on the appeal of your books for most customers. The support functions contribute most to the publishing program, then, when they perform on an *adequate* level at the lowest feasible cost (and thus help the business manager widen that operating margin), rather than seeking top-quality performance at higher cost.

This subjugation of quality to cost poses a morale problem, since most of us are conditioned from childhood to seek excellence in the performance of our work. The problem can only be circumvented by constantly defining cost-control objectives (lowering those budget percentages and unit costs so that the strategic prima donnas can have more resources to quicken the pace or broaden the scope of the program) as the essential goals that define excellence in support-function performance. Business managers and support supervisors must back up this set of values by being quick to reward (with praise, pay raises and promotions) the people who find ways to cut their own budgets!

CHAPTER 34
Developing and Refining
the Financial Planning Model

As we pointed out in Chapter 10, the budgeting process (and similar planning exercises) should start with a common understanding of ground rules and expectations. With that in mind, then, we've suggested that the business manager should go first, in that vital sequence in which each of the core function managers submits a single-sheet "strategic planning model" to the publisher (for discussion by the core group) to summarize their game plans. Each of these models should explain the priorities the originating manager has applied to the basic ingredient of their function. That means acquisition strategy models focus on product subject-categories, marketing models on audience categories, pre-press models on time-sequences (deadlines!), and business/operations models on *money*—the absolutely necessary commodity in the business manager's quest for the largest-feasible "bottom line" operating margin

For that reason, then, the business manager's most appropriate strategy focus (and summary) is a *financial* model. A good one looks something like Figure 34a (a repeat of Figure 9a, shown here to save wear-and-tear on your book binding!), on the next page.

The first section of the model ("function goals") simply identifies the business manager's recommended targets for each component of the monthly Performance Index illustrated in Figure 7b (and explained in Chapter 7). The "budget ratios" offer the business manager's recommendation as to what pattern of apportionment of financial resources will best meet the objectives of the Mission Statement (Figure 6a); these ratios—when/if approved by the publisher after core management group discussion—become the starting place for the next budgeting cycle or session. The "planning assumptions" provide guidelines for managers in all functions when they attempt to estimate costs and risks of particular decisions or projects, set prices, or evaluate staffing levels.

There is no universally "correct" number for any one of those lines in Figure 34a, for any specific publisher. Essentially, the business manager begins by saying: "These are the basic things we need to keep in mind to stay out of financial trouble while planning aggressively." (A good business manager

Figure 34a—Sample Financial Strategy Model

Function Goals

Sales Volume Growth Rate	11.0% over previous year
New Title Contribution	35.0% of sales volume
Pre-Press Page Cost	$20.00 (including copy-edit)
Operating Margin	11.0% of sales volume
Inventory Investment	25.0% of annual sales level

Budget Ratios (percent of anticipated revenue)

Publisher's Office (Mgmt)	7.0% *
Acquisition Staff/Expenses	5.5%
Royalty Liability	9.0% **
Pre-Press Editing/Page Prdn	10.0% ***
Marketing (Sales, Promo)	17.5%
Business Mgr's Office	2.0%
Financial Administration	2.5% ****
Paper/Printing/Binding	22.5% ***
Warehousing and Shipping	4.0%
Rebillable Transport Charges	3.5%
Facilities & Equipment	5.5%
Operating Margin	11.0%

(* includes interest costs)
(** includes royalty advance cost-of-goods)
(*** as expensed via cost-of-goods recovery)
(**** including bad debt and inventory write-offs)

Planning Assumptions

Payroll/Benefits	24.0% of revenue
F/t/e Employees*****	1.0 per $100,000 sales
Returns	7.0% of sales volume
Bad Debts	0.7% of sales volume
Inventory Write-Offs	1.0% of sales volume
Average Discount	35.0% off list price
Maximum Regular Discount	50.0% off list price
Per-Page Pre-Press Cost	$20.00 including copy-edit
Per-Impression P/P/B Cost	$0.01 per copy per page
Pricing Multiplier	5.8 x unit inventory cost

(***** F/t/e = full-time equivalent)

never forgets that low margin-for-error, and that high level-of-risk, characteristic of fast-moving, informally-managed independent publishing houses!)

The place to start in developing the "right" numbers for each element in the model, then, is with your own organization's recent performance. If you'll annualize data as illustrated in both Figure 7b and Figure 35a (next chapter), it will be fairly easy to establish the *actual* numbers your publishing house "scored" on each line of the financial strategy model over the most recent 12 months. It is then the business manager's responsibility to recommend how those current numbers in future plans/budgets should be changed—to push the enterprise in the direction of better over-all performance.

Perhaps the first gross generalization to consider in seeking such improvement is that smart publishing managers are always attempting to *decrease* the percentage of available working capital (usually more-or-less synonymous with sales revenue) absorbed by all other lines in the budget, in order to *maximize* the percentage to be devoted to any-or-all of three specific budget lines: (a) *acquisition salaries,* (b) *total marketing costs,* and (c) *the operating margin* ("bottom line," or before-tax profit). This is because only the more effective, more ambitious acquisition of new manuscripts and the enlarged outreach of an effective marketing program can really increase what you do to the world, how much of it you do, and how much money you make doing it. Otherwise, you're better off "taking your money and running" (banking it for an enhanced bottom line). Even author royalties, publishers have found, make little impact on quality; good authors expect the industry's normal 10 percent "cut"—but can seldom be bribed away from another publisher by a larger percentage (which does not eventually guarantee them a larger net income). So you're more likely to get more and better books (acquisition) by hiring more and better acquisition editors than by boosting royalties.

The business manager must constantly review financial results and trends (from feedback such as Figure 35a) to identify—as the scale of operations and available technology and prevailing circumstances change—what other functions and budget lines can be cut proportionally (as a percentage, not necessarily in actual dollars) quarter-by-quarter, in order to leave more money for acquisition staffing, expanded marketing, or "the bottom line" (eventually convertible into "retained earnings" or a not-for-profit's financing of other non-revenue-generating activities).

So every budgeting process and review should begin with the question: "How can we squeeze more out of other functions and lines to make more available for those three legitimate contenders?" And (because anybody else would simply have to come to the business office and learn all those numbers to make a stab at it), the business manager is the most appropriate person to establish the initial "frame of reference" for addressing that critical question—by updating the financial strategy model.

He does that most effectively by determining the current (annualized) *actual* numbers and ratios, proposing very modest and gradual changes (usually one-, two-, or three-tenths of a percent) in allocations to specific activities within the various functions, and reflecting what he thinks will happen by way of adjustments in the functional goals by which performance is to be measured, and the planning assumptions by which future projects and proposals are to be evaluated. From that process, every publishing house will come forth with its own distinctive version of Figure 34a—or some sensible equivalent.

By creating and constantly refining such a financial strategy model, the business manager does not automatically decide all financial issues for the publishing house. The budgeting process described in Chapter 10 only uses this model as a starting point for actual planning. And even then, the model itself should not be considered "in force" until it has been discussed by the entire core management group (with the acquisition, pre-press and marketing managers getting their shots)—and the publisher has eventually decided what to amend and what to endorse.

The heart of this discussion, in a healthy publishing organization, will revolve around how to split surplus resources (after bare-bones financing of all essential functions) between those three vital contenders—acquisition staffing (the pituitary gland of any publishing house), marketing outreach (its blood stream), and the bank account (operating margin—available [after taxes] for whatever purposes the owners choose). And the very same set of priorities must be argued when *cutting back* a budget (in times of sales decline or cash flow crisis)—to decide (since everything else has presumably already been held to a realistic minimum) which of these once-fatted calves must now be skinned to make up a deficit.

Very clearly, each of the three strategic options has a partisan in the core management group. (The pre-press managing editor, alas, can only react to how much work acquisition strategies push onto his staff ... and how cost-effectively he's already shown the business manager he can get that work done. But since acquisition quota-cuts often make possible pre-press staffing cuts—because fewer new titles require fewer copy editors—he tends to end up as a rather partisan ally of the editor-in-chief in such arguments.)

The editor-in-chief says: "Give me more people and I'll give you more new books." The marketing manager says: "Give me more money, and I'll give you more orders—thus multiplying that money—by effectively telling more people about the books we already have." The business manager says: "That's all highly speculative. The safest thing to do with available money is to put it in the bank (as operating margin, or retained earnings)."

The point is that *this is healthy contention.* When those three voices go at it hammer-and-tong, you've got a grown-up publishing team strong enough to generate synergy. A wise publisher will continue to referee such contention until (hopefully) a consensus begins to take shape. If consensus doesn't emerge, the publisher must eventually earn his pay by making hard choices himself and reminding the other core managers: "That's why I get paid more than you do."

The atmosphere gets even warmer when budget *reductions* are necessary—to adjust to disappointing results. Once again, each of those managers should campaign "whole hog" in defense of her-or-his previous plans and spending levels. The aim of the exercise is to convince the publisher which feasible cuts will hurt end results least.

This leads to one observation unpopular with most business managers. In times of belt-tightening, it has generally been *marketing* budgets that have tended to suffer most—simply because they're laden with external commitments to ad media, mailing programs, catalog printing, exhibit displays, etc., which will jolt external vendors, but cause relatively little disruption of the lives of internal colleagues if abandoned. Unfortunately, such abandonment is very likely to *accelerate* the revenue (sales) decline or failure to achieve targets—which is at the heart of most financial crises. So automatically choosing the "easy" marketing cuts rather than trimming back the operating margin or acquisition staff can be a self-defeating process, adding momentum to a downward spiral.

But it takes a long time to bring replacement acquisition editors "up to speed" once the crisis is over. So the least disruptive place to squeeze the budget in a crisis is usually the "bottom line." When things are rough, there's nothing wrong with taking an occasional vacation from "making money" to protect the integrity and continuity of well-planned acquisition and marketing strategies. Once you start trimming parts off such intricate plans, you can easily cripple their basic logic and render the entire exercise ineffective.

But it's *never the business manager* who should propose to cut margin goals (i.e., agree to lose money temporarily, or make a little less) in such circumstances. A mature core management meeting is like a courtroom; to get the best end result, every appropriate point-of-view must have a strong, partisan advocate. Let the editor-in-chief emote on behalf of future masterpieces; let the marketing manager make the case for avoiding that dangerous downward sales spiral (or "striking while the irons are hot"); let the managing editor campaign for desktop systems and operators that eventually eliminate designers and typesetters. It's the business manager's job to campaign unapologetically for that bottom line!

And this means that as he proposes a basic financial strategy (Figure 34a)—and future refinements of that strategy—he persistently campaigns for more-challenging performance standards that will enhance profitability. In the long run, a strong bottom line satisfies much more than greed. It's no secret that some of America's most profitable mid-sized publishers are *not-for-profit* enterprises, with tough-minded business managers who've convinced their bosses that "the more we make, the more good works we can perform on the morrow."

CHAPTER 35
Creating the Chart of Accounts and Reporting Format

How well a publishing enterprise is performing at any given time (and where management needs to intervene to solve obvious problems) can be expressed not only in terms of the workflow (procedures, schedules, etc.), but in terms of the moneyflow—the economic bloodstream of the corporate entity.

It is a major responsibility of the finance administrator (whether that is the business manager wearing a second hat, or a subordinate controller or accountant) to see that comprehensive feedback on the financial performance of the enterprise is regularly available to the core management group. And *if they are different people,* it is the business manager's responsibility to make certain the reporting format used for such feedback serves the *managerial* needs of the publisher and core management group even before it serves the pure accounting needs of the auditors and tax collectors.

While some organizations have misgivings about dissemination of such financial data beyond the core management group (mostly because they fear good news will encourage employees to seek raises, and bad news will scare vendors), common sense suggests that this feedback should also go to everyone who has responsibility for controlling any line of the budget (expense or revenue)—so they can see how results compare to plans, and how their particular financial concern fits into the overall picture. The cost of paranoid secrecy, in the form of warped planning perspectives, far outweighs the disadvantages of openness. A business manager who makes this point, and assures reasonable financial feedback on a regular basis, has a much better chance of promoting general concern for profitability than one who joins the conspiracy of financial silence that pervades too many publishing houses.

A good financial reporting format will parallel the organizational structure, so that it's easy to relate the responsible people to the numbers. You'll save a lot of redundant work it you use the same format for maintaining accounting data (your general ledger), budgeting, and reporting results. The format illustrated in Figure 35a (a repeat of Figure 10a, shown earlier), on the next page, can easily be modified for publishers whose staffs or marketing channels are structured differently.

Figure 35a—Sample Chart of Accounts and Budgeting Format

	1 SAMPLE CHART OF ACCOUNTS	2 Jul 93	3 Aug 92	4	5 Jun 93	6 Last 12 Mos.	7 Actual %	8 Budg %	9 Budget
2	++++++++++++++								
3	Trade Book Sales	$56,882.84	$51,194.55		$58,521.44	$731,517.96	70.2%	68.3%	$750,000.00
4	Special Market Book Sales	$13,776.95	$12,399.25		$14,173.81	$177,172.65	17.0%	18.2%	$200,000.00
5	Direct Response Book Sales	$14,448.24	$13,003.42		$14,864.45	$185,805.59	17.8%	18.2%	$200,000.00
6	GROSS BOOK SALES	$85,108.02	$76,597.22		$87,559.70	$1,094,496.20	105.0%	104.8%	$1,150,000.00
7	Return Credits	$6,442.31	$5,798.08		$6,627.89	$82,848.67	7.9%	7.7%	$85,000.00
8	NET BOOK SALES	$78,665.71	$70,799.14		$80,931.80	$1,011,647.53	97.0%	97.0%	$1,065,000.00
9	Sub Rights Revenue	$214.22	$192.80		$220.39	$2,754.87	0.3%	0.3%	$3,500.00
10	Shipping Reimbursements	$2,101.01	$1,890.91		$2,161.54	$27,019.20	2.6%	2.6%	$28,000.00
11	Other Revenue	$75.96	$68.36		$78.14	$976.80	0.1%	0.1%	·$1,221.61
12	TOTAL NET REVENUE	$81,056.90	$72,951.21		$83,391.87	$1,042,398.40	100.0%	100.0%	$1,097,721.61
13									
14	MANAGEMENT COMPENSATION	$5,697.12	$5,127.41		$5,861.24	$73,265.47	7.0%	6.7%	$73,619.46
15	Mgmt Professional Fees	$0.00	$0.00		$0.00	$0.00	0.0%	0.0%	$0.00
16	Mgmt Travel/Entertainment	$165.19	$148.67		$169.94	$2,124.30	0.2%	0.2%	$2,356.69
17	Board Honoraria	$155.52	$139.97		$160.00	$2,000.00	0.2%	0.2%	$2,000.00
18	Board Expenses	$34.04	$30.64		$35.02	$437.81	0.0%	0.0%	$500.00
19	Interest	$18.01	$16.21		$18.53	$231.62	0.0%	0.0%	$300.00
20	Misc Mgmt Expenses	$53.04	$47.73		$54.57	$682.08	0.1%	0.1%	$1,000.00
21	TOTAL MGMT EXPENSE	$6,122.92	$5,510.63		$6,299.30	$78,741.28	7.6%	7.3%	$79,776.15
22									
23	ACQUISITION COMPENSATION	$4,057.39	$3,651.65		$4,174.27	$52,178.36	5.0%	4.8%	$52,520.78
24	ROYALTY ADVANCE C/G/S	$1,822.49	$1,640.24		$1,874.99	$23,437.40	2.2%	2.2%	$24,450.00
25	Roy Liability Accrued	$6,166.43	$5,549.79		$6,344.06	$79,300.80	7.6%	8.0%	$87,486.63
26	Honoraria/Prof Fees	$27.22	$24.49		$28.00	$350.00	0.0%	0.0%	$500.00
27	Acqui Travel & Entrnt	$54.10	$40.70		$55.71	$696.80	0.1%	0.1%	$750.00
28	Misc Acqui Expenses	$151.87	$136.69		$156.25	$1,953.10	0.2%	0.2%	$2,200.00
29	TOTAL ACQUI EXPENSES	$12,279.58	$11,051.63		$12,633.32	$157,916.46	15.1%	15.3%	$167,907.41
30									
31	PRE-PRESS COMPENSATION	$4,006.88	$3,606.20		$4,122.31	$51,528.87	4.9%	4.7%	$52,077.20
32	COPYEDITING C/G/S	$3,084.27	$2,775.84		$3,173.12	$39,663.95	3.8%	3.7%	$40,750.00
33	PAGE-PREP C/G/S	$1,033.64	$930.28		$1,063.42	$13,292.74	1.3%	1.5%	$16,300.00
34	Pre-Press T&E	$0.00	$0.00		$0.00	$0.00	0.0%	0.0%	$200.00
35	Misc Pre-Press Expenses	$60.57	$54.51		$62.31	$778.90	0.1%	0.1%	$800.00
36	TOTAL PRE-PRESS EXPENSE	$8,185.36	$7,366.83		$8,421.16	$105,264.46	10.1%	10.0%	$110,127.20
37									
38	MARKETING COMPENSATION	$4,919.63	$4,427.67		$5,061.35	$63,266.85	6.1%	5.8%	$63,727.27
39	Publicity	$806.49	$725.84		$829.72	$10,371.50	1.0%	1.0%	$10,717.71
40	Trade Selling	$4,142.37	$3,728.13		$4,261.70	$53,271.20	5.1%	5.1%	$55,609.66
41	Co-op Ad Credits	$317.26	$285.53		$326.40	$4,080.00	0.4%	0.4%	$4,102.53
42	PROMO C/G/S	$1,321.51	$1,189.35		$1,359.57	$16,994.67	1.6%	1.5%	$16,300.00
43	Special Market Selling	$1,088.89	$980.00		$1,120.26	$14,003.23	1.3%	1.3%	$14,402.48
44	Direct Response Selling	$297.28	$267.55		$305.84	$3,823.00	0.4%	0.4%	$4,381.12
45	Marketing T&E	$3,478.58	$3,130.72		$3,578.78	$44,734.81	4.3%	4.1%	$45,000.00
46	Misc Marketing Expense	$265.22	$238.69		$272.86	$3,410.70	0.3%	0.3%	$3,500.00
47	TOTAL MARKETING EXPENSE	$16,637.22	$14,973.49		$17,116.48	$213,955.96	20.5%	19.8%	$217,740.77
48									
49	BUS/OPS COMPENSATION	$4,446.46	$4,001.81		$4,574.55	$57,181.82	5.5%	5.3%	$57,790.31
50	Fulfillment Supplies	$374.45	$337.01		$385.24	$4,815.50	0.5%	0.5%	$5,200.00
51	Mfg. Freight In	$628.90	$566.01		$647.02	$8,087.70	0.8%	0.8%	$8,314.65
52	Prepaid Pstg/Trans Out	$1,643.92	$1,479.53		$1,691.28	$21,141.00	2.0%	2.1%	$23,438.38
53	External Storage/Handling	$782.82	$704.54		$805.37	$10,067.14	1.0%	1.0%	$10,590.18
54	Misc Fulf Expenses	$19.44	$17.50		$20.00	$250.00	0.0%	0.0%	$300.00
55	Pin Adm Prof Fees	$0.00	$0.00		$0.00	$0.00	0.0%	0.0%	$0.00
56	MFG (PPB) C/G/S	$14,510.82	$13,059.74		$14,928.82	$186,610.30	17.9%	16.7%	$183,000.00

Figure 35a—Sample Chart of Accounts and Budgeting Format (cont.)

	1	2	3	4	5	6	7	8	9
1	SAMPLE CHART OF ACCOUNTS	Jul 93	Aug 92		Jun 93	Last 12 Mos.	Actual %	Budg %	Budget
2	**************								
57	INVENTORY WRITEOFF C/G/S	$1,227.40	$1,104.66		$1,262.76	$15,784.44	1.5%	1.5%	$16,300.00
58	Bad Debt Write-Offs	$91.36	$82.22		$93.99	$1,174.90	0.1%	0.1%	$1,200.00
59	Misc Fin Adm Expenses	$124.05	$111.65		$127.62	$1,595.30	0.2%	0.1%	$1,500.00
60	Rent and Utilities	$2,177.51	$1,959.76		$2,240.24	$28,002.98	2.7%	2.7%	$30,021.11
61	Equipment Lease/Maint	$2,213.92	$1,992.53		$2,277.70	$28,471.19	2.7%	2.9%	$31,643.62
62	DEPRECIATION	$98.71	$88.84		$101.55	$1,269.43	0.1%	0.1%	$1,300.00
63	Office Supplies	$1,122.67	$1,010.40		$1,155.01	$14,437.62	1.4%	1.3%	$14,000.00
64	Routine Postage	$286.79	$258.11		$295.05	$3,688.10	0.4%	0.4%	$4,112.41
65	Phone/Wire/Courier	$1,167.47	$1,050.72		$1,201.10	$15,013.77	1.4%	1.4%	$15,000.00
66	Ref/Libr Materials	$57.40	$51.66		$59.05	$738.17	0.1%	0.1%	$823.17
67	Misc Facility Exp	$165.84	$149.25		$170.62	$2,132.69	0.2%	0.2%	$2,400.00
68	TOTAL BUS/OPS EXPENSE	$31,139.93	$28,025.94		$32,036.96	$400,462.05	38.4%	37.1%	$406,933.83
69									
70	TOTAL GROSS REVENUE	$87,499.21	$78,749.29		$90,019.77	$1,125,247.07	107.9%	107.7%	$1,182,721.61
71	RETURNS/REFUNDS	$6,442.31	$5,798.08		$6,627.89	$82,848.67	7.9%	7.7%	$85,000.00
72	TOTAL NET REVENUE	$81,056.90	$72,951.21		$83,391.87	$1,042,398.40	100.0%	100.0%	$1,097,721.61
73	TOTAL COST OF GOODS	$23,000.12	$20,700.11		$23,662.68	$295,783.50	28.4%	27.1%	$297,100.00
74	TOTAL OPERATING REVENUE	$58,056.77	$52,251.10		$59,729.19	$746,614.90	71.6%	72.9%	$800,621.61
75	TOTAL OPERATING EXPENSES	$51,364.89	$46,228.40		$52,844.54	$660,556.71	63.4%	62.4%	$685,385.36
76	TOTAL OPERATING MARGIN	$6,691.88	$6,022.70		$6,884.66	$86,058.19	8.3%	10.5%	$115,236.25
77									
78	REFERENCE ACCOUNTS*****								
79									
80	Mfg C/G/S to Bus/Ops	$14,510.82	$13,059.74		$14,928.82	$186,610.30	17.9%	16.7%	$183,000.00
81	Inv WriteOffs Exp'd to Fin	$1,227.40	$1,104.66		$1,262.76	$15,784.44	1.5%	1.5%	$16,300.00
82	Roy Adv C/G/S to Acqui	$1,822.49	$1,640.24		$1,874.99	$23,437.40	2.2%	2.2%	$24,450.00
83	Copy-Ed C/G/S to Pr-Pr	$3,084.27	$2,775.84		$3,173.12	$39,663.95	3.8%	3.7%	$40,750.00
84	Page-Prep C/G/S to Pr-Pr	$1,033.64	$930.28		$1,063.42	$13,292.74	1.3%	1.5%	$16,300.00
85	Promo PPB C/G/S to Marktg	$1,321.51	$1,189.35		$1,359.57	$16,994.67	1.6%	1.5%	$16,300.00
86	COST OF GOODS SOLD	$23,000.12	$20,700.11		$23,662.68	$295,783.50	28.4%	27.1%	$297,100.00
87									
88	Royalty Advances	$1,788.48	$1,609.63		$1,840.00	$23,000.00	2.2%	2.3%	$25,000.00
89	Copy-Editing Investment	$3,031.33	$2,728.20		$3,118.66	$38,983.20	3.7%	4.0%	$43,753.21
90	Pre-Page Investment	$2,715.18	$2,443.66		$2,793.39	$34,917.40	3.3%	3.4%	$37,668.43
91	New Title P/P/B Investment	$8,394.67	$7,555.20		$8,636.49	$107,956.12	10.4%	10.8%	$118,113.92
92	Reprinting P/P/B Investment	$4,194.50	$3,775.05		$4,315.33	$53,941.60	5.2%	5.0%	$54,886.08
93	TOTAL INVENTORY INVESTMENT	$20,124.16	$18,111.74		$20,703.87	$258,798.32	24.8%	25.5%	$279,421.64
94	RECOVERED C/G/S	$23,000.12	$20,700.11		$23,662.68	$295,783.50	28.4%	27.1%	$297,100.00
95	NET INVENTORY INVESTMENT	($2,875.97)	($2,588.37)		($2,958.81)	($36,985.18)	-3.5%	-1.6%	($17,678.36)
96									
97	Capital Equipment Investment	$0.00	$1,000.00		$0.00	$1,432.00	0.1%	0.1%	$1,097.72
98	Depreciation Expensed to #62	$0.00	$0.00		$0.00	$1,269.43	0.1%	0.1%	$1,300.00
99	NET EQUIPMENT INVESTMENT	$0.00	$1,000.00		$0.00	$162.57	0.0%	0.1%	($202.28)
100									
101	Non-Capitalized Salaries	$16,853.21	$15,167.89		$17,338.69	$216,733.62	20.8%	19.9%	$217,922.82
102	Contract Labor	$141.52	$127.37		$145.60	$1,820.00	0.2%	0.2%	$2,000.00
103	Company FICA Contrib	$1,119.91	$1,007.92		$1,152.17	$14,402.08	1.4%	1.3%	$14,535.00
104	Other Payroll Taxes	$538.75	$484.88		$554.27	$6,928.40	0.7%	0.6%	$7,000.00
105	Employee Benefits	$48.99	$44.09		$50.40	$630.00	0.1%	0.1%	$700.00
106	Payroll Insurance	$319.16	$287.24		$328.35	$4,104.40	0.4%	0.4%	$4,200.00
107	Personnel Miscellaneous	$99.07	$89.16		$101.92	$1,274.00	0.1%	0.1%	$1,300.00
108	TOTAL NON-CAPL COMPENSATION	$19,120.60	$17,208.54		$19,671.40	$245,892.50	23.6%	22.6%	$247,657.82

This model represented in Figure 35a draws its data from a computer "transaction file" database (replacing the conventional "general ledger") in which all sales and/or expense transactions are entered as they occur (see Chapter 36). End-of-the-month subtotals for each line item can then be provided quickly by the computer, and key-stroked into the appropriate monthly column on the spreadsheet. In the space indicated by the jagged line, there is a column for *each* of the 12 months; when a month comes around again the following year, you just replace the old numbers (and the year-designation at the top) with the new. In that "Last 12 Months" column, then, the computer (using any good, basic spreadsheet program) constantly retotals the previous 12 (monthly) columns, giving you a new *annual* total at the end of every month. This eliminates seasonal distortion by allowing you always to look at the *most recent full year.*

The lines in capital letters are automatically calculated by the computer, from a reference account and/or a spreadsheet formula. The other lines are entered monthly (from the database sub-totals) by the finance function.

Note the four "reference accounts" at the bottom of the chart. These enable the finance function to keep up with certain categories of cost that it will need to treat specially (for a variety of reasons), and then have the computer automatically distribute the results to the right portions of the organization-paralleling operating statement above. Distribution of various segments of cost-of-goods (inventory depletion) charges to appropriate departments is suggested by the abbreviations in lines 80-85. Capitalized prepublication investments in the inventory are tracked and budgeted in lines 88-92, to enable management to assess the cash flow impact of different levels of new title generation. (Note that the amount of inventory investment *recovered* through cost-of-goods charges is subtracted from the total to determine the actual net inventory capital needed.) While major equipment purchases (as opposed to leasing) usually must be capitalized over several years, this year-by-year expensing via "depreciation" (line 98) should be charged to facilities costs (line 62) to reflect gradual depletion of such capital investments. Payroll and related compensation costs (lines 101-107) should be consolidated in one reference account to simplify all of those payroll tax returns you must file—but can then be distributed among the work-sections by percentages (periodically recalculated by the core managers) or on an actual person-by-person basis, to give managers a better picture of the *true total cost* of each function—and the trade-offs between internal staffing, free-lancers, labor-saving equipment, etc.

In column 6, then, the spreadsheet has translated the last-12-month totals into percentages of annual net receipts. Column 8 contains the current annual budget as established by the core managers (and perhaps endorsed by the Board of Directors). Column 7 translates the budget to percentages of net receipts, for easy comparison with actual result percentages in the previous column.

The budget may represent a given calendar or fiscal year, or may be a quarterly-updated plan for the forthcoming (at any time) 12 months. The same spreadsheet can easily be extended to project (by applying trend formulas) over a number of years—perhaps even providing a continuous estimate of the fair market value of the enterprise (as per Chapter 4).

By establishing a basic financial format that reflects the organization and workflow, the business manager and/or finance administrator build staff identity with (and responsibility for) appropriate aspects of the financial operation of the publishing house. But the basic "chart of accounts" (the numbered line-captions that tell you what each entry represents) can extend beyond the "operating feedback" format you see in Figure 35a. You may want other reference accounts lower on the spreadsheet (which will virtually never be printed out for general distribution) to track everything from the status of your bank line-of-credit to back pay due an owner/operator, or pension credits, or a line-by-line "balance sheet."

How, then, do you decide what specific line items should be identified in your "chart of accounts?" First, establish the major sections in which information can be most usefully summarized for the core managers. Essentially, this dictates at least one income section ("profit center") for book sales, plus an expense section ("cost center") for each major function or department—including the publisher's office (lines 14-21 of Figure 35a).

The marketing manager should be consulted as to whether revenue should be broken into several "profit centers." Many like to distinguish between frontlist and backlist book sales, subsidiary rights, and such non-marketing revenue as shipping charges, sales tax collections, interest on cash reserves, etc. Some even want separate "profit sub-centers" for each major category of book customer (see lines 3-5 of the sample in Figure 35a) and/or subsidiary rights buyer. The marketing function will probably find it useful to accompany *each* book-purchase category reflected under income with a negative adjustment for returns—to help it identify the causes of excessive returns—rather than simply lumping them into one adjustment as in Figure 35a.

Some business managers prefer that the distinct segments of the business/operations function (inventory maintenance/shipping, financial administration, facilities administration) be subtotaled to help them evaluate the separate supervisors of these activities (even when it means splitting the business manager's own salary between the three).

Each function (or operations sub-function) manager or administrator (including the publisher herself) should then be interviewed as to the planning categories ("line items") for which they'd find financial feedback most useful. But the business manager and publisher must make hardnosed decisions about who automatically assumes responsibility for some automatic "negative charges" that nobody may wish to own. Thus, you'll see, Figure 35a charges not only the expenses of the Board of Directors, but interest costs—which represent a decision by that Board to borrow money rather than raise more capital—to the publisher's office ... because the publisher (COO) is ownership's "representative" on the operating team; none of the other functions are really in a position to influence such costs. And you'll see that Figure 35a charges business/operations (finance) for both obsolete inventory write-offs (line 81, distributed to line 57—because it had control of original print quantities) and bad debt write-offs (line 58—because it's responsible for "credit and collections").

The design of the reference accounts should be left pretty much to the financial administrator; the main object here is to consolidate numbers that must eventually be collected for tax returns, periodic income statements (lines 70-76 of Figure 35a), balance sheets, audits, etc. But it is very important that all such reference account results then be distributed among the appropriate cost centers *in a logical manner*—to reflect true, comparative trends and ratios in the total, month-to-month operation of the enterprise.

No one will appreciate the complications that arise when significant changes are made in the chart of accounts more than the finance administrator. Nevertheless, it is vital that the chart *be flexible* enough to change when the organizational structure changes (new departments require new sub-categories), or when the work procedures or tactics adopted within a department shift so much that function costs can no longer be clearly tracked by the people doing (and planning) the work.

Therefore, it behooves the finance officer—at any point at which the chart is being significantly revised—to make a major project of interviewing key people, offering to chair departmental brainstorming sessions, etc., so that the adjustments will be thorough, and will not have to be repeated too often.

Whenever changes are made in the chart of accounts (the house's basic scorecard), the finance officer should also execute two follow-up steps: (1) Immediately print out a new list of the categories, with identifying line numbers (usually adapted straight from the computer spreadsheet program), so that all concerned can adjust the codes they use to approve bills, calculate performance indices, etc. (2) Go back to the last 2 or 3 years' annual summaries of results and adjust the numbers (by combining lines that have since coalesced, and estimating the division of those for functions that have since been split) so others will still be able to make meaningful comparisons with past norms.

CHAPTER 36
Basic Financial Administration and Routine Feedback

Whether on a full-time basis, or as a second-hat responsibility of the business manager, the primary task of the financial administrator is to organize such staff as will be required to handle the intake, distribution, and recording of the publisher's money and such other tangible assets as inventory—and to establish effective procedures for doing that work. Of course, if the publishing house is small enough, the financial administrator may be expected to do all of this alone. If a single additional employee is justified, this should probably be a clerical assistant competent in elementary bookkeeping and database key-punching (for routine computer input).

When the finance office grows to three people, the financial administrator might consider dividing basic tasks between one assistant who specializes in accounts receivable and credits-and-collection (taking money in), and another who focuses on accounts payable (including royalties, commissions, payroll, and taxes ... disbursing money out)—with both contributing to the upkeep of the general ledger (transaction database). Any fourth employee might function as a general assistant to both—but by this point you should begin getting critical about staffing levels; three or four people with a small computer can usually handle a publishing cash flow of several million dollars a year effectively.

Most of the analytical responsibilities of the finance office should continue to reside with the business manager, or a financial controller with sufficient accounting credentials to have been designated the chief financial officer. This chief financial officer should also maintain a systematic checklist of all the routines involved in meeting the function's responsibilities, and review that checklist with the administrative supervisor or staff periodically.

The financial administrator should be responsible for scheduling and obtaining such audits as are required by law, or by the corporate directors or owners, to provide independent verification that the assets of the publishing house (inventory and other property, as well as money) have been handled and reported honestly and accurately. This is usually accomplished (provided the owners feel the cost is justified) by retaining a non-affiliated firm of certified public accountants for annual examination and certification of the balance sheet, the inventory reports, and additional appropriate records.

It is not our intention to attempt a full course in financial accounting in these few pages. Suffice to say that the work of the finance function (and thus, the responsibilities of the finance administrator) consists essentially of seven tasks: (1) recording financial transactions for later summary, verification, and analysis; (2) monitoring and collecting the "receivables" (money others owe you); (3) monitoring and administering settlement of the "payables" (what you owe others); (4) verifying corporate assets and liabilities; (5) providing useful management feedback; (6) monitoring and adjusting cash flow; and (7) preparing/filing tax returns.

Let's look first at the fundamental task of recording financial data. There are generic accounting packages available in computer stores, and directly from software publishers, that provide a framework into which you can enter basic data from/about every transaction (whether a sale or a purchase) and end up with monthly and annual summaries. Some of the more elaborate order processing programs will also handle this accounting for you (at least with respect to income). But the fact is that, for most small publishing houses, such programs aren't really necessary. And, too often, they lock you into somebody else's logic—and are keyed more to answering government's (generic, tax) questions than serving management's (unique strategy feedback) needs.

It is fairly simple to preserve the data you'll need for financial administration, feedback, and tax returns in a basic file generated by any good database software—by utilizing a self-made form such as that illustrated by Figure 36a below. If you have an accounting package that *is flexible enough* to serve as a general database, and will also write your checks for you—it may be worth the cost. But except for that check-writing, it won't give you much you can't get from any straight-forward database program using this "transaction file" form. The transaction file, then, becomes your general ledger.

Figure 36a—Sample Transaction File Data-Form

```
                            Transaction File
LINE:_____    ACCRUAL DATE:_____    CASH DATE :_____   AMOUNT $:_____
PARTY:_____  BOOK:_____   TALLY1:____   TALLY2:_____
NOTES:_____
```

Use the line numbers from your chart of accounts in the first space to define the nature of each transaction (whether a debit or a credit). When an expense is divided between more than one function, complete a separate form for each function's portion.

Enter the date on which the transaction (financial obligation) occurred as the "accrual date" (for accrual accounting). Use a six-digit dating number (first two digits for year, next two for month, last two for day—940115 for 15 January 1994), so the computer will be able to rearrange data in chronological sequence for periodic reports. Until each entry is settled (paid or collected), put arbitrary alphabetical symbols (such as "x" for receivables, "y" short-term for payables, "z" for long-term obligations) in the "cash date" blank to help the computer assemble lists of aged payables or receivables or long-term indebtedness as you need them. As each item is settled (because you collect receivables, pay bills, or retire long-term debt), substitute enter a six-digit dating number to indicate when that happened. Thus the computer will be able to use this simple database to produce either accrual-basis or cash-basis summaries whenever you need them.

Obviously, you enter the dollar-amount involved in the fourth blank, and identify the party with whom you transacted in the next.

If the transaction involved inventory investment (a typesetting, color separation, printing, etc.) which is later to be "capitalized," enter a code for the specific product in the "book" blank; then the computer will be able to recapitulate all such front-money expenditures (even capitalized payroll charges) to determine unit cost-of-goods charge-backs for entry into your order processing program when the finished goods are actually added to the inventory.

The "Tally1" and "Tally2" blanks are there for whatever special analyses the financial administrator may wish to make from time-to-time. (For example, you might want to track charges for using freelancers in various departments over a given period of time—for comparison with the projected cost of hiring additional staff to do such work.) And "Notes" is simply a general-purpose opportunity to record explanations about items anyone suspects might be questioned later.

Recording transactions through such a database will be greatly simplified if you do *not* attempt to enter routine book sales item-by-item, but simply use your order processing program (usually from a separate, dedicated computer system—as described in Chapter 40) to transfer end-of-month summaries directly to the financial score sheet illustrated by Figure 35a. Since any good order entry software will also report aged receivables at any time, the only receivables you need track through this transaction database are such non-routine items as subsidiary rights income—which do not go through the normal order processing procedure.

Payroll, and such routine non-billed expenses as the rent, royalties, sales commissions, and payment of withheld payroll taxes, should be outlined on a reference checklist and automatically entered as obligations on each appropriate weekly, monthly, quarterly or annual date. If (as in the case of payroll) an entry is settled on the same date it's entered, the "accrual" and "cash" dates will be the same. When you *prepay* expenses (such as paying next month's rent a few days before the end of this month), you may actually enter occasional "cash" dates that are *earlier* than the transaction dates.

Once a publishing house is established, it is assumed that the finance function must *collect* money owed it in order to have the resources to *pay out* what it owes others (including payroll). So once transactions are recorded (on either your order processing program, or a transaction database such as illustrated by Figure 36a), the finance administrator's second major responsibility is disciplining the flow of money *into* the operation, through collection of sales revenues. And since such collections are obviously dependent upon the credit-worthiness of the people to whom you sell your books, extending credit is normally seen as part-and-parcel of this collections responsibility.

The first step, then, in establishing sound procedures for controlling credit and collections is to clarify your ground rules as to who can buy your books on credit. These are the "open accounts" that most publishing houses establish with trustworthy bookstores and wholesalers, libraries and schools, and other credible organizations or individuals.

Most publishers do not extend open credit to individuals who would likely buy only one book at a time, regardless of their financial trustworthiness, simply because the cost of accounting and billing often exceeds any potential profit on such sales. For customer convenience (and impulse purchase encouragement) of such individuals, many small publishers have made arrangements to honor one or more of the commonly used consumer credit cards, as a substitute for credit. (MasterCard and Visa are by far the most popular cards with such publishers; both are accepted by over 70 percent of all book publishers. Arrangements for both of these card programs are handled by participating local banks, which can be identified by a few telephone inquiries.)

However, quite a few publishers selling directly to responsible professionals or even selling low-priced books directly to general consumers—have found that the 2-4 percent most banks charge on credit card transactions is higher than both their normal bad-debt losses (which averaged only 1 percent of independent publishers' sales in 1991) and the interest-value of waiting a month to collect. Those whose order processing systems can easily enclose automatic invoices in the jiffy bags with their books sometimes decide that extending consumer credit is a workable alternative to lost sales.

The major credit risks small publishers encounter are bookstores. Some publishers go overboard in refusing to open a credit account for any new bookstore customer until they've checked references. A more sensible, realistic policy is to authorize order entry personnel to open new accounts automatically when first-time orders arrive from bookstores, or other business or institutional buyers, who use a printed letterhead or purchase form, or appear in any of the basic industry directories you might consult (such as Bowker's *American Book Trade Directory*; see Appendix 2)—as long as those orders don't exceed some modest level (frequently $100) which you're willing to risk. Set the same top-limit amount as the maximum accumulative credit authorized, so that subsequent orders (before the first is paid) won't increase your risk beyond the acceptable level. Should an account later seek to exceed this limit, consult the payment record it has then established; if the account has paid its bills regularly, an automatic extension is probably justifiable. This means that a major portion of your open credit accounts can be established and adjusted without incurring either significant risk or the administrative work of checking credit.

When you receive an order in an amount larger than a customer's automatic or accumulated credit limit (or from a customer whose credibility you suspect for any other reason), you should promptly contact the customer and ask for at least three credit references, plus identification of his/her bank. You should then ask those references to verify the amount of credit they normally extend to that account, and how long it normally takes the account to pay; you should ask the bank reference to tell you how long the customer has had an account with the bank, and what that customer's average deposit balance is (in round numbers, such as how-many-digits). You can use form letters for these queries, but most publishers make all of these inquiries by telephone to speed the process—since it usually only applies to large orders, and only has to be done once to establish what is hopefully a long-term account.

Customers might be informed, while you're asking for references, that they can avoid delay on the current order by paying in advance. It is customary in such cases to send a *pro forma invoice* (a bill for advance payment) with your explanation, promising prompt shipment of the order *as soon as their payment arrives.* This can even be phone/faxed if the new buyer is in a hurry.)

Financial administrators often find that knowing their counterparts in several other publishing houses enables them to compare notes on a new customer's payment habits (especially a bookstore) much more quickly, and more reliably, than by checking the references the customer provides.

If you discover that a customer has a record of not paying bills, or taking an inordinately long time to do so, it is the duty of the financial administrator to decline to open the account. This means informing the marketing department, and then (unless marketing wishes to handle it) also informing the customer—meanwhile providing a pro forma invoice so he/she can still get the books by paying in advance. This is a point at which financial administrators owe it to the integrity of the process to dig in their heels, and resist being soft-soaped into extending credit to avoid offending people, if they have reason to suspect the customer's credibility. And the publisher must stand behind them, if your business is to limit its risks and operate in a financially responsible manner.

Once you've decided to issue credit, the basic data on the customer (including the determined credit limit—the maximum amount for which you're presently willing to trust that customer), should be entered into your order processing customer-file so that these questions need not be redundantly answered with each subsequent order—as long as the buyer maintains an acceptable payment record. If he *doesn't*—the account should remain on your customer file, clearly flagged as a credit risk, so the computer will *stop* any future shipments to that account except on a pro forma basis.

It is customary to send invoices (bills) for each customer-order you fulfill, at the time the books are shipped. These can be mailed separately from the book shipment, or attached to the book carton, or enclosed within that carton (and the post office no longer requires separate first-class postage for such routine invoice enclosures). However, many book dealers do not pay on the basis of such invoices, but wait until the publisher has recapitulated what is owed in an end-of-the-month statement. So if you do a substantial amount of credit business, you should make sure your customers get both invoices and monthly statements.

Use some form of aged receivables checklist (which can be easily compiled by most order processing systems, or a transaction database such as Figure 36a) to identify those accounts who do not pay within 30 days of the statement, so you can apply additional collection pressure—perhaps initially by just stamping "Past Due" on the next monthly statement. Send a letter with the monthly statement to every customer with unpaid items more than 60 days old, pointing out that you'll have to not only suspend further shipments but possibly deny future credit if the account is not paid promptly. Telephone all accounts with unpaid items which have appeared on three statements (and are thus more than 90 days old), reminding them of the letter they received and ignored the previous month—and asking for a specific commitment as to when you can expect payment; press for at least a modest partial-payment very soon. This is probably also the right time to announce that you can ship no more books until payment is received—though some publishers do this even earlier (after 60 days).

At the point at which future shipments are suspended, be sure your order processing customer-file is updated to record it, so the now-risky account will not become even more of a risk through lack of interdepartmental communication. If invoices remain unpaid more than 120 days, you should phone again and warn that you will not only cancel future credit, but will report the delinquency to other publishers with whom you exchange credit information. If you've found a collection agency whose fees and performance are acceptable, 30 days after this last warning (i.e., 150 days after the oldest invoice date), it's probably time to hand the matter over to them. And by 365 days, you should be writing off this hypothetical asset, and charging the bad debt loss to the finance function accordingly (as per line 58 of Figure 35a) to offset the earlier revenue credited to the original sale.

Don't be bashful about applying such reasonable collection pressures as strenuously to your large trade accounts as to small ones; the larger they are, the less risk you should take with them. Most large book dealers have attempted from time to time to stretch their inventory budgets by slow payments, and are therefore used to being dealt with firmly by prudent publishers; you'll win more respect than you'll lose sales, by showing them you can't be victimized this way.

Publishers have generally found that hard cases, which don't pay up even after you've stopped shipments and made repeated calls, can't be scared by threats of legal action. Sadly, in most cases, forceful collection will cost you more than you're owed. Your best protection is establishing *and following* systematic and disciplined procedures for extending credit, billing, sending statements, and applying early collection pressure *before* an account gets in too deeply.

The third major responsibility of the finance administrator, monitoring and administering settlement of the "payables" (what you owe others) is greatly assisted by using some database such as in Figure 36a to produce an easy aged-payables list every week. Then it's simply a matter of determining how much cash is left after non-discretionary items (such as the payroll, the withheld taxes, and the bank loan) are settled, determining which (if any) are sensitive enough to be paid out-of-order, and using your remaining cash to issue checks as far down the date-list as possible.

Finance administrators usually find it feasible, once each incoming bill has been entered into the database, to hold the actual paper documentation in a simple file-folder for use in executing the settlement. This folder, then, becomes a double-checking duplicate of the aged payables report obtained regularly from the transaction database.

Perhaps the most complex aspect of administering accounts-payable is the payroll. To keep the staff working, someone in the finance office must regularly initiate periodic paychecks (usually weekly, but sometimes biweekly, semi-monthly, or monthly—especially for higher pay grades). To make this an easy task, develop a *payroll spreadsheet* for your PC, on which you enter (by date each payday) a line for each individual that properly divides their gross pay into various withholding categories, plus the net take-home amount. As you write paychecks from this reference each subsequent payday, simply computer-copy each individual's previous entry, changing the date, unless you've been notified of a change (usually a raise). Such a payroll spreadsheet will look something like Figure 36b, on the next page.

At the end of each month, quarter, and year, then—just use the math capabilities of your spreadsheet program to add up individual and over-all totals for any period (as with the monthly recapitulation illustrated at the bottom of Figure 36b) to calculate withholding tax payments, W-2 forms, etc. Meanwhile, require that all managers or supervisors authorized to hire, fire, or promote provide the finance function with *written* memoranda regarding any additions, deletions, or changes to the most recent payroll entries.

The finance administrator should create two special forms for proper accounting of reimbursements for business-related expenditures by your employees. One is a *petty cash voucher* for recording each use of any modest cash reserve you keep in the office for nominal on-the-spot payments. Require the responsible party to initial each entry and attach any receipts. Limit use of

Figure 36b—Sample Payroll Withholdings Spreadsheet

NAME	DATE	GROSS	FICA	MEDICARE	WSTAX	STATE TAX	MED INS	WITHHELD	PAID	NOTES
CMA	920319	$749.64	$46.48	$10.87	$94.00	$38.00	$40.56	$229.91	$519.73	
PPG	920319	$566.00	$35.09	$8.21	$103.00	$32.90	$40.56	$219.76	$346.24	
RFA	920319	$449.79	$27.89	$6.52	$50.00	$25.38	$0.00	$109.79	$340.00	
JJG	920319	$125.63	$7.79	$1.82	$9.00	$0.00	$0.00	$18.61	$107.02	
MEH	920319	$393.57	$24.40	$5.71	$49.00	$22.22	$40.56	$141.89	$251.68	
SSB	920319	$763.78	$47.35	$11.07	$115.00	$45.41	$40.56	$259.40	$504.38	
MEH	920319	$393.57	$24.40	$5.71	$49.00	$22.22	$40.56	$141.89	$251.68	
JJG	920319	$125.63	$7.79	$1.82	$9.00	$0.00	$0.00	$18.61	$107.02	
RFA	920319	$468.29	$29.03	$6.79	$52.00	$26.77	$0.00	$114.59	$353.70	Review/Raise
PPG	920319	$566.00	$35.09	$8.21	$103.00	$32.90	$40.56	$219.76	$346.24	
CMA	920319	$749.64	$46.48	$10.87	$94.00	$38.00	$40.56	$229.91	$519.73	
SSB	920319	$763.78	$47.35	$11.07	$115.00	$45.41	$40.56	$259.40	$504.38	
MEH	920319	$393.57	$24.40	$5.71	$49.00	$22.22	$40.56	$141.89	$251.68	
JJG	920319	$125.63	$7.79	$1.82	$9.00	$0.00	$0.00	$18.61	$107.02	
SSB	920319	$753.78	$47.35	$11.07	$115.00	$45.41	$40.56	$259.40	$504.38	
MONTH	March	$12230.64	$758.30	$177.34	$684.00	$658.42	$648.96	$3927.02	$8303.62	
March	CMA	$2998.56	$185.91	$43.48	$376.00	$152.00	$162.24	$919.63	$2078.93	
March	PPG	$2264.00	$140.37	$32.83	$412.00	$131.60	$162.24	$879.04	$1384.96	
March	RFA	$1836.16	$113.84	$26.62	$204.00	$104.30	$0.00	$448.77	$1387.39	
March	JJG	$502.52	$31.16	$7.29	$36.00	$0.00	$0.00	$74.44	$428.08	
March	MEH	$1574.23	$97.61	$22.83	$196.00	$88.88	$162.24	$567.55	$1006.73	
March	SSB	$3055.12	$189.42	$44.30	$460.00	$181.64	$162.24	$1037.60	$2017.52	
CHECK	March	$12230.64	$758.30	$177.34	$684.00	$658.42	$648.96	$3927.02	$8303.62	

this fund to items costing less than $20-or-so, and only keep a modest amount of cash (say $50) on hand at any time. When the accumulative entries on the *petty cash voucher* add up to a major portion of that amount, replenish the fund by putting the voucher through the bill-paying process, issuing a cash check for the amount accounted for by the voucher, and having someone cash it for the "cookie jar."

The other form you will need is a *reimbursable expense voucher* on which authorized employees can record travel, entertainment, and other appropriate business-related expenses for later reimbursement. Ask your local IRS field office for guidelines as to what items can be reimbursed without income tax liability, and ask management for clear rules as to what is allowed, and what isn't. Require employees to attach receipts for all items over $25, since IRS may eventually require the same of you; credit card carbons will provide this documentation in most cases. As each *reimbursable expense voucher* is submitted (with any required supervisory approval), just enter it into the payable file with appropriate notations to insure prompt payment.

Your accounting system should also make provision for certain adjustments that don't involve money changing hands. The most obvious of these is an *internal cost transfer* from one department to another, a routine form for shifting appropriate costs—and even revenue—to reflect work one function does for another. Other examples include the "expensing" of depreciation of capitalized equipment, and the write-off of discarded or lost inventory—by subtracting those values from the balance sheet, and charging them to the appropriate functions (in these cases, facilities and finance). Such transfers are important if your financial records are to reflect the true costs of each department/function. But make the people involved initial routine, written transfer memos to avoid future arguments.

All such internal transactions should be "run through" the transaction database system (Figure 36a) as though they involved external vendors—so the resulting financial records will accurately reflect the operation of each department or function.

The fourth routine financial administration role, verifying corporate assets and liabilities, is largely a matter of updating and confirming the balance sheet, your on-going accounting to the owners of the status of their investment. The federal corporate income tax form dictates a balance sheet format, which can be easily modified to reflect peculiarities of your situation, addressing the needs of owners and the IRS. Along with routine summarization of the financial situation, updating that balance sheet essentially involves two continuous documentations of non-cash assets: inventory accounting, and verification of non-inventory/non-cash assets.

Because the book inventory normally constitutes the single biggest asset of a publishing house, tracking and verifying its value is especially important.

So a layman's tour of the arcane subject of inventory accounting is in order at this point.

Actually, the mumbo-jumbo accountants talk when they manipulate inventories of unsold (or recently sold) books has very real and useful meaning when/if you learn to decipher it. The "inventory value" of a new book is simply the capital investment you made to put that book into the warehouse—where it retains that value until it is sold or discarded. The total of the accumulated unit inventory values of *all* the books in your warehouse (or on consignment to "distributors"—but still legally "yours") at any given time is a major asset on your balance sheet (which reflects the "book value" of your publishing house ... frequently quite different from its "fair market value")

While some publishers (mostly not-for-profits) periodically depreciate the values of old books in inventory on the assumption that they've become partially obsolete, the landmark *Thor Power Tool* decision of the Supreme Court (affirming an IRS policy) now stipulates that it is illegal for taxpaying publishers to "write down" an inventory value—and thus take a tax deduction for the loss—until they've actually lost the money (by selling books for less than their inventory cost) or destroyed/discarded the books themselves.

So once a book is in your inventory, the only proper ways to get it out (and claim its production cost as a tax-deductible expense) are to sell it, give it away (as a promotional sample), discard it, or lose it and adjust your permanent count accordingly. When you do so, the computer (or the bookkeeper, if you're tracking inventory manually) then subtracts its unit cost from that balance sheet "inventory value" reflecting the fact that you've now "used up" that little portion of your capital investment; it's finally become a true "expense."

So when you pay your printing bills—or pre-press bills for copy-editing, design, typesetting, and other processes necessary to get a book onto the press—those are not really "costs" in the profit-or-loss sense. They are instead *capital investments* in inventory value. Instead of entering them on the books as part of the current month's cost of doing business (expenses), the financial administrator properly *adds them to your inventory value* as part of your accumulative capital investment. Thus accountants describe this manner of deferring costs (until the books are disposed of) as "capitalizing" those costs.

A properly programmed order processing computer, then, will record the unit inventory value of every book as it goes into the warehouse (and the computer's "product file"), and make an appropriate deduction from your total inventory value as each book is sold, shipped, or discarded. (These subtracted values are normally referred to as "cost of goods.") It is at the time this "cost of goods" is subtracted from inventory value that the book is actually charged to your current operating expenses (against whatever department, or cost category, you specify) as a true, timely "cost of doing business." This process of actually making the deferred charge against current operations is referred to as "expensing" of inventory.

Moderately sophisticated order processing software or manual bookkeeping procedures will actually divide the unit cost of each book into capitalized sub-components (royalty advances, pre-press costs, paper/printing/binding)—so each component can be appropriately charged back to a *different* department or function as each book is "expensed" as "cost of goods."

Unit "manufacturing costs" for paper/printing/binding are almost always calculated on the basis of each print-order. While it's theoretically more appropriate to amortize pre-press costs over the estimated first-year sales quantity (and some publishers actually spread it over several assumed printings)—for practical purposes, a majority also spread those costs over the first printing alone.

Incidentally, the first-year assumptions made in pre-contract evaluations and pricing (as per Figure 18a) need *not* coincide with the inventory values you enter into your order processing "product file" and use as a basis for expensing the monthly "cost of goods." Those preliminary evaluation numbers were hypothetical, for pricing purposes; whether your financial administrator eventually uses first-printing, first-year, or long-term amortization of pre-press costs should depend on which (legally defensible) option renders the lowest tax bill.

Because they're not concerned with tax maneuvers, not-for-profit publishers sometimes spread pre-press expenses over several assumed future reprintings to reduce the unitized, near-future "cost of goods"—and thus defer the actual admission of some expenses to a later year/budget. Unfortunately, this is usually a self-deception; someday the piper will have to be paid. And it's one reason why accumulated inventory values among not-for-profit publishers average 40 percent of annual sales volume—compared to only about 27 percent for commercial publishers.

Before the recent U.S. "tax reform," book publishers were not required to capitalize internal copy-editing costs; now *all* expenses of developing new books (including portions of the payroll reported on the tax return as "263A costs") are supposed to be capitalized rather than immediately "expensed." Not being a tax accountant, the author must leave it to you, your finance administrator, and your IRS field office to sort out just what staff costs this includes.

Some finance administrators "capitalize" royalty advances, and some treat them as "prepaid expenses." Some include freight costs (from the printer to the warehouse) in paper/printing/binding capitalization—while some "expense" those freight costs immediately. Again, we won't attempt to referee the nuances; let the tax experts be your guide. We suspect the actual impact on tax bills is less than generally assumed.

If your order processing software doesn't break inventory data down the way you want it, you can easily reorganize that data by transferring a few end-of-the-month numbers from that computer's sales reports to a self-programmed spreadsheet that will accomplish all of the inventory *and* the royalty accounting you're likely to need. You're free to copy the sample format depicted in Figure 36c, on the next page.

This spreadsheet is simply recopied (vertically) on the computer for each subsequent month. Program the spreadsheet to carry over (copy) all "closing" numbers each month as "opening" numbers in the same category for the following month. By putting in actual inventory values as each book is published (and thus moved from "works in progress" to "finished goods")—and programming the spreadsheet to (1) multiply those values by the number of copies moved (or, for royalties, the sales dollar-volume) each month and (2) subtract the results from the "opening balances," you'll get automatic monthly updates of each category of inventory investment for each title.

The first column of numbers in Figure 36c totals the counts in all of the individual-book columns. The second column totals only those books already in the warehouse ("finished goods"), while the third totals those books still under development ("works in progress"). Each subsequent column summarizes the month's activity relative to a single title (indicated by the 4-letter codes from author names at the tops of the columns).

Note that Ms. Boynton's book ("Boyn") has not yet been published. But in October, the publisher paid an additional $300 on her royalty advance (bringing the total to $1,000). They also began copy-editing the book, and "capitalized" $973.65 (in staff or freelance editing costs) as inventory investment in this future title. Both of these items have contributed, then, to the $18,760.16 "total inventory value" we have invested in not-yet-published ("works in progress") books.

Also note that of the titles shown, only the Brownter book ("Brow") has earned back its royalty advance. So by moving the royalty percentage from the "advance" section down to the "royalty liability" section at the bottom of the monthly block, the finance administrator has re-set the computer to begin registering royalties that are actually to be paid to the author (rather than retained to offset advances). And since the "Brew" inventory is almost exhausted, it is not surprising to see (by peeking ahead at the next month) that a new printing was added to the inventory at that time.

All one has to do to update this record at the end of each month is to enter (from the order processing summary) the quantities of each title moved into or out of the inventory, the sales volume (in dollars), and the new ("accrued") costs charged to each title in each category. The spreadsheet (adaptable to any basic spreadsheet software) then serves virtually all of your inventory and royalty accounting needs.

In addition to inventory accounting, asset verification involves other non-cash assets likely to appear on your balance sheet. The others are normally monitored and maintained by departments other than finance. But the financial administrator should be accountable for confirming that they do indeed have the value indicated on that balance sheet. The easiest way to do this is to circulate a checklist of such assets monthly, asking each responsible party to certify by initials that the assets are secure—and indicate any changes in value other than routine tax-depreciation. This should be coupled with actual inspection of the assets by the financial administrator at least once a year. (If your publishing house is audited, others might want to be included in this inspection.)

Figure 36c—Sample Inventory/Royalty Recording Form

INVENTORY/ROYALTY RECORD	Total	Fin Gds	Wk-Prog	Aran	Boyn	Brew	Cart	Davi
Opening Balance - Oct 92	242026	242026	0	1826	0	540	1850	929
New Mfg (+)	10221	10221	0	0	0	0	0	0
Good Returns (+)	496	496	0	0	0	0	0	0
Shipped Sales (-)	10824	10824	0	86	0	325	7	5
Shipped Comp (-)	905	905	0	15	0	0	0	0
Hurt/Lost/Discarded (-)	212	212	0	0	0	0	0	0
Closing Balance	240802	240802	0	1725	0	215	1843	924
$ Net Book Rev - Returns	$117865.27	$117865.27	$0.00	$403.26	$0.00	$1132.93	$41.39	$45.17
$ Sub Rights Revenue	$2426.96	$2426.96	$0.00	$0.00	$0.00	$0.00	$0.00	$0.00
Royalty Advance Opening	$12409.46	$9809.46	$2600.00	$962.80	$700.00	$0.00	$467.60	$165.47
Royalty Adv Accrued	$2100.00	$0.00	$2100.00	$0.00	$300.00	$0.00	$0.00	$0.00
* Royalty Adv %	n/a	n/a	n/a	13.0%	12.5%	0.0%	12.5%	12.5%
Book Roy Adv Expensed	$3389.59	$3389.59	$0.00	$52.42	$0.00	$0.00	$5.17	$5.65
Sub Rts Roy Expensed	$208.42	$208.42	$0.00	$0.00	$0.00	$0.00	$0.00	$0.00
Royalty Adv Closing	$10911.45	$6511.45	$4400.00	$910.37	$1000.00	$0.00	$462.42	$159.83
Editing Opening	$24294.59	$19560.08	$4734.51	$1755.21	$0.00	$0.00	$829.13	$36.13
Editing Accrued	$4772.81	$0.00	$4772.81	$0.00	$973.65	$0.00	$0.00	$0.00
* Editing ProRata	$11.66	$11.66	$0.00	$0.96	$0.00	$0.00	$0.45	$0.07
Editing Expensed	$3008.72	$3008.72	$0.00	$96.96	$0.00	$0.00	$3.15	$0.36
Editing Closing	$26058.68	$16551.36	$9507.32	$1658.25	$973.65	$0.00	$825.98	$35.77
Prepress Opening	$16615.34	$13986.57	$2628.77	$230.97	$0.00	$0.00	$273.06	$449.17
Prepress Accrued	$2246.07	$22.00	$2224.07	$0.00	$0.00	$0.00	$0.00	$0.00
* PrePress ProRata	$6.47	$6.47	$0.00	$0.13	$0.00	$0.00	$0.15	$0.74
Prepress Expensed	$2452.50	$2452.50	$0.00	$13.13	$0.00	$0.00	$1.04	$3.71
Prepress Closing	$16408.91	$11556.07	$4852.84	$217.84	$0.00	$0.00	$272.02	$445.46
Mfg Opening	$146203.61	$146203.61	$0.00	$2943.51	$0.00	$434.32	$2306.32	$582.11
Mfg Accrued	$5000.08	$5000.08	$0.00	$0.00	$0.00	$0.00	$0.00	$0.00
* Mfg ProRata	$34.70	$34.70	$0.00	$1.61	$0.00	$1.22	$1.25	$1.06
Mfg Expensed	$12268.84	$12268.84	$0.00	$162.61	$0.00	$396.50	$8.76	$5.30
Mfg Closing	$138934.84	$138934.84	$0.00	$2780.90	$0.00	$37.82	$2297.55	$576.81
TOTAL INVENTORY VALUE	$192313.88	$173553.72	$18760.16	$5567.36	$1973.65	$37.82	$3857.98	$1217.87
Royalty Liability Opening	$37783.20	$37783.20	$0.00	$0.00	$0.00	$181.13	$0.00	$0.00
* Royalty Percentage	n/a	n/a	n/a	0.0%	0.0%	12.5%	0.0%	0.0%
Book Royalty Accrued	$4104.60	$4104.60	$0.00	$0.00	$0.00	$141.62	$0.00	$0.00
SubRt Royalty Accrued	$949.01	$949.01	$0.00	$0.00	$0.00	$0.00	$0.00	$0.00
Royalty Liability Paid	$37783.21	$37783.21	$0.00	$0.00	$0.00	$181.13	$0.00	$0.00
Royalty Liability Closing	$5053.60	$5053.60	$0.00	$0.00	$0.00	$141.62	$0.00	$0.00
INVENTORY/ROYALTY RECORD	Total	Fin Gds	Wk-Prog	Aran	Boyn	Brew	Cart	Davi
Opening Balance - Nov 92	240802	240802	0	1725	0	215	1843	924
New Mfg (+)	8381	8381	0	0	0	2944	0	0
Good Returns (+)	0	0	0	0	0	0	0	0
Shipped Sales (-)	0	0	0	0	0	0	0	0
Etc, etc, etc ...								

The facilities administrator, or building or office manager, should be able to document the value of real estate and equipment from a *property file;* it should include serial numbers and other identification, original invoices or tax assessments or other indications of monetary value, warranties, service contracts, and whatever else might be of use if questions or problems relating to the property (such as insurance claims) ever arise. The same individual should maintain an *insurance file* containing all policies, and summarizing their coverage, their expiration dates, and their premiums. The office manager should have available a *supply inventory file* or checklist, from which you can quickly determine the value of accumulated supplies.

The editorial department should maintain a fireproof *contract file,* documenting all those precious agreements with authors which are the very heart of a publishing house's value. And marketing should have some type of *mailing list inventory,* indicating how many useful names it has accumulated in each market category at any given time. Discuss with your lawyer and tax advisor whether and how these should most advantageously be reflected on your balance sheet.

Effective strategic management of a book publishing house consists of discovering what is working and *doing more of it,* while discovering what is not working well and *doing less of it*—or, if it absolutely can't be de-emphasized, focusing a spotlight on the mal-performing function so it can be "fixed." The key to being able to manage in this manner lies in creating an effective measurement structure (the chart of accounts), determining that results are expected (budgeting), and then telling all concerned which parts of the performance are living up to (or beyond) those expectations—and which are faltering (feedback).

The fifth, and perhaps most important, basic responsibility of the financial administrator, then, is to feed results back to the organization at regular intervals (in the most precise score-keeping language we have—dollars and cents). This is normally done monthly—and to make sure all concerned are responding to changing events promptly and realistically, efficient finance departments make sure their summaries are distributed within 10 days after the end of each month.

Some staff members will have a need for relatively detailed feedback on specific functions; this can most easily be accomplished by printing out the entire spreadsheet illustrated in Figure 35a (or your equivalent), including the monthly entries for the past year, and giving a copy to each core manager or department head; they can then photocopy and distribute whatever portions of that display they think various people in their areas might find useful.

However, there are other people who want to know what's happening in general, but don't need this much detail. This will include your Board members, the bank (if you maintain a credit line), and perhaps major vendors/creditors. It may even include the publisher! For these people, you might prepare a summary (departmental totals only) which can be distributed with your updated balance sheet.

Another critical piece of monthly feedback is that inventory report—which if well designed) can not only provide cost-of-goods data for the monthly financial report, but enables the inventory administration function to spot depleted titles before you're out-of-stock and trigger reprint decisions, and provides the data needed for periodic calculation and reporting of author royalties. Good integrated order-entry software will generate this report as a by-product of routine order processing; it will be up to the finance officer to see that all of the concerned parties get their monthly copies promptly.

Traditionally, accountants have insisted on conforming both financial projections (budgets) and financial feedback to the *fiscal year* calendar on which they pay taxes or (in a tax-exempt organization report to their annual meetings and/or auditors. These tend to start over at the beginning of each fiscal year—thereafter generating partial "year to date" summaries which can be very misleading in an industry as seasonal as book publishing.

But with the easy availability of small computers and good spreadsheet programs, it has become very easy for finance offices to retotal the most-recent 12 months' data at the end of *every* month—as suggested by Figure 35a—and thus show everybody how the latest month's results effected the *annual* pattern. The finance officer willing to do this has recognized the difference between mere bookkeeping and true "managerial accounting" (to guide sound decision-making). The finance officer who isn't willing to do this is, in many cases, displaying more loyalty to the tax-collectors and the auditors than to his own organization!

Good feedback is as obvious and meaningful as possible; today's amazing PCs and spreadsheet programs make it easy to deliver.

Planning the financial patterns you expect your publishing program to follow (budgeting), maintaining reasonable control over spending (by providing feedback relative to budgets and other plans), and insuring that you're actually paid the money you've earned within a reasonable time (credit and collections), should enable you (at any given time) to project several months ahead approximately how much money you will have on hand, and how much you'll owe, on any future date. Making sure there's enough "cash flow" on hand to keep the operation functioning smoothly at all times (without disrupting the timing of intricate strategies) is the sixth basic responsibility of the finance administrator.

Assuming you pay your bills in about the same length of time as it takes your customers to pay theirs, the financial overview illustrated by Figure 35a (or some comparable format) will give you a fairly good idea as to the general financial health of the enterprise. But it does not include short-term (month-by-month) projections to tell you whether you'll be able (for instance) to meet any specific week's payroll.

Therefore, for the 3 months immediately ahead, the financial administrator may want to maintain a more precise cash flow projection. You can do it by querying department heads every month about minor departures they foresee over the next quarter from the pattern of the previous year or the limits established by your budget.

To the greatest extent possible, you should break this quarterly cash flow projection down on a weekly basis (for the next 13 weeks), extending it an additional month at the end of every month. If cash is likely to be in short supply, ask major function managers (especially in print-buying and marketing) to go over their actual schedules with the financial administrator, to get anticipated major expenditures into the right weeks. Then summarize the projection for general management—to provide 13 weeks advance notice of any extraordinary steps which must be taken to minimize the negative impact of any "cash flow crises" (temporary cash shortages) that can be predicted.

In warning of a cash flow crisis, the financial administrator should provide general management with a checklist of options for meeting the crisis without upsetting the momentum or the strategic direction of the publishing program. Adjustments to such crises short of selling equity (a complicated last resort) fall into two categories: those which speed up income, and those which slow down disbursements.

The most common ways of speeding up income are (a) accelerating pressure on accounts receivable for faster collections, (b) adjusting schedules to enable earlier billing of advance shipments of appropriate books, (c) adjusting marketing schedules to produce earlier cash—especially through prepublication and subsidiary rights sales, and (d) borrowing.

The most common ways of slowing down disbursements include (a) slower payment of those vendors who aren't in a position to retaliate significantly, (b) slowing inventory investment by delaying marginal or loosely scheduled projects, (c) reducing inventory investment by automatic reduction of print quantities, and (d) reducing marginal staff—especially by asking your core staff to take over certain tasks usually assigned to temporary, part-time, or freelance help.

The financial administrator who accepts the creative challenge of cash flow management can usually see that, once a publishing program has passed the break-even point, strategic plans seldom have to be adjusted for cash flow reasons, as long as they remain within budgetary limits.

Finally, the seventh basic responsibility of the financial administrator is to settle with the tax collector. If your capital position is sufficiently complex, this may simply consist of providing the necessary data (from the transaction database and the order processing computer) to an external tax accountant—who may or may not massage that data in consultation with the chief finance officer to get the owners the best deal (lowest tax bill) legally allowable. But in a majority of independent publishing houses, finance administrators willing to wade through the instruction books that come with the federal and state tax returns—and refer to previous years' returns for additional guidance—should be able to handle this task without paying outside professionals.

Commercial publishers' budgets commonly include "before tax" operating margin projections; how that gets divided between taxes, retained earnings, and later dividend disbursements need concern no one except the publisher, the financial administrator, and the Board of Directors. But there are other tax costs involved with routine operating decisions (for instance, increases in unemployment tax liability when you have a high staff turnover in some states, or property taxes when you own your own facilities), and the financial administrator is generally responsible for understanding the options in such cases and advising the core managers as to which are best for you.

Among the practical issues on which a tax strategy should be developed, in the light of your particular circumstances in any given year are: whether it's more advantageous to buy office equipment or lease it ... whether you pay more in fringe and payroll tax costs for putting a specialist on the payroll than you do for hiring a freelancer ... the impact of amortizing pre-press costs over several anticipated printings of a book rather than absorbing them all in the first printing ... whether the delayed tax deductions of large inventories offset the economies-of-scale assumed for long press runs ... and whether your expense account procedures expose the company to potential future retaliation from the tax collector.

Your regional Internal Revenue Service field office and your state tax department have ample libraries of publications, and a willing staff of consultants, to help you decipher all of these implications. When you call them to fill in the gaps in your own knowledge of tax regulations, be sure to ask IRS to show you (and explain) its Ruling #80-60, implementing the *Thor Power Tool* decision of the U.S. Supreme Court (1979) which changed the ground rules for writing off inventory as obsolete (and thus a deductible loss). Also request an explanation of how much editorial payroll should be capitalized (rather than immediately expensed) under Section 263A of the Tax Reform Act of 1986.

To make certain tax decisions, you'll find it helpful to calculate a "trial balance" estimating your year-end figures about a month prior to the end of your fiscal year (which can be anytime you and the tax people find agreeable). This projection will help you identify tax liabilities while there is still time to do something about them. You can usually manipulate expenses upward or downward by last-month rescheduling of certain commitments. This may be particularly important when you have tax-deductible loss carry-overs from prior years; you lose these deductions if they're not taken within 7 years.

Of course, the financial administrator is not supposed to make policy decisions related to tax strategy on a unilateral, arbitrary basis. His job is to anticipate the options, and make firm recommendations (through the business manager) to the core management group and the Board of Directors.

In addition to plotting strategy to minimize the tax bite, the financial administrator has a considerable task in simply complying with legal requirements for tax data reports. This can be minimized by establishing a chronological file in which photocopies of all previous years' tax forms and returns are available as guidance when the same form is due next year. Such a file can also become the basis of a systematic tax calendar, forewarning all concerned of the periodic deadlines for major reports.

CHAPTER 37
Pricing and Other Keys to Profitability

Perhaps in no single way can a business manager do more to insure the profitability of segments of the publishing process outside his control than by periodically reviewing, and campaigning for refinement of, the process by which a publishing house prices its books. We'll look at some other opportunities for "stacking the deck" to nudge the other strategic functions (acquisition, marketing) toward more profitable decision-making later in this chapter, but first let's examine this main-chance mechanism of the pricing formula.

Most publishers base their "list (before discount) prices" on the unit inventory-investment (pre-press, printing) cost of each book, as estimated in advance of publication. This makes sense, because this is the largest component of the total (direct and/or indirect) cost of publishing any book which can be fairly accurately estimated (from those unit-cost performance indices in Figure 8b) far in advance.

Properly calculated for pricing purposes, this unit production cost consists of two basic components: (a) the *pre-press* (or "plant") cost of getting the raw manuscript onto the printing press (including copy editing, if you're to observe IRS's letter-of-the-law), and (b) the *manufacturing* cost (for paper, printing, and binding)—both estimated on the basis of the number of units marketing is reasonably sure it can sell *in the first year* (or 18 months for a textbook, since the first six are largely spent giving away free samples). Be leery of arguments that such costs should be amortized over a longer period; normal budgeting formulas seldom assume more than one year of storage—or prepayment of printing costs.

Figure 18a demonstrated how these two unit production costs can be utilized not only to determine in advance what *minimum* price you'll have to charge to expect a proposed book to support your (Figure 34a) financial strategy—but what kind of commitment you can expect from the critical marketing function. By campaigning constantly against proceeding with any new products that have not undergone this test, the business manager can do much to avoid future financial crises.

Bear in mind that the 1-year sales quantity estimate that results from this process is *not* necessarily the proper print quantity. At the bottom on Figure 18a, you'll see that provision has been made for the finance officer (who should essentially control such major capital investments) to second-guess routine procedures and base the actual decision on cash flow and other circumstances at the time the printing is ordered.

To determine by what number the finance administrator should multiply ("mark up") that estimated unit production cost of the first year's sales, to set a price that essentially guarantees acceptable profitability (if everybody's estimates are sound), use six columns on a spreadsheet to perform (on one line, for the specific discount category applicable to the proposed book) the calculation illustrated by each line of Figure 37a.

Figure 37a—Representative Pricing Mark-Up Formulas

MARKET/TERMS [1991 Data]	Max Norm Discount	Left for Publisher	PrePress Budget	P/P/B Budget	Col 3 x (Col 4 + 5)	Multiplier = 100/Col 6
78 Secular Trade Publrs	52.7%	47.3%	11.6%	23.6%	16.6	6.0
27 Religious Trade Publrs	55.7%	44.3%	6.5%	27.1%	14.9	6.7
11 El-High Publishers	37.0%	63.0%	9.2%	27.8%	23.3	4.3
55 Professional Book Publrs	45.5%	54.5%	10.0%	21.0%	16.9	5.9
40 Secular Not-for-Profits	46.3%	53.7%	13.3%	20.2%	18.0	5.6

In the first column of numbers, enter the *highest normal discount* percentage you offer, for large quantities to your most-favored customer category. (*Don't* use you "average" discount; that simply tends to make large sales unprofitable!) Now subtract that discount from 100 to determine (second column of figures) what percentage of the eventual list price will (under the least-favorable circumstances) end up in the publisher's hands. In the next two columns, enter the respective percentages of your total budget you plan to use (according to your Figure 34a Financial Strategy Model) for pre-press development, and for paper/printing/binding. Multiply that combined number by the "percentage of list price left for publisher" (second-from-left column)— and you'll have calculated (in the second-from-right column) what percentage of the retail ("list") price should be allocated (in support of your financial strategy) for inventory investment. Divide that number into 100, and you'll know (in the final right-hand column) by what factor you must mark up (multiply) the estimated unit cost (per Figure 18a) in order to determine the *minimum* price that supports your financial strategy. (Note that Figure 18a subsequently queries the marketing function as to whether any higher price would be acceptable; never insult a book by under-pricing it!)

When you reprint a backlist title for which the pre-press development cost has already been amortized, there's frequently a tendency not to review the price (or even a temptation to reduce it) because you no longer have to recover copy editing and typesetting from future sales. This gives your customers—rather than you—the principal reward for that acquisition and marketing savvy and that financial risk-taking you invested in pulling off a publishing success. For every book that survives to be reprinted, two or three gather dust eating up storage money, or have to be remaindered. Give yourself the benefit of your successes by either sticking with your original price, or using the same formula (with nothing in the pre-press column) to generate a bigger cost/price mark-up anytime you recalculate the price for a reprint. You *earned* it!

You'll often be tempted to make a sales, rights, or distribution deal that doesn't meet your normal pricing-profitability standards—but which represents some small increment of revenue you wouldn't have gotten otherwise. The argument for such a deal says "it adds on to our revenue total without adding anything directly to expenses—so why not?" But almost all such "add-on" deals make small, incremental demands for more personnel, more computer capacity, and more inventory investment that can't be directly traced. Eventually, they undermine your profitability by allowing your publishing operation to be exploited by somebody else (a high-discount distributor, an aggressive co-publisher, a tough-bargaining book club), on terms you couldn't afford to offer across-the-board. A strong policy *against* making such special "add-on" deals that violate your normal business terms and/or pricing standards may force you to by-pass an occasional windfall, but it will build a healthier publishing program (and prevent potential fair trade violations) over the long run. Once your staff, authors, major customers, or vendors learn that you can be exploited in this way, you'll be surprised how fast your normal operating margin shrinks.

Even after the business manager or finance officer has defended the profitability requirements of a proposed new title through the preliminary pricing process described on the preceding page, those profits can evaporate automatically if the publishing house is locked into a financially unsound deal with the author. A periodic review of basic author contract terms (as outlined in Chapter 14), with emphasis on "bottom line" results, should thus be a routine exercise for the conscientious business manager. (The publisher must, of course, be prepared to referee if differences develop between the business manager and the acquisition function.)

Three essential elements of the basic contract (see Figure 14a) are of particular interest to the business manager. The first is the royalty clause, specifying what percent of net receipts or list price will be paid to the author for each book sold. The second is the advance payment against future royalties (if any) which the publisher agrees to pay the author to seal the deal. The third is the subsidiary rights clause, establishing how proceeds from licenses to third parties to adapt the manuscript to other uses will be divided between author and publisher. By agreeing to modest adjustments in these three contract elements, when profitability is consistently low, the editor-in-chief (or the publisher) can fine-tune the contract pattern to enhance the resulting operating margin.

The royalty issue is the most critical one. Typically, well over half of the cost of obtaining manuscript rights is paid to the authors; less than half goes for acquisition salaries and related expenses. By limiting royalties to profitable levels through your basic contract—and adopting disciplined rules about negotiating changes in those contract terms—you can insure that editors will spend at least a majority of that creative money on a profitable basis.

How much royalty you can afford depends on the complex interplay of your budget and pricing strategies. However, the publishing industry (without conspiring illegally) has traditionally paid fairly standard royalty percentages, which are affordable if one also assumes reasonable sales terms and pricing formulas.

For trade books (those intended primarily for the bookstore and public library markets), publishers have traditionally paid the author 10 percent of the "list" or "cover" price that the consumer will eventually pay the store, on all books sold through trade channels at no more than 50 percent discounts. Often their contracts have reduced the royalty to 5 percent when books were sold at discounts greater than 50 percent, or outside trade channels (for example, directly to readers).

However, according to the Huenefeld consultants' survey of 1991 policies, 77 percent of secular trade publishers and 65 percent of religious trade publishers (and even higher percentages of classroom and direct-marketing publishers) now base their royalties on their *net receipts* rather than list prices. Both authors and publishers find such net-receipt accounting more straight forward; most also agree that it is fairer than list-price royalties. On this net-receipt basis, trade and non-trade royalties both usually range from 10 to 13 percent (averaging about 11 percent).

When acquisition editors need bargaining leeway, it is better to encourage them to increase *advances* than to increase royalties—and since this is "instant money," hard-to-get authors can usually be mollified by such higher advances. However, it behooves the business manager to argue for sensible limits on advances. Given the contemporary cost of tying up investment (operating capital) in royalty advances, they should generally not exceed the royalty the author will earn on the books your marketing department estimates it will sell during a title's first year. (The average paid by the 71 percent of independent publishers who gave authors such advances in 1991 was $1,975.)

Subsidiary rights income is customarily divided between author and publisher. Traditionally, the split has been 50/50 on payments (including advances) from third parties for subsidiary *print* rights to use the manuscript (or portions of it) in another book or periodical (even in translation). Income from *adaptation* rights to use the material in another medium (stage, screen, software, etc.) has customarily been divided 90/10 or 80/20 in favor of the author. However, unless the publisher's share is at least 20 percent, few small houses can afford any serious effort to sell such rights; many, in fact, now insist on a 50/50 split of *all* subsidiary rights income. This is especially important regarding rights to adapt manuscripts to electronic media that compete directly with the publisher's books.

Some authors (particularly if represented by agents) bargain to retain 100 percent of subsidiary rights and market them independently of the publisher. When that happens, the business manager should insist that an evaluation be made of the potential of those rights, and the viability of the project without them.

Frequently the star authors of small publishing houses argue that they should be rewarded for their loyalty (and the supposed bestseller status they've sacrificed by staying away from the big houses) by royalties substantially above your normal levels. This is usually a deception; *if* the big houses were willing, most independent publishers' star authors would change homes in a hurry! Don't make special deals here that will undermine the relative profitability of your best books. If your royalties are *below* the industry norms (10 percent of list price, or 10-13 percent of net receipts), you may indeed find good authors reluctant to talk to you unless they're increased. But if they're at normal levels, you aren't likely to lure many best-selling authors away from the larger publishers by increasing them—and you may seriously undermine your profitability by attempting it.

In the 1980s, religious trade publishers serving the Protestant bookstore market were jolted when one of the larger commercial houses began offering extremely high royalties (20 percent or more) in an attempt to lure away the star authors of some of the smaller (mostly not-for-profit) houses. The "bidding war" that this instigated had such severe financial repercussions that religious trade publishing was, for several years, the most unprofitable segment of the industry. Only after smaller publishers learned to stand their ground by limiting royalty offers to sensible budgeting levels did religious trade publishing profits recover. There is no convincing evidence that either publishers or authors really gained from this exercise.

Just as a carefully planned basic author contract can help keep the acquisition function operating profitably even when its attention is focused on other priorities, a properly developed set of sales terms can do the same for the marketing function. So the business manager also has a stake in reviewing the profitability of sales terms periodically, and recommending potential improvements to the core management group (and thus to the publisher).

The aspect of sales terms that has the greatest impact on profitability is your *discount schedule*. But you can't afford to be arbitrary about it, if you hope to sell through middlemen. Both the realities of their continued solvency, and the practices of your competitors, virtually dictate certain minimum discount levels.

If you have any serious expectations of substantial sales through bookstores, those stores must normally get your books for at least 40 percent less than the "cover" price they'll charge customers. If wholesalers are to have any incentive to stock your books in bulk and make them more easily available to stores, libraries, and schools—you'll have to see that they normally get at least 46 percent discounts; most will tell you they need 50 percent.

Schools and libraries are less interested in the discount percentage than in their actual net cost per book. Over the years, schools have pressured publishers into keeping prices low by keeping discounts low. So publishers of textbooks and supplementary classroom materials have traditionally offered "short" discounts of only 20 percent on bulk classroom orders—but have compensated by pricing their books lower than other books in relation to production costs. Sometimes they do offer somewhat higher (30-35 percent) discounts to dealers buying for resale (either as school wholesalers, or through school supply stores), but this usually requires a modest upward adjustment in prices.

In recent years, however, an increasing number of small textbook publishers have adopted "net pricing," whereby they keep prices at the lowest feasible level and offer *no* discounts. These are publishers who maintain well-targeted contact with the educators who make classroom materials decisions, feel no need to accommodate middleman dealers, and want to see that schools get the best possible break on the purchase of their books.

Individuals buying books directly from publishers by mail or phone (from print or broadcast ads, direct mail promotions, etc.) are usually less price conscious, and less concerned with discounts, than trade or institutional buyers. However, discounts are often used to provide direct response copywriters with dramatic ammunition—especially in calling attention to (and speeding up cash from) forthcoming new titles. So it behooves the business manager to see that reasonable limits for such copy-appeal discounts are firmly established.

It is a common (and sensible) practice to apply different discount schedules to different types of books. Many publishers establish a "trade" schedule (with high discounts) that applies *only* to a limited selection of their most popular general-interest titles—clearly identified in catalogs and order forms, and a reference/textbook or "short" discount schedule that applies to all other titles. Some make the discounts available only to dealers purchasing for resale; others extend their "short" discounts to schools, and to libraries; a few even extend bulk discounts to individual mail order customers who buy enough books. Discounts are usually based on the total number of units in an order, whatever the mix of titles—but a few publishers base them on the dollar-size of each order rather than the number of books included.

Perhaps the single discount practice business managers have the greatest stake in "policing" is the marketing temptation to give bookstores discounts on single-copy orders. Even when these are paid in advance (so-called "SCOP orders"), their processing usually eats up any potential profit from the transaction. And since the order itself is evidence that the bookstore didn't "play ball" by pre-stocking your books—why reward people who aren't doing anything for you? Generally speaking, it makes very little sense to give anybody a discount on anything less than five books—except in the case of selective pre-publication or "stock reduction" (remaindering) promotions directly to readers.

In recent years, many publishers have sought to discourage trade accounts from returning unsold merchandise, by offering extra 3-5 percent bonus discounts on "nonreturnable" purchases. However, most trade buyers have been relatively unreceptive to this tactic.

Others have met with more success in helping wholesalers deal with their burdensome "margin squeeze," by giving their major wholesale accounts bonus discounts for very large orders submitted in advance of printing (either initially, or when titles go back to press).

There is, of course, no "standard" discount schedule; the FTC would consider that an illegal conspiracy, restraining competition between publishers. So every publisher must take steps to communicate its terms to its principal market-audiences. The discount schedule, as well as other basic sales terms, should be available on a printed sheet for interested accounts, and should be incorporated into trade and institutional catalogs and order forms. Making it available in printed form assures all concerned (including the FTC) that you are dealing fairly and evenly with all comers.

Marketing personnel are often pressured by dealers to make special discount concessions to close important sales. The business manager should occasionally remind these marketing colleagues (if the marketing manager hasn't) that the FTC's "fair trade guidelines" (which are enshrined in law, with stiff penalties for deliberate or continued violation) require that all terms you offer one customer must also be made available (at your initiative) to all of that customer's competitors.

If you're seriously interested in trade (bookstore, wholesale) or institutional (library, school) business, you must be prepared to extend credit. Cash purchases are simply so difficult for business and public organizations to administer that you'll lose a major percentage of your sales (and spend a lot of time in repetitive explanations) if you require advance payment from most such buyers. But credit should be extended only with the understanding (written into the formal terms statement) that invoices are payable within a reasonable time. The most common payment terms in book publishing are "30 days e/o/m"—which means within 30 days of your end-of-the-month statement. (Some booksellers ignore invoices and pay publishers on the basis of their end-of-the-month statements, so it is important that open accounts receive such statements *in addition* to the invoices you send at the time you ship books.) Review Chapter 36 regarding your enforcement of these terms.

One concession you almost have to be willing to make if you expect significant sales to bookstores and wholesalers is the privilege of returning unsold books within a stated time for credit to their accounts. (Some publishers offer actual refunds, but most insist that returns can only be credited against accounts receivable, or future purchases.) Such return privileges are often limited to "not less than 90 days, or more than 365 days" after purchase. Some publishers, however, think it's simpler and more straightforward to accept returns for as long as a book remains "in print" (in the publisher's active sales list). In the book trade, the classified ad section of *Publishers Weekly* is generally recognized as the appropriate place to forewarn the trade that a title is being declared "out of print," and will not be accepted for return credit beyond a specified date.

There has been a pronounced trend in recent years for publishers to exact some penalty for returns, rather than crediting stores with exactly what they paid for the books. Perhaps the most common penalty is a modest deduction (10 percent or so) from the original purchase amount.

Some publishers require that customers obtain *prior permission* to return specified numbers of copies of specified titles. This gives the publisher an opportunity to confirm that the customer is eligible to make the return, and provide the account a warehouse address, before unwieldy cartons end up in your editorial or production offices.

Return privileges are almost universally based on the requirement that the books sent back be in undamaged "mint" condition. The business manager should make certain this is clear in the printed terms statement, and that procedures are in place for checking incoming books and eliminating any too damaged for resale from both the credit memo and the inventory.

It is traditional in the book trade that customers pay shipping costs (the actual postage or other transportation) on all credit orders (by addition to the invoice) and all merchandise returns. Often publishers offer to prepay shipping costs on bulk trade and institutional orders that are paid in advance—but those are relatively rare. It has also become customary to add "shipping and handling charges" (usually some set amount) to prepaid mail order terms—usually by making it a preprinted entry on the last line of all order forms. In recent years, some publishers have attempted to use "free freight" on large quantities as an inducement to get trade accounts to consolidate their orders—but results have been (at best) mixed.

A final condition frequently included in the business terms of trade publishers is some provision for credits to reimburse stores and wholesalers for their promotion of specified books. The most common such arrangement offers a credit to the customer's account of 75 percent of the documented cost of local promotions of specified new titles, provided those promotions have been approved in advance by the publisher, and limited to some percentage (usually 7.5-to-10 percent) of the net (after-discount) amount of that customer's actual purchases of the book in question.

Funneling normal promotion-budget support for a new book through the outlets that will present it to the public, in this fashion, not only improves the targeting of such support, but can be used as an additional inducement to stores to stock the book. However, those are marketing considerations. It is the responsibility of the business manager to see that such allowances are charged against the authorized marketing budget (just as internally-sponsored ad bills would have been), so that they don't undermine the profitability of your sales.

As we noted in Chapter 24, proposing workable sales terms is really the province of the marketing manager, not the business manager. But the business manager should periodically review such terms, and suggest revisions to the core management group if they seem to be unduly undermining profitability. At the same time, all concerned must realize that marketing cannot sell effectively in many markets (especially the book trade) unless it is able to offer terms competitive with the conventions of the industry.

A fourth general policy issue which the business manager should periodically review for opportunities to "stack the deck" in favor of greater profitability is the method of establishing press quantities when a book is initially printed, or subsequently reprinted. But since this is an issue that should not only be reviewed periodically, but *actually applied within the business office,* it deserves a chapter of its own.

CHAPTER 38
Inventory Management and Print Buying

As we've noted earlier, its inventory of printed, unsold books is usually the biggest (by far) tangible asset of any publishing house—greater even than its accounts receivable. Obtaining, monitoring, and periodically replenishing this inventory—in a manner which minimizes both capital investment and the costly redundancy of processing out-of-stock back orders—is a particularly grave responsibility of the business manager.

The most critical aspect of fulfilling this responsibility is the actual purchasing of printed reproductions of each new title—or for replenishment of established titles. Clearly there are trade-offs between the lower unit costs you'll get from printers for larger print-order quantities, and the greater likelihood of obsolescence (which eventually eats up 2 percent of the typical independent publisher's sales revenue in the form of inventory write-offs) when you stock books for a longer period of time. The financial complexities of this trade-off are such that they should be dealt with in the finance function (and the business office) rather than in non-financial functions.

Every business office should have one person (most often, in small companies, the business manager herself) clearly designated as the "print buyer." Even though she may work from bids presented by the pre-press function (though many prefer to develop their own bids), this designated print buyer should be the final arbiter (subject to over-rule only by the publisher) of actual print-order quantities.

As suggested by Figure 34a, buying paper/printing/binding is normally the single biggest expense of operating a book publishing house. So how well you manage it has an enormous impact on eventual profitability. The key to cost-effective print buying is the solicitation of competitive bids from the considerable range of vendors available to North American publishers (not only in the U.S. and Canada, but overseas). Yet despite this array of eagerly competing printers, an astonishing number of small, independent publishers still by-pass the process by automatically sending most of their printing jobs to a "favorite vendor" who has "done them the honor" of giving them his "standard" price schedule so they can make their own estimates of his "quote" for any job. That's really buying wooden nickels!

Time after time, when aggressive print buyers examine the range of prices they get back from asking ten-or-so vendors to quote on a specific job, they find price spreads of 25-30 percent between the high and the low bids. And despite assurances to "give you the best possible prices," no printer comes up as the "low bidder" for an aggressively-shopping publisher *every* time.

Printers have mortgages just like the rest of us—and their bankers are no more impressed than ours when their cash flow dries up. So whether they like to admit it or not, they have to adjust their pricing formulas from time-to-time when they see idle presses on their near-future schedules. It's better for them to slice profits on a few jobs, than to have presses (and sometimes crews) standing idle while the mortgage payments go on. But when you buy on the basis of anyone's "standard price schedule," you're automatically excluded from the benefits of those bidding adjustments printers routinely make to avoid press "downtime."

Book publishing is a competitive industry—and modest-sized book publishers don't get many breaks in it that they haven't engineered for themselves. If you're not rigorously and consistently soliciting and comparing competitive bids on your book paper-printing-binding, you are almost certainly skimming thousands of dollars right off your own bottom line and handing them to that favorite printer as a gift.

Getting competitive bids is an easy process if you make intelligent use of your word-processor. Just set up a basic bid-invitation letter similar to Figure 21c, change the book title and other data from job-to-job, and run off personalized versions for each of the printers you want to approach. Once you've revised the letter/form once for each book, it's simply a matter of typing in the printers' names/addresses one-by-one and letting the word-processor "crank 'em out."

You'll find 379 printers who'd like to do your work listed (and partially described) in Ad-Lib Publications' *Directory of Book Printers* (Appendix 1). Unless you're absolutely convinced you know the best ones, there's no reason why you shouldn't invite a score or more (including those with whom you've had the best luck in the past) to bid on your next book. Don't be bashful about "inconveniencing" them—they love it! And most of them calculate those quotes by computer, in very little time, anyhow.

If you're printing several different titles within a brief period, you may find it worthwhile to "gang" them into a single bid request—simply by listing them *all* (with page counts) on separate lines in your request letter. In this case, it's a good idea to add a line for a "Production Batch Number"—so you can identify the resulting bids more accurately over a period of time. Print-buyers are divided as to whether such "batching" really gets them significant price breaks (though it logically should)—but they agree that it definitely cuts down the staff time needed to buy printing and supervise the printers.

Of course, batching also results in bigger cash flow demands (for several books at a time)—but if you're really going to need them within a short period, that's a financial problem you'll have to face anyhow.

Some publishers—especially those with a considerable number of very short (1,000-1,500 copy) runs—find it advantageous to solicit "term bids" for a minimum number of page-impressions (page counts multiplied by quantities) over a 6-month or 1-year period. It would certainly seem reasonable that this approach should entice some printers to shave their prices—and also reduce the supervisory time required for liaison once you and the winning printer have "gotten used to" each other. But you have to shop very carefully in such cases—since you're making it harder for the printer to match your work to anticipated press "down time."

All of which points to the need for having a good index of basic printing-cost levels for your normal type of book, and your normal print quantities. The best such index is a running last-12-months' average of the actual "price per page impression" you've paid for recent books. You can calculate this (as in Figure 7b) by simply recording the dollar amounts and page-impression counts from all of your paper/printing/binding bills in a month-by-month database, and dividing the most-recent-12-month accumulated dollar amount by the most-recent-12-month total page-impression count. Tough-buying publishers manage to keep this per-page-impression price *under one cent* on a (paperback) book-at-a-time basis, with typical 3 to 4,000-book press runs.

Such a calculation will also give you an index for determining how much (if anything) you'll save by "ganging" print jobs or inviting bids (for a minimum total quantity) on a term basis.

You can also cut printing costs by adapting your specifications to the capabilities and paper-stocks of particular printers. Note in the sample bid-request letter in Figure 21c that the publisher has *not* insisted on a specific kind of paper (for either the interior or the cover), but has invited each printer to submit (with the bid) samples of the material he proposes to use.

Even bigger (pre-press) cost-savings are possible from screening your vendor list to eliminate the need for expensive paste-ups or camera-ready pages. You do this by prescreening potential printers, with a word-processed letter asking if they can prepare their plates from a disk-copy of your desktop publishing file rather than from actual camera-ready (laser or paste-up) pages. An increasing number of printers are now obtaining equipment that enables them to make this transfer; by the mid-1990s, you can expect almost all main-line book manufacturers to be able to do it.

You should also adjust each printer's bid (*especially* if you buy any printing overseas) by estimated freight costs for getting the books from their plant to your warehouse. Note how the sample letter in Figure 21c, on the previous page, asks the printer to help you with this estimate. Examining freight costs on recent books will give you a double-check on these estimates.

Once you've received bids from those interested in any job for which you've issued requests, you'll probably find two-or-three in a fairly close race for "low bidder." It'll be worth your while to phone *each* of these, talk through each bid to make sure you understand any peculiarities, and invite each printer to suggest any reasonable alterations in your specifications that would lower their price.

While you're phoning, *request references* to at least five other publishers for whom any unfamiliar printer has produced books. (Ask for plenty of references just to make it harder for a printer to "stack the deck." You needn't phone all the names provided—but should spot-check at least three of them.)

When you've carried it this far, you needn't be compulsive about sticking with "the low bidder." Assuming you have several within a few dollars of each other, "go with your hunches" about quality and reliability, after the reference-checks. Meanwhile, each round of bidding adds more information about the next-time candidates in your vendor pool—making it feasible to keep comparing new possibilities (book after book) with the most competitive and reliable printers you've identified from previous rounds.

As we've noted before, the actual quantity you purchase in each print order should depend not only on sales expectations, but on your current cash flow situation. Just remember that the odds of ending up with obsolete inventory increase *geometrically* when you buy books you expect to warehouse for more than a year—not because the subject matter itself will be outdated, but because of the increased time-span that allows for some competitor to come up with a more appealing book on the same topic.

As important as it is for the business office to campaign for consistent inter-departmental evaluations (as per Figure 18a) before new titles are contracted, it's equally important to remember that the first-year sales estimate (even though it was the pricing basis) need *not* be the actual print quantity; it is only a hypothetical number. The financially-oriented print buyer should be free to adjust the quantity to both the prospects of the book, and the cash flow situation, as reviewed just before you write the print order. (Remember, incidentally, that the "customs of the trade" allow the printer to deliver 10 percent above-or-below your prescribed quantity—and bill for the difference on a pro-rated basis—because of the spoilage uncertainties in getting each "up and running" on the press.)

Once you've written a print order, your print buyer must remain vigilant to make sure you get what you ordered. When you choose a printer for any job, write a letter summarizing *your understanding* of the main points of their bid (including total cost and delivery schedule), and asking reassurances on any particular quality concerns you have about that specific job. Ask them to initial or countersign a copy of that letter and return it. They won't particularly like this—but they'll do it ... and it may be the only insurance you have against a hopefully-rare botched job. Use the sample in Figure 38a, if you wish.

Figure 38a—Sample Print-Purchase Confirmation Letter

[WORD-PROCESSED ON YOUR LETTERHEAD]

8 February 1993

Mr. James James
James Printing Company
4444 James Boulevard
Jamestown, Ohio 44444

Dear Jim:

I'm happy to advise you that we will accept your Quotation #93167 and designate you as our chosen printer for the book *Duty of a Teacher* referred to therein, in a quantity of 3000 (give-or-take 10 percent) at your quoted base price of $1.63 per copy, if you will acknowledge the understandings summarized below by signing and returning the enclosed confirmation copy of this letter no later than February 22.

In addition to performing the job as specified by your quotation, we want your assurance on the following of special concerns:

(1) The background color on the reverse-plate cover must be solid and unblemished (for bookstore display).
(2) The adhesive binding must be sufficiently durable that pages will not come loose in the course of normal usage of books.
(3) Each carton must be separately stenciled to indicate the book title, the quantity, and our (Roberts Publishing) name.
(4) At least 1000 copies of the book must be out of your plant and enroute to our warehouse no later than March 31. (You will receive the camera-ready pages and cover separations no later than February 26.)

If you cannot confirm any of these understandings, please phone me immediately. Otherwise, please acknowledge your agreement below, and we'll proceed promptly from there.

Cordially,

Publisher

Agreed:

_____
Robert Roberts

_____
For James Printing Company

Date _____

While you're routinizing your new-title print-bid process, keep in mind those reprints of existing (backlist) titles that you'll need from time to time. Here is frequently an opportunity to save money by "ganging" books—even if the chosen printer didn't do each original job. As more-and-more printers learn to make their plates from your desktop disks, it will become easier-and-easier to move titles from one printer to another in search of lower reprinting prices.

The key to cost-effective reprinting is a disciplined procedure for monitoring inventory status, reviewing which titles actually *deserve* to be reprinted (because they continue to support your profitability objectives), and ganging reprint needs to reduce your purchasing and printer-supervision chores. A routine procedure that covers all of the important bases consists of six steps:

(1) The inventory monitor (print buyer) should check a reliable inventory status report (as illustrated in Figure 36c) monthly, and provide the next core management meeting with a list of all titles (not already in the reprint process) that are expected to run out within the next 6 months;

(2) The editor-in-chief (for the acquisition function) should promptly certify which books on that list are obsolete, and which require updating before re-issue in revised editions. On agreement of the publisher, these titles should be removed from the list—and the order processing supervisor should be instructed to reprogram the computer to report them "out of print" when present inventory is exhausted;

(3) Revised editions of those books the acquisition function wants to update should be requalified through the normal new-title approval process and entered on the acquisition schedule for appropriate future seasons. Marketing may arrange for advance news release announcements of the new editions to be automatically sent to any interim orderers, with the out-of-print notices.

(4) The marketing manager, meanwhile, should provide the core group with an estimate of unit sales of each remaining title on the list for each of the next 3 years. If the core managers (or the publisher) approve, those for which this accumulative 3-year quantity is at least a minimally-feasible press run (1,000 or more) are then approved for reprinting. The order processing supervisor is instructed to declare the remaining books on the list out-of-print as soon as existing stock is depleted.

(5) The appropriate acquisition (series) editor is then given 3 weeks to specify any necessary corrections before the reprinting of each title. Any changes must be endorsed by both the editor-in-chief and the publisher. (Expensive corrections of harmless errors are seldom justified.)

(6) Meanwhile, the print buyer proceeds to request bids and arrange reprinting of the titles in question, in financially acceptable quantities—for delivery before current stock is exhausted.

In recent years, the introduction of "on-demand printing" installations in many lettershops and office service centers has made it feasible to reprint and perfect-bind in paperback quantities as low as five or ten books at a time. Some service bureaus have achieved per-page-impression costs as low as 3 cents in such modest quantities. This option makes it possible for a publisher to keep a slow-moving "classic" in the catalog for a long time with very little inventory investment. This is an option smart print buyers are learning to take very seriously!

CHAPTER 39
Coordinating Storage and Shipping

In addition to buying the printing, in fulfillment of its responsibility for managing the inventory, the business office must also arrange to store those books—and to ship the right combinations out the door in response to individual customers' orders. In most independent publishing houses, the storage/shipping function is coordinated (and sometimes single-handedly performed) by a designated shipping supervisor who reports directly to the business manager. Assuming the business manager or finance administrator also doubles as print-buyer, this shipping supervisor becomes the principal custodian of the physical inventory. (He may even be responsible for monitoring quantity-levels and triggering the reprint process described in the previous chapter.)

The first requirement for fulfilling this responsibility is the planning and arrangement of physical storage and package-processing space. The best way to understand the requirements of good warehouse or storage-area layout for all sizes of book publishers is to envision the components of a comprehensive storage area for a multi-million dollar publisher, and then rethink their application to a smaller operation, With that in mind, then, there are usually *five* key locations in a good book warehouse—all but the first of them clustered closely together:

(1) The bulk storage skid-racks or bins—most of the warehouse space—where the complete inventory of all titles, miscellaneous items the warehouse has been asked to store (office supplies, etc.), and any bulky materials-handling equipment are kept;

(2) The office area, where records are kept and supervision is arranged;

(3) The picking line, where a short-term supply of currently-active titles is kept so that most orders can be filled without touring the warehouse;

(4) The packing table(s), where most orders are bagged, cartons sealed, postage and labels affixed, and other final touches performed;

(5) The loading dock, where trucks bring new inventory and take away mail bags and cartons filled with outgoing orders.

For most publishers, a good warehouse layout clusters the packing table(s) near the loading dock, to minimize the hauling of finished orders to the trucks; the picking line must obviously be adjacent to the packing table(s), to minimize carrying filled cartons to be labeled, sealed, etc. And since most of the activity takes place around these three locations, the office area should be nearby (it usually has glass windows) so the supervisor can see what is going on. The large bulk storage area, then, spreads out from this center of activity—with clear access from the loading dock.

In a very small publishing program, you may eliminate the "picking line"—if you have so few titles that it is easy to "tour the warehouse" (or storage room) and fill each batch of orders from bulk inventory.

Judicious purchasing of auxiliary materials-handling equipment is fundamental to good warehouse management. While most small publishers order their books shipped from the printer in cartons, some find it advantageous to accept large print runs of fast-moving titles on skids—large wooden pallets on which may be strapped a thousand-or-so books; this option simply is not available to you unless you own a fork lift. But you'll also find this mobile lifter-and-mover useful if you have to move large numbers of cartons any distance—especially when unloading truckload printings of new titles. With tracks embedded in the warehouse floor, you might also find a system of sturdy carts (your own miniature railroad!) a good investment in higher warehouse productivity and lower workmen's compensation costs (for busted backs).

Conveyor belts or overhead wires that carry cartons along the picking line to the packing table, and carry mailbags from there to the loading dock, are also usually a good investment in warehouse productivity. Some publishers even extend the belt system past most of the bins in the bulk storage area, to help with the constant transfer of stock to the picking line. Others find overhead conveyors—along which suspended baskets can be easily pulled by hand—a more satisfactory way of moving books. Some even settle for supermarket-style shopping carts.

Whatever equipment combination you choose, remember to investigate maintenance arrangements before you buy.

The warehouse supervisor is also generally responsible for the *security* of the inventory. Its Number 1 Enemy is *water*. This not only means making sure the roof is patched promptly, and that the warehouse wasn't built in a dry riverbed to begin with; it may also involve obtaining and using dehumidifiers in muggy weather in certain parts of the country.

The Number 2 Enemy of inventory security is *pilferage*. Provide access to the fulfillment office by other routes than through the warehouse, and discourage non-fulfillment traffic there. Establish clear rules prohibiting *anyone* (from the shipper to the publisher) from removing a single book without proper documentation *through the order processing (inventory accounting) system*.

The Number 3 Enemy is *fire*. This not only suggests prohibiting smoking in the warehouse area, but suggests why neat, clean warehouses and regular trash disposal are of more than aesthetic importance.

The ultimate security precaution is to schedule regular, periodic reviews (between the warehouse supervisor and the finance officer) of the insurance coverage you carry on your inventory.

An important function of the person supervising storage/shipping of your book inventory is the receipt of new books from the printer. Since the inventory supervisor is simply verifying delivery of whatever you ordered—the process must be a collaboration between the two functions.

Before the inventory/shipping supervisor even allows an incoming truck to unload books, he should:
   (1) Identify the book(s) by title;
   (2) Verify (by thorough carton inspection) the absence of serious transit damage;
   (3) Verify that packaging and labeling conform to instructions.

When the books are unloaded, the supervisor should:
   (4) Store the shipment temporarily in a nearby holding area;
   (5) Estimate unit counts (by counting cartons, etc.);
   (6) Verify the contents of cartons by spot sampling;
   (7) Spot-check inside random cartons for damaged books;
   (8) Verify and forward (to accounting) any freight charges;
   (9) Route a prescribed number of copies to the print buyer with confirmation of all of the above;
  (10) Retain enough books near the picking line or packing table to process accumulated "back orders";
  (11) Remove the rest of this inventory to the bulk storage area.

It then becomes the responsibility of the print buyer to:
  (12) Distribute shelf-copies of the book to designated people in the rest of the organization (the acquisition editor, pre-press project manager, marketing department, etc.)—so that all can scan them for problems, and enter them into their various systems, schedules, or reference shelves;
  (13) Reconcile the quantity received with the printer's bill;
  (14) Notify the order processing supervisor that the new stock is ready to be used—and supply counts and unit costs to update the computer's product file.

The general daily workflow of the warehouse and shipping area, then, begins in the office, with the hand-delivery or computer print-out of batches of packing slips and shipping labels (and possibly actual invoices) from the order entry function. Normally, in a fairly large operation, the shipping process begins with a batch-by-batch (or daily) title-by-title consolidation of the total quantities of each book that will be needed to fill the orders at hand. (A computer can be programmed to handle this consolidation automatically—but if yours isn't, avoiding a manual calculation probably isn't worth the programming time to arrange it.)

Then the shipper(s) "tour" the warehouse with a fork lift, large cart, etc., and move the necessary quantities of each title from their bins to the picking line.

Some publishers skip this consolidation process, and eliminate the entire picking line, by sending *every* order on a conveyor belt "warehouse tour"—to be assembled from the bulk stock, in a wire basket that goes right to the packing table. But if you have any significant number of titles in stock, this requires a computer program that will rearrange the packing slips in bin-location order. (Very small publishing operations, functioning in a limited area with relatively few titles, can usually do it this way without a computer. That's where those shopping carts come in handy!)

Special procedures should be established for filling large orders for books in *carton lots* directly from bulk storage, rather than exhausting the limited picking line stock.

Next, assuming you do use a picking line, the packing slips and shipping labels are clipped to picking baskets, or actual (size-selected) cartons or jiffy bags, at the head of that picking line. The requisite titles are then collected from along that picking line, as per each packing slip, and moved to the head of the packing table. There (if not earlier) suitable cartons or shipping bags are taken from a nearby stock, the books *and the packing slips* are inserted, the package is sealed, and the shipping label is affixed.

You should establish some procedure for determining how many shipping labels will be needed for a large order—based on the number of books involved—and prepare the necessary duplicates at this stage of the process. Since large orders will usually be a separate "batch" category, this need not interrupt the normal flow of one-label order processing via your computer or manual multiple-copy forms. Most such orders will come from a few big, regular accounts—and you may find it useful to maintain a separate label-addressing file and system in the office area just for them.

You must also establish clear-cut procedures for what the shipper does with the invoices—if you use a "one-pass" system whereby the computer pre-calculates shipping charges and prints out those invoices with the packing slips and labels. Do you want them put in the cartons, attached outside, or mailed separately? Since many publishers do not add the shipping charges to credit orders until *after* actual postage or express charges are calculated, and because a separate handling of the invoice gives the order clerk an opportunity to double-check on the shipping performance, the majority of publishers mail them *separately*. Most agree that separate invoices get better handling in their customer's offices than do those inserted in cartons (which the receiving clerks may confuse with packing slips).

Then the shipper(s) calculate actual postage, UPS, or other delivery charges from reference charts posted right beside an accurate scale and a postage meter, or through a computer database terminal, at the opposite end of the packing table. It's probably best (except in a very small operation) that you put a separate postage meter from the one in your general office here—since these costs should be charged against shipping rather than routine administration.

The packing table is also a good location for a phone extension. This not only enables the shipper to call the parcel service or other carriers when they're needed, but will enable this individual—who dispatches most of your orders—to respond to customer-service queries and forward tracer-requests to the carriers without significantly interrupting the workflow.

From here, then, the finished cartons or mail bags move on (via conveyor, cart, or muscle-power) to the loading dock. Some publishers manage to crowd the packing table(s) right against sliding doors that open onto the loading docks, so that bags and cartons can be moved directly from the postage meter or manifest printer into the trucks that will take them away.

And if your shipping volume is sufficient, you may find your local post-master willing to locate an official "substation" right in your warehouse—or at least designate it as a regular pick-up point—so you won't even have to haul the books to the post office. Your parcel delivery service will offer the same service, if you're a regular customer.

Finally, the shipper(s) make appropriate notations on the batch control forms or invoice duplicates, provide shipping charge data if needed, and return the documentation (on paper or by computer) to the order entry function. By overseeing this documentation process, the shipping supervisor keeps fully informed about the status of the day's work.

Warehousing/shipping supervisors should plan ahead for periods of time when shippers are not busy, and can be utilized to shift bulk stock to more convenient locations. This means constantly moving inactive titles to the farthest bins away from the picking/packing area, and making sure the most frequently ordered titles are right there by the picking line, since you'll be needing large quantities of them almost every day.

Many shipping departments that have developed smooth systems for handling routine orders still encounter difficulty with transactions that do not fit the most-common pattern. The handling of such situations requires close coordination between shippers and the marketing department's order processing and customer service functions. At least three situations present such incongruities on a fairly regular basis:

(1) *Back-Orders* are accumulated obligations to ship books that were not in stock at the time the orders arrived; even in the best-controlled inventories, these occur when orders for new titles beat the actual books to the warehouse.

(2) *Returns* are unsold books that trade accounts (stores or wholesalers) have sent back, expecting credit or a refund.

(3) *Complimentaries* are books to be shipped free on instructions from the promotion coordinator, acquisition editors, or other authorized parties. In textbook houses, free samples to educators constitute such a heavy flow that they are usually treated as a separate sub-category.

In order to handle back-orders correctly, it is first necessary to communicate with customers to explain shortages in their original shipments. The best way to do this is to enter *on the invoice,* after the title (in place of the quantity, discount, and net due) an abbreviated code that gives a status report. You should explain your codes in a small-type footnote at the bottom or on the back of the invoice form, particularly if you expect to do much business with trade (bookstores, wholesale) buyers. Good order processing software will do this automatically. Most publishers use standardized abbreviations such as:

NOB = "not our book" (wrong publisher!)
NYP = "not yet published"
TOS = "temporarily out-of-stock"
OP = "out of print" (no longer published)

Many trade buyers include on their orders a routine instruction to "cancel back-orders," or to cancel them after a certain number of days. This means that if you don't currently have the book in stock, you should notify them (by those codes on the invoice) and then forget about it (unless you get more stock within the time frame they've allowed). This instruction should *not* be interpreted to apply to advance orders of new titles, however. (And some publishers find it advisable to keep a record of such canceled back-orders so they can at least inform the customer when the inventory is replenished, in hopes of a rejuvenated order.)

Otherwise, it is customary industry practice to accumulate back-orders for out-of-stock books and ship them (with separate invoices) whenever the new stock becomes available. Your "TOS" report on the original invoice, and your footnote explaining that code, should make it clear what policy you're following. You'll find it wise, even after such explanations, to *query* all back-order recipients before shipping if these orders are more than 30 days old. This suggests maintaining *two* back-order files (on the computer, or on paper)—one consisting of those you plan to ship to automatically, the other of those who should be queried as to whether they still want the books.

Prepublication orders for forthcoming new titles are normally treated like back-orders except that they are not automatically canceled because of the obvious delay in waiting for them to come off the press. However, you can prevent a lot of needless tracer queries if you'll not only use the notation "NYP" (not yet published) in reporting on such titles when you fill partial orders (for backlist titles), but also indicate by footnote or inserted memo the anticipated shipping dates of all near-future new titles.

When you accept prepayment for books that are not yet in stock, or are temporarily out-of-stock (as with many prepublication mail order campaigns), the FTC's "Fair Trade Guidelines" require you to ship the books within 30 days, or by a more-distant date that was specified in your promotion, or otherwise take special steps to reassure customers. When you miss the first shipping deadline, you must contact every prepayer, announce a new shipping date, and offer their money back *if they'll ask for it.* If you miss that second deadline, you must send their money back *unless they'll give you explicit permission to keep it* pending a still-later announced shipping date.

When new stock arrives, then, back-orders are simply fed into the system as though they were new orders.

Obviously, the same computerized or manual filing and recovery system that keeps track of orders for out-of-stock books can be used for advance orders of forthcoming new books. In fact, in most publishing houses, the *new title* orders constitute *most* of the back-order file. Since none of these transactions have yet been entered into sales volume totals (because they aren't invoiced as accounts receivables until the books are actually available and shipped), the accumulative dollar total in the back-order file is usually of great interest to the marketing department; it constitutes "sales volume in reserve." The unit sales accumulated for not yet published titles is also the earliest indicator of the market's reception of those new books, and thus anxiously watched by editors.

It is customary for "trade" publishers to guarantee bookstores and wholesalers credit (against balances due or future purchases) for any unsold "returns" that arrive at your warehouse (or other designated location) *in undamaged, resalable condition* within a time frame specified in the publisher's business terms (usually at least 90 days after purchase, and while the book is still "in print"). Textbook publishers often make similar guarantees to dealers. It is good tactics for mail order publishers (selling directly to the ultimate readers) to offer "money-back guarantees" to any dissatisfied customers who return undamaged books within 30 days; if your books are reasonably good, the takers will seldom exceed 1 percent.

It is the generally understood custom of the trade that the customers prepay shipping costs for returns—just as they pay shipping costs for outbound orders. Trade publishers also usually indicate in their terms statements that returns will be "credited against balances due or future purchases; no refunds."

Most publishers also replace (or refund) any *damaged* books returned promptly if the customer certifies that they were damaged in transit, and arrived in that condition. These are known in book warehouses as "hurt books," and are often accumulated for special sales, donations to prisons, or periodic sprees on the paper shredder.

Many publishers require customers returning undamaged books for credit to first inform them of the circumstances, and the titles and quantities they want to return, to get formal permission before doing so. Some obviously feel this inhibits accounts who're inclined to respond to collection pressure by premature returns. But the most legitimate rationale for doing this is so that the publisher can provide the customer with *special shipping labels*—thus making sure these cartons go directly to your warehouse, rather than being routed through offices (often at other locations), to avoid excess handling.

Remember that the ground rules are whatever you *say* they are. Return privileges are not a constitutional right of bookstores; the FTC confirms that *only you* can set your business terms. So insist that customers do it *your* way!

Whatever their rules, many publishers undermine the discipline and the economics of return guarantees by neglecting to insist that the books (as usually stated in trade terms), must be in *undamaged, resalable* condition. The warehousing/shipping function should verify the undamaged quality of returned books before credits are issued. If bookstores return merchandise with scratched covers, etc., you should (after so stating your terms) *not include* those copies in the credit you issue. Send a form letter advising these customers that so-many books were deducted from their claim because of damage, and offer to return those useless copies to them if they'll pay shipping costs; otherwise, simply add the damaged books to your "hurt books" collection. A few such notifications will (after the theatrical indignation runs its course) make problem customers more careful with your books.

The third type of special transaction for which procedures should be clearly established is the handling of *complimentary* book shipments to reviewers, educators examining prospective texts, etc. Dispatch of such books should be carefully *controlled* by either giving the shipping supervisor the list of the only people entitled to authorize them, or requiring use of a special memo-form (available only to appropriate departments) for such authorizations. All such complimentary authorizations should be put through the basic order entry process (as 100-percent-discount transactions), so that inventory records will be properly updated.

The vast majority of customer complaints most book publishers receive relate to book orders that have gone awry in processing or transit. Fielding such complaints is normally and properly the responsibility of the customer service function in the marketing department. But those customer service people must (off-line, after promising to call the customer back) refer many questions to the shipping function, since that's where most of the answers are likely to be found.

A major portion of complaints arise because customers get impatient about slow service by the carriers that dispatch the goods. While the customer may insist that you send a replacement shipment immediately, you should (unless you'd previously promised fast delivery) resist this *until the carrier confirms* that the shipment is probably lost. If you will immediately and willingly trace the shipment, and promise to report back to the customer as soon as you get a response, this will mollify most complaints without duplicate shipments.

Unfortunately, unless you've insured or certified a shipment (unlikely without special instructions), all the books you've shipped by parcel post *can't be traced* on request. In those cases, you'll have to settle for asking the postmaster's advice as to what is a reasonable time frame for assuming a missing parcel is indeed lost, not just delayed. All other carriers should be queried when you first do business with them about tracing procedures; this information should be kept on file in the shipping department. The carrier involved can then be called immediately on receipt of any non-delivery complaint or tracer-request from a customer.

Finally, in handling complaints, don't overlook the easy way out when small orders go awry in complicated ways. If it's going to cost more than the inventory and shipping cost of replacing the shipment just to trace it and/or report back to the customer (which is often the case with errant single-book shipments), you're better off simply dispatching an immediate duplicate shipment.

Most publishers are in a position to generate extra income by systematically inserting promotional flyers in all shipping bags and cartons before they are sealed and labeled. The post office says that "incidental" promotional material (including catalogs) may be inserted without adding first class postage, and other carriers do not set rates by type of material—but only by weight and size. However, you should check with your postmaster if you are in doubt about any particular insert.

We've already discussed the planning and utilization of such cross-sell promotion in the section on marketing. Such items should be given stock numbers, and entered onto packing slips (as free additions) by order entry personnel. In the shipping department, the inventory of such materials should be located within the picking line, so the insert(s) can be selected and incorporated without invoking separate, redundant procedures.

You can also use these insertion procedures to generate extra income by agreeing to insert *other people's* promotional materials in your shipping containers, at an agreed cost per thousand (comparable to list, processing, and postage costs for bulk rate mailings). Or you can *swap* inserts with other publishers—agreeing to send so-many thousands of theirs out in your cartons, if they'll send an equal number of your flyers out in their cartons.

The shipping department can show its support for the sales effort by calling this whole area of possibilities to marketing's attention, and volunteering its cooperation.

The Huenefeld Consultants' 1988 survey found that about two-thirds of independent (under-$2-million) publishing houses handled all of their inventory storage and shipping internally; about 10 percent said they delegated this function entirely to external fulfillment services; about one-fourth utilized a combination of internal and external storage/shipping arrangements.

With the plummeting prices of computer systems, and the variety of software now on the market, there is little reason for any small publisher to give up the tight control and flexibility of internal order processing to an external service, in order to keep up with expanding sales volume. It often makes good sense, however, to delegate the maintenance of large storage space, and the muscle-work of moving skids and large cartons, to someone who is more appropriately equipped and staffed to handle such work than is the typical small publishing organization.

The most common usage of external fulfillment services, then, is for bulk storage, and the picking-packing-shipping of bulk orders (for, say, five-or-more books) from packing slips and address labels supplied by the publisher's order processing system. The best way to determine whether such a division of labor is advisable is to get a unit price list (monthly storage per book or square foot, handling per order and per unit, etc.) from any interested warehousing/fulfillment services listed in your metropolitan phone directory and calculate how much they'd add to monthly fulfillment costs (after you subtract the shipping personnel, excess rental space, etc., they'd eliminate from your present budget).

Generally, using such an external service will double the typical 5 percent storage/shipping cost of a small publisher. There is a phase in the development of a publishing house (usually between $100,000 and $1,000,000 in sales volume) when convenience may justify that extra expense. Beyond $1 million in sales, you'll probably find it more cost-effective to rent suitable warehouse space and perform these functions with your own staff.

CHAPTER 40
Facilities, Equipment, and Computer Configurations

The kind of work that goes on in a publishing house is often so esoteric (as with acquisition editors or promotional copywriters) or so attention-demanding (as with order processors or copy editors) that minor nuances of work environment (from frequent interruptions to anxiety-producing decor) can make a significant difference in how much productive work you actually get for your payroll. The potential for improving that productivity (getting 120 invoices a day from an order processor instead of 100, or 50 lines of good prose each hour from a copywriter instead of 35, or 5,000 finished pages a year from a copy editor instead of 4,000) by imaginative planning, coordination, and administration of working facilities is enormous.

But few small book publishing houses have enough people or space or money to justify hiring a specialist to plan and administer the physical facilities within which their staffs perform. Many, as a consequence, essentially settle for whatever they found when they signed the lease—and day-to-day responsibility for keeping it running is casually bucked to someone without enough managerial clout to do the job creatively.

As the basic asset-manager of the enterprise, the business manager is the most appropriate party *with clout* to take on responsibility for making this function contribute significantly to the end results achieved by the enterprise. That doesn't mean business managers should function as office administrators; this (like financial administration, print buying, or storage/shipping) is only one aspect of their work. Not long after that first million dollars in sales volume, they usually find it necessary to delegate the day-to-day details of administering the physical facilities.

The traditional title given this delegated overseer is "office manager"—though we would suggest that "facilities administrator" is more precise and appropriate, since this individual needn't be directly involved in the top-strategy deliberations of the core management group. Nevertheless, there's more to the function than just running an office. The basic responsibilities of effective facilities administration include:

(1) Negotiating lease (or purchase) of appropriate space;
(2) Arranging appropriate furnishings and decorations;
(3) Arranging for installation and maintenance of utilities;

(4) Obtaining cost-effective office equipment;

(5) Establishing, monitoring and maintaining an effectively configured computer system for the organization;

(6) Arranging maintenance and repair of building and equipment;

(7) Maintaining an inventory of basic office supplies;

(8) Providing appropriate communication facilities (phone, mail delivery, express couriers, bulletin boards, etc.);

(9) Providing appropriate general reference materials;

(10) Providing for reception of visitors, messages, packages;

(11) Arranging appropriate centralized services (from typing pools to envelope stuffing to computer programming).

The most challenging, and productivity-impacting, aspect of facilities administration has to do with *planning* the individual environments in which the organization's personnel perform their work. The first requirement of sound facilities planning is to *identify* the work stations the organization needs. The next is to *locate* each work station for maximum convenience of those who must consult each other frequently (while at the same time minimizing work disruptions and inappropriate environments). The third is to *equip* each work station for the most cost-effective performance of the tasks to be done there. The fourth is to *personalize* each work station (within reasonable limits) to maximize the comfort and motivation of the individual who will use it.

But few office administrators are trained environmental engineers, and few have the time to do a lot of daydreaming about other people's walls and desks. So they often find that they can get more creative ideas by organizing and chairing a Facilities Committee—a representative ad hoc group from all echelons and functions of the organization which meets periodically to brainstorm possibilities.

Such a group will work best if you establish a procedure whereby all concerned can propose (by a deadline) facility problems to appear on a written agenda, circulated *before* each meeting. Additions to that agenda might also be specifically requested from the core management group, and even from general staff suggestion boxes. At the meeting, the presiding facilities administrator should then invite the group to brainstorm solutions to each problem, and alternatives to each possible improvement, on the agenda.

This group should be periodically reminded that not all work stations are associated with specific individuals. Specialized installations such as photocopiers, light tables, certain special-purpose computer terminals, etc., may be used by a variety of people—and should be planned and located accordingly. But each person should be associated with one primary work station (even if part-timers have to share), so each has a place to leave work-in-progress and personal accessories—and each should be encouraged to individualize that station to suit his/her own working habits and psychological make-up.

Significant productivity or morale benefits can often be achieved by planning for double use of certain, frequently unoccupied common spaces. For example, conference rooms may double not only as central libraries, but as pleasant employee luncheon areas. Central filing areas might be decorated and equipped to provide private visitor interview rooms for those whose own work stations don't offer such privacy.

Traditionally, publishing houses (like all offices) have suffered from the industrial-era compulsion of managers to standardize. But in work as creative and esoteric and individualistic as publishing, it costs little more to make available some variety of materials (paint, etc.) and equipment, and allow each employee some latitude in developing a productive working "home," than it does to enshrine the deadening universality of institutionalized wall paint and houseplant prohibitions.

Facilities administrators can prevent many future office crises by systematically documenting facilities arrangements. It's amazing how many small publishing houses can't readily find a copy of their building lease, or the purchase agreement for their computer, or the telephone number of a good repairman, when they need it. To avoid such frustrations, it makes sense to establish a documentation program that includes:

(1) A "property file" containing all leases, deeds, titles, purchase agreements, etc.;

(2) An "insurance file" containing all policies;

(3) A "maintenance file" containing all warranties, instructions, service contracts, etc.;

(4) A "supply inventory" file with monitoring checklists and sources/prices of replenishments.

In addition to supporting all sections of the organization by maintaining a productive environment for their own work, the facilities function may be able to help restrain the total payroll by providing some centralized services that few departments could justify alone (without wasteful redundancy). These services might include everything from secretarial pools to computer programming. One useful possibility often overlooked is a centralized filing service, which combines all available editorial, production, promotion, and other material on each book once it has been published—so all concerned can find what they need without bothering each other.

Certainly one of the most challenging responsibilities of the facilities administrator is the maintenance and constant improvement (updating) of the organization's computer system. If you publish within a large parent organization, this sub-function may have been separately delegated to a specialized "management information systems" department—but the expert help available there may cause more problems (by insisting on conforming the peculiarities of the publishing process to non-publishing logic) than it solves. This tends to lead to a syndrome we'll call "compulsive over-networking." By that we refer to the unreasoned insistence of cybernetic perfectionists on tying everything and everybody into one single computer network.

When that syndrome prevails, such organizations sometimes spend ten times as much having programmers modify their non-publishing software to handle order processing, manuscript development, and other tasks strange to the parent group as good publisher-specific "off-the-shelf" hardware would cost—and they usually still get poor results! Thus too many victimized "publications departments" end up with charts of accounts more appropriate to nursery schools—and have to "farm out" such things as mailing list maintenance, type-setting, and manuscript archiving for lack of file storage capacity.

Unfortunately, those institutional "MIS" specialists sometimes become so enamored of their own trade that they're overly-inclined to mix apples and oranges. Once raw data (either text or numerical) goes into the system, they insist that it remain "untouched by human hands"; all the programs have to interact in one big network; the idea that somebody might reasonably retype a hundred month-end summary numbers to move them from one system to another is heresy!

But trying to conform the complex, creative *publishing* process to the cybernetic logic of another kind of institution (a denominational or association headquarters, a university, a financial conglomerate) seriously waters down the effectiveness (and the creativity) of that publishing program. In such cases, you're much better off buying off-the-shelf, publisher-specific software ... unlinking the publishing enterprise from the larger institutional network ... and periodically retyping the modest summary publishing data the parent system really needs.

A majority of effective, independent publishing houses create separate systems *without any custom programmed software*. They buy, at any good computer store, the three basic programs most of the staff will need for most of their work: ordinary word processing, database, and spreadsheet software compatible with the basic operating system of their hardware. (Despite the popularity of the Macs, IBM-compatible DOS remains by far the most common operating system—probably because there's more [and more varied] off-the-shelf software available for the DOS systems.)

Word processing programs are essentially computerized typewriters that save everything on an electronic file, offer numerous aids in manipulating ("editing") those files, and print out "hard copy" (on paper) as needed. Well over half of today's authors are writing on word processors—and conversion from one program to another is increasingly practical—so book manuscripts themselves account for a major portion of an up-to-date publishing house's word processing volume. (This book was written on a word-processor program, that was then "imported" into a desktop page-generating program/file which created the type and laid out the pages.)

Database programs are "electronic card files"—that allow you to design a file-structure (outline and data-entry form) for each specific purpose (from schedules to mailing lists), accumulate entries over a period of time, and print out various cross-referencing analyses (as well as mailing-address labels) on demand. Figures 15a, 26a, and 36a in this book are typical examples of such database entry forms.

Spreadsheet programs are essentially "chart-makers" that cross-reference data from horizontal "rows" with vertical "columns" for a wide variety of displays and analyses. Once you enter brief instructions as to how certain data may be derived, a spreadsheet can continuously update fairly complex reports with very little new input. Figures 7b, 8b, 9d, and 10a are typical computer-generated spreadsheets.

The facilities administrator should (with the business manager's endorsement) select-and-decree a *specific* software program for each of these three basic uses, for *everybody* in the organization—so that people can easily exchange and consolidate information. (It's easy to deny unauthorized access to confidential files, by employing program features requiring a secret "password" before such a file can be examined.) Often all of the computer terminals (keyboard work stations) in the publishing house are "networked" (electronically linked), so that everybody's files end up in the same "library" and (unless password-protected) can be "called up" at any terminal.

But until a publishing program is using more than half-a-dozen terminals, the advantages of electronic "networking" should not be taken for granted. Smaller organizations have little difficulty in making quick disk-copies when they wish to transfer a file from one work station (or one person) to another—and this virtually eliminates any person's unintentional mangling of another person's files.

Two other types of software are utilized by most well-managed publishing houses (whether on networks or unlinked computers). We'll call one category "special purpose" programs which might be useful to various people as adjuncts to the basic software. These usually require some intensive training (or self-study)—so once any individual elects to add such software to the library, it's wise to designate that individual as the "trainer" who will conduct periodic workshops (or offer one-on-one guidance) for others who might wish to learn to use it. Perhaps the most common special purpose programs in book publishing houses are word processing *conversion* programs (which convert authors' disks from their different software packages to yours), *graphics* programs (increasingly used to generate art for book covers), and *archiving* programs (which compress huge files into reduced disk space for transit or storage).

The other "extra" software category found in most publishing houses today consists of "dedicated" (single-purpose), integrated programs that go beyond the basics to perform fairly complex multiple-step operations from fairly simple inputs. Because they significantly reduce the time/cost involved in work absolutely essential to the publishing process, two kinds of dedicated programs are found in most (even very small) publishing houses today:

Order processing systems allow fulfillment personnel (increasingly, the "tel-ereps" in sales departments) to key in minimal data (zip-based finder codes, customer account numbers, book codes, quantities, etc.) and get back finished packing slips, shipping/mailing address labels, and properly-discounted invoices—while automatically updating each customer's account (for month-end statements), each author's royalty record, and each book's inventory status.

Desktop page-generating systems (popularly called "desktop publishing") convert input from the word processor to chosen type fonts and sizes, lay out the type on each page as you want it, add running heads and page numbers, leave appropriate blank space for illustrations, actually import line art (and increasingly, even halftones and four-color art) into those blanks, and either print out camera-ready pages (via an attached laser printer) or produce an electronic (disk or tape) copy of the "desktop" file which a well-equipped book manufacturer can use to prepare the necessary plates for the printing press.

It's generally a good idea to limit access to dedicated *order processing* and *desktop* files to those who actually create them, and the very few managers with a real and immediate "need to know"—rather than leaving these complex systems on the open-access "network." A menu of available reports from such a system can then enable others (within reason) to tap into the resulting bank of information when appropriate—without cluttering up (and frequently man-gling) such files through ill-informed intrusions.

Note that we haven't included "accounting packages" among these inte-grated, dedicated, special purpose programs. As we noted earlier, some mid-sized publishers do find the database and check-writing features of such packages useful—but hardly essential. Many more, however, find that being locked into somebody else's (often non-publishing) concept of what financial data and analyses are most important is *too high a price to pay* for the modest amount of work saved by such a "package."

The "software publishing" industry has made an extensive assortment of programs for each of these uses (word processing, database files, spreadsheet analyses, disk conversion, graphics, archiving, order processing, page genera-tion) available at reasonable prices. You can get a good version of any package we've described above for under $1,000—though the most popular, more sophisticated order processing systems cost several times that amount. For a fascinating array of what's available, consult R. R. Bowker Company's two-volume directory *The Software Encyclopedia* (listed in Appendix 2).

Epilogue
Adjusting to the Drama of Your Enterprise's Evolution

It has been this author's intention, in the 40 chapters contained here, to provide a sufficient overview of all aspects of the management and operation of the book publishing process to help experienced general and function ("core") managers keep abreast of the rapid structural, technological, and marketplace changes that are so rapidly enhancing the opportunities and compounding the challenges of independent publishers—as they apply creative, flexible small-group dynamics to their inevitable competition with those slow-moving but durable dinosaurs, the publishing conglomerates. At the same time, we hope we have provided you with an inexpensive training aid to help the bright, energetic newcomers you recruit to your enterprise live up to—nay, exceed!—your expectations of them.

But as you apply what we've presented here, remember that publishing houses—like human beings—tend to evolve through an organizational life-cycle. Stay awake; what worked once may not work the next time around. How you respond to any specific opportunity or problem should be conditioned by the stage of evolution which your enterprise is currently experiencing.

In the *pre-planning* stage (before you've actually started publishing), you have a precious opportunity to explore alternatives and speed eventual progress by mentally "dry-running" the publishing process while it isn't costing you money. Have the patience to work your way through this phase carefully and thoroughly; it'll be much less expensive than subsequent "trial and error" explorations.

But once you're actually committed to the *start-up* phase of entrepreneuring (or intrepreneuring—within a larger organization) a new publishing house or program, you have to remember that *time is money*. It's vital at this stage to move forward boldly, to generate sufficient revenue to make the enterprise self-sufficient before it becomes vulnerable to strategy-warping financial compromises.

After you've reached break-even, be aware that it is virtually impossible to maintain for long the high level of emotional energy, and even personal sacrifice, of the start-up period. Now it's time to *institutionalize* the enterprise—so its future development can be quantitatively projected, deliberately staffed, and endlessly extended without too much wear and tear on the people (or capital resources) involved.

At times, that development will involve *fast growth* spurts, which (because of fortuitous breaks, market changes, etc.) require the enterprise to revert to the hectic style of the start-up phase. To create an enterprise that can shift back into high gear without serious damage to mental health, personal relationships, or its balance sheet, you need to maintain a reasonable level of the kind of organizational discipline and accountability implicit in impersonalized performance indices (Figure 7b) and job reviews (Figure 11b).

And there'll be the converse of such growth spurts—revenue declines, competitive challenges, key-person departures, and other situations that thrust the enterprise into a temporary phase of *crisis operation*. When that happens, you'll find it especially important to have those formal job descriptions (Figure 5a, 22a, 27a, etc.) and strategy models (Figures 9a-b-c-d) in place, so that problem-solving personnel (even the boss!) can step quickly and decisively into unfamiliar roles without throwing the rest of the team out of focus.

The most severe form of crisis management you're likely to encounter is the *turn-around* challenge of reversing general decline in an overly-matured publishing house—to bring it back to new vigor and profitability. Good turn-around managers usually leave so much emotional carnage on the landscape that they tend to move on from situation-to-situation as the well-paid, never-bored "hired guns" of the industry. And there's virtually *nothing* in this book they don't need to know about and think about.

And both entrepreneurs and the publishing houses they create may eventually elect to (corporately) self-destruct—by *selling-out or liquidating*. Once past break-even, wise publishers have this option continually in mind—because it's so much happier an experience when it's pre-planned and deliberate than when it's forced on you, and has to be faced from a position of weakness.

As your own publishing house and career evolve from stage to stage, this author wishes you the best of luck—and feels confident about *promising* you it won't be dull.

APPENDIX LISTINGS

Resources you should learn about
... by requesting current catalogs and/or mailing list counts

Appendix 1:

Ad-Lib Publications
P.O. Box 1102
Fairfield, IA 52556
For more information, *phone 800-669-0773*

Ad-Lib, now headed by Marie Kiefer, maintains and markets the directories, idea-books, and databases initially created by independent publishing's most prolific informational pack-rat—John Kremer. Their computer has well-categorized addresses of virtually every type of potential customer or vendor you're likely to encounter in your publishing career. Most of this information is available both in printed directories and on computer disks. Their nicely-condensed annotated price list makes it easy to find what you want. Highlights include:

Book Publishing Resource Guide, by Marie Kiefer. Addresses of more than 8,000 key marketing contacts—from book clubs to chain stores, catalogue merchandisers to reviewers, talk show hosts to card deck media. 1992, $25.00

Directory of Book Printers, by Marie Kiefer and John Kremer. Over 700 manufacturers of books, catalogs and magazines—with clues about the quantities, trim sizes and bindings they handle best. 1992, $9.95

Phone Radio Interview Shows. Along with how-to discussion, you get 32 pages of photocopyable address labels listing 971 such shows, and 53 pages of details about each. 1992, $30.00

Mailing Lists. Over 20,500 names/addresses, categorized by the subject-interests of bookstores, reviewers and other vital contacts. Prices quoted by category.

Appendix 2: (Publishers of the Bowker directories)

Reed Reference Publishing
121 Chanlon Road
New Providence, NJ 07974
For more information, *phone 800-521-8110*

Bowker is the most comprehensive compiler of basic book industry and bibliographic information in American publishing today. Among the Bowker directories most frequently referred to in the foregoing chapters:

Literary Market Place, the single most widely-used guide to who's who in American publishing. While it includes address-sections on reviewers, sub-rights buyers, wholesalers, printers, fulfillment houses, etc., it is especially noteworthy for its key-person index to the managers of more than 3,000 major and mid-sized U.S. and Canadian publishing houses, 10,000 services and suppliers and the subject-interests of over 2,500 U.S. publishers. 1993, $148.00

International Literary Market Place, a guide to co-publishing, rights buying/ selling, distribution, and other contacts in 160 countries beyond the U.S. and Canada. 1993, $164.00

Subject Guide to Books in Print, cross-indexing non-fiction titles into Library of Congress subject headings. The absolutely essential starting place when evaluating the uniqueness of a prospective new title. 1992-93 (5 volumes), $281.00

American Book Trade Directory, the definitive guide to over 30,000 U.S. and Canadian bookstores, chains, wholesalers, and distributors—what each buys, and who buys it. 1992-93, $205.00

American Library Directory, contact names and addresses in some 35,000 U.S./Canadian public, academic, special, and government libraries. 1992-93, $215.00

Ulrich's International Periodicals Directory, the most useful world-wide guide to specialized book-review contacts—subject-categorizing 120,000 periodicals from 65,000 publishers. 1992-93 (3 volumes), $364.00)

The Software Encyclopedia, describing (with prices) over 16,000 micro-computer software programs from 4,000 sources—cross-referenced by title, and by application. 1993 (2 volumes), $209.95

K. G. Saur
P.O. Box 31
New Providence, NJ 07974-9903
For more information, *phone 800-521-8110*

The K. G. Saur database is, in many ways, the international equivalent of the R. R. Bowker treasure-trove. Highlights:

International Books in Print. 210,000 non-fiction titles currently available in English from some 6,000 publishers in 150 countries outside the U.S. and Canada ... categorized by more than 150 Dewey subject groupings. 1992-93 (4 volumes), $600.00; subject guide only (2 volumes), $350.00

Publishers' International ISBN Directory. The most definitive directory of worldwide book-publishing you'll find, detailing some 252,000 publishing houses in 189 countries. 1992-93, $315.00

Cahners Direct Mail Services—R.R. Bowker
249 West 17th Street
New York, NY 10011
For more information, *phone 800-537-7930*

These are the people who rent the definitive mailing lists that are the by-products of the Bowker, Saur, and other Reed-affiliated directory databases. Probably the best source available for library lists, and Ad-Lib's worthy competitor in access to bookstores. Their complimentary catalogs contain complete price and list-quantity data.

Appendix 3:

CMG Information Services
Fifty Cross Street
Winchester, MA 01890
For more information, *phone 800-677-7959*

The former "College Marketing Group," CMG has become one of the two (also see MDR below) most definitive sources of faculty names and addresses—subject-by-subject—for classroom adoption and scholarly book promotions to over 3,500 U.S. and Canadian two-and-four-year colleges and universities. Their list catalog is a fascinating demographic profile of the academic world.

Appendix 4:

Gale Research, Inc.
835 Penobscot Building
Detroit, MI 48226
For more information, *phone 800-347-GALE (ext. 1321)*

A leading compiler of library reference materials and address directories on all aspects of American intellectual endeavor, Gale is particularly appreciated in book marketing departments for:

Encyclopedia of Associations. The most comprehensive available guide to over 22,000 not-for-profit U.S. organizations: who they represent, what they do, who runs them, what they publish (all those journals and newsletters book publishers find so vital to specialized promotion) ... and those special marketing contacts who often use or promote other people's books in support of their own programs and causes. 1992 (3 volumes), $320.00

Trade Shows Worldwide. A directory of over 5,000 conferences and conventions where you can exhibit books—approximately a third of them outside the U.S. and Canada. 1992, $195.00

Appendix 5:

Market Data Retrieval
16 Progress Drive
Shelton, CT 06494
For more information, *phone 800-333-8802*

Market Data Retrieval offers one-stop rental access to the most comprehensive, definitive mailing lists of public and private elementary and secondary educators in over 100,000 U.S. and Canadian schools (selectable by function, subject, grade level, and/or buying power); more than half-a-million of those teachers at home addresses; over 130,000 public, school, and college libraries; and some 650,000 college faculty members in 4,216 two-and-four-year institutions. Altogether, here are carefully-categorized addresses of more than 2,600,000 educators. Free catalog also details markets for other information packages besides books.

Appendix 6:

Standard Rate and Data Service
3004 Glenview Road
Wilmette, IL 60091
For more information, *phone 800-344-0208*

SRDS is to the advertising industry essentially what the R.R. Bowker database is to the book publishing industry—the most comprehensive source of U.S. and Canadian contact addresses, demographics, and rates for all major media (direct mail lists, business publications, consumer magazines, newspapers, radio/television, card decks, trade shows—you name it) available to promotion planners. Book publishers' favorite SRDS directories:

Direct Mail List Rates & Data—a constantly-updated directory of over 10,000 mailing lists available for rental ... with selection criteria, prices, test requirements, etc. ... all conveniently organized into some 600 business/professional, consumer-interest, and agricultural categories. Very current (6 issues a year), $329.00

The SRDS Tradeshow Catalog—Published semi-annually in May and November. A geographical, alphabetical (by sponsor), and product-categorized guide to exhibit opportunities. 1992, $299.00 (2 issues)

INDEX